The Pleasure Gardens of Virginia

PETER MARTIN

The Pleasure Gardens
of Virginia

FROM JAMESTOWN TO JEFFERSON

UNIVERSITY PRESS OF VIRGINIA
CHARLOTTESVILLE AND LONDON

The University Press of Virginia
Originally published in 1991 by Princeton University Press
©1991 by Princeton University Press
All rights reserved
Printed in the United States of America on acid-free paper

First University Press of Virginia edition published 2001

ISBN 0-8139-2053-1 (paper)

Library of Congress Cataloging-in-Publication Data
Martin, Peter, 1940–
The pleasure gardens of Virginia : from Jamestown to Jefferson / Peter
Martin.— 1st University Press of Virginia ed.
p. cm.
Originally published: Princeton, N.J. : Princeton University Press, c1991.
Includes bibliographical references (p.   ).
ISBN 0-8139-2053-1 (pbk. : alk. paper)
1. Gardens—Virginia—History. I. Title.
SB466.U65 V86   2001
712'.6'09755—dc21
2001033327

For my mother

and

in memory of my father

Contents

List of Illustrations   ix
Preface   xiii
Introduction   xvii

1   The Beginnings: Garden Images in the Seventeenth Century   3

2   Gardens in Early Williamsburg   28

3   John Custis and William Byrd II: Crosscurrents of Virginia
    Gardening 1720–1750   54

4   Williamsburg Gardens in the Second Half of the
    Eighteenth Century   79

5   The Plantations   100

6   Landscape Gardening at Mount Vernon and Monticello   134

7   Two Gardeners in Williamsburg after the War:
    Joseph Prentis and St. George Tucker   165

Conclusion   182
Notes   187
Bibliographical Essay   225
Index   233

Illustrations

1. Remnant of mid-seventeenth-century terraced garden at Jamestown, Virginia. Recovered in archaeological excavations (after field drawings, National Park Service, 1940). Colonial Williamsburg Foundation.

2. Surveyor's plat of 1697 showing the Charles County, Maryland, courthouse and adjacent land. Colonial Williamsburg Foundation.

3. Drawing of the Green Spring archaeological excavations in the 1920s (after Arthur Shurcliff [1929] and Desandrouins [1782]).

4. Green Spring. Watercolor by Benjamin Latrobe, late 1790s. Maryland Historical Society, Baltimore.

5. House lot, gardens, and orchard of Bacon's Castle, Surry County, Virginia, 1911 (after an 1843 survey plan). Association for the Preservation of Virginia Antiquities.

6. Aerial view of the gardens of Bacon's Castle. Photograph: Nick Luccketti.

7. Reverend James Blair. Oil painting by Charles Bridges. Muscarelle Museum of Art, The College of William and Mary, 1941.005.

8. Desandrouins Map of Williamsburg (ca. 1781–1782). Library of Congress.

9. Francis Louis Michel's drawing of the Wren Building, College of William and Mary (ca. 1702). Burgerbibliothek Bern, Mss.h.h. 152, f.63r.

10. Bodleian Plate (ca. 1736–1740). Colonial Williamsburg Foundation.

11. "A Plan of Westover" (1701). Author unknown. William Byrd II Title Book, Virginia Historical Society.

12. Alexander Spotswood. Oil painting by Charles Bridges, early eighteenth century; Neg. #A9-1715. Library of Virginia.

13. Plan of Annapolis, Maryland (1781). Drawn by Major Capitaine. Ministère de la Défense—Service Historique de l'Armée de Terre, Paris.

14. Frenchman's Map of Williamsburg (1782). Swem Library, College of William and Mary.

15. Survey of the "Virginia Peninsula" (1818), by Major James Kearney. Colonial Williamsburg Foundation.

16. Town plan of Williamsburg, last quarter of the eighteenth century, showing major topographical features, landmarks, and gardens (after Desandrouins, 1781; Frenchman's Map, 1782; and Bucktrout Map, 1800).

17. View of the Magazine along South England Street. Photograph: Colonial Williamsburg Foundation.

18. View south along the Palace Green from the Palace. Photograph: Colonial Williamsburg Foundation.

19. View north from the Palace over the gardens and

toward the Governor's "Park." Photograph: Colonial Williamsburg Foundation.

20. Simcoe Map of Williamsburg (ca. 1781–1782). Colonial Williamsburg Foundation

21. Governor's Palace and gardens. Detail from the Bodleian Plate (ca. 1736–1740). Colonial Williamsburg Foundation.

22. Williamsburg environs showing major public and private gardens, including original Palace lands 1699 (A), and additions 1760–1775 (B–D).

23. Plan of the "Governor's Park" on a map showing "Williamsburg and the Slip of Land Between the York and James Rivers" (ca. 1781). Author unknown. Clements Library, University of Michigan.

24. The terraces in the Palace gardens. Photograph: Colonial Williamsburg Foundation.

25. The canal and terraces in the Palace gardens. Photograph: Colonial Williamsburg Foundation.

26. Drawing of the Dutch-style gardens at Crossy Hall in South Holland, Lincolnshire, by William Stukeley (1735). (Gough maps 16, folio 29). Bodleian Library, Oxford.

27a and b.   Hand-colored engravings of plants in *Catalogus Plantarum* (1730). Attributed to Philip Miller. Colonial Williamsburg Foundation.

28. Watercolor painting of a dogwood taken from Mark Catesby's *Natural History of Carolina, Florida, and the Bahama Islands* (1731), vol. 1, plate 27. Colonial Williamsburg Foundation

29. Robert Furber's oil painting of the flowers of "September," from *The Flower-Garden Displayed* (1732). Colonial Williamsburg Foundation

30. Fragments of an earthenware urn with decorated arms found in the Custis well, Williamsburg. Photograph: Colonial Williamsburg Foundation.

31. Pedestal base from an eighteenth-century earthenware flower urn, covered with gray and pink paint, found at the site of the Custis gardens. Photograph: Colonial Williamsburg Foundation.

32. John Custis. Unknown American artist. Washington-Custis-Lee collection, Washington and Lee University, Lexington, Virginia.

33. William Byrd II. Oil painting by Sir Godfrey Kneller, early eighteenth century. Virginia Historical Society.

34. "A View of Cliefden in Buckinghamshire." Drawn by Luke Sullivan (1759). Victoria and Albert Museum.

35. Westover plantation. Photograph: Colonial Williamsburg Foundation.

36. Iron gate at Westover, eighteenth century. Photograph: Colonial Williamsburg Foundation.

37. Figure of a martlet on top of one of the main gate piers at Westover. Photograph: Colonial Williamsburg Foundation.

38. Stone pier ornament along the clairvoyée at Westover. Photograph: Colonial Williamsburg Foundation.

39. Stone pier ornament along the clairvoyée at Westover. Photograph: Colonial Williamsburg Foundation.

40. Stone pier ornament along the clairvoyée at Westover. Photograph: Colonial Williamsburg Foundation.

41. Westover landscape, 1783. After the sketch by Thomas Lee Shippen. Library of Congress.

42a–f. Sale advertisement vignettes from the *Virginia Gazette*, ed. William Rind, 1766–1770. Virginia Historical Society.

43. Waller garden in Williamsburg, ca. 1807, after a sketch by Luty Blow. Redrawing by Mary Stephenson from a lost sketch in the Blow Family Papers. College of William and Mary.

44. Plan of Richard Blow's house and garden in Norfolk, Virginia, late eighteenth century. Colonial Williamsburg Foundation.

45. George Wythe House gardens, Williamsburg, ca. 1837–1844, after Kate Millington Blankenship. Colonial Williamsburg Foundation.

46. View of the restored George Wythe House gardens. Photograph: Colonial Williamsburg Foundation.

47. Tazewell Hall, Williamsburg. Photograph: Colonial Williamsburg Foundation.

48. Bassett Hall, Williamsburg. Photograph: Colonial Williamsburg Foundation.

49. Bassett Hall plantation environs on the outskirts of Williamsburg, mid-nineteenth century (after an anonymous drawing). Colonial Williamsburg Foundation.

50. Belvidere. Watercolor by Benjamin Latrobe, late 1790s. Maryland Historical Society, Baltimore.

51. Simcoe Map, 1781–1782. Simcoe Collection, Colonial Williamsburg Foundation.

52. Kingsmill garden archaeological excavations. Photograph: Anheuser Busch Company.

53. House lot and garden plan, Kingsmill plantation. After a drawing by Fraser Neiman, based on archaeological excavations directed by William Kelso, 1975. Virginia Department of Historic Resources.

54. Kingsmill. Excavated terrace steps. Photograph: Anheuser Busch Company.

55. Kingsmill. Excavated volute from river-front entrance steps. Photograph: Anheuser Busch Company.

56. Kingsmill. Excavated fragments of carved sandstone. Photograph: Anheuser Busch Company.

57. View of the James River from the restored gardens of Carter's Grove. Photograph: Colonial Williamsburg Foundation.

58. View of Carter's Grove and its restored gardens. Photograph: Colonial Williamsburg Foundation.

59. Reconstructed garden plan, Carter's Grove. Based on archaeological excavations (after William Kelso, 1972). Colonial Williamsburg Foundation.

60. Plan of Middleton Place garden, Charleston County, South Carolina. After a plan from Samuel Stoney, *Plantations of the Carolina Low Country* (Charleston, 1938).

61. Mid-nineteenth-century watercolor of Carter's Grove and its terraces. Artist unknown. Colonial Williamsburg Foundation.

62. Landon Carter. Oil painting, artist unknown, late eighteenth century. Virginia Historical Society.

63. Sabine Hall. Reprinted from *Virginia Plantation Homes,* by David King Gleason. Copyright ©1989 by Louisiana State University Press.

64. Mrs. Charles Carter of Cleve plantation. Oil portrait attributed to William Dering (ca. 1745–1749). Colonial Williamsburg Foundation.

65. Nomini Hall. Mid-nineteenth-century watercolor by E. Mound. Colonial Williamsburg Foundation.

66. Urns in the Mount Airy gardens. Photograph: Colonial Williamsburg Foundation.

67. Mount Airy. Measured drawing of the gardens by Arthur Shurcliff (1931). Colonial Williamsburg Foundation.

68. Gunston Hall. House lot and garden plan (after Fiske Kimball and Erling Pederson, 1949). Philadelphia Museum of Art.

69. Plan of Prestwould plantation, 1798 (after John Hill). Skipwith Papers, Swem Library, College of William and Mary.

70. Garden plans for Prestwould plantation, ca. 1790 (after plans attributed to Lady Jean Skipwith). Skipwith Papers, Swem Library, College of William and Mary.

71. Manuscript page of notes by Lady Jean Skipwith. Skipwith Papers, Special Collections, Swem Library, College of William and Mary.

72. Aerial view of the restored gardens at Mount Vernon. Photograph: Colonial Williamsburg Foundation.

73. Plan of the Mount Vernon gardens by Samuel Vaughan (1787). The Mount Vernon Ladies' Association of the Union.

74. "View to the North from the Lawn at Mount Vernon." Watercolor by Benjamin Latrobe (1796). Maryland Historical Society, Baltimore.

75. "View of Mount Vernon looking to the North. July 17th 1796." Watercolor by Benjamin Latrobe. Maryland Historical Society, Baltimore.

76. Robertson-Jukes view of the east lawn and front of Mount Vernon (1800). The Mount Vernon Ladies' Association of the Union.

77. Plan of the restored gardens at Mount Vernon (after a plan of Mount Vernon by Samuel Vaughan, 1787, and a drawing from Elizabeth Kellam de Forest, *The Grounds and Gardens at Mount Vernon* [Mount Vernon, 1982]).

78. Courtyard garden at Mount Vernon. Anonymous oil painting (1792). The Mount Vernon Ladies' Association of the Union.

79. View of Mount Vernon from the northwest. Aquatint by George Parkyns (1798). The Mount Vernon Ladies' Association of the Union.

80. Claremont (Esher, Surrey). Engraved plan by John Rocque (ca. 1739). The National Trust.

81. Esher Place (Esher, Surrey). Engraved view by

Luke Sullivan (1759). Victoria and Albert Museum.

82. Monticello landscape (after a study-plan by William L. Beiswanger, 1990). Monticello/Thomas Jefferson Memorial Foundation, Inc.

83. Jefferson's sketch of two rectangular flower beds for Monticello (ca. 1772). Coolidge Collection, Massachusetts Historical Society (Nichols 57).

84. Jeffeson's sketch of the house and adjacent grounds at Monticello (ca. 1772–1808[9]). Coolidge Collection, Massachusetts Historical Society (Nichols 61).

85. View of Montalto from the vegetable garden at Monticello. Monticello/Thomas Jefferson Memorial Foundation, Inc.

86. Jefferson's sketch of the first vegetable garden proposed along Mulberry Row, Monticello (ca. 1774). Coolidge Collection, Massachusetts Historical Society (Nichols 87).

87. Conjectural drawing of the Garden Pavilion at Monticello, based upon archaeological excavations. Monticello/Thomas Jefferson Memorial Foundation, Inc.

88. Aerial photograph of the Monticello grounds. Monticello/Thomas Jefferson Memorial Foundation, Inc.

89. Jefferson's first sketch for the orchards at Monticello (1778). Coolidge Collection, Massachusetts Historical Society (Nichols 127).

90a and b. Thomas Jefferson's "General ideas for the improvement of Monticello" (ca. 1804). Coolidge Collection, Massachusetts Historical Society (Nichols 171, pp.1–2)

91. Jefferson's drawing of the top of Monticello's gardens (1806). Jefferson Papers, Massachusetts Historical Society (Nichols 61).

92. Jefferson's sketch of the planned oval flower beds for the east and west lawns at Monticello (1807). Historical Society of Pennsylvania.

93. Jefferson's rough sketch of the proposed serpentine walk around his west lawn, with oval flower beds (1807). Coolidge Collection, Massachusetts Historical Society (Nichols 147-gg).

94. Jefferson's "Plan of the Spring Roundabout at Monticello" (1790s). By permission of The Huntington Library, San Marino, California (Nichols 197).

95. View of the west front and lawn at Monticello. Watercolor by Jane Bradick (Peticoles), 1825. Monticello/Thomas Jefferson Memorial Foundation, Inc.

96. View of the St. George Tucker House, Williamsburg, from the Wythe House across the Palace Green. Photograph: Colonial Williamsburg Foundation.

97. Manuscript memorandum in an almanac belonging to St. George Tucker (1792). Tucker-Coleman Papers, Swem Library, College of William and Mary, Williamsburg.

Preface

Early American garden history is as yet undeveloped, and the scholarship is still uneven. It is perhaps understandable, then, that no thorough study of Virginia gardens in this period has been available. Architecture, literature, music, and painting in colonial Virginia have received more attention than gardening, either as a fine art or in the horticultural sense. Only the history of botany has been less neglected than the history of garden design or the stories of individual gardeners. This book, I hope, will help adjust the imbalance.

Although I am concerned primarily with the eighteenth century, the scope of this study ranges beyond the colonial period because two of the most important Virginia gardeners, Thomas Jefferson and St. George Tucker, lived into the first quarter of the nineteenth century. Moreover, my emphasis is on pleasure, not practical, gardening, except when the evidence suggests that a gardener or garden provided for orchards, vegetables, and herbs in a deliberately decorative manner. It is clear that American colonial gardeners often grew fruit, vegetables, and herbs together with ornamental plantings. My interest in them, however, extends neither to their roles as essential elements of household economy nor to the care that had to be taken to ensure that the greatest productivity would be realized.

A book about the gardening of eighteenth-century Virginia must necessarily deal with both plantation and town gardens, but it must also be selective. Although I bring in other towns from time to time, notably in the Tidewater region, Williamsburg is the central focus. As the capital of Virginia for most of the eighteenth century and one of the colony's economic centers, it was a gathering place for the individuals most important to the life, society, art, and government of the colony. Some loosely scattered evidence exists for gardening in Alexandria, Fredericksburg, Norfolk, Portsmouth, Richmond, and York-town, but most of what is known about colonial town gardening in Virginia revolves around the capital.

Decisions about which plantation gardens to discuss were more difficult to make. For the most part, I have been guided by available historical and archaeological evidence. In other cases, the determining factors have been the people who owned and gardened the plantations or the significance, however slight the evidence, of what is known about them. Several plantation gardens from other colonies occasionally find their way into this account in order to elucidate and provide some context for the practices in Virginia.

The amateur garden restorer or landscaper probably will not find this book useful if his or her objective is chiefly to lay out a colonial-style garden. I hope instead that it will go some way toward reconstructing a world almost completely lost to us. Garden history is an especially elusive aspect of art history. Unlike most other works of art, gardens cannot be preserved by museums and libraries, nor are they even capable of the longevity of buildings. Through neglect, one season alone can modify a garden, five can alter it in major ways, and ten can destroy it. Moreover, the ease of redesigning means that gardens continuously evolve, either by intention or by default, and eventually most of them disappear. Very few eighteenth-century English gardens, for example, survive today in anything approximating their original forms; in the United States, still fewer have survived. The garden historian must therefore rely heavily on what graphic and documentary evidence may still exist. But there is not much of that for Virginia, except for Monticello and, to a lesser degree, Mount Vernon.

Despite these obstacles, the effort to recover what we can of this aspect of cultural history is well worth the effort. What may emerge are not only ideas about what gardens looked like in the colonial period but also broader themes about what gardens could mean to the people and culture at the time.

. . .

In the process of researching and writing this book, I have benefited from an enormous amount of help that I am now pleased to acknowledge. My principal debt is to Cary Carson, Vice President of Research at the Colonial Williamsburg Foundation. It was he who first suggested this subject and provided me with all manner of assistance and encouragement to enable me to complete it. He also read two drafts

and offered helpful and intelligent suggestions. Without him, I would not have written it.

Present and past members of the Department of Historical Research at the Colonial Williamsburg Foundation have willingly offered detailed help and advice: Linda Rowe, who in the latter stages expedited all manner of business for me, especially the acquisition of several illustrations; Patricia Gibbs and John Hemphill II, both of whom checked the manuscript for accuracy and hunted up lost references; Harold Gill; John Ingram; Julie Richter; and Susan Berg. I should also like to thank the Foundation's Department of Architectural Research, whose assistance has been vital. The Director, Edward Chappell, read an early draft and made many constructive suggestions. Mark R. Wenger, an expert on Westover, read the chapter on that plantation and shared helpful insights. I am also indebted to Richard Stinely for expertly drawing fifteen garden plans and to James Garrett, Director of the Audio-Visual Department at Colonial Williamsburg, for helping me to collect the photographs for the plates. Foundation help has also been forthcoming from Graham Hood, Joan Dolmesch, and Margaret Pritchard. My thanks also to Margaret Cook, Curator of Manuscripts and Rare Books in Swem Library, College of William and Mary, who helped me through the Tucker-Coleman, Blow, and Skipwith papers in that repository. A special word of appreciation also goes to Camille Wells, who gave two of my drafts thoughtful readings and suggested useful revisions, and to Carl Lounsbury for last-minute help.

Other individuals to whom I am indebted for their reading of this study in manuscript stage are Thad Tate, Kevin Kelly, Donna Sheppard, and Audrey Noel-Hume. William L. Beiswanger, Resident Architect of the Thomas Jefferson Memorial Foundation, helped me immeasurably in the reading of the Monticello gardens and supplied illustrative material. Gregory A. Johnson of the University of Virginia Library assisted me at a critical time in sorting out the Jefferson drawings. Finally, I take pleasure in mentioning my gratitude to Robert Birney, Senior Vice President of Colonial Williamsburg Foundation, who generously authorized funding and other means whereby I could begin, carry on, and complete this book.

In addition to these individuals, I am grateful to the repositories and collections that have allowed me to use documentary and graphic material. These include the Alderman Library, University of Virginia; the British Library; the Bodleian Library, Oxford; the Gloucestershire Record Office; Sir Bryan Gooch's family papers at Benacre Hall, Suffolk; the Huntington Library; the Library of Congress; the Manuscript and Rare Books Department and the Joseph and Margaret Muscarelle Museum of Art at the College of William and Mary; the Maryland Historical Society; the Massachusetts Historical Society; the Mount Vernon Ladies' Association; the National Trust of Great Britain; the New Jersey Historical Society; the University of North Carolina Library; the Pennsylvania Historical Society; the Public Record Office, London; the Service Historique de l'Armée de Terre, Paris; Special Collections, Swem Library, College of William and Mary; the Victoria and Albert Museum; the Virginia Historical Landmarks Commission; the Virginia Historical Society; and the West Sussex Record Office. Individual acknowledgments of permission to use illustrative material are included in the List of Illustrations.

A final word of thanks goes to Cynthia, Andrew, and Claire for their buoyant support and to my caring parents, to whom I dedicate this book.

Bury, West Sussex, England
September 1990

Introduction

Between the towns and the plantations of eighteenth-century Virginia there necessarily existed links—economic, social, artistic, and cultural—that affected the quality of life in both. Such links made life both easier and more pleasurable. Once commercially and culturally viable towns had been established in the colony early in the century, plantation and town could each depend on the other's resources and thereby enhance one another. In fact, a recurring complaint throughout the seventeenth century was that the plantations lacked the unifying and cohesive influences that could have been provided by towns and thus remained too isolated from one another and failed to promote quickly enough the growth of civilization in North America's oldest colony. Alexander Spotswood was struck by the scattered character of what he called "luxurious" living up and down the plantations when he arrived in 1711 to take up his governorship.

Spotswood was fortunate. He was moving into a new town, the young capital named Williamsburg, which would soon begin to create a focal point of civilization in the colony, at the same time drawing the plantations to itself and to each other. More than that, he himself brought to the town and colony architectural as-

pirations that included garden design. His gardening at the newly built Governor's Palace, together with the town plan conceived and directed by the former governor, Francis Nicholson (1698–1705), endowed Williamsburg with the beginnings of a gardening tradition that developed immediately through the botanical and designing virtuosity of John Custis, the fortuitous arrival of the English naturalist Mark Catesby, and the ornamental garden layout at the College of William and Mary. Broadening from mid-century onward—through the efforts of tradesmen, artisans, professional classes like lawyers and doctors, and planter oligarchs who set up town residences in addition to their country seats—a practical and decorative garden tradition determined much of the character of the capital as it grew. That tradition lasted, moreover, well into the next century and was a source of nostalgia for old residents like St. George Tucker.

The gardening going on in Williamsburg's public places and in the grounds of its more affluent and powerful residents commanded greater attention from travelers than did town gardening anywhere else in the colony. More valuable for the general pursuit of gardening in the colony, though, were the planters who frequently came to the capital from their seats, chiefly in the Tidewater region. There they saw the college and Palace gardens, perhaps consulted with the gardeners in charge at both places—who were among the most competent practitioners around—exchanged ideas with one another, and took home with them gardening books, advice, plants (from the college, Palace, or local residents), tools, and renewed enthusiasm. The capital also enjoyed more leisure time and money; not surprisingly, then, ornamental plantation gardening in Virginia began to evolve and grow more confident simultaneously with Williamsburg's increasing distinction. And, in turn, numbers of planters, especially those who acquired town properties but not excluding families like the Byrds and Burwells who lived close enough to be in town frequently without having to purchase residences, exercised their own influences on gardening in the capital. William Byrd II contributed many of his own plants at Westover to the gardens of his town friends and acquaintances, including Spotswood's Palace gardens.

. . .

The interrelatedness of plantation and town gardens in the minds of gardeners was one of the bright effects of Williamsburg's creation and development, but it was not a phenomenon of early colonial cultural life without precedent in European garden history. Garden historians have shown how the gardens of ancient Rome, Renaissance Italy, seventeenth-century Holland, and eighteenth-century England, to name but a few examples, were distinguished by modes of exchangeability between the rural and the urban.[1] In Virginia, however, the kinship between town and rural gardens was more complicated. When Williamsburg was finally established as the capital at the end of the seventeenth century, the colony still did not have a pervasive "landscape" or "countryside" with which to embrace the town. Both these words call up images of land that has been lived on, enjoyed, and profitably used and improved long enough to have generated particular associations and values. In

Western thought, the word *countryside* for centuries, but especially since the Renaissance, has evoked positive and benign images of peace and beauty amid comfort and security. And the emotional appeal of the countryside has been heightened by the latter's contrast to urban areas.[2]

Until the eighteenth century, however, Virginia had neither a substantial urban area to juxtapose with the countryside nor much countryside itself. Instead, it had wilderness. The individual plantations that Spotswood noted scattered up and down the land may be seen only as pockets of landscape within the wilderness. They were too few and too isolated from one another to compose collectively a "countryside." Individually, there was about them relatively little of that traditional European sense of retirement and rural bliss. Except to some undetermined extent for places like Sir William Berkeley's Green Spring, William Byrd I's Westover, his son-in-law Robert Beverley's Beverley Park, or William Fitzhugh's Eagle's Nest, seventeenth-century plantations were little industrial complexes keynoted by economy rather than luxury or rural recreational pastimes. Not until three decades after Williamsburg's establishment did owners of plantations more commonly begin to cultivate images of countryside life in their demesnes, and not until mid-century or later did they begin to evolve a landscape out of the wilderness—one that could relate functionally as well as emblematically to the town. Significantly, that imaginative interplay between landscape (or the *rus*) and town, and between landscape garden and town, occurred most energetically along the major rivers, where the concentration of plantations was greatest. Indeed, travelers from time to time referred to these river landscapes—perhaps struck by the analogy to the Thames from Putney to Twickenham or to Italy's Brenta—as the "gardens" of Virginia.

Regarding the exchangeability of garden designs between town and country, I have not been able to find explicit documentary evidence that any garden in Williamsburg or another town directly affected the design of a plantation garden. There are several indefinite clues, as well as credible traditions, that certain Williamsburg gardens did exert such influence. Benjamin Waller's Williamsburg garden, for example, may well have determined something of the shape of Richard Blow's garden at Tower Hill; similarly, from their garden on the Palace Green, Robert and Eliza Carter almost certainly took design ideas for their gardens at Nomini Hall. But such links cannot be pinned down by a casual diary entry, a passage from a letter, or (best of all) graphic evidence. Not even the Governor's Palace, which has been shown clearly to have influenced plantation architecture in the colony, provides such authority.

Nonetheless, one of the purposes of this book is to illustrate and document the reciprocity between town and plantation in eighteenth-century Virginia, one of the effects of which was to cultivate a sense of civilized living and grace. Such reciprocity or diffusion of genteel culture began in earnest in the 1720s and 1730s, when the "great house" became interwoven with the Virginia plantation way of life. Gardens—utilitarian and ornamental but especially the latter—like other trappings of a domicile, tended to make people take heart that they were not as completely exiled from the Old World culture as they felt. The garden became a powerful metaphor for improvement, progress, and culture in the minds of many Virginians during this period of the colony's history. It could project order amid disorder, a sense of controlling, or wishing to control, one's environment. It could represent an impulse to escape to a civilization on the other side of the Atlantic, an impulse suffused with nostalgia. Byrd II and Custis, who were brothers-in-law and shared an almost compulsive interest in gardening, both felt this impulse profoundly. The garden also had the value of a reassuring artifact that had been redeemed from the wilderness but still retained fresh associations with it. From Robert Beverly, who at the end of the seventeenth century pastoralized the plantations with images of their "fragrant and delightful Walks," to Thomas Jefferson and his patriotic mythologizing of the American landscape as a latter-day agrarian Eden, the garden

frequently was seen to relate to natural scenery much as art did to nature. Gardens stood for improvements and refinements of nature, but nature in return endowed gardens with associations of paradise-like settings.

For many plantation patriarchs, and perhaps also town planners and gardeners like Nicholson and Spotswood, gardening doubtless was chiefly another means by which they were able to dominate and prevail over their environment—an assertion of will and ego. But for most of the personalities who figure prominently in this book, it was a more subtle and sensitive activity—a very personal art. There was a strongly emotive and individual element of landscaping keenly felt by a number of them. "As is the Gardener, so is the Garden," Thomas Fuller observed in 1732.[3] John Custis is the best example of a Virginia gardener using his garden for self-projection, as a repository of his personal values and a reflection of his identity. This is also an important theme in early-eighteenth-century England, when a garden's associative meaning came to be understood as part of its value and beauty.

The Virginia gardener, however, encountered special physical problems on the way to making his garden, and these tended to dramatize his personal relation to it. Skilled gardeners were in great demand, and few were to be found for hire. Apparently, English gardeners, if they came at all, did not stay long. Moreover, the seasons were extreme, plants (early in the century especially) scarce or still unclassified, ornaments hard to come by, and gardening books (notwithstanding the efforts of the office of the *Virginia Gazette*) not easily obtainable. If a Custis, Byrd, Tucker, Jefferson, or Joseph Prentis could overcome these obstacles, he cultivated in the process a gratifyingly proud link between himself and his landscape. If he failed, as Custis in his old age felt he had, the distress was very real.

• • •

Entirely separate from the matter of garden design and more completely documented is the botanical connection between the colonies and England. Plant exchanges had taken place even in the seventeenth century. The most active promoter of exchanges in Virginia was Custis, beginning about 1715, when he built a house in Williamsburg. For more than twenty years he regularly received English plants of many varieties, sent to him chiefly by the Quaker botanist Peter Collinson. Many others indulged in this means of stocking their gardens, so that English flora had a decided effect on the look of colonial gardens. According to existing evidence, this dependence on English flora was more characteristic of the first than the second half of the eighteenth century. The exchange worked the other way, too, as colonists steadily supplied the botanists and gardeners of the mother country with native Virginia flora, thereby not only helping to generate, through the Royal Society, a new energy in English plant research and catalog ing but also affecting somewhat the appearance of English gardens. At Badminton House in Gloucestershire, for example, a large folio volume dating from early in the century is filled with color paintings of innumerable Virginia plants. These presumably were done by some member of the Beaufort household to record plantings at Badminton.

Special note needs to be taken of the Virginia climate and soil, both of which complicate and confuse the theme of how much gardening in England influenced that in eighteenth-century Virginia. The early colonists did not understand that Virginia, along with most of the eastern coast, had an extreme climate. Since the colony had the same latitude as Spain, they reasoned that the same sorts of plants would flourish there—citrus, grape vines, mulberry trees, pomegranates, olives, almonds, and other exotic species of a warm and temperate climate. This expectation not only induced great excitement about the colony's agricultural and horticultural promise; it also encouraged the vision of Virginia and a few of the other colonies as temperate paradises or Edens where just a little labor would bear rich rewards. As regarded gardening specifically, colonists assumed that in such a mild climate they could easily re-create the pleasures of the English garden, but with far more varied and exotic plants. It would be like realizing in actual greenery Milton's Garden of Eden or stepping into the idealized garden of Ben Jonson's "To Penshurst": man and nature would cooperate easily and harmoniously to bless each other. As historians have pointed out,[4] however, the early settlers—and their descendants for nearly a century—did not appreciate that Virginia's was a continental climate, whereas Spain's and England's had the benefit of the tempering effect of the ocean. Not grasping this, colonial gardeners persistently miscalculated what could and could not thrive in their gardens. Failure tended to raise suspicions of indolence rather than induce reform of methods. Even Custis, as late as the 1730s and 1740s, continued to mourn the loss of his plants in extremes of cold, heat, and drought without readily giving up cherished ideas of having certain English flora in his Williamsburg garden. Eventually, he saw the light. "If I were a young man," he wrote to Collinson in 1741, "I would never plant any trees that would not endure our winters."[5] The scale of the problem is suggested by a letter from Collinson to Custis in 1736 regarding where "Delicious Fruites" like watermelons might be grown: "If you Look into the Map and see the Northern Latitude of Petersburg or Muscow one wou'd reasonably conclude such Delicious Fruites are not to be expected in that Climate. They are Indeed beholden to a more Souther[n] situation for their production."[6] He may be right about melons, but in spite of Custis's frequent complaints to him about how vicious frosts had destroyed many of his plants, Collinson still concludes that latitude is about all one needs to know when judging what will grow in a particular "situation." After reading Custis's recitation of the havoc wrought on his garden by freezing weather in 1741, Collinson had to confess that "Its Effects in your southern latitude is very surpriseing."[7]

The Virginia climate forced changes in the rules of gardening on anyone who had ideas of gardening with a European, especially an English, perspective. And yet, until the nineteenth century there was almost no written guidance for the gardener in the colony. Philip Miller's *Gardener's Dictionary* (first edition, 1737)—a Bible in the colonies and, incidently, heartily recommended by Collinson to Custis in 1737—did not address itself at all to the problems posed by the climate of the eastern coast. The aesthetic impulse to design gardens according to more naturalized criteria did grow slowly in Virginia, but the gardener who was thus inclined found that he could not simply transplant the English garden to the colony's climate and soil.

And toward soil, a similarly unscientific attitude prevailed. As John Stilgoe has put it, "Colonists carried to North America the soil lore of their fathers' fields and wrote always with old-country standards in mind."[8] According to Old World lore, for example, the color of the soil was reckoned one of the best clues to its fertility, as was the presence of trees. The more trees, the better the soil. Since Virginia was well endowed with forests, there was a consensus that its soil was generally and vigorously fertile. The effect of such an assumption was a remarkable inattention by gardeners and botanists alike to specific soil variations and, consequently, no little confusion about why certain plants would not grow in particular places. William Byrd II almost never mentions soil in an analytical vein in his letters and other writings about plants and landscape. Neither does Custis in his gardening correspondence with Collinson. There appears to have been a shared and simple understanding between them that the best plants grew in the woods and forests. Whenever Custis wanted some hardy specimens to send Collinson, he journeyed into the forests to get them. In Collinson's mind, most of Virginia consisted of a wilderness of trees, of untamed land; therefore, most of its soil had to be excellent. It was of such wilderness-endowed soil that he was thinking when he suggested that the reason variegated English plants in Virginia tended to lose what he called the "sicklyness" of their varied shades of green in favor of their "Native Verdure" was "the

Vigorousness of your soil & Climate," for "your fine Country is a Meare Monpelier to their Natural Complection."[9] In fact, however, soil fertility varied considerably in Williamsburg alone. One would have thought Custis, Byrd, and other Virginians would have made this abundantly clear to their European friends in order to displace or discredit their Old World lore, but existing evidence suggests they did not.

. . .

English influences on Virginia garden design and practice are difficult to document closely, mainly because few plans of colonial gardens survive and because English ideas had to be adapted to the Virginia landscape and economy as well as to the climate and soil, with the result that they may not have turned out to be recognizably English. At times, colonists do specifically state their debts to English taste, or possess English gardening manuals and treatises that suggest their debts, or introduce features that are clearly English. Certain individuals moved back and forth frequently between Virginia and England and so kept up with English garden styles. Others attempted to do this through what they read or heard others say. Although the seventeenth-century European garden tradition is difficult (but not entirely impossible) to trace in Virginia plantations during the second half of that century, the eighteenth-century English garden represented a stronger cultural and aesthetic statement that did not go ignored in the colony. American practice generally lagged behind that in England—and even English practice lagged behind English theory on the subject at the start of the century—although perhaps by only a couple of decades and not by as much as half a century, as has long been supposed. What evidence there is suggests that the English landscape garden inspired, in one way or another, some of the garden designing, especially on the plantations, in all the colonies during the second half of the century.

It is plausible to assume that whatever ideas for garden design arrived in Virginia with seventeenth-century planters derived from contemporary English fashion. Apart from features of the Tudor garden that continued in favor late into the seventeenth century—small walled gardens containing geometrically shaped sections divided by rails or similarly obtrusive separators and stocked with elaborate, sometimes emblematic, arrangements of flowers—the English garden was then more European than native. The garden may have been the chief art form England contributed to Europe after the Renaissance, but that transfer did not begin to occur until the beginning of the eighteenth century. The indigenous eighteenth-century creation that became known in France as the *jardin anglais* was based principally on a rejection of autocratic French formality on a vast scale. The relentlessly dominating axial design of the French layout, with its seemingly endless vistas, intricate parterres, geometric settings, and rigid canals, constituted the largest European influence on English gardens of the seventeenth century. It was augmented (especially after William and Mary assumed the throne in 1688) by the fastidious Dutch taste for topiary (clipped evergreens) and less pretentious roomlike or compartmentalized garden areas. An Italian element also made an appearance, one that was more sympathetic with the emerging *jardin anglais*. It showed itself through a use of water more expressive than the regular French and Dutch canal and in a more subtle and less clearly defined management of space.

Geometric formality in the shape of square or rectangular garden areas divided into quadrants, or split into two halves by a central path, or laid out in some sort of balanced or symmetrical scheme and enclosed by wooden fences is evident in seventeenth- and eighteenth-century Virginia, but whether it was consciously indebted to the European tradition is far from clear. Certainly the intricate flower gardening of the Tudor and French styles was economically beyond the planter; it would have struck him, in the middle of his other household and estate concerns, as a tasteless extravagance. The virtue of a

fenced garden in colonial Virginia, separated visually as well as practically from surrounding ground, had little to do with the concept of a *hortus conclusus*, the garden as an isolated and sacred aid to devotion and contemplation. It was in the main an actual, not a symbolic, world to which the gardener addressed himself as he looked around him to decide what to do with his ground. There can be no doubt that the geometric regularity evident, in one way or another, in most seventeenth- and early-eighteenth-century American gardens was a manifestation of the gardener's practical need to protect and control efficiently the gardening that he was doing. But if at the same time he could satisfy himself that to some extent he was recalling images and ideas inherent in the English garden—or, through the English garden, features of the Renaissance Italian garden—then all to the good. Evidence of English influence is almost nonexistent for the seventeenth century but becomes less scarce throughout the eighteenth century. Without replacing the plain and pervasive squares and rectangles of ornamental gardens in Virginia, touches of irregularity and the picturesque began to appear, in varying degrees, in this and that garden. Plans and maps may tend to overlook them, but they were there. We know this from descriptions in letters, diaries, and journals, as well as from archaeological excavations—all of which, it should be noted, also reveal the preponderance of squares and rectangles. The aesthetic, in other words, of the naturalized English garden of the early eighteenth century, with its congenial Italian overtones, was present in the gardening consciousness of many Virginians in the century. This is evident not only in existing descriptions but also in the gardening books that took up space on Virginia shelves—books that could not be read without imparting aspects of this aesthetic.[10]

· · ·

This is not the place to go into the history of the English landscape garden of the eighteenth century; but since a few of its features are manifested at different times in Virginia, it will be useful to mention them. It is important to remember that these features were themselves constantly evolving in England and that there was no such thing as a spontaneous and sudden "revolution" of taste that made them current. A similarly gradual evolution occurred in eighteenth-and early-nineteenth-century Virginia.

Quite early in the century, impatient and dissatisfied chiefly with both the grand manner and the ornate splendor of the French style, and impelled by new ideas about nature and man's relationship to it, the English began to object to the wasteful use of land in huge landscaped estates that performed little function other than self-aggrandizement of the owner. Joseph Addison and Stephen Switzer both urged in their different ways that a landscape be used for profit as well as pleasure. This idea, which was a prelude to a greater integration between house, immediate garden, and surrounding landscape, and which may strike us today as obvious good sense, inevitably appealed to planters in the New World, who could not afford to squander real estate for the sake of mere aesthetics. Addison's essays and Switzer's books were available in the colony and, along with other writings on gardening, had their places in several libraries whose inventories are extant. By the 1730s, or perhaps a little later, the pleasure-profit principle led to the popularization of a new garden art form, the *ferme ornée* or ornamental farm. Jefferson wrote about seeing examples of such English landscape gardens, and at Monticello he employed the idea to encompass most of the acreage around his house. There were other earlier, but less explicitly described, examples in the colony.

Greater economy, which was one of the premises encouraging this reaction against the French garden, also accounted for increased simplicity of design. If one reads Robert Beverley's *History and Present State of Virginia* (1705) with these new themes of usefulness and simplicity in mind, his comments on landscapes and gardens appear timely in that they are framed by a similar spirit of freedom and industry. The same is true

of John Lawson's writings on the Carolinas at about the same time, although Lawson was interested even more in productive as distinct from decorative gardening. Since people like Beverley and Lawson, the Byrds, Custis, the Carters, and the Burwells did not, so far as we know, themselves make the connection between their landscaping and the more practical directions the English were taking, it is not possible to argue confidently that in the early part of the century they deliberately emulated English trends. After all, even in England practice lagged behind theory, and well into the century the European models continued to leave their mark. But in England the Enlightenment principles of liberty and equality increasingly made those old autocratic gardens seem outdated, and in Virginia there were signs of this new spirit in town and plantation. Jefferson's and Washington's landscapes ultimately represent the fulfillment of this process, where gardening, economics, politics, and philosophy inform and support one another.

Jefferson, especially, understood that the fortunes of the landscape garden involved the history of ideas as well as design, as his writings, not to mention his garden plans, amply bear witness. In much more fragmented ways, this notion is evident throughout the colony in the eighteenth century. Spotswood's gardening at the Palace was perhaps motivated by politics as much as by an architectural sense. He appears to have had a minimal interest in horticulture. His and Nicholson's town plans, in which vistas and public gardens figured prominently, were determined by ideas regarding social order. Custis, too, saw gardening in political terms, but also in pictorial terms suggesting that he, like his English counterparts, likened gardening to pictures. Had he been familiar with it, he would have agreed with Alexander Pope's remark in 1734: "All gardening is landscape-painting. . . . Just like a landscape hung up."[11] The relish with which travelers and observers after mid-century comment on the views from Virginia gardens highlights the growing importance of this theme.

Given the famous and interesting personalities involved, the problems to be surmounted, the ideas generated, and the varied garden effects created, the progress of gardening appears as an engaging drama in the growth of colonial Virginia, the like of which has not been enjoyed since Prentis, Tucker, Washington, and Jefferson passed from the scene.

The Pleasure Gardens of Virginia

1

The Beginnings: Garden Images in the Seventeenth Century

On one of the first days after his landing in the New World in May 1607, George Percy, a member of the original Jamestown settlement, excitedly recorded seeing in the forests, fields, and swamps "ground all flowing over with fair flowers of sundry colors and kinds, as though it had been any garden or orchard in England."[1] A century later, when Alexander Spotswood arrived in Williamsburg in 1710 to take up his duties as lieutenant-governor of Virginia, he wrote back happily to his brother in Edinburgh: "The Life I lead here is neither in a Crowd of Company nor in a Throng of Business, but rather after a quiet Country manner: & now I am sufficiently amused with planting Orchard & Gardens, & with finishing a large House which is design'd (at the Country's Charge) for the reception of their Governours."[2] In the century that intervened between these two remarks, a tradition developed in Virginia of seeing, or wanting to see, the wilderness as a garden.

Percy was one of the first writers in the seventeenth century to apply garden images to the wilderness, images that performed the imaginative function of taming and controlling the wilderness—making it seem more like the soft and sylvan gardens, fields, and woods of England that the settlers had left far behind them.[3] To be sure, these pioneering settlers were honest with themselves when in the formless wilderness they saw garden-like scenes of incredible fecundity and luxuriance. Their immediate desire to describe the flora and fauna of this newfound paradise evinces their genuine wonder and amazement.[4]

The immense and exciting natural riches the colonists found gave them hope that with this recently revealed part of God's creation the lost Garden of Eden could be restored in its botanical and horticultural fullness. Their first efforts to list and describe plants in America were part of a new and popular literary art form in England—natural history and travel literature—that coincided with the early stages of a fascination with plants that eventually led to the founding of the Royal Society in 1660.

The settlements at Roanoke Island and Jamestown were founded just in time to gratify this great interest in plants. A few months after he safely arrived in Jamestown, Richard (or Robert) Rich wrote about the entire experience in a news ballad, "Newes from Virginia," that expresses his delight in the landscape:

> Great store of Fowle, of Venison,
> of Grapes, and Mulberries,
> Of Chestnuts, Walnuts, and such like,
> of fruits and Strawberries,
> There is indeed no want at all. . . .

In this paradise, Rich wrote, every laborer shall have his daily wages, "and for his more content, / A house and garden plot shall have."[5]

. . .

The tendency to see a garden in the wilderness grew out of the settlers' profound emotional need to sell this virgin wilderness to themselves as well as to those still in England whom they wanted to follow them there. So many features of the Virginia wilderness were quite unlike a paradise that their enthusiastic citing of and response to the landscape stands out as a species of rationalization for their loss of, among other things, the English garden. They could imagine that Eden was, in a sense, reconstituted with all its pastoral and primitive simplicity in the glades of Virginia. Looked at in this way, the compulsion of seventeenth-century Virginia settlers to see or imagine gardens around them could have become a key ingredient, fired by nostalgia, in the evolution of their gardens.

We cannot always be certain, however, whether a writer like Robert Beverley is giving us fact or fancy with allusions to Virginia gardens in his *History and Present State of Virginia* (1705). In one instance, Beverley informs his English readers, with a touch of the pastoral, that the Virginians' "Plantations, Orchards, and Gardens constantly afford 'em fragrant and delightful Walks" and that "a Garden is no where sooner made than there, either for Fruits, or Flowers." But then, in the more realistic style of a reformer, he judges that "yet they han't many Gardens in the Country, fit to bear that name." Elsewhere, he states that in Virginia and adjacent colonies "Paradice it self seem'd to be there" and that the colonies "are reckon'd the Gardens of the World"— an allusion to the copiousness of nature in America, to the idea that within it one may find the prelapsarian fullness of the world.[6] Beverley's apparent contradictions may be explained by the ratio of art to nature that he varyingly adopts as he writes from one perspective or another. As James Kornwolf has perceptively put it, this is an instance not so much of a conflict

between the primitive and the pastoral, the savage and the picturesque, as an illustration of changing attitudes—even within a week or day—toward formal, informal, and "artificial" elements in landscape.[7] Over the next hundred years the aesthetics of garden design in America, as in England, would develop in terms of those changing attitudes.

The paradox Beverley presents us may also partly be explained by the enormous gulf between the dream and the reality of the seventeenth-century colonial South, between what these early settlers wrote idealistically and promotionally for their countrymen at home and for their own sense of well-being in the wilderness and what they quickly discovered were the facts of life about survival in that wilderness. As Edmund Morgan has dramatically shown, for even the more affluent settlers by mid- and late century—the Beverleys, Fitzhughs, Wormeleys, Byrds, Carters, Diggeses, and others on plantations—life in the colony hardly measured up to a comfortable squirearchy tasting the niceties of rural life.[8] The plantation economy required extraordinary industry and stamina and, until near the end of the century, left little time even for the elite to act out their images of garden pleasures or other forms of social diversion.[9] Indeed, whatever else Virginia promotional literature of the seventeenth century pictured in the way of riches, land, freedom, and so on, it did not promise gentility, certainly not the kind associated with pleasure gardening.[10]

Another factor behind Beverley's complaint that there were too few gardens in Virginia was his chagrin that little in the way of a pervasive and unifying culture, of which gardens could have been a part, had been encouraged in Virginia because of the lack of a substantial town or city. By the time Beverley wrote, South Carolina had enjoyed for more than twenty years a capital city that was far more substantial than Jamestown. There, in Charleston, a sufficient local demand for plants and seeds had induced John Lawson to set up a nursery business in 1701. Lawson—apparently sent over in that year by the well-known English botanist James Petiver on a plant-finding mission—wrote that Charleston in 1701 had "very regular and fair Streets, in which are good Buildings of Brick and Wood."[11] Although he was thinking chiefly of plantations near Charleston, Thomas Ashe in 1682 also had in mind the gardening of the two-year-old capital when he wrote that in addition to planting vegetables the new gardeners of that area were beautifying their grounds: "Their Gardens also begin to be beautified and adorned with such Herbs and Flowers which to the Smell or Eye are pleasing and agreable, viz. The Rose, Tulip, Carnation and Lilly, etc."[12]

Since Williamsburg was not even conceived of until 1680, Virginia throughout the seventeenth century was deprived of the urbane cultural and social as well as political center that would certainly have stimulated town gardening and inaugurated at a much earlier date the gardening activity that is the subject of this book. In 1705 Beverley did not write much about gardening in Virginia—he only recognized the potential. He would have accepted, one feels, the appropriateness of the garden analogy used in 1662 by a country parson who lamented the fragmented state of the Church of England in the colony and pleaded with the bishop of London (in whose gardens at Fulham Palace numerous Virginia plants were already represented) to consider the unifying effects a major town would have: "contemplate the poor Church (whose plants now grow wilde in that Wildernesse) become like a garden enclosed, like a Vineyard fenced . . . all of which are the promised fruites of well ordered Towns."[13]

Beverley said nothing in his *History* about gardens in Jamestown, and there is little enough known about them from any other source. Undoubtedly, almost the only function of gardening there throughout the century was practical. In 1624, for example, the House of Burgesses decided that the best way to establish self-sufficient vegetable and fruit gardens in the capital was to compel residents to fence in their gardens. It therefore threatened fines against settlers who did not do so.[14] Beyond that, only a handful of hints—curiously, all but one from the first half of the century—indicates that a few Jamestown residents attempted to ornament their grounds with flowers and fruit.

Not surprisingly, these residents were among the wealthier and more important—Sir Thomas Gates, for one. Next to the governor's mansion, which he built in Jamestown between 1611 and 1614 as his "chiefest residence," he apparently created an area that a resident, Ralph Hamor, identified as a garden. Hamor wrote in 1615: "in Sir Thomas *Gates* his garden at Jamestown, many forward apple & peare trees come up, of the kernels set the yeere before."[15] William Pierce, about whom we know disappointingly little, harvested one hundred bushels of figs annually from his orchards; George Sandys, a poet and treasurer of the colony, who lived in Pierce's house, called them "the fairest in Virginia."[16] In 1624 Captain John Harvey acquired a large piece of land in the so-called New Town section of the settlement, near the river, in order to accommodate, as he put it, his "gardening and planting of sundry fruit trees."[17] Finally, by mid-century, according to William Berkeley's promotional tract, *A Perfect Description of Virginia* (1649), Jamestown's residents more generally were cultivating herbs and flowers having medicinal uses: "*Herbes* they have of all kinds for Garden, and *Physicke* Flowers." The writer went on to tempt his English readers with a list of native flora that could be or were being cultivated at Jamestown and elsewhere.[18]

In addition to these descriptions, we have some evidence of a garden layout at Jamestown that dates from the second half of the seventeenth century (figure 1). Among the surviving stone foundations, which have long been interpreted exclusively as the remains of seventeenth-century houses, is a brick wall about forty-four feet long that is interrupted in the middle by a flight of steps. The archaeological evidence suggests that this wall makes perfect sense not as part of a house but rather as a terraced garden wall. The steps appear to have led up to a higher

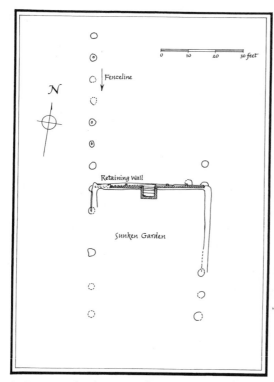

N

Fenceline

Retaining Wall

Sunken Garden

0   10   20   30 feet

1. *Remnant of mid-seventeenth-century terraced garden at Jamestown, Virginia. Recovered in archaeological excavations (after field drawings, National Park Service, 1940).*

been in continuous use from about 1650 to 1690.[19]

. . .

By mid-century numerous small- to medium-sized plantations had been established and their grounds developed and arranged chiefly to grow foodstuffs. These were ordinary cultivated landscapes with scarcely any provision for ornamental patterns other than those that would encourage utilitarian horticulture. To begin with, the siting of a dwelling place was chosen for how conducive it could be to the growth of produce, not for aesthetic reasons. And for the most part, outbuildings determined how the ground was laid out around the house. The opportunity was always there of course—especially in a warmer climate like Virginia's, where vegetables were grown without much concern for cold winds—for the small planter to arrange his buildings in a manner that pleased the eye and lent itself to the planting of an attractive set of beds between them. Herbs and flowers could in an abbreviated way ornament this or that vegetable bed. The need for food, however, not aesthetic considerations, overwhelmingly guided the energies of this planter.

There is little graphic evidence from the seventeenth century with which to illustrate the appearance of a small- to medium-sized plantation layout in the colonial South. Fortunately, a surviving plan of a site in Charles County, Maryland, dating from 1697, provides just a glimpse (figure 2). The site is not a plantation but a courthouse, built initially in 1674 as a private home with outlying grounds.[20] The sketchy plan shows a rectangular "Parsell [of] ould peach Trees" enclosed in a worm rail fence extending southeast along the perimeter of the property. Since the plan describes these trees as old in 1697, it is likely they were planted about twenty years earlier, close to the time when the house was first built. South of the orchard and not too far from the house, uncleared forests (identified on the plan as "Thickitt") remain, bounding the orchard and an area of cleared fields immedi-

terrace. Moreover, archaeologists have discovered ditches, carefully squared and leveled at the bottom, that look as if they bordered the lower garden terrace on the east and west sides, having replaced perhaps an earlier post fence, the holes of which have also been found outside the enclosure. These parallel ditches extend south in the direction of the James, so that the terraces could have taken in river views. The southern ditch, if there ever was one, has been completely obliterated; so it is not clear how near to the river the enclosed area ended. North of the upper terrace and close to it are the foundations of the later Ambler House. If this were a terraced garden, it apparently disappeared or was destroyed by the time, or when, that house was built late in the century. Most of the artifacts turned up by excavations indicate that the garden would have

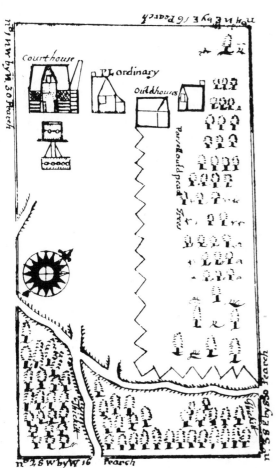

2. *Surveyor's plat of 1697 showing the Charles County, Maryland, courthouse and adjacent land.*

ately southeast of the house where sundry crops vital to the domestic economy of the household grew. Next to the house stand the outbuildings, separating it from the orchard. The plan is not detailed enough to suggest what kind of planting was done near the house, but the whole scene has a functional, utilitarian aspect.

. . .

Evidence of any gardening other than the practical, whether at Jamestown or on outlying plantations, is so meager as to suggest that for most of the seventeenth century Virginia did not begin to develop a clear tradition of gardening as an art, as a pleasurable pastime, or as a way of enhancing the setting for a house. There were, however, two known exceptions: Bacon's Castle and Governor William Berkeley's Green Spring.

Sir William Berkeley built his famous seat, Green Spring, in the late 1640s, about four miles north of Jamestown and five from Williamsburg (then known as Middle Plantation). The estate became a center of social and political activity in the half century before Williamsburg was created as the colonial capital. After the Ludwell family acquired it through marriage in 1680, it survived as a place of social importance throughout most of the next century until William Lee demolished the house and built another in 1796–1797.[21] With its well-stocked gardens and nurseries, the estate was a source of plants and, in a few instances, gardeners for gardens all over Virginia for much of the eighteenth century. It is difficult, even with the archaeological excavations that have been done on the site, to recapture a feeling for the design and layout of the seventeenth-century gardens, but we know that William Byrd II liked to walk there and, especially, play bowls on the bowling green. So did John Custis. Neither of them has endeared himself to garden historians by leaving descriptions of the gardens.

When in the early 1640s Berkeley acquired one thousand acres in the area of Green Spring and three thousand nearby along the James River, he entertained certain social aspirations in connection with this new land. He wrote about Virginia to a friend in England in 1662, saying that "men of as good Families as any Subjects in England have resided there."[22] Whether that statement was or was not true, it is clear he hoped it would be if enough Englishmen like himself were to cast their lots on these western shores of the Atlantic. He himself was not going to equivocate. He must have begun construction of his original house without delay, because he was in residence as a bachelor in 1649. For most of the 1640s, during his first tenure as governor, he was busy planting fruit trees. Henry Hyde, earl of Clarendon, was impressed enough by Berkeley's orchards to mention the "15 hundred fruit-trees, besides his Apricocks, Peaches, Mellicotons [a peach grafted on a quince], Quinces, Wardens [an old variety of baking pear], and such like fruits."[23]

After he resigned the governorship in 1652 and settled into "retirement" at Green Spring, Berkeley could devote full attention to the management of his estate and the culture of his orchards and gardens. Thomas Povey, receiver-general for rents and revenues of the plantations in Africa and America, praised Berkeley's scientific attention to agriculture and botany during those years in a letter of 1661 to Edward Digges of Bellefield plantation on the York River. On behalf of naturalists at Gresham College, London, Povey asked Digges to answer a few questions about natural products and flora with the help of "Noble and Ingenuous" men like Sir William, "who is known to bee a Person of most eminent Ingenuitie; and one that hath made verie many Tryalls and Experiments."[24]

By 1678, the year after Sir William's death, Lady Berkeley was proud enough of her residence to write to her cousin in England, judging that it was then "the finest seat in America & the only tollerable place for a Governor."[25] At some point late in the century, either in Berkeley's closing years or in the early stages of Philip Ludwell's subsequent ownership as Lady Berkeley's new husband,[26] the original house was enlarged and made to face south, in a somewhat Italian fashion, overlooking some terraces and a central path down them leading to the drive. This drive established the principal axis for the garden in what appears to have been a symmetrical and balanced layout. Archaeological excavations have revealed that sometime in the early eighteenth century the straight brick walls flanking the terraces were relaxed into a flourish of curving walls enclosing a larger garden area and arching decoratively out from the house (figure 3). These walls shaped what had been a strictly rectangular garden into an area of ornamental interest, somewhat resembling John Tayloe's splen-

did Mount Airy garden in the 1760s. The walls were still standing at the end of the eighteenth century when Latrobe painted the house (figure 4). They appear to have been even more elaborate in outline than those at the Governor's Palace, which are pictured in the engraving known as the Bodleian Plate (figures 10 and 20). A military map of Green Spring, drawn in 1781 by the French colonel Desandrouins (see also figure 3), also shows the position of the garden walls (not curved) and the main axis of the layout.

As Williamsburg's urbanity increased, so did Green Spring's, especially under Philip Ludwell II, who inherited the estate from his father in 1710. Byrd II recorded his frequent visits to Green Spring after 1705 in his diary, and Spotswood was entertained there when he first arrived in Virginia in 1710.[27] John Custis was also a regular guest, as was James Blair, president of the College of William and Mary. The Green Spring gardens therefore became widely known, and their plants began to find their way to London and to other plantations in the colony.

Word seems to have spread that the Green Spring nursery was a good source of Virginia flora, and thus its owners were among the first Virginians to engage in sustained transatlantic plant shipments. Almost certainly, they also received plants from England. Nathaniel Blakiston, governor of Maryland from 1698 to 1701 and later London agent for both Virginia and Maryland, wrote to Ludwell I in the early years of the century asking for plants. On March 12, 1708, he alluded to trees from Green Spring that Ludwell had sent to Bishop Compton at Fulham: "I am obliged to you for your kind overture of sending me some trees. I know you sent some over to the Bishop of London and if you will be soe kind as to remember me with a few I can place them where they will be very acceptable. . . . Since you are soe Franke to send me a few

3. Drawing of the Green Spring archaeological excavations in the 1920s, showing such prominent features as the garden enclosure facing the south front of the house (after Arthur Shurcliff [1929] and Desandrouins [1782]).

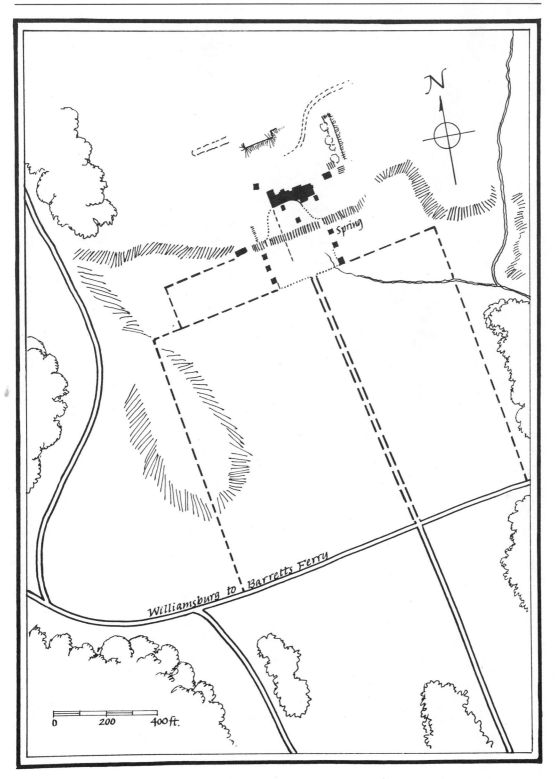

Spring

Williamsburg to Barretts Ferry

N

0   200   400 ft.

4. *Green Spring. Watercolor by Benjamin Latrobe, late 1790s.*

trees, I am informed amongst the rest the popler tree is very acceptable here."[28] William Blathwayt of Dyrham Park (Gloucestershire) was also the happy recipient of plants from Green Spring. He told Ludwell II in 1715 that Green Spring evergreens had "given an agreeable Entertainment in my Garden."[29]

If Alexander Spotswood spent any amount of time at Green Spring during the early years of his governorship, before he fell out with Ludwell II, it is likely he would have found the setting congenial. The pleasures to be enjoyed at Green Spring, according to Byrd's "Secret Diary," included cricket, Green Spring asparagus, horse racing on the grounds, and fencing. It all sounds unlikely in early eighteenth-century Tidewater Virginia, but for Byrd—who really wanted to be back in England—and very likely for Spotswood, Green Spring's cricket, gardens, bowling green, and general ambience were of enormous social value.

. . .

Bacon's Castle is a Jacobean brick manor house built in 1665 by Arthur Allen, a justice of the peace, about twenty miles from Williamsburg and about six miles from Jamestown, on the south side of the James River. Its gardens are not as well documented in personal terms as those of Green Spring because less is known of Allen and his more affluent son, Major Arthur Allen, who laid out the gardens, than of Governor Berkeley and the Ludwells. But archaeology carried out there in the mid-1980s has revealed gardens dating from about 1680 that are of considerable scale and design interest. The large size of these gardens and a few modest touches of ornamentation that varied their otherwise geometric plainness suggest that Major Allen, like Berkeley, took pleasure and interest in what his gardens could introduce aesthetically, as well as functionally, into his plantation demesne. With Green Spring's, they are the earliest documented ornamental gardens in the colonies.[30]

Located to the southwest of the large house—the earliest known house still standing from the seventeenth century—the gardens discovered by archaeologists do not appear to have been as expressive and varied as those of Green Spring. They consisted of a large rectangular area about 195 by 360 feet, which is shown clearly in an 1843 survey plan of the house and adjacent landscape (see figure 5). This huge garden area,

the length of which runs north-south, with the northern end directly west of the house, was originally fenced on the western, eastern, and southern sides. The northern boundary, which was built of brick, was more substantial and undoubtedly more attractive. The main features within the enclosure were six large, raised planting beds, each measuring 74 by about 97 feet (figure 6). Separated by a long 12-foot-wide central north-south axis in the form of a path surfaced with firmly packed white sand and by two 8-foot-wide east-west crosswalks, also of sand, and with a 10-foot-wide perimeter walk around them, the planting beds must have been impressive chiefly because of their scale and rigid geometry in a setting that must have seemed wild

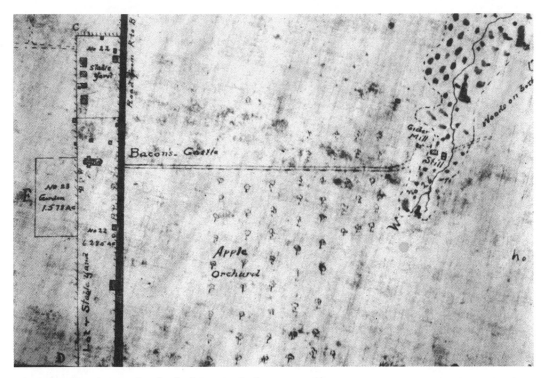

5. *House lot, gardens, and orchard of Bacon's Castle, Surry County, Virginia, 1911 (after an 1843 survey plan).*

6. *Aerial view of the gardens of Bacon's Castle.*

and desolate. The archaeologists are satisfied that there is no evidence of ornamental planting in these beds in the form of orchard, vineyard, or parterres. Neither have they found clues suggesting ornamental planting along the 6-foot-wide planting beds extending all the way along the inside of the east, west, and south fences. On the contrary, evidence of planting furrows indicates that the beds were used exclusively for vegetables and herbs.

There are signs of embellishment and ornamentation elsewhere in these gardens, however, indicating that Major Allen was not entirely content with a purely functional rectangular enclosure. Just south of the northern brick wall, along most of its length, he laid out two smaller planting beds, measuring about twenty by eighty feet each. They would appear to have been straightforward enough except for their curved inside

ends, which create a centrally placed bell-shaped area between them with clipped corners. Lined up with the north-south axis, this bell-shaped area (containing a hole of uncertain use) was positioned in a commanding spot from which to view the gardens southward. Conceivably, that spot was made more attractive by plantings, such as espaliered fruit, in front of or against the south face of the brick wall.

Another, more fascinating hint of ornamentation is the evidence of three brick structures built at the western ends of the three middle and northern crosswalks. Were these three-sided structures, the openings of which faced the walks, examples of exedras—glorified seats, in effect—where one could sit and leisurely look down the crosswalks? Indeed, remains have been found of at least one bench, which stood at the back of one of these structures and not against the sides as in European examples of the period. On the other hand, did the little buildings have some more prosaic function? The archaeologists disagree. But since all three are lined up perfectly with the crosswalks, and since there are two-foot breaks in the border beds for access directly in front of them, there is at least an even chance that they were exedras. Favoring that theory is their placement on the west side facing east—toward the house, related buildings, and possibly orchards. In other words, they would have taken in pleasant and reassuring views of the little plantation world that was evolving, just as late-seventeenth-century French and Dutch gardens were designed to unfold views within the gardens and not of the adjacent countryside, with the house as the centerpiece symbolically representing man's control and domination of the landscape.

· · ·

Both Green Spring and Bacon's Castle were singular exceptions to the general pattern of plantation life at this time. Before turning to a few of the turn-of-the-century planter-aristocrats who sought to re-create a measure of the comforts of English landed gentility, it is important to recognize more clearly some of the psychological and material constraints weighing against any aspiring Virginia planter, howsoever capable or successful, who may have wished to turn the pastoral dream into the reality of a pleasure garden.

In any country, the history of pleasure or ornamental gardening does not concern chiefly the lower or so-called working classes, or even what we think of as the middle classes. As a complex and articulate art, gardening historically has been the expression of generally educated and affluent people—people who turn to it as a way of enhancing their social identity and sense of well-being. Focusing on such people in seventeenth- and eighteenth-century Virginia, therefore, does not imply a disinterest in or deliberate neglect of the vast majority of the Virginia population that was simply out to make a living or establish a comfortable existence. It is true that

the canvas widens throughout the eighteenth century to include a more varied group of gardeners and a broader cultural base, especially beginning in the late 1720s and 1730s, when the so-called great house became interwoven with the Virginia plantation way of life and the "ideal of cultivation"—with its requirement that there be fitting environments for the assemblage of people who strove for civility and refinement—showed signs of becoming part of the middle-class as well as elite consciousness. Indeed, the striving for this ideal did not proceed independently of the vernacular culture but drew upon it and thus was tinged by a native air of rusticity—or at least Europeans thought so.[31] Nonetheless, certainly up to the mid-eighteenth century, pleasure gardening delineates a pastime predominantly limited to the well read, better educated, and socially ambitious. Moreover, the anonymous multitude of gardeners in our period who quietly contented themselves with introducing a few flowers, bushes, and trees into their essentially practical gardens did not, with rare exception, record what they were doing, draw plans of their grounds, or write letters about it all. In short, the garden historian knows relatively little about them as individual gardeners.

As it happens, similar problems hinder the study of the elite of seventeenth-century Virginia. Those (chiefly immigrant) owners of large plantations—the Fitzhughs, Wormeleys, Carters, Beverleys, and Byrds—went to great lengths to acquire from England the furnishings, silver, paintings, books, carriages, and clothing that served as symbols of their status and compensated them for their feelings of isolation from English society. But they have left us little record of any gardening they did.[32] Nor does much survive by way of contemporary plans or descriptions of their gardens, perhaps because they did not bother to record any pleasure gardening they carried on, but more likely because carefully laid out pleasure gardens, even in the last quarter of the century, were either not a high priority for them or involved almost insurmountable obstacles.

To begin with, too few competent gardeners were brought over from England to advise the new planter-aristocracy. The age of the amateur gentleman-gardener had not yet fully dawned in England, much less in Virginia. Although increasing numbers of gardening manuals were published to help the English landowner design and manage his grounds—several of which found their way to the colony—they did not provide much impetus. And if a good gardener was a rare luxury, there was also the problem of insufficient labor available for the considerable work required to lay out and maintain terraces, parterres, and walks. This constraint began to disappear as black slaves replaced indentured servants in the plantation labor force, although the accelerating influence of slavery on the development of gardens would not become clearly discernible until the second quarter of the eighteenth century.[33]

Even with the rise of slavery and its promotion of the large planters' wealth, the number of planters who counted themselves among the elite and were inclined to create for themselves gentry-like settings was small. One historian has judged that only one in fifty planters fell into this class by the end of the century.[34] Even within this class, not many were convinced that the elaborate trappings of their rank in Virginia amounted to anything more than a vague allusion to English country house life, although people like William Fitzhugh and Byrd I put brave faces on their efforts.[35] This lurking feeling of inferiority to the English landed aristocracy and gentry—that they were big fish in what the English thought was a little, or at least unimproved, New World pond—may have acted as a psychological impediment to their desires to design elegant settings for their houses. It was one thing simply to purchase commodities and luxury items from England; it was a rather more ambitious, costly, and demonstrative statement to move large amounts of earth in order to create gardens that would make themselves feel and their landscapes appear more European. If Virginia planters were reluctant to take themselves too seriously as gentlemen of honor and position

in a colony to which many believed they had emigrated because they could not succeed socially and economically back home, it would not be surprising to find that ambitious landscape projects before the turn of the century seemed to them a bit bizarre, foolish, or even presumptuous.[36] "I neither live in poverty nor pomp," Fitzhugh wrote to his mother on April 22, 1686, "but in a very good indifferency."[37] A landscape garden for pleasure and show, even for this patriarch, would have registered a more highly pitched pomp than the display of his considerable collection of fine silver.

In 1686, Fitzhugh, looking for an English buyer, described his plantation, Eagle's Nest, in Stafford County near the Potomac River.[38] Although he failed to mention any ornamental gardens, large orchards and a one-hundred-foot-square paled-in garden, undoubtedly for vegetables, merited comment. But even if he did not have any ornamental gardens of significant size and character to attract the attention of potential English purchasers, one is surprised at his failure to interest them with some description of the situation of his land or its proximity to the river—some evocation, in other words, of the Virginia countryside, the "vision of pastoral contentment," which Louis Wright thought Fitzhugh's account of his house and land conjured up,[39] of domestic and utilitarian, not pastoral, images of locust fences, brick walls, orchards, livestock, a mill, and vast acreage up river with "commodious seats."

Another chronicler, a French Huguenot named Durand, who visited Eagle's Nest and Ralph Wormeley II's Rosegill plantation on the Rappahannock River in 1686–1687, hinted at these pastoral beauties when he fondly alluded in his journal to the riverside scenes at Port Tobago, another of Wormeley's estates on the Rappahannock: "I went walking . . . delighted with the sight of those lovely hills, the fountains & brooks flowing out of them, as well as with the quantity of wild grapevines all about."[40] Fitzhugh's sensibility to landscape need not have been undeveloped or dormant; nor can one conclude that his landscape was bereft of pictorial beauties. Rather, in his letter of advertisement he emphasized his estate's productivity and efficiency, not its aesthetic merits.[41]

One planter who took a greater interest in gardens was Robert Beverley. His *History and Present State of Virginia* reads felicitously and convincingly enough in the promotional vein, but it also contains much that is useful to the garden historian. It suggests attitudes to the Virginia landscape and flora at the end of the century that may be termed transitional. His proud rehearsal of the resources of this land points the way to the next century's gardening. It also dramatizes the new interest in American plants that was being encouraged in London by the Royal Society and a number of eminent English botanists. Sadly, we know nothing of any gardening in which Berverley may have been engaged at Beverley Park (in King and Queen County), but his feelings about pleasure gardening, or about the pleasure gardening that could be done in Virginia, emerge clearly from his *History*.

Beverley displays an enthusiasm for plants of the colony, but he was more the keen observer than the trained botanist. As one of the first colonists to write about native flora, he signals the importance that the study of American plants was beginning to assume in English intellectual and scientific circles. This line of inquiry would command much attention in early eighteenth-century Virginia among men of culture and education, including those who applied themselves to gardening. It was an intellectual or scientific current that characterized the Enlightenment in England and America—what one writer has called the mechanistic view of nature.[42] But Beverley writes not in the manner of a collector or researcher like his friend John Banister or the Reverend John Clayton, but like a man who loves plants and the decorative and utilitarian uses to which they could be put in a garden. He is delighted with the natural settings of plants and in their adaptation as garden ornaments. Of particular interest is his fusion of that delight with the image of the well-planted garden. Thirty years later, Byrd II would achieve the same coherent vision of man's re-creating eye in

pictorial and garden compositions that collaborated with nature's beautiful handiwork.

Beverley sees dramatic possibilities for gardens at the heads of Virginia's rivers, where the landscape is hilly or mountainous: "many of them flow out of the Sides of Banks very high above the Vales, which are the most suitable Places for Gardens."[43] His own Beverley Park faced a river (as did many plantations) but was sited on flat terrain, so that in this passage he seems to imply a preference for gardens with more variety of elevation. To counter a prevailing misconception that the Virginia landscape is all essentially flat, he announces that "upon the Heads of the great Rivers, there are vast high Hills; and even among the Settlements, there are some so topping, that I have stood upon them, and view'd the Country all around over the Tops of the highest Trees, for many Leagues together." "These Hills," he goes on, "are not without their Advantages."[44] He also likes waterworks, which in English gardening of the early part of the century were becoming particularly popular and varied. They were expensive, however. Yet in romantic scenery like Virginia's, Beverley notes, "the finest Waterworks in the World may be made, at a very small Expence." A garden in a wilder and visually dramatic setting appears to be what he likes.[45]

Aiming to whet the appetite of the English gardener, Beverley turns to the flower kingdom of Virginia:

> Of spontaneous Flowers they have an unknown Variety: The finest Crown Imperial in the World; the Cardinal-Flower, so much extoll'd for its Scarlet Colour, is almost in every Branch; the Moccasin Flower, and a Thousand others, not yet known, to *English* Herbalists. Almost all the Year round, the Levels and Vales are beautified with Flowers of one Kind or other, which make their Woods as fragrant as a Garden.[46]

Landscape has a magical, idyllic quality: "spontaneous," "unknown," pervasive, ever-blooming, "fragrant as a Garden."

Writing as an Elizabethan might have, sensitive to sounds and fragrance in a garden, Beverley delivers an encomium on Virginia's uncommon landscape beauties. Owners of plantations, he observes,

> enjoy all the benefits of a warm Sun, and by their shady Groves, are protected from its Inconvenience. Here all their Senses are entertain'd with an endless Succession of Native Pleasures. Their Eyes are ravished with the Beauties of naked Nature. Their Ears are Serenaded with the perpetual murmur of Brooks, and the thorow-base which the Wind plays, when it wantons through the Trees; the merry Birds, too, join their pleasing Notes to this rural Consort, especially the Mock-birds. . . . Their [the planters'] Taste is regaled with the most delicious Fruits, which without Art, they have in great Variety and Perfection. And then their smell is refreshed with an eternal fragrancy of Flowers and Sweets, with which Nature perfumes and adorns the Woods almost the whole year round.[47]

Perpetual springtime in the garden of Virginia, where art has relatively little role and "naked Nature" need not be clothed with "improvements"—this is the pastoral fiction Beverley serves up for his Old World readers. The opposition he sets up between art and nature parallels a thesis running through the entire *History*: the artificial Old World versus the fresh and spontaneous New World. Although one feels that he genuinely believes a "Garden is no where sooner made than there, either for Fruits, or Flowers,"[48] it is inevitable that art played its part in the making of Beverley Park's gardens. "I don't know any *English* Plant, Grain, or Fruit, that miscarries in *Virginia*," he writes; "Have you pleasure in a Garden? All things thrive in it."[49] Yet he surely knew that some English plants would not thrive in the Virginia climate. His and other planters' efforts to cultivate gardens had to rely heavily on the decorative uses of native plants and trees; the sarsaparilla vine, for example, with its red berries, has "divers Ornamental uses."[50] Considerable experimentation was required before Virginia gardeners could discover both what native flora could be propagated for garden uses and

which English plants could thrive in this climate. Until botanists like John Banister, John Clayton, John Lawson, John Custis, John Bartram, and John Mitchell put botanical studies on a stronger footing in the colonial South, a man like Beverley had to rely on trial and error. It was no easy matter, despite what he told his English readers, to create a pleasure garden in Virginia.

•   •   •

The scientific, botanical current of Enlightenment thinking in Virginia flowed strongly in Beverley's accounts of the colony's native flora. There is a vigor in his descriptions of plants, partly because he linked them to his theme about the purity and beauty of the landscape before English settlers arrived and to his idea that these settlers, the affluent planters not excepted, were too unimaginative and idle to consult properly the spirit of the landscape, which the Indians understood simply and well. He was willing to acknowledge that the English had altered, but not improved, Virginia by 1705.[51] Yet his detailed lists of flowers, fruit, trees, bushes, vegetables, and herbs also reflect the burgeoning English botanical curiosity about colonial plants.

English naturalists found the colonies a source of entirely new and exciting plants and trees, and they came to study the flora and collect specimens to send or carry back home. A few wrote treatises on the subject. Some planters like William Byrd II and John Custis engaged English botanists in correspondence and plant exchanges, while others attempted to develop their own nurseries of native flora.[52] These nurseries served chiefly for the collection and study of plants, not for ornamental uses, and their designs were accordingly functional rather than aesthetic.

The two botanists who made their homes in or near Jamestown toward the end of the seventeenth century, the Reverend John Clayton[53] and John Banister, probably started botanical gardens of sorts, but nothing is known of them.[54] Both were sent to Virginia by Henry Compton, bishop of London, as much for their plant collecting and identifying skills as for any other reason. Clayton, who lived in Jamestown as rector from 1684 to 1686, wrote a long letter in 1687 to the English scientist Robert Boyle (also intended for the members of the Royal Society), in which he gave an "Account of Virginia" that included the first scientific description of Virginia from a strictly natural history standpoint. Disappointingly, his "Account" and letters to the Royal Society from 1684 to 1686 fail to describe or even mention any existing gardens in Virginia.[55]

Banister died along the Roanoke River in 1692 before he could write his *magnum opus* on Virginia, thereby disappointing the Royal Society, Bishop Compton, and many of Europe's leading botanists. His Virginia garden also disappeared, apparently without anyone having taken the trouble to describe it, although the bishop's garden at Fulham—probably the greatest private collection of exotic plants and trees in England at the time—harbored a number of species that Banister sent from his own collection.[56]

Apparently both Beverley and John Lawson, the chronicler of North Carolina's natural history, found themselves somewhat confused where native flowers were concerned and shied away from listing them. Lawson probably articulated Beverley's own thoughts when he complained: "Had not the ingenious Mr. *Banister* (the greatest Virtuoso we ever had on the Continent) been unfortunately taken out of this World, he would have given the best Account of the Plants of *America*."[57]

On the subject of specimens for the flower garden, Beverley had little to say, merely that they were of "an unknown Variety," that Byrd I's garden at Westover was full of "sweet Flowers," and that gardens were easily made with "Fruits, or Flowers."[58] Most of the ornamental flowers he had in mind probably came from Europe and by then had been in Virginia for many years. Lawson, in his *Description of North-Carolina* (1718), was also sparing in his lists of such ornamental flowers, but he gave a reason for this, one that applies as well to Virginia. "The Flower-garden in *Carolina*," he observed, "is as yet arriv'd but to

a very poor and jejune Perfection. We have only two sorts of Roses; the Clove-July [clove gilly] Flowers, Violets, Princes Feather, and *Tres Colores*. There has been nothing more cultivated in the Flower-Garden which, at present, occurs to my Memory; but as for the wild spontaneous Flowers of this Country, Nature has been . . . liberal."[59] He felt, as did Beverley, that the lack of variety was owing in part to a measure of indifference or indolence. A scarcity of appropriate plants was the more significant factor, however, as well as ignorance about which so-called immigrant specimens could thrive. Beyond that, Lawson, like Beverley, reveals his wonder at the fecundity and "spontaneous" (or natural) character of native flora.

When recording fruit, trees, bushes, herbs, and vegetables, Beverley is chiefly concerned with portraying for his English readers how Virginia plantations were self-sufficient, anticipating the early-eighteenth-century revival of the concept of the self-sustaining villa or country house, the latter-day version of Pliny the Younger's ancient Roman delineation of the *villa rustica*.[60] If the reader desires a fresh example of the Renaissance model, Beverley seems to say by way of a vignette of plantation life, he should go not to Italy but to Virginia. Note also his distinction between seedsmen and gardeners:

> The Families being altogether on Country-Seats, they have their Graziers, Seedsmen, Gardiners, Brewers, Bakers, Butchers, and Cooks within themselves: they have a great Plenty and Variety of Provisions for their Table; and as for Spicery, and other things that the Country don't produce, they have constant supplies of 'em from *England*. The gentry pretend to have their Victuals drest, and serv'd up as Nicely, as at the best Tables in *London*.[61]

In the realm of the "Plenty and Variety of Provisions," Beverley delighted especially in fruit, as did Banister and Lawson for more scientific reasons.[62] In English literature, fruit had long been a symbol of nature's prolific goodness and cooperative spirit, and its celebration in early accounts of the colony is not surprising. In his 1676 *Account of Virginia*, for example, Thomas Glover had written in the most general approving terms about fruit on plantations: there are "few planters but that have fair and large orchards, some whereof have 1200 trees and upward bearing all sorts of English apples . . . of which they make great store of cider . . . likewise great peach-orchards, which bear such an infinite quantity of peaches."[63] Still earlier, in the 1640s, William Bullock had lauded the colony's riches of fruit, which grew "all on standing Trees, & not against Walls" as in England.[64] The writing about fruit provides another example of the merging of science and romantic pastoralism, where fruit becomes a convenient symbol of Virginia as the new promised land as well as a subject of horticultural interest.

. . .

The gardens at Westover plantation and the College of William and Mary, because they are the best documented of the late seventeenth century, provide further ideas of Virginia thinking about gardening at the time. For both, a few details have survived about their inception and early layouts. Perhaps most important is that the patriarch of Westover, William Byrd I, and the founders of the college saw to the development of the gardens as much because they wished to promote scientific knowledge of native plants and the effects of the climate on English plants as because they desired ornamental garden settings. Both gardens, then, may be identified to some extent with the dawning of the Enlightenment in Virginia.

Byrd I's gardening at Westover, on the James River about twenty miles west of Williamsburg, was inspired in the main by his serious study of plants in the colony during the last fifteen years of the seventeenth century. Significantly, he was a member in good standing of the Royal Society. When the Reverend Clayton called him in 1688 "one of the most intelligent Gentlemen in all *Virginia*," he was thinking of, among other things, Byrd's ability to solve botanical problems posed

by climate and soil.[65] Two years later Byrd built a wooden house on his land and called the place Westover. He immediately began to lay out the grounds around it into gardens that he planted with both English and exotic native plants. Thus began the history of one of the best-known colonial plantation gardens in America.

Even before he built Westover, Byrd had been collecting plants, many from botanist friends in England. Despite his many important duties on the Governor's Council, which made him one of the most influential citizens of Virginia in the 1680s, Byrd found time to write to England for plants and seeds of many kinds. One of his earliest botanical friendships was with Jacob Bobart, keeper of the Physic Garden at Oxford University, from whom he received sundry roots and seeds that, at least on one occasion, sprouted aboard ship because they had been placed in the very warm hold. In May 1684 he told Bobart that the "iris, crocus, tulips, & anemos flower'd this year"—apparently Bobart had sent them the year before.[66] In 1688 Bobart sent him trees and shrubs, probably for Westover. Byrd also corresponded with Dr. Hans Sloane, famous collector and eventually founder of the British Museum, Leonard Plunkenett, keeper of the Royal Gardens at Hampton Court, and the Honorable Charles Howard of Castle Howard in Yorkshire, whose gardens were shortly to be designed by Sir John Vanbrugh.[67]

Byrd relied on these naturalists and botanists mostly in the early 1690s, when he was first laying out some grounds at Westover. After his son William visited him at Westover in 1696 and returned to England in 1697, it is possible that Byrd I relied on his son for most of his botanical needs. The son doubtlessly pleased his father with the news of his election to the Royal Society. When Byrd I himself returned to London in 1697, he developed friendships with leading botanists like James Petiver, Sloane, Dr. Martin Lister, the Reverend Clayton, Dr. Plunkenett, and others, making himself into the kind of informed naturalist that Virginia badly needed in the early eighteenth century. When the young

Byrd finally left England to take up his inheritance at Westover in 1705, he found there many of the plants he himself had helped procure for his father.

The most valuable immediate help for the Westover gardens almost certainly came to Byrd from John Banister. Banister's name appears several times in Byrd's letters to botanists, almost in a patron-like manner, as if he is doing his best to facilitate his friend's researches and plant needs. "I wish it lay in my power any way to doe you or Mr. Banister any acceptable service," he wrote to Bobart in 1684, about five years before the Westover gardening began.[68] "Let him not be disheartened," Dr. Plunkenett appealed to Byrd in 1687, "but proceed in the noble design of improving a natural knowledge that comes so neer the divine & which alone can make us rich unto salvation."[69] Banister's gardening at Westover in the two years before his death in 1692 may have been his repayment for Byrd's encouragement and patronage. When he died, his botanical papers (chiefly the plant catalogue) were all sent to Bishop Compton; but his practical gardening legacy remained in Virginia, undocumented, at Westover and very likely at the plantations of friends such as Ralph Wormeley of Rosegill and at William and Mary through his role in its establishment. Another of Banister's legacies in Virginia was his botanical library, part of which ended up in the famous Byrd library at Westover.[70]

It was not only the "curious" botanist in England who was fascinated by Virginia plants in these early years. So was the English country house owner. Three big estates, all in Gloucestershire, lead the way into the world of Virginia plants at the end of the century: King's Weston, the seat of Sir Robert Southwell, secretary of state for Ireland and intimate friend of both Byrd I and Sloane; William Blathwayt's Dyrham Park; and Badminton House, the duke of Beaufort's enormous estate. In the 1690s, it seems Beaufort's gardeners were in touch with George London, then Bishop Compton's gardener at Fulham Palace and later royal gardener to Queen Anne, in an effort to collect plants from Virginia for Badminton. Several gardening volumes still in the private collection at Badminton, richly illustrated with unpublished paintings of Virginia plants, appear to testify to this. Perhaps Byrd I had a hand in sending plants to Badminton; he certainly sent some to King's Weston and Dyrham.[71] Between 1693 and 1698 Blathwayt completely altered his gardens along Dutch lines and simultaneously naturalized them by introducing exotic Virginia flora. Blathwayt continued to receive plants from Virginia up to his death in 1717, in later years from Philip Ludwell of Green Spring.[72] As for King's Weston, in 1699 Byrd I was sending Southwell countless seeds and plants.[73] Southwell's gardens at King's Weston were also Dutch in conception, boasting a particularly fine canal, so that on his and Blathwayt's grounds the Dutch and the Virginian joined up for early English essays in international gardening.

. . .

At the College of William and Mary in Williamsburg, founded in 1693 largely through the efforts of its first president, James Blair (figure 7), the emphasis was probably more on scientific discovery initially than on garden design, although the earliest reference to the college gardens was made in the latter context. From London the eminent horticulturist and garden designer John Evelyn wrote in 1694 to John Walker in Richneck, Virginia, informing him that George London, "his Majs Gardner here," had arranged to have "an ingenious Servant of his" sent to Virginia "on purpose to make and plant the Garden, designed for the new Colledge, newly built in your Country." Evelyn was ever on the lookout for new plants from new sources. He asked Walker "to enquire out, what plants, rare in this Kingdome, may be transported hither."[74]

Walker's cousin, Daniel Parke II, John Custis's father-in-law, had for years been supplying the eager Evelyn with Virginia flora and other natural curiosities. "By this insitigation of Mr.

7. *James Blair. Oil painting by Charles Bridges, early eighteenth century. The College of William and Mary is shown at left.*

Daniel Park," Walker wrote to Evelyn in 1693, "I have presumed these rude lines with a quart bottle of sassafras oyle and a letter by him, my meeting with Mr. Parke as I was packing away some trees and plants for our governor [Edmund Andros][75] [to send to] England [and] fell into discourse concerning you." Walker wrote again to Evelyn in December 1693: "I understand by Mr. Daniell Parke that you are desiris of some Raireitis of our Country which if I had some timely notis of it, would have made you a present; I have put . . . up for Sr. Edmund Andros severall things as plants, trees, shrub seeds and stone." Intending to please Evelyn, Walker enclosed "a Draught of dryed plants to show what is in our American parts with some sorts of trees and plants." The great man in London was delighted: "The Catalogue of plants you set downe," he wrote back, "are many of them Rare with us;

but thro' . . . your generous Communication, we may hope to be further inrich'd."[76]

Evelyn's well-known study of plants makes his interest in the new College of William and Mary more understandable; there was little other reason that the founding of such an institution in such a place should have kept his attention. John Locke, too, recognized the opportunity for scientific investigation represented by this new center of learning in the colonies. In October 1699 he wrote to James Blair, who had first been sent out to Virginia by Bishop Compton at least as much for his botanical interests as for his spiritual distinctions, requesting his share of the scientific booty: "I know your country has many natural curiosities, such of them as come in yr way & are of noe difficult transportation I should receive as an obligation from you, more particularly all seeds of all strange & curious plants, with an account of the soyles they grow in, & the best season yu observe there for sowing them."[77] Here emerged a role for the college garden as a sort of nursery or physic garden.[78]

• • •

All this searching after plants still left time for some attention to garden design at both Westover and the college as the century drew to a close. The few details that have survived about either garden during those early years impart a feeling for their character and spirit. These, of course, were two gardens with entirely different situations and functions. While Westover enjoyed a rural setting next to a river, the college's position at the west end of the main street in Middle Plantation invited gardens suitable for a public building and public occasions and open to public view in the village. In this sense, at least, the two gardens define a paradigm of contrast and reciprocity that existed throughout the eighteenth century between urban and (for want of a more accurate term) country gardening in the colony. The contrast that developed—and that is a recurring theme in these pages—manifested itself chiefly in a process of cooperation between the two types. Plantation gardens supplied plants, tools, and even gardeners for the town; in return, especially when it had grown enough to look like a civilized urban center, the town offered a venue of gardening where people could conveniently meet and talk. It also presented an urban complement to gardening that gradually enabled plantation owners to see their own gardens not as isolated green spaces redeemed from the wilderness but as elements in a type of circular community. In this way the town brought a measure of coherence to the colony.

Most of the early garden layout at the College of William and Mary appears to have existed on the west side of the original building, not on the east side facing the main street (later called Duke of Gloucester Street), where in the 1720s and 1730s the elegant garden design evolved as a setting for the college building (the Wren Building), the Brafferton, and the President's House. From the evidence available, it is noteworthy that certain features of the college gardens from the outset could be traced to Renaissance Italian garden designs.

When in 1705 Beverley referred to the "piazzas of the College," he was thinking of a portico on the west side with steps leading down to a courtyard that, flanked then only by the wing containing the Great Hall, was awaiting the wing that would house the chapel. We know the piazzas were on the west side because Hugh Jones wrote in 1724 of "a spacious piazza on the west side, from one wing to the other." Jones added that this piazza was "approached by a good walk, and a grand entrance by steps, with good courts and gardens about it."[79] Clearly, some of the earliest gardens were laid out on that side, where today the area is dominated by a so-called sunken garden.

This garden treatment involving piazzas and courtyard, and the creation of a type of garden space that could be used for dramatic events—if not for plays, then simply for commencement exercises, speeches, and other academic events—has a distinctly Italian ambience about it. In the Italian Renaissance garden, as John Dixon Hunt has shown, architectural features such as loggias, pavilions, courtyards, steps, and galleries could invoke a sense of the garden being both inside and outside, resulting in "the organization of garden space either to cater for theatrical representations or to suggest that they might take place."[80] Although this organization of shapes and space was not the same as actually creating theaters, it did, as Hunt points out, enforce connections between garden and theater that made a deep impression on the English imagination in the seventeenth century. The chapel wing that would complete the theatrical symmetry of the college courtyard was not built until a few years later, but the intention of the designers, which appears to be suggested by Jones's adoption of the word *piazza*, could well have been inspired by seventeenth-century English images of Italian designs. Indeed, Evelyn, who took such an interest in the college and who traveled widely in Italy and kept copious journals of what he saw, especially in gardens, was one of the first Englishmen explicitly to link the garden and the theater.

Virtually identical maps of Williamsburg drawn in 1781 and 1782 and known as the Rochambeau and Desandrouins maps (see figure 8 for the latter) show large separate gardens to the west of the main building.[81] Moreover, Beverley suggested the proximity of the garden to the piazza when he wrote of Governor Francis Nicholson's quarrel with Colonel Edmund Jennings in "the garden" nearby.[82] It is tempting to imagine some graceful garden treatment of Oxford- and Cambridge-type quadrangles adorning the west side of the college, but it is more probable that a nursery or botanical garden was there, or simple beds for vegetables and herbs. As such, the garden would again recall the Italian model, as well as the Dutch.

The Dutch influence here would have been logical, given King William and Queen Mary's demonstrable enthusiasm for garden design and

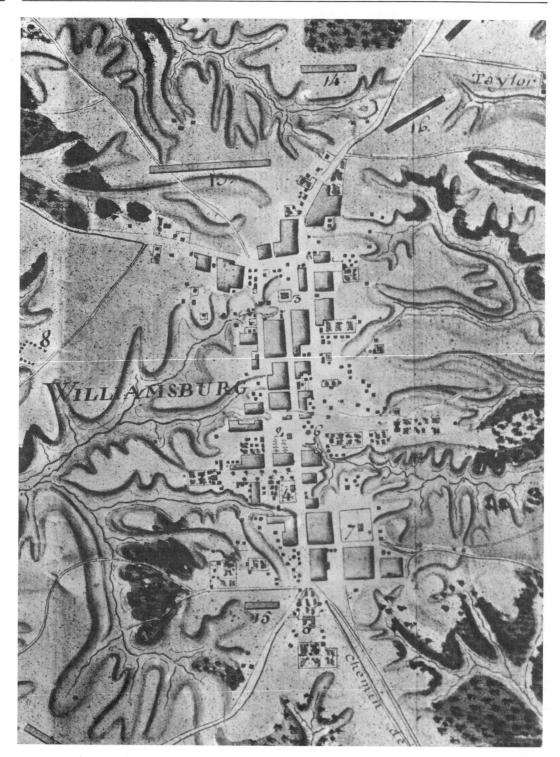

the ideological assumptions underlying it. Their Protestantism, hostility toward the type of absolute monarchy embodied by France and its grand gardens, and preference for their own nation's more "piecemeal and incremental" gardening—one that disdained a single overpowering, coherent, autocratic statement—all composed a sympathetic "republican" background to and authority for what the people who founded and developed the college hoped it would become.[83] Moreover, the compartmentalized character of the Dutch style was ideal for botanical gardens. As we have seen, Evelyn's interest in the college appears to have been heightened partly by his desire to have organized knowledge of American flora. Since he knew Dutch gardens well, he could be counted on to understand how the Dutch style and botany might be ideally joined at the college. He, the English naturalist John Ray, and others in the Royal Society had also assimilated the connection in Italy between gardens and so-called cabinets, or display areas for rare and exotic plants. The college afforded splendid opportunities to obtain this knowledge, so why not fashion a botanical garden there for the purpose? It would fit in perfectly with the contemporary zeal for collecting rare plants and exhibiting them, even in a theatrically exhibitionist way that would complement the concept of the garden as a type of theater, as in the Tradescant brothers' famous botanical garden at Lambeth. As Hunt suggests, it was in Italy that people like Evelyn absorbed the idea that one of the functions of a garden was to "comprehend the principall and most useful plants, and to be as a rich and noble Compendium of what the whole Globe of the Earth has flourishing upon her boosome."[84] In America, the newfound land, the botanical garden could be seen as one aspect of the metaphoric search for the recovery of Eden.[85]

It is likely that by 1702 there was little in the way of gardens to the east of the college build-

8. *Desandrouins Map of Williamsburg, ca. 1781–1782, showing a number of prominent gardens.*

ing. Francis Louis Michel, a Frenchman passing through the brand new capital that year, drew what is the earliest known sketch of the Wren building (figure 9) and described a fireworks display in the grounds facing the east front of the building.[86] The hundreds of people who crammed the small area to see the event, which was both a memorial service for King William and a celebration of the proclamation of Queen Anne, would not have had a beneficent effect on whatever gardens were there. Still, the theatricality of the event, whether there were gardens yet or not, suggests an Italianate use of the area as theater, in which members of the audience were participants as well as spectators. The fireworks and their celebration of two monarchs are also reminiscent of the seventeenth-century English use of gardens for court entertainments.[87]

When Alexander Spotswood arrived in Williamsburg in 1710 to take up the governorship, the college had been in ruins since a fire in 1705, and he immediately began to promote its rebuilding. Perhaps soon after, the gardens to the east began to be laid out, eventually, by the late 1730s, composing the design pictured in the Bodleian Plate (figure 10).[88] In light of Spotswood's immediate attention to the town's overall appearance and the design of the gardens connected to the governor's house, it is feasible that he worked on the college's eastern gardens, too. That spot has always been a public part of the townscape—public in the sense that it can easily be seen from the main street—so it may have had priority in Spotswood's list of improvements. He has been credited with a revision of the east front of the building to include, in the Italian Renaissance garden motif, a classically pedimented relief with steps. Perhaps this, with the gardens, was part of a plan to render this public building equal in elegance to the Capitol, which Beverley had called a "stately Fabrick."[89] Hugh Jones unhesitatingly announced in the *Present State of Virginia* that the college was "rebuilt, & nicely contrived, altered and adorned by the ingenious Direction of Governor Spotswood; and is not altogether unlike Chelsea Hos-

10. Bodleian Plate, featuring the public buildings and
gardens of Williamsburg, ca. 1736–1740.

pital."[90] The comparison with Chelsea Hospital
refers, however, more to the building than to the
garden setting.

• • •

While the College of William and Mary was being established in the 1690s, Byrd I began to lay
out his own setting at Westover. Plans of colonial gardens are today among the rarest of artifacts in the history of American art, but fortunately for us Westover is the subject of two that
are extant. One that was drawn in the 1760s, we
shall turn to later. The other dates from 1701

9. *Wren Building, College of William and Mary. Drawing by Francis Louis Michel, ca. 1702. The "Governor" to
whom Michel refers at the base of the drawing was
Francis Nicholson.*

and shows the overall layout (figure 11).[91] This
plan reveals no garden detail whatsoever next to
the house, but it does give an idea of the east-
west and north-south axes of the gardens and
the position of the house and gardens relative to
the river. It also suggests that the west avenue
of trees lined up with the main (still wooden)
house. Byrd's placement of his north axis may
also have been determined by the location of
Gut Landing a short distance to the north, so
that the avenue of trees could lead directly from
the landing to the house. Part of the east-west
axis extends east of the house, suggesting garden
areas at some distance in that direction as well as
to the west and south. The row of dots shown on
three sides of the house may indicate either paling or, more likely, some line of planting such as
bushes. Those dots argue, at any rate, that the

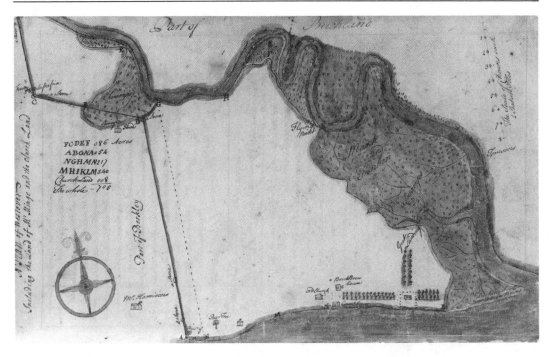

11. *"A Plan of Westover," 1701.*

principal pleasure gardens faced the river front of the house, where there may have been more room.

This plan is enormously important because the subsequent architectural history of the main house and its flanking kitchen and library invites the conclusion that this early axial landscape may have remained unaltered throughout the lifetimes of Byrd II and his son, Byrd III. The plan also shows conclusively that a Virginia plantation owner in the seventeenth century was capable of designing a fairly sophisticated landscape setting in a Dutch manner with avenues radiating out from the house.

Robert Beverley entertained little doubt as to the quality of the Westover garden of the late seventeenth century. In his *History*, he wrote Westover's praises not long before Byrd I died in 1704 and the first stage of its gardens had ended. By then, Byrd had been experimenting with plants in his garden for about fifteen years and had become one of Virginia's botanical ex-

perts. As Byrd's son-in-law, Beverley knew Westover intimately. Allowing for some family pride, we nonetheless ought to credit his sentiments: "Colonel *Byrd*, in his Garden, which is the finest in that Country, has a Summer-House set round with *Indian* Honey-Suckle, which all the Summer is continually full of sweet Flowers, in which these Birds [hummingbirds] delight exceedingly. Upon these Flowers, I have seen ten or a dozen of these Beautiful Creatures together, which sported about me so familiarly, that with their little Wings they often fann'd my Face."[92] Clearly still thinking of Westover, Beverley then adds a significant gardening detail. His observation that the grotto was prevalent in Virginia at the time suggests the occasional use of some kinds of grottoes for cooling, natural effects. A desire to minimize the summer heat was the impetus behind them and several other gardening embellishments: "that Inconvenience is made easie by cool Shades, by open Airy rooms, Summer-Houses, Arbors, and Grottos."[93] Here again, incidentally, although Beverley never visited Italy, the conflation of architectural features such as cool rooms and summerhouses with natural features like grottoes and arbors suggests that his perception of the garden partakes of, or is shaped by, interpenetration of the immediate garden with the house itself, such as was to be seen in Italy and was being reproduced in England.

. . .

It is well to consider what sort of adjustment between garden and open landscape men like Byrd and Beverley were countenancing in their own grounds. When George Percy, Beverley, and others in the seventeenth century romanticized the Tidewater Virginia landscape and pretended to see pastoral images reminiscent of English meadows and gardens, they were not projecting visions of actual English landscape but rather calling up Edenic metaphors replete with classical overtones of pursuits such as appear highly stylized in the Renaissance English pastoral poem.[94] Their vocabulary of description, therefore, can mislead one into thinking they saw a landscape more English than it was. Byrd II is more reliable in his descriptions of Virginia and North Carolina forests in the 1720s. His verbal sketches possess a pictorial beauty such as might have pleased him had he been able to reify them as he laid out his Westover gardens in relation to the adjacent scenery. But in the first part of the century he appears to have been an exception to the norm.

Rhys Isaac has described Virginia landscape scenery with the right tone of pastoral-gothic. In the passage that opens his book he conveys a medley of visual effects ranging from dark forests to luminous riverbanks and lofty prospects of hill and dale. Plantation garden designers, depending on the situations of their grounds, had to assimilate elements of this varied *theatrum mundi* (the world as a theater) as they planned their gardens throughout the century:

> Water and trees—trees and water. These are the features that now dominate the impressions of a traveler in Tidewater Virginia. In some parts the woods are so dense that one can see but a few yards into them. Elsewhere they thin out, and standing water marks the edge of a swamp. The lay of the land is better revealed in those places where the road crosses or runs alongside one of the great rivers. There, oaks and pines stand thick along the banks, almost down to the high-water mark. From the air the terrain is even more fully revealed, and the eye can take in a total pattern of dense green or black forest, lighter-colored swamps, and the silver arms and fingers of the sea that reach far into the land spread out below. Moving to the west, in the region between the rocky falls and the heaving lines of the Blue Ridge, the land is a series of rolling hills, and the river inlets become fast-flowing streams.[95]

Variety through elevation and the prospects of water and wood were nature's pervasive gift to the plantation gardener. So was the prolific plant life to be cultivated within walls or fences. It was essentially an American equation, although the aesthetic premises and conclusions of the English clearly left their mark as the eighteenth century toiled on.

2

Gardens in
Early Williamsburg

*T*he more ambitious and affluent Virginia planters at the turn of the seventeenth century may have aspired to realize an Edenic newfound land through various garden patterns—patterns that, for all their straightforward, prosaic, and not particularly imaginative character, nevertheless point to a desire for embellished enclaves. Such ornamented gardens as there were, apart from their utilitarian functions, also imply the planters' hopes that the lives they were establishing in the wilderness would be sustained and consolidated. They could imagine their gardens as metaphors of control and civilization as well as reassuring artifacts at such a distance from Europe. The native flora particularly excited them because they could anticipate these riches thriving at their doorsteps. But gardening at the turn of the century was a fragile and thin achievement, aptly underlined by the entirely unpredictable fate of plants that were sent to the colonists from England. If these immigrant plants survived the journey, the American climate might yet destroy them. Even hopes of classifying and cultivating native flora could be suddenly dashed by the untimely deaths of visiting English naturalists. Perseverance and resilience were necessary. Needed even more was a credible and promising colonial capital. With-

out that, the planters were masters of enclaves but not citizens of a community. They were isolated gardeners.

With the single exception of the new garden at the College of William and Mary, there was not much at Middle Plantation to attract the interest of plantation gardeners before it was selected as the colonial capital in 1699. The cooperation between plantation and town gardeners that eventually began to characterize Virginia gardening was at least two decades away. Even by 1710, when Alexander Spotswood arrived, there was little in the town by way of gardens. The Palace[1] was far from completion, and probably no one had given serious thought to its gardens.

Spotswood quickly emerged as the town's chief, self-appointed gardening promoter (figure 12). His excitement about garden possibilities, perhaps intensified by visits to plantations like Green Spring and Westover, has already been mentioned in connection with the college. He discovered that Virginia, the civilized culture of which he identified with a succession of plantations, was not the hopeless wilderness outpost that he and his countrymen at home had thought. He fancied that he could himself easily become a country squire in the English mold. At

12. Alexander Spotswood. Oil painting by Charles Bridges, early eighteenth century.

grant innocence," as the English poet Andrew Marvell had described land untamed by the mower, his symbol of cramping art and social custom.[4] In another way, however, this absence of history and culture was a disadvantage, and it was so felt. What Virginians wanted in a capital was not only an economic and political center but also a center of culture, a focal point for civilized living within which they could play out their versions of a materially improving life. The town needed to be beautiful and at the same time allow for a diversity of attitudes and habits and the opportunity to accommodate both affluent planters and humbler tradespeople, the educated and the uneducated, the cultured and uncultured. Williamsburg obviously never became a Boston or New York, or even a Charleston or Philadelphia, as a William and Mary student in 1699 hoped it would.[5] But neither Francis Nicholson nor Alexander Spotswood doubted Williamsburg's ultimate greatness as an American city, and they acted accordingly. And by the time Hugh Jones wrote his historical progress report, the capital had begun to realize these hopes.

Certain garden-related factors helped the town to develop. The town plan, designed by Governor Nicholson and then refined by Spotswood, contributed to a sense of ordered life in the community. It suggested urbanity and reflected a developing civic consciousness and pride on the part of many Virginians. Spotswood's particular contribution in this vein was his garden design at the Palace, but he also enhanced the appearance of the town generally by highlighting perspectives through the development of vistas and open spaces and the placement of buildings. One aspect of Nicholson's and Spotswood's town that demands special attention is one to which they devoted much care: the human dimension of the arrangement of buildings, public and private, in relation to streets, neighborhoods, vistas, public green spaces, and individual gardens. As for the college gardens, they continued to unfold ornamentally in the 1720s and 1730s. While providing a graceful setting for a

the same time, however, he knew he had to live in the new and culturally undeveloped town, and he immediately understood the critical importance of encouraging the arts of gardening and architecture. In an early letter to his brother, he mentions a new activity in which he had begun to indulge: "I am sufficiently amused," he wrote, perhaps with the Palace and college in mind, "with planting orchard and gardens."[2] Contemporary descriptions in this early period are very rare, but Spotswood's success after a little more than a decade of presiding over the nascent stages of the town's culture and growth is announced by Hugh Jones in *The Present State of Virginia* (1724). Jones found that the residents "dwell comfortably, genteely, pleasantly, and plentifully in this delightful, healthful, and (I hope) thriving city of Williamsburgh."[3]

The newness of Williamsburg as a town proved to be an advantage. It was a city of promise and new opportunities in the context of the colony, a landscape of freedom—"a wild and fra-

public building, open to view, they also (along with the Palace gardens) illustrated a style of pleasure garden that could be realized in the town.

. . .

The story of how Williamsburg was established and designed begins with Francis Nicholson. After a term as Virginia's lieutenant governor from 1690 to 1692, Nicholson went back to England, where he lived from 1692 to 1694. He then served as governor of Maryland from 1694 to 1697, finally returning to Virginia in 1698 to preside over the removal of the capital to the new town. It may have been in England that he studied city planning. We know at least that he brought to Maryland an informed enthusiasm for that subject, which found expression immediately in his design for Annapolis. When later he moved to Virginia, he was in a position to experiment further with urban planning ideas, a few of which he had not used in Annapolis and the ancestry of which reached back through Christopher Wren and Inigo Jones to Renaissance towns of England and Europe.[6]

Nicholson appears to have been an urban planner with more than just a passing interest in gardening and the role gardens could play in the disposition of a town. His personal library in Williamsburg contained several well-known English and French works on horticulture and garden design, including Jean de la Quintinie's *The Compleat Gard'ner*, translated and published by John Evelyn in 1693 while Nicholson was in London.[7] Unfortunately, these books burned in the college fire in 1705, just after he had donated them, so they cannot be examined for signs that might have revealed which he relied on most.[8]

In part, Nicholson's objective in his layout of the streets, buildings, and open spaces in Williamsburg was to enhance pictorial variety and interest. Spotswood continued this approach, so that as a pedestrian walks about the town certain prospects and vistas open to view. Many of Nicholson's decisions about Williamsburg's appearance, and their elaboration by Spotswood,

were calculated to evolve a visual sense of unity through a comprehensive interplay of pictorial scenes. There is an analogy here to the landscape designer who relates different areas and terrain with avenues, "rides," perspectives, monuments and buildings, and plantings. Such a design does not require vast tracts of land but can be accomplished with a handful of acres or even less. The smaller the landscape, in fact, the greater the virtuosity displayed.

There was historical and literary precedent for seeing and designing a townscape, or parts of it, in terms of garden and landscape images, or for laying out a landscape garden by invoking patterns of urban planning or including views of towns and cities from it. In Roman gardens, for example, as Nicholas Purcell writes, "*both* town and country and their mutual connections were part of the total landscape into which the house of the wealthy man was inserted."[9] Many of the villa gardens outside Rome in the first century A.D. were designed deliberately to command distant views either of the city itself or other villas. At the same time, the Romans brought gardens and versions of landscape into their cities and thereby influenced the arrangements of urban areas. In Renaissance Italy, similar reciprocation found expression through town in country and country in town. Judith Kinnard has explained how the appearance of urban images in villa gardens derived from the Renaissance concept of the ideal city—a city free from dirt, noise, and general disorder.[10] John Evelyn perceived the town in the garden when in 1644 he visited Villa Borghese, just outside Rome: "an house and ample Gardens on Mons Pincius, yet somewhat without the Citty-Wales; circumscrib'd by another wall full of small turrets and banqueting houses, which makes it appeare at a distance like a little Towne, within it tis an Elysium of delight."[11]

We may note in passing (for we shall turn to them later) that certain features of colonial American plantations and their gardens appear to have derived specifically from the introduction of townlike settings, perhaps for reasons having to do with the need for a sense of community and security. Conversely, an "ideal" urban area that would encourage order, peace, harmony, beauty, the pursuit of the arts, enlightened government, and a balanced culture—in short, the civilized community—required a design that would welcome a few of the multifarious forms of the garden. Evelyn, when he visited Dutch towns, recognized garden elements in their designs; and Maximilian Misson interpreted Leiden's streets in 1664 as "so many Alleys of a well-adorn'd Garden."[12]

From a literary and more symbolic point of view in the Age of Enlightenment, only three decades after the creation of Williamsburg, there is the example of Alexander Pope, himself an informed and influential gardener in the classical tradition. His mythopoeic imagination, bred as it was on Renaissance examples, could compose a detailed poem on tasteful gardening in the more naturalized vein that ends by imploring Richard Boyle, the third earl of Burlington, to embark on urban building works—works that, with gardening, will help bring in the new golden age of good communities:

> To build, to plant, whatever you intend,
> To rear the Column, or the Arch to bend,
> To swell the Terras, or to sink the Grot;
> In all, let Nature never be forgot.
>
> . . . . . .
>
> Bid Harbors open, public Ways extend,
> Bid Temples, worthier of the God, ascend;
> Bid the broad Arch the dang'rous Flood
>   contain . . .
> These Honours, Peace to happy Britain brings,
> These are Imperial Works, and worthy Kings.[13]

Nicholson and Spotswood did not necessarily have such grand ideas as they set to work on Annapolis and Williamsburg, but clearly they were aware of the exchangeability of town and garden in their architectural heritage.

Nicholson attempted the landscaper's approach first at Annapolis. While the plan (figure 13) is Wren-like in its deployment of radiating and diagonal streets leading to open areas featuring important public buildings or churches, John Reps observes that it more closely resembles Evelyn's plan for London in the casual and imprecise manner that the streets are lined up with these circular or square open areas. Reps even finds evidence that Nicholson borrowed Evelyn's design of a garden layout in *The Compleat Gardener* (1693) for a treatment of streets and open space in one section of Annapolis.[14] The treatment is unusual enough and the circumstantial evidence convincing enough to make this suggestion credible. In his book Evelyn appended an account of landscape gardening principles that he had culled from Moses Cook's *The Manner of Raising, Ordering, and Improving Forrest-Trees* (1676). Reps cites one passage that Nicholson may have kept especially before him as he planned both Annapolis and Williamsburg: "Walks should not terminate abruptly, but rather in some capacious, pretty figure, be it *Circle, Oval, Semi-Circle, Triangle,* or *Square.*"[15] Elsewhere in that book, Evelyn reiterated that openings or clearings in a landscape garden must vary in shape. If Nicholson learned nothing else from Evelyn, he gleaned from him the value of pictorial variety and perspective in laying out a town.

Annapolis had two advantages over Williamsburg that Nicholson's designing eye appears to have exploited. First, the site for the town was propitiously chosen next to the Severn River, which, apart from its commercial advantages, opened up prospects from the town and afforded picturesque views and terminal perspectives along some streets and from various buildings.[16] Second, the topography of the site offered greater variety of elevation so that Nicholson could more easily position buildings to command prospects. Williamsburg's ravines and gullies presented annoying problems as well as potential opportunities.

. . .

What was it, then, about Nicholson's townscape and Spotswood's projects that especially promoted gardening in Williamsburg? The town's

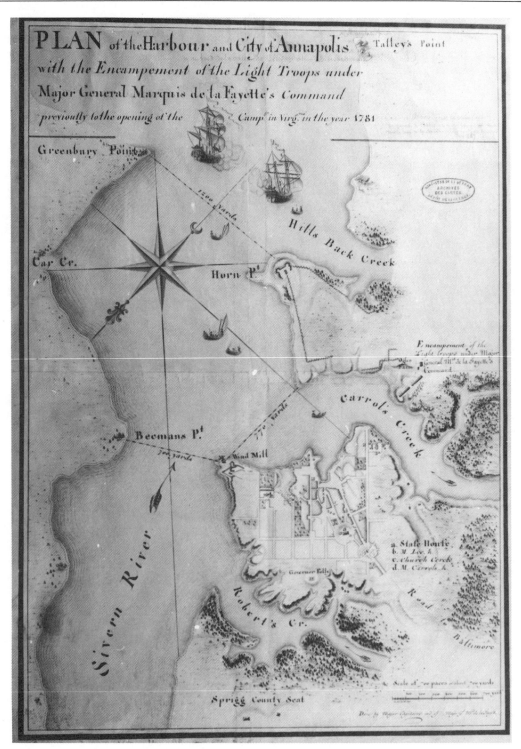

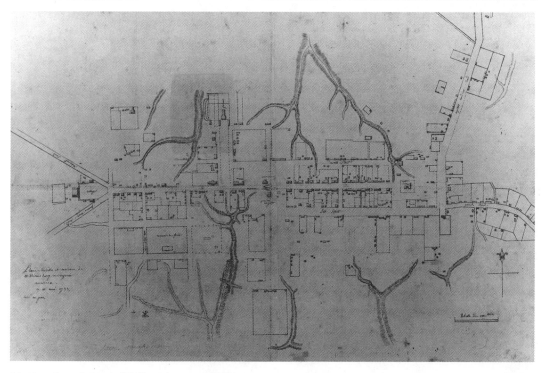

14. *Frenchman's Map of Williamsburg, ca. 1782.*

topography endowed it with three natural, inescapable features that immediately determined its character and layout: a ridge almost equidistant from the James and York rivers, running east-west, at the western end of which stood the college; numerous ravines and gullies; and several springs that supplied the town with its water. The ridge that ran east-west needed "improvement" in 1700. By removing some seventeenth-century houses that stood in the way and by filling in hollows, the earliest town planners after a few years were able to create a straight, level road extending from the college to the new Capitol building, which was under construction by 1701. This road, named Duke of Gloucester Street in honor of Queen Anne's young son, engraved a dominant axis upon the town plan (as shown in the so-called Frenchman's Map, figure

13. *Plan of Annapolis, Maryland, 1781. Drawn by Major Capitaine.*

14) and accounts for several of the features in Nicholson's master plan and Spotswood's refinements.[17] In much the same way that a central avenue or "ride" in an eighteenth-century landscape park could create variety as well as symmetry deriving from a dominant axial pattern, Williamsburg's main avenue encouraged symmetry, balance, moderation, and harmony of design in subsequent development of the townscape.[18]

Most visitors in the eighteenth century who bothered to record what they saw in Williamsburg noted its dominant axial pattern, and most of them liked it, although they may have had reservations about the appearance of the houses and street surfaces. Both Nicholson and Spotswood, however, faced some opposition as they proceeded with their ambitious plans. Wishing to complete the full length of Duke of Gloucester Street, Nicholson wrote, somewhat autocratically it seems, to the House of Burgesses in 1704,

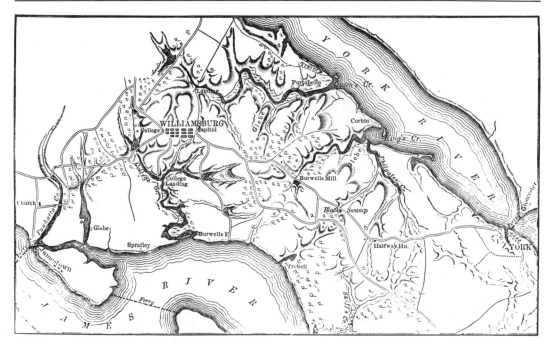

15. *Survey of the "Virginia Peninsula," drawn by Major James Kearney, 1818.*

ordering it to have John Page's "old House" removed so that "the Prospect of the Street between the Capitol and Colledge may be cleer."[19] The next year, Robert Beverley scoffed at what he construed as Nicholson's pride, observing that he "flatter'd himself with the fond Imagination, of being the Founder of a new City."[20] Later Spotswood fell foul of John Custis when he overstepped his authority and cut down several of Custis's trees in order to open up a "visto" from the Palace.[21]

Still, both Beverley and Custis had to admit that the unfolding of this urban plan was likely to perpetuate civic pride. Beverley went on to give Nicholson credit for the stately Capitol at the other end of the wide avenue from the college and also for having "mark'd out the Streets in many Places, so as that they might represent the Figure of a W. . . . he procur'd a stately Fabrick [the Capitol] to be erected, which he placed opposite to the College."[22] Today it seems that the east-west ridge was an obvious choice for the

site of Duke of Gloucester Street, especially since the college stood at one end of it; but Nicholson must nonetheless be credited with skillfully "reading" the landscape there.

Two other topographical features of Williamsburg that Nicholson and Spotswood had to read and study were (and still are) the zig-zag pattern

16. *Town plan of Williamsburg, last quarter of the eighteenth century, showing major topographical features, landmarks, and gardens (after Desandrouins, 1781; Frenchman's Map, 1782; and Bucktrout Map, 1800).*

FEATURES: *A, "Waller's Grove"; B, Waller's lots; C, Capitol Square; D, James Hubard's garden; E, Coke's lots; F, Bellett's nursery; G, Bassett Hall garden; H, Tazewell Hall garden; J, St. George Tucker lots; K, Joseph Prentis' lots; L, Dr. Amson's garden; M, Cocke-Jones garden; N, Robert Carter Nicholas's garden. 1, ravines; 2, Market Square; 3, Magazine; 4, Palace Green; 5, Bruton Parish Church; 6, College of William and Mary gardens; 7, Capitol Building; 8, Palace gardens; 9, South England Street; 10, Duke of Gloucester Street; 11, Custis Square; 12, Francis Street; 13, Nicholson Street.*

of ravines and gullies and the numerous springs that watered the town, running down and away from the ridge to the north and south (see figure 15). It was as if a colossal giant had pressed his hands into the landscape here to form the ravines, with the fingertips of both his hands not quite touching each other so that Duke of Gloucester Street could pass in between (see figures 8 and 16). Spring water passed down there and eventually fed into College Creek and Queen's Creek.

These ravines were a nuisance to the town planners and to individual residents throughout the century because they stood in the way of intended roads and rendered portions of several lots unusable for cultivation or any other purpose. On the other hand, the ravines provided some variety of elevation and increased the sense of space within those half-acre lots.[23] The additional perspectives also had pictorial value. One example, over which Nicholson had control, is the site of the Capitol building. In addition to

the W and M patterns of roads and paths that, as Reps has surmised, Nicholson may have wished to introduce through the siting of the Capitol and layout of diagonal streets, a ravine with a small creek north-northwest of that building originally crossed the main street and ran down to Nicholson Street. The descent was and still is fairly steep, and the Capitol looked over it. In spite of the essentially flat area in which it stands, then, the Capitol appears from several angles to the north to crown a knoll, much as Nicholson's statehouse did at Annapolis. If Nicholson had placed the Capitol farther east or west, it would have ended up in the ravine or he would have missed the chance to win some pictorial variety from a flat situation. Numerous such opportunities presented themselves to gardeners in lots next to ravines or sloping ground, as well as to Spotswood in the Palace gardens.

Nicholson, Spotswood, and the others who concerned themselves with the layout of the town knew that public buildings in England

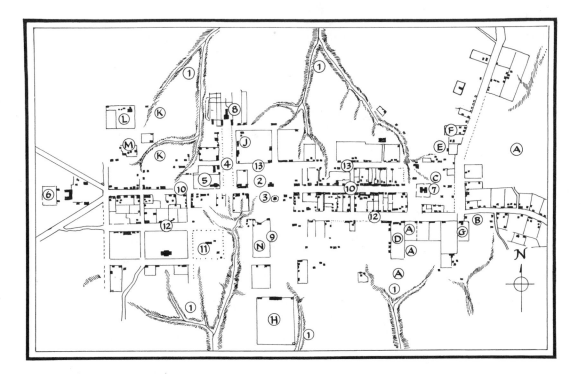

were unthinkable without gardens to frame and signal their importance.[24] There is, however, no evidence of gardens around the Capitol, either the first building, which burned down in 1747, or the second, built soon after. The Bodleian Plate (figure 10) shows none, although it does feature gardens at the college and Palace. Indeed, the act of 1699 that authorized a square for the Capitol grounds cryptically specifies that this square "shall not be built upon planted or occupied for ever." Even contemporary descriptions of the second building, while praising its elegance, fail to mention any gardens. Lord Adam Gordon thought it "very handsome" in 1765. An anonymous Frenchman in the same year called it "a very good building," which terminated the "very spacious" main street and made "a very good appearance." William Eddis singled it out in 1769 as "neat and elegant." John Smyth in 1770 thought it made an "elegant public building," and for the Chevalier de Bore it was "a very beautiful building."[25] Still, it is worth pausing to wonder whether the first Capitol possessed the elegance of the second and, if so, whether either building would have been left with the prosaic adornment normally associated with a traditional Virginia courthouse compound. It does not seem plausible that Byrd II, for example, who greatly admired Williamsburg's public buildings, would have been content with such a plain setting for the seat of the colonial government.

. . .

From the very beginning, it is obvious, the Market Square occupied space in Williamsburg comparable to a rond-point in a landscape garden. (See the modern drawing of the eighteenth-century town, with features identified, in figure 16.) The square may have been as close as Nicholson got in Williamsburg to a public garden idea he had in mind in 1696 for Annapolis. In that year he requested of the Maryland Assembly that "a Certain parcell of land in the publick pasture [be] . . . layd down in the Platt of the Town for planting or makeing a Garden, Vineard, or Somerhouse or other use."[26] In Williamsburg, vistas in the form of streets radiated out from the square in several directions, creating residential areas with separate identities. For the most part, the areas in or toward the west end of town were the more affluent. Benjamin Waller's little "corner" of the town and the homes along South England Street were also choice, as were the homes fronting Market Square on Nicholson Street.

It was no coincidence, of course, that the finest gardens in town were located in these neighborhoods. One reason was the "situation" or character of those areas. Another was that people living in them could afford to purchase more than one lot on which to build their houses. "Custis Square" and Joseph Prentis's Green Hill, for example, possessed exceptional gardens because they each comprised eight lots, one entire block. Robert Carter Nicholas's gardens and those of Tazewell Hall on South England Street also encompassed multiple lots. Frequently, *Virginia Gazette* advertisements for houses selling in these neighborhoods were carefully worded to emphasize their locations in desirable parts of town and mentioned their spacious gardens. And often a succession of enthusiastic gardeners would own these houses and gardens, suggesting that the areas or the gardens or both especially attracted them. Of course, the most prestigious area of all came to be along the Palace Green, because the Palace gardens were at the northern end of it and in a sense dominated those of everyone else. The Rochambeau and Desandrouins maps (see figure 8 for the latter) indicate that the pursuit of gardening for pleasure and ornament proceeded in several of these areas and determined their character.

The Market Square (feature 2 in figure 16), a large open green eventually surrounded by houses built mostly on two or more lots joined together, opened up views in all directions. By mid-century, the views of the houses around the perimeter of the square were varied, especially north toward Nicholson Street, where there stood what are now known as the Grissell Hay Lodging House, Peyton Randolph House, and Ludwell Tenement. Houses across Francis Street, on the south side of the green, such as Philip Lightfoot's in the 1750s or Robert Carter Nicholas's in the 1770s, took good advantage of these views across the green.

The Magazine (feature 3 in figure 16) provided a visual focus within the square itself. Since it was built during Spotswood's tenure as governor, it is conceivable that he designed and placed it. It was enhanced as a focus by its octagonal design (in the manner of Lord Allen Bathurst's Octagon Building at Cirencester Park, Gloucestershire), because it thus could be appreciated from any angle. An important English translation (by John James, 1712) of A. J. Dézallier d'Argenville's *The Theory and Practice of Gardening* describes the formal French use of structures resembling the Magazine in a landscape: "The Ends and Extremities of a Park are beautified with Pavilions of Masonry, which the *French* call *Belvederes*, or Pavilions of *Aurora*, which are as pleasant to rest one's self in, after a long Walk, as they are to the Eye, for the handsome Figure they make at a distance."[27] The owners of houses along Nicholson Street commanded a good view of the Magazine and, in fact, could regard the entire square as something of a park-like adjunct of their gardens. Except for minor encroachments upon the square, it remained open and picturesque throughout the century and added significantly to the attractiveness of the town, as St. George Tucker's appreciation of the square's "delightful verdure" bears witness.[28]

At the end of South England Street, John Randolph[29] built a house in the 1760s (see figure 16) that straddled the street so that through the front windows he could see the Magazine at the other end and beyond to the houses on the north side of the green (figure 17). In this way, Randolph also made his own house function as a terminating focus as seen down the street from the green and Magazine. Over a period of ten years he laid

17. *View of the Magazine along South England Street, Williamsburg.*

out in back of his house one of the largest gardens in town.

To the west of the Magazine, along the route of what was first known as France Street and later became Francis Street, there was a prospect created by sloping ground. The slope descended to a ravine that cut its way parallel to the roadway and along the gardens behind houses on Duke of Gloucester Street. In Spotswood's time, after 1717, probably the only noteworthy pleasure garden overlooking that ravine belonged to John Custis (see figure 16), and it is not improbable that Custis could see the Magazine across and up the ravine from his house (which no longer exists). He was deeply attached to his garden at "Custis Square" and fond of the views from his elevated demesne. He once proudly remarked, following a violent wind storm that blew down trees in the town, that "I myself have as strong and as high a house as any in the Government. [It] stands on high ground." It pleased him to observe that from his doorstep he could see the courthouse on the corner of Francis and South England streets.[30]

· · ·

One particular vista in Williamsburg, already mentioned, created a controversy and no small amount of ill feeling in 1717. The incident is of interest because it involves the two leading Williamsburg gardeners in the first quarter of the century, Custis and Spotswood. Custis, who was ill and cranky, fell into a quarrel with Spotswood about trees. Custis recounted his side of the story for Philip Ludwell in April 1717: "I happened to be at the Governors, and he was pleased to ask my consent, to cut down some trees that grew on my Land to make an opening, I think he called it a visto, and told me would cut nothing but what was only fitt for the fire, and for that he would pay as much as anyone gave for firewood. . . . I told him he might if he pleased cutt such Trees down."[31] That seems generous enough. But apparently unknown to Custis, Spotswood also wanted to cut down some of his swamp trees in another spot for a second "visto." According to Custis, Spotswood interpreted the original permission as a license to decimate his woods. "As to the clearing his visto," he complained, "he cut down all before him such a wideness as he thought fitt" and managed in the process to destroy some good oak and ash that, among other purposes, had been earmarked for one of Custis's tenements. Custis also claimed that Spotswood denuded some of the swamp woods and that he finally had to ask the governor to desist. He ended with the grumble that the governor had been saying "little mean things" of him. A note on the manuscript letter, possibly written by Ludwell, goes one step further in charging Spotswood with not paying for the wood, "no more than he has the gardener for laying out his garden above a year past."

The two men disliked each other, and it would be understandable if in his self-pitying letter Custis had distorted the incident, though we can be grateful to him for the information that the governor had been "laying out his garden" at the Palace during 1715–1716. More important, what emerges from this letter, apart from Custis's disdain for what he construed as Spotswood's pretentious gardening (implied by his requiring a vista from the Palace), is Spotswood's continuation of Nicholson's high valuation of prospects and angles of perspective within the

18. *View south along the Palace Green from the Palace, Williamsburg.*

town and his desire to incorporate into his Palace gardening a vista of the adjacent countryside. It is likely, though not certain, that one of Spotswood's desired vistas was from the Palace down the Palace Green (see figure 18 and feature 4 on figure 16), across the main street, along what was known as King Street to a corner of "Custis Square." Another was north over the gardens and toward open landscape (figure 19).

With his intended vistas, Spotswood was merely attempting to take advantage of Nicholson's original plan. When Nicholson arrived in Virginia in 1698, one of the directives he brought from the Board of Trade, or from John Locke specifically, was that a house for the royal governors be built in the colony as soon as possible. When the seat of government moved to Williamsburg, a suitable site for such a house took high priority in Nicholson's town plan. Around 1700 the Governor's Council accordingly selected twelve acres along the town's northern boundary, plus some sixty-five acres adjacent to the north.[32] In deciding to site the governor's residence on this northern boundary of the town, Nicholson undoubtedly planned to lay out an approach to the house from the south, the width and prominence of which would establish another north-south axis to complement the one created by South England Street. Since the Bruton Parish Church (feature 5 on figure 16) already stood on the line of the intended Duke of Gloucester Street, and since both the church and the governor's house would represent the most visible royal prerogatives in town, Nicholson apparently concluded that they ought to be not only near each other but also connected by an avenue approach extending to the governor's residence from a point on the main street next to which the church sits. This avenue came to be called the Palace Street sometime after the governor's house took on the name "Palace"; and it

has remained ever since a major, though sometimes forlorn, element in the town's layout. But it was Spotswood's pursuit of a vista, in fact, not so much Nicholson's, that appears to have been chiefly responsible for determining the full breadth and length of the axis established by the Palace Green as it is shown in late-eighteenth-century maps. The Palace was far from complete when he arrived in 1710; the same may have been true for the avenue in front of it.

In 1737, when William Gooch was governor, the appearance and function of the avenue changed somewhat. Philip Finch was paid ten pounds in December for "laying and planting

19. View north from the Palace over the gardens and toward the Governor's "Park."

the Avenue to the Governors House."[33] Whereas before the avenue may have been simply a roadway, providing a vista but not landscaped, after Finch's work it must have been more pleasant to look at, planted perhaps with a row of trees on either side as it is today, though not necessarily with catalpa trees as Thomas Jefferson noted when he drew a plan of the Palace sometime between 1779 and 1781.[34] With Finch's planting in 1737, what started out as Nicholson's thousand-foot-long approach to the Palace, and may have become part of Spotswood's landscape vista, also became something of a public promenade.

St. George Tucker, who lived next to the Green, obviously cherished its beauty as a public place. It appears in the title of one of his poems, "Lines Supposed to have been found upon the Palace Green at Williamsburg, on May-day 1816," which begins:

> O, the sweet, bewitching Scene
> Palace Grounds, or College-green,
> When the Beaus and Belles, assembling. . . .[35]

The poem also alludes to the two public gardens, those of the college and the Palace, which, a century after Spotswood's presence on the Williamsburg scene and after considerable neglect, remained the pride of the town.

. . .

It remains in this chapter to take a closer look at the landscaping that went on in those two gardens during the second and third decades of the eighteenth century. Although there is no evidence that Spotswood had anything to do with the college gardens before his departure in 1721, he is the person most likely to have exerted leadership in the landscaping that went on there in the 1720s, of which there is little evidence. As for the Palace gardens, his distinguished and better documented performance there illustrated to the town residents and also to the planters at least one kind of garden that could be laid out in the colony. It must have been an inspiring exam-

ple, one that forged an artistic link between plantation and capital and supplied many ideas for ambitious gardeners.

At least by 1729, after the completion of the Brafferton building, the grounds facing the east front of the college had been landscaped a little (see feature 6 on figure 16). A document dated February 1729 and titled "The Transfer of the College of William and Mary, Virginia" could just as likely be describing the eastern gardens as the western ones when it speaks of the college as "adorned with a handsome garden" laid out "all in . . . courts, gardens, and orchards,"[36] though the orchards were surely accommodated within the more spacious areas to the west, near the pasture.[37] Robert "King" Carter vaguely alludes to the eastern area in his diary for September 11, 1727. His note that the proclamation welcoming the arrival of Governor William Gooch was read on the "Colledge green" presents an image of a sward of grass, not flower beds.[38] Governor Gooch himself, excited by the unexpected gentility of the young capital, wrote promptly and assuringly to his brother, offering a glimpse of the gardens: "I promise you the College is very large and well built, with gardens and outhouses proportioned."[39]

In August 1732, when the President's House was being built on the northern side of the eastern courtyard, the Reverend William Dawson (James Blair's eventual successor as president) informed the bishop of London about the gardens there. "The foundations of a common brick House," he proudly wrote, were to be "laid opposite to Brafferton," so that the two buildings "will appear at a small distance from the East Front of the College," symmetrically and elegantly framing an existing "Garden planted with Ever-Greens kept in a very good Order." Here we have a clear image of an elegant setting decorated by clipped evergreens. Dawson continues, describing the layout on the western side: "The [Great] Hall and Chapel, joining to the West-Front towards the Kitchen-Garden, form two handsome Wings."[40]

Between Dawson's remarks in 1732 and the Bodleian Plate (figure 10) in the late 1730s, there is little evidence to indicate what the college gardens looked like until 1777, when Ebenezer Hazard wrote a brief account. A New York bookseller who took notes on his travels to the South for an intended geography of America, Hazard had a sharp eye. During a ten-day stay in Williamsburg he wrote the most complete extant description of the town. "At this [east] Front of the College," he observed, "is a large Court Yard, ornamented with Gravel Walks, Trees cut into different Forms, & Grass.—The Wings are on the West Front, between them is a covered Parade [piazza], which reaches from the one to the other, the Portico is supported by Stone Pillars: opposite to this Parade is a Court Yard and a large Kitchen Garden."[41] His description of the eastern gardens agrees well with the picture of them on the Bodleian Plate. (Archaeological investigations in the 1930s proved the Bodleian Plate's depiction of the Palace gardens to be correct in outline and shape, so there is every reason to trust what it shows of the college gardens.)

Both Hazard and the Bodleian Plate reveal a symmetrical, formal garden treatment such as Europeans felt was appropriate for a public building. There is no hint whatever of irregularity or variety. The design conveys firmly that this is a building of importance in the town. A central walk leading to the main building is flanked on either side by two rows of clipped evergreens and bushes. This topiary in the rows closest to the path is either planted on long low walls or has long trimmed hedges as ornamental bases, rather like long pedestals. Between the central path and the Brafferton to the left and the President's House to the right are rectangular grass plats framed by more bushes and topiary. A row of the same sort of planting stretches across the garden directly in front of the main building. Wooden paling connects all three buildings, completing the enclosure of the garden and separating it from the eastern gardens. It is notable

that no large trees interrupt the geometric pattern, which is open and free of the shade that would inhibit plant growth within.[42] From the windows of the buildings, the view of the garden would have presented ideas of order and grace—an emblem of what the college stood for in the New World.

The thirty-some years separating the Bodleian Plate from Hazard do not appear to have brought any obvious changes in the college's eastern gardens. With their simple, regular, and elegant lines, they were easy to maintain, especially since there were apparently no flower beds there.[43] Other visual evidence of the eastern gardens is available in what is known as the Simcoe Map (figure 20), drawn around 1781, about four years after Hazard saw the gardens.[44] Although there are good reasons for doubting the map's accuracy, the layout shown is historically interesting simply because the draftsman has the gardens bordered with a curving path, bisected by the central walk. The appearance is symmetrical, as it is on the Frenchman's Map drawn at about the same time, but the impression is softer and more natural owing to the curving path.

It is not known who designed the college gardens in the 1720s and 1730s, but there was an interesting Williamsburg personality who from the late 1720s was head gardener there. Thomas Crease also held the plum position of head gardener at the Palace until at least 1726, when the Council, soon after Governor Drysdale's death, authorized "that Thomas Crease be paid for his Service and labourers in assisting in putting in order the Gardens belonging to the Governor's house."[45] In 1724 he is identified simply as a gardener of Williamsburg, married and owning a half-acre lot.[46] With Governor Drysdale's death and the completion of the first (Spotswood's) stage of the Palace gardens, Crease may have been ready for a change. He stayed at the college a long time, judging by his *Virginia Gazette* advertisement in January 1738. Probably from the college gardens, "Thomas Crease, Gardener to the College, in Williamsburg," was selling for

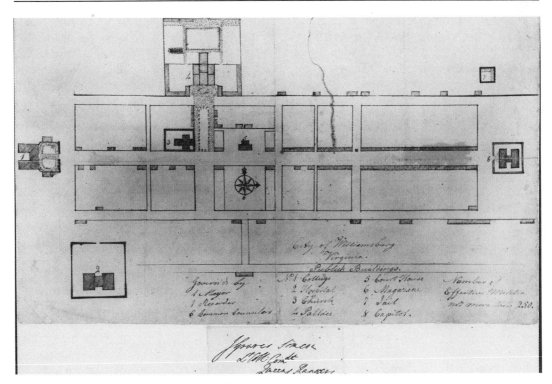

20. *Simcoe Map of Williamsburg, ca. 1781–1782.*

"Gentlemen and others . . . good Garden Pease, Beans, and several other Sorts of Garden Seeds." The rest of the advertisement is more significant. He also had for sale "great Choice of Flower Roots; likewise Trees of several Sorts and Sizes, fit to plant, as ornaments in Gentlemen's Gardens, at very reasonable Rates."[47] The latter were for "Gentlemen" only, not the "others." This is the first known reference in the colony not only to "Gentlemen's Gardens" but also to ornamental plants being sold for such gardens. These must have been both plantation and town gardens, since Crease made no distinction in his advertisement. At the very least, the advertisement tells us that amateur gentlemen gardeners were sufficient in number to constitute a market for ornamental flowers, bushes, and trees. To be able to sell plants on a scale justifying an advertisement like this, Crease must have been able to draw on the college nurseries, suggesting that they were developed and large enough to supply his private enterprise. Conceivably, he had engaged in such business at the Palace.

. . .

The Palace gardens, above all others, provided the strong lead for garden designers and horticulturists, both in the town and at the plantations, and epitomized the manner of living that Spotswood hoped to promote for himself in the town. It was the governor's gardens, not his house, that the House of Burgesses cited in November 1718 as an instance of how Spotswood, with his grand ideas for propping himself up, "lavishes away the Country's [colony's] money."[48] When he arrived, the house already had its roof, thanks to his predecessor Edward Nott's efforts to make the burgesses appreciate the urgent need for a governor's residence;[49] but only later were specific plans drawn up for the gardens and money appropriated. Spotswood therefore had more scope for self-expression in the creation of the gardens than in the completion of the house. And the available evidence suggests that he distinguished himself with the gardens, perhaps calculating their size and dignity as one means of lifting himself artistically above the leading planters like Byrd and Ludwell or the town luminaries like Blair and Custis. It will be recalled that when he arrived in Virginia, the squire-like, "perfect retir'd country life" being lived by Ludwell, Byrd, and other planters surprised him and inspired him to adopt a similar pose in a "Country manner." It was a pose more relaxed and countrified than he apparently had expected. Of course, he had the colonial purse to help him achieve his social ambitions through gardening. In that first letter to his brother, he mentions his new gardening amusements with the twin perspective of royal representative and squire—all at "the Country's Charge."[50]

Whereas his colleagues the planters had to pay for their gardening and architectural projects out of their own pockets, Spotswood could play the squire with the best of them and still let the colony pay for most of the expenses.[51] Back home in England he did not have the financial means to become "propertied"; but in Williamsburg, wearing the governor's robes and spending public monies, he could conveniently embark on imperial projects, such as gardens that symbolized his political and social role.[52] To this end, he apparently gained little understanding or appreciation from fellow Virginia gardeners. If they admired what he did, they did so grudgingly. This might be one of the reasons, for example, that Custis's highly descriptive letters never once commend or detail what the governor had achieved as a gardener. Byrd II mentioned only the fruit and poplar trees that he arranged to be sent to the Palace and said nothing about the governor's gardening, at least not until the 1730s, when Spotswood was only a squire gardening at Germanna.

In the beginning of his tenure, Spotswood understandably enjoyed good and hopeful relations with the powerful planters of the colony, including William Byrd II, with whom he shared gardening interests. He may indeed have come to the colony with genuine goals as a reformer, to do good for the crown and English colonial policy. But he was not averse to personal gain. After a series of political defeats that frustrated his self-esteem as a political and social reformer, he turned to the more satisfying and lucrative business of land acquisition. Land, especially in Germanna along the Rappahannock River, served his ambitions, and he did well for himself, although at the same time he further alienated the planters and, more generally, the House of Burgesses. The author of the anti-Spotswood "Memorandum for His Excellency" testified in 1721 to the resentment of the planters when he accused Spotswood of neglecting the Palace gardens, and Williamsburg too, while devoting his energies and skills to his own interests in Germanna: "He is building a very fine House there & has encouraged artificers of all sorts to people his new town which I hear is regularly laid out in streets and squares and a pretty many houses are already built." Spotswood had ambitions, said the writer, to be "a very great man."[53]

It is astonishing how little is known about the gardens Spotswood laid out and nurtured around the Palace during his tenure in Williamsburg—possibly the finest in America in the first half of the century. We might expect at least a few of the numerous visitors to the gardens throughout the century—participants in the annual Birth Night celebrations or house guests simply gazing at the gardens through the windows—to have been impressed enough to record the sight in a journal or letter. And undoubtedly people did write such accounts, which have been lost or have not turned up. This is as dismal a fact for American garden history as it would be for English garden history if there were no known descriptions of Hampton Court in the seventeenth century. It is a blank that is maddeningly reinforced by the almost total absence of graphic evidence. The detail of the Palace on the Bodleian Plate (figure 21) is the

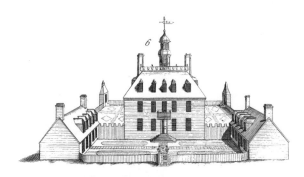

21. *Governor's Palace and gardens. Detail from the Bodleian Plate, ca. 1736–1740.*

only exception. It shows the so-called North Garden laid out in parterres with diamond-shaped centers and the forecourt garden taken up with oval flower beds separated by gravel walks. But the engraver of this plate was, not unnaturally, more interested in the Palace than the gardens and did not bother to include the gardens that we know existed east and west, and perhaps north, of the North Garden. Of greater interest are the gardens to the west and the view of the landscape to the north. That is where the potential existed for imaginative gardening, for variety, the pictorial, and the natural.

It is no coincidence that four months after Spotswood's arrival the General Assembly was persuaded to pass "An Act for finishing a House for the Governor of this Colony and Dominion," which in effect rescued the project from the inertia to which it had again succumbed. Considering especially his ambitions and the pose he sought to cultivate, Spotswood must have been appalled at the ragged environs of the house. No effort had yet been organized to lay out a garden setting. He saw years of waiting ahead of him. Certainly he must have been behind the act's resolution to render the house, without further delay, "more complete and commodious" along the lines that the 1705 act had prescribed, with its insistence that "severall buildings, gardens and other ornaments" be built and laid out. The act also "freely and unamimously" granted the £635 for such ornaments, words that imply a

past record of foot-dragging. Regardless, in the same precise fashion that the 1700 act authorized the building of the Capitol, the new act commanded:

> That a Court-Yard, of dimentions proportionable to the said house, be laid out, levelled and encompassed with a brick wall four feet high, with the ballustrades of wood thereupon, on the said land, and that a Garden of the length of two hundred fifty-four foot and of the breadth of one hundred forty-four foot from out to out, adjoining to the said house, to be laid out and levelled and enclosed with a brick wall, four feet high, with ballustrades of wood upon the said wall, and that handsome gates be made to the said court-yard and garden.[54]

Such detail as this about garden dimensions—known in this case simply because the gardening was paid for by public funds—is not to be found for any other garden in Williamsburg or for any Virginia garden until Jefferson began to pace out his gardens at Monticello in the 1770s and recorded their dimensions and plantings in his "Garden Book." The dimensions cited in the act were for the North Garden plus the so-called Ballroom Garden and the ground on which the mid-century ballroom and supper room wing was built. Archaeologists have confirmed that the garden's width, which they reckoned by excavating the foundations of the brick walls, and its length, determined by the foundations of the house and gate, answered very closely to the dimensions.

The four-foot-high brick walls enclosing the garden on the east and west sides, topped with the wooden balustrades, offer another clue about the garden. Obviously, at a height of four feet the brick walls did not completely cut off outside views from inside the garden, as did the high brick walls, for example, of English Tudor and Jacobean gardens. The wooden balustrades could be seen through—just how much depending upon the spacing of the balusters. While the balustrade was an effort at ornamentation, construed doubtless as more elegant than a plain brick wall and as a way of encouraging the circulation of air in the garden, it is possible that Spotswood decided on the brick-and-balustrade combination in order to diminish the feeling of separation between this central part of the garden and the garden areas west and east of it. If other parts of the garden could be seen through the wall, there would be a greater sense of movement from one part of the garden to another. The increased openness would lend itself also to the creation of visual angles and perspectives. If Spotswood already had in mind turning the ravine and little stream to the west into a canal faced by terraces or falling gardens, less substantial walls would have encouraged a person to move in that direction.

From "a proposal For rendring the new House Convenient as well as Ornamental,"[55] also in 1710, it would appear that some form of parkland, including orchard and pasture, was intended for the governor's house. The act of 1700 had specified the purchase of sixty-three adjoining acres to the north (in York County), so that from the beginning the governor's residence and lands were intended to appear somewhat as a plantation in its relation to the adjacent landscape (see figure 22). The orchard and pasture were probably to be located within the sixty-three-acre tract of land, not within the twelve acres straddling the northern boundary of the town on which the house was sited. According to the "proposal," the orchard, as well as a kitchen garden,[56] had to be fenced in. The 1710 act, in mentioning the orchard in the same breath with the pasture and requiring that both be "enclosed with a good ditch and fence," suggests that the orchard would be planted next to the pasture in the sixty-three-acre tract and that the entire acreage would be surrounded by the subsequently well-known French and English device, a "ha-ha," or sunken fence. The "proposal" indirectly confirms this arrangement by adding that the tract "be enclosed with a Ditch and Fence for a Pasture."

The ditch used as a fence or boundary, with respect to the adjacent parkland that Spotswood seems to have been determined to procure and lay out,[57] is important. Although such uses of a ditch—sometimes, as in the Palace grounds, combined with a fence—occurred rarely in the seventeenth-century French garden, it was advocated for the first time in garden literature in A. J. Dézallier d'Argenville's *Theory and Practice of Gardening* (French edition, 1709). The ha-ha revolutionized English gardening. It was a sunken barrier deep enough to keep livestock out of gardens without interfering with prospects or views of the surrounding countryside. In thinking back on its effect on the English landscape garden, Horace Walpole, in his *Observations on Modern Gardening* (1760), judged that the ha-ha exerted the single greatest influence in leading English gardening away from French and Dutch styles into the new era of the uniquely English landscape garden. "The capital stroke," he wrote, "the leading step to all that has followed, was (I believe the first thought [practice] was [Charles] Bridgeman's) the destruction of walls for boundaries, and the invention of fosses [ditches]—an attempt then deemed so astonishing that the common people called them Ha! Ha's! to express their surprise at finding a sudden and unperceived check to their walk."[58] D'Argenville called it an "Ah, Ah," which in John James's English translation (1712) is described as "on some Occasions, to be preferred, for that it does not shut up the Prospect, as the Bars of a Grill do."[59]

In light of how the 1710 documents specified that the Palace pasture should be managed, it appears that this land became a park-like extension of the house and gardens. By this means, Spotswood was able to enhance the governor's residence and make it seem more like a plantation. In a sense, he introduced elements of a plantation landscape into his life in Williamsburg, which he appears to have coveted from the earliest of his days in the colony. The result may be seen as a paradigm of the reciprocity between plantation and town gardening that at the time only uncertainly existed in the minds of people such as himself and Byrd II but that gradually

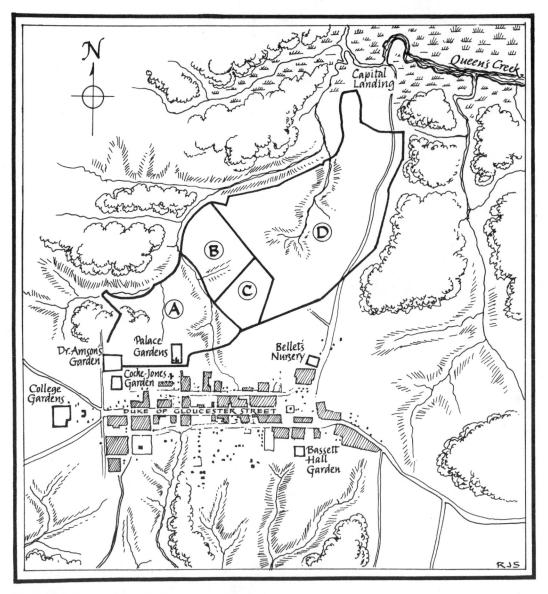

22. *Williamsburg environs showing major public and private gardens, including original Palace lands 1699 (A), and additions 1760–1775 (B–D).*

strengthened as the culture of both the town and the plantations developed. Bassett Hall and Tazewell Hall in Williamsburg are later, if more modest, examples of this paradigm. Janus-like, the Palace grounds had two faces: one looked out to the surrounding fields, the other to the town. In them, the rural and the urban settings were joined.

Later references to the pasture as the governor's "park" underline Spotswood's achievement.

The English park, of course, became an integral part of the English landscape garden and was deliberately designed for visual effects; later references to the Palace pasture as a "park" substantiate the integration of the Palace within a landscape garden scheme.

Governor William Gooch was so taken with Spotswood's landscape when he first saw it in 1727 that he wrote a brief description for his brother Thomas in England, one of the few known accounts: "The house is an excellent one indeed, all manner of conveniences that you can imagine, an handsome garden, an orchard full of fruit, and a very large Park, now turn'd to better use I think than deer, which is feeding all sorts of Cattle, as soon as I can stock it."[60] Judging from Gooch's mention of deer, Spotswood's pose as an English squire in Virginia evidently included stocking the park with deer, a common practice in English parkland. But more interesting is Gooch's pragmatic banishment of the deer and substitution of cattle. His revealing word here is *use*, which by 1727 had become a central principle of the new English landscaping. As Addison, Switzer, and Pope, among others, had urged, it was far better to combine pleasure with "profit" in one's landscape than to continue extravagantly to turn vast tracts of land over for ornamentation and the self-aggrandizement of the owner. Writing with an eye more on cultivation than pasturage, Addison had put it this way in 1712:

> It might, indeed, be of ill Consequence to the Publick, as well as unprofitable to private Persons, to alienate so much Ground from Pasturage, and the Plow, in many Parts of a Country that is so well peopled, and cultivated to a far greater Advantage. But why may not a whole Estate be thrown into a kind of Garden by frequent Plantations, that may turn as much to the Profit, as the Pleasure of the Owner?[61]

Furthermore, Homer, Horace, Virgil, Ovid, and other classical writers—the ultimate authorities—had taught that there was much beauty in a scene of grazing cows and sheep adjacent to a house, beauty that was enhanced by implied values about usefulness and industriousness. And in the Italian Renaissance garden these values were re-enacted in the incorporation of the *vigna*, an outlying area that could include vineyard or simply farmland, into the villa complex with its immediate gardens. In the governor's park and orchards, in fact, we may well have an early American example of the Italian vigna, mediated by English taste for the "congruence of villas and fields" in seventeenth-century estates.[62] Gooch's brief remark does not articulate these values, but it makes the general point clearly enough.

After a lapse of forty years, there is further evidence that the pasture or park was regarded as part of a landscape garden. In December 1770, just after Governor Lord Botetourt died, William Nelson of Yorktown wrote to Samuel Athawes of London, noting that Botetourt's "Gardener is also being continued, that the Garden-Park etc. may be in good order for the next Governor."[63] Nelson's terminology suggests he was thinking of these two parts of the Palace land as one landscape garden. Soon after he arrived at the Palace in 1768, Botetourt had written to the secretary of state: "My house is admirable, the ground behind it is much broke, well planted and watered by beautiful Rills, and the whole in every respect just as I could wish." That he was referring, in part at least, to the natural landscape in the park is borne out by another, more expressive letter he wrote at about the same time: "I . . . repaired to my Palace which is an excellent house. Behind it are about 150 acres of beautiful ground, finely broke, planted with tulip trees, oaks and pines, and watered by rivulets. I am told that the meadows are covered with white clover in the spring."[64] There is also a description in 1771 of a pit in the Palace "Garden," which was really in the park, that supplied shells and fossils for "Walks instead of Gravel." These materials, said Mr. F. Feilde in a letter to a Dr. McKenzie, were to be found only along the "banks of little Riverlets" in the park.[65] Lord Dunmore, in May 1775, complained that the re-

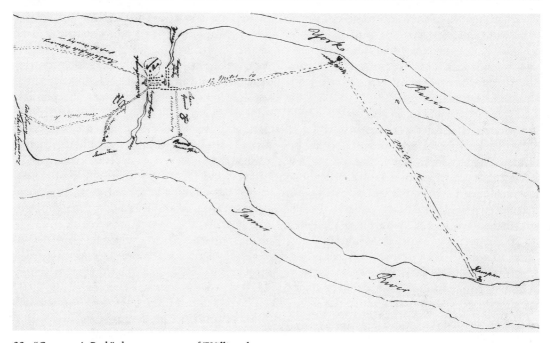

23. *"Governor's Park" shown on a map of "Williamsburg and the Slip of Land Between the York and James Rivers,"* ca. 1781.

belliousness of the people had reached such a pitch that they had taken possession of the "park"—"a considerable piece of land," he explained, "adjoining and belonging to the Governor's house"—"wantonly cutting and maiming my cattle."[66] A most interesting map of 1781 (figure 23) shows clearly the location of the park.

Spotswood's orchards, to which he looked forward in his letter to his brother, were located at a considerable distance from the house—certainly not in the immediate gardens. The ditch-and-fence combination appears to have separated them from the gardens and house, although they were also separately enclosed by paling to keep roaming livestock away. If the orchard had been planted on the garden side of the ha-ha and thus been protected by it from hungry livestock, there would have been little point in fencing it. According to the topography of the Palace area today, the orchards would have been

planted on the other side of the main (Lafayette) road that now marks the northern boundary of the restored gardens.

That Spotswood's orchards were large and that he took a special, immediate interest in them is evident from Byrd II's diary. On October 8, 1711, one year after Spotswood arrived in Williamsburg, Byrd records that the governor took him "to the house that is building for the Governor where he showed me abundance of faults and found great exception to the proceedings of the workmen." Byrd may or may not have been admiring Spotswood's talents and personal role as an amateur architect at the governor's house, but he left Spotswood resolved upon helping him plant his orchard. He adds in this entry that he immediately went out to Colonel Henry Duke's plantation, "where I got 50 black cherry trees for the Governor." On February 5, 1712, Byrd notes that he ordered his sloop "to go to Colonel Eppes's for some poplar trees for the Governor," which though not for the orchard itself shows at least Byrd's early commitment to help Spotswood with the Palace gardens. Three days later he sent from Westover, via the James River, "some fruit trees for the Governor." In March, Byrd entertained Spotswood at Westover, after which occasion he sent him more fruit trees.[67] It is likely that Byrd was using plants to enhance his rapport with Spotswood, just as he and his father had done with influential politicians in England, but his earnestness regarding matters horticultural argues that for the most part he was perfectly sincere in wanting to help the governor with his exciting new planting schemes.[68]

Adjacent to the Palace, Spotswood's flower gardens remain a mystery, except for this brief allusion to them in the 1710 "proposal": "That a Flower Garden behind [north of] the House as well as the Courtyard before it be enclosed with a Brick Wall 4 foot high with a Ballustrade of Wood on the Top." This explicitly states that the garden, 254 by 144 feet, prescribed in the 1710 act was in fact a flower garden. It could hardly have been anything else. It has already been noted that the diamond-patterned parterres shown in the Bodleian Plate suggest one version of the garden's layout; but gardens change frequently, and that design existed almost thirty years after Spotswood's flower beds had first been planted. We do not even know if Spotswood took much of an interest in the flower garden. His town-planning and landscaping interests—large-scale projects—argue that he was more enthusiastic about the architectural than the horticultural.

Although the Bodleian Plate reveals sketchily what the parterre garden facing the north front of the Palace looked like in the late 1730s, the archaeological discoveries on the site supply more precise evidence about dimensions, elevations, pathways, terraces, walls, and steps. Whatever Spotswood's North Garden looked like, it was altered after the addition, sometime between 1749 and 1752, of a ballroom and dining room wing onto the original house's north

front. Archaeologists have determined that when the wing was built the ground between the east and west walls of the garden was filled in and leveled northward up to the point where a low wall ran east-west across the garden.[69] This earth-moving project was designed to create a flat, even, and formally elegant setting on the three sides of the new wing. It also created two levels in the garden, so that from the upper or Ballroom Garden one looked down on the lower North Garden. These revelations about the effects of the new wing on the gardens were confirmed by the discovery of three sets of steps leading from the upper to the lower garden. The steps stood on the lines of three north-south paths or walks, two on the sides of the garden enclosure and the middle one centered on the house and main north iron gate.[70] The two side paths terminated at the northeast and northwest corners with two necessary houses, the foundations of which were also discovered. A crosswalk was located by the discovery of the foundations of east and west gates in the brick walls. The three sets of steps descended directly onto that crosswalk, which established the principal east-west axis of the entire garden layout extending west through the wall and over to and down the terraces.

The flower garden preceding the new wing, then, which presumably did not alter much in shape and in the grading of the ground between Spotswood's time and mid-century, was a single-level garden. It probably had two north-south side paths for the sake of convenience, in addition to the central one, although the Bodleian Plate shows only the eastern one. The Bodleian Plate does show that the diamond-patterned layout of beds extended all the way to the north, with the necessary houses at the corners. The house itself obscures the central axis on the plate, as well as the low east-west wall, but archaeologists have found the remains of a sixteen-foot-wide path that came almost up to the steps descending from the original dwelling. This central axis, therefore, was longer and more dominant before the wing was added.[71]

A more public part of the gardens is the little courtyard facing the south front of the house, at the head of the Palace Green. Brick walls enclosed that courtyard, too, although the Bodleian Plate shows higher ones than the four-foot walls with wooden balustrades designated by the 1710 documents. This little garden with four oval flower beds provided a pleasant forecourt for welcoming visitors. It would have been needed as a turn-around area for vehicles so that visitors did not have to alight from their carriages in the street. It is possible, however, that the walls enclosing this courtyard, together with the garden, were removed later in the century to provide more room for vehicular access to the Palace, for none of the maps and plans dating from near the end of the Revolution—Rochambeau's, Desandrouins's, the Frenchman's, Simcoe's, or Jefferson's— shows the walls and garden there. The Simcoe Map (figure 20) seems the most informative of all about the Palace garden features after the north wing was added. It shows the courtyard open to the Palace Green, with a little garden area (grass or flowers) in the center circled by a drive.

Also suggestive is the Simcoe Map's rendering of the North Garden as it existed after the wing was added. Its reliability in this area of the gardens may be contested forever, but the fact that it illustrates the garden layout with some detail is historically important. The map shows the opening for the north gate, with what looks like part of a circular drive outside the gate, but there is no central drive or even path establishing a principal axis. Instead, the large rectangle (with its length incorrectly stretching east-west instead of north-south) dominates the foreshortened North Garden, which is bordered with side paths and crosswalk. Several of the dimensions and proportions are wrong here, such as the sizes of the kitchen and stable yards and the size of the main house relative to the wing, but the author must have been exceedingly forgetful or unobservant if he could not get right whether or not the North Garden had a main north-south axis. As it happens, neither does the reliable

Frenchman's Map indicate a central, north-south path there, although it does include several other paths and divisions.

The most interesting landscaping Spotswood did was west and northwest of the North Garden.[72] His trouble with the House of Burgesses over his gardens probably began, however, when he decided to transform the ravine west of the house into elaborate terraces facing west over a formal canal that opened out into a fish pond, possibly (as today) at its northern end. The project necessarily involved much earth moving and tree felling, as well as the canalization and damming up of the rivulet. Then there was the fish pond (of unknown shape) to dig out as the canal's extension. This sizable area, reaching from Scotland Path north all the way to and beyond the north wall, had to be landscaped too and maintained, presumably at no small expense.

These terraces were the earliest known in Williamsburg (figure 24). Spotswood laid them out with three sets of steps (foundations of which were discovered by archaeologists), two at either end of the terraces and one near the center, lined up with the east-west cross axis. Whether the terraces were naturalized through the planting of fruit trees and shrubs, it is impossible to say, but they certainly were broad enough to accommodate some planting. A distinctive garden form in Renaissance Italy and in seventeenth-century England, one which created that blessed quality of variety as well as a theatrically conceived and shaped space, terraces became common in southern colonial plantations during the eighteenth century. Those at the Palace, however, are the only ones that we know for certain existed in Williamsburg. And remarkably successful ones they were, lending a neat theatrical aspect to an otherwise desperately inconvenient feature of the terrain. It is not being too fanciful, in fact, to think of these terraces as part of a large theater in which people could walk, observe the plantings, and appreciate the formal water treatment below.

Spotswood was equally ambitious with the ca-

Gardens in Early Williamsburg 51

24. *The terraces in the Palace gardens.*

nal at the foot of the terraces (figure 25). Garden canals were a Dutch contribution to the seventeenth-century English garden, remaining popular in the first half of the next century, as at Lord Burlington's Chiswick House. The fish pond, which Spotswood stocked with fish for his table, provided an attractive ornamental feature at the northern end of the canal. When the canal and pond were introduced, they represented the only known water gardens in Virginia.

The canal was obviously a Dutch feature, but so was the series of room-like garden areas just above the terraces, including the large North Garden. The layout had a piecemeal look to it, with the several areas not relating to one another—an instance of parts not adding up to a whole. Although there is no extant drawing of the canal and the adjacent gardens, an idea of the Dutch appearance of the design, but without the terraces, may be obtained from a drawing in 1735 by William Stukeley of the seventeenth-century gardens at Crossy Hall in South Hol-

25. *The canal and terraces in the Palace gardens.*

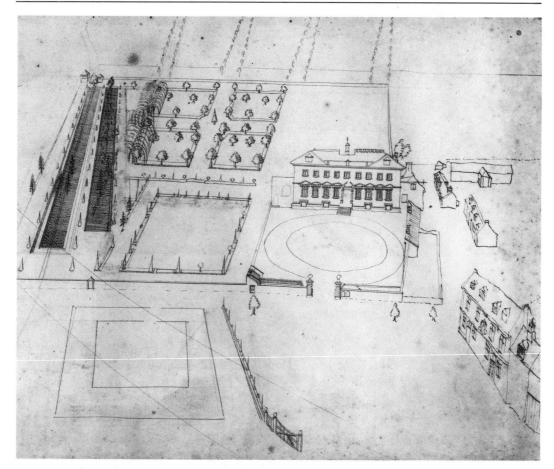

26. *The Dutch-style gardens at Crossy Hall in South Holland, Lincolnshire. Drawing by William Stukeley, 1735.*

land, Lincolnshire. The drawing is reproduced here (figure 26) because those gardens reveal an uncanny resemblance to what we know about the layout at the Palace.

The burgesses, however, remained unimpressed. To them the water effects seemed almost prodigal, a frittering away of the colony's money so that Spotswood could conveniently have fish for dinner. It is true that he ended up spending far more money on his gardens than the House, probably in its most generous estimates, ever thought possible. The burgesses were appalled. If this man wished to live the high life, they may have thought, he ought to pay for it out of his own pocket. They asked him

in November 1718 whether the gardens and palace were yet completed and, if not, how much more money would be required to bring the whole business to an end. Spotswood's delayed reply was petulant: "I am loath to offer any valuation of my own Gardeners . . . performances."[73]

His responses in early 1719 to the House's charges mention chiefly the gardens, which suggests that the Assembly was disturbed mostly by his gardening expenses. Eventually he rose defiantly to his own defense: "I have expended about their Building and Gardens but little above Two Hundred pounds per annum," he told the burgesses, adding that in May he had offered "to be at the Expence of the Fish-Pond and Falling gardens, to take them to my Self; these improvements happening to be upon the Town Land and such as would not long want Purchasers." He reminded them that he had personally overseen all the improvements—in effect, had served the colony as a landscape architect free of charge—and at the same time had saved the public about £100 annually. If it had not been for him, he added, the four-man select committee set up by the House to inspect the house and gardens would have tried to "pull to pieces" the 1710 legislation that "allows an Orchard, Gardens, and other Appurtenances."[74]

Still the burgesses were unimpressed. The quarrel and rivalry had taken on a life and energy of their own and refused to subside. In November 1720 the Assembly, determined not to be obliged to Spotswood, requested him to walk around the garden to "view all the Improvements that had been made since Christmas 1717 in the Gardens for the ornament and preservation thereof and compute the Charge of the whole."[75] He told them that his patience had worn out and that from then on they could hire their own overseer. Accordingly, they appointed a committee to compute charges for work to be done. Significantly, the committee allowed no money whatever for more gardening and earmarked only £52 for Henry Cary to finish up the house and an insulting £1 for the completion of a "bannio"—some sort of ornamental Italianate bathhouse. By now, Spotswood had given up the gardens and turned his artistic attention to his house and town at Germanna. Not surprisingly, the author of the "Memorandum for His Excellency" announced in the fall of 1721 that the "fine Gardens and Fish pond, etc. are not so much regarded as Formerly."[76]

That was a self-serving report, however. Even if not supervised by Spotswood, the gardens would have been cared for by the head gardener, so it is doubtful that they would have deteriorated so quickly. Deliberately, Robert Beverley praised them in the 1722 edition of his *History*,

giving Spotswood full credit for their beauty. And two years after Spotswood had been removed from office, Hugh Jones, in his *Present State of Virginia* (1724), published this resounding endorsement of Spotswood's gardens: "The Palace, or governor's house, [is] a magnificent structure, finished and beautified with gates, fine gardens, offices, walks, a fine canal, orchards. . . ."[77]

If this controversy had any positive value, it is not that it stopped Spotswood from doing any more gardening at the Palace; rather, it confirms that he had not created the terraces, canal, and fishing pond until about 1717. It also points up that these landscape elements were among the most expensive and last of Spotswood's improvements. Political history aside, it is undeniably a shame that Spotswood did not stay on with the Assembly's cooperation. If he had, he doubtless would have embellished the gardens further. As it was, he enjoyed them for only six years, his innovative canal, pond, and terraces taking shape only after he had moved into the Palace.[78]

By the end of the first quarter of the century, partly through Spotswood's own efforts, Williamsburg had become a more attractive and settled town than the one he had found when he arrived about fifteen years earlier. His encouragement of building, the gardening virtuosity he demonstrated, the college's own evolving ornamental gardens, and the layout of the town itself had helped to promote the capital's development toward a more gracious center for the colony's life, culture, and government. Much of Spotswood's incentive derived from his social ambition to enjoy in Virginia a way of life that he could not afford back in England but one that would at the same time remind him of England. When he had taken these ambitions as far as he could, or as far as he was permitted in Williamsburg, he transferred them to Germanna. By that time he had amassed property, chiefly in the form of land, that enabled him to pursue his ambitions in his own private sphere.

3

John Custis and William Byrd II: Crosscurrents of Virginia Gardening 1720–1750

William Byrd II and John Custis felt much as Spotswood did about encouraging around themselves a culture and society that would make early eighteenth-century Virginia seem not quite so remote from Europe. Like Spotswood, Byrd II felt keenly his removal from England and loss of the cosmopolitan world of London. If he had possessed the means, he would have quickly returned to the theaters, coffeehouses, high society, country houses, gardens, and women of his native land. Instead, his destiny was to remain in Virginia and, at Westover and in Williamsburg, to cultivate as best he could the society he so sorely missed. Gardens, plants, and landscapes played no little part in the complex of values he tried to construct, especially at Westover. Byrd even demonstrated a capacity for picturesque composition through his writing about landscape. As for John Custis, his love for Williamsburg was best expressed through his love for his garden there and his introduction of countless native and English plants into it. He was obsessed with plants, and both he and Byrd did much to advance the science of botany in the colony. Through their gardening, they also helped to bring plantation and town life closer together. They illustrated the very personal, even emotional, character that gardening could assume. And each distinguished himself by suggesting the beauty of the natural and pictorial in gardens and landscape.

These two men were among the boldest and most scientifically curious promotors of Virginia gardening and horticulture before 1750. Spotswood had been determined—ostentatiously and somewhat egocentrically—to create pleasure gardens at the Palace; but his gardening interest was not then in horticulture as much as in staged architectural effects—with himself as their principal focus. For example, having received a valuable packet of seeds for Bishop Compton from the botanist and illustrator Mark Catesby, who was then living in Williamsburg, all Spotswood could manage by way of comment on Catesby's scientific interests was the vague remark that he was "very curious in such things."[1] Byrd, by contrast, was excited about Catesby's talents. Similarly, for Spotswood, Virginia was of incidental importance as the setting for his gardening projects, whereas for both Custis and Byrd (especially in the later stages at Westover) the colony's horticultural resources, environment, and society offered major inducements to gardening. They saw themselves as *Virginia* gardeners, even if they looked to England for much of their inspiration and many of their plants.

As Custis in Williamsburg and Byrd at Westover involved themselves in the tasks of laying out the grounds around their homes, they advanced three developments of critical importance to eighteenth-century Virginia gardening. The first was the persistence of plant exchanges between the colony and England.[2] Custis's enthusiasm for plant exchanges, chiefly with Peter Collinson (1694–1768), is well known today because of the extraordinarily detailed letters he and Collinson exchanged about Virginia and English plants. An English Quaker, Collinson did much in the first half of the eighteenth century to encourage botanical study in the American colonies, especially through John Bartram, the Philadelphia naturalist and nurseryman. Custis, Bartram, and several other horticulturists ceaselessly sent him American plants, which he planted in his own famous garden at Mill Hill near London and which were studied and scientifically identified by the Royal Society. In return, Collinson shipped to the Americans countless English plants for experimentation and ornamentation in their gardens.[3] Byrd was also keen about this form of transatlantic trade, which he, too, carried on with Collinson as well as with such eminent botanical personalities as Sir Hans Sloane and Leonard Plunkenett. But whereas little is known about the plants in Byrd's Westover plantation garden, it is clear that Custis's plant exchanges thoroughly determined the character and look of his Williamsburg garden. This dimension of Custis's gardening, in fact, represents an important element in American garden history: although plant exchanges with England were going on throughout the colonies early in the century, their influence on colonial gardens is seldom as clear as in the case of Custis.

The gardening careers of Custis and Byrd also strengthened the balance or complement between urban and plantation gardening in Virginia. This second important development was characterized, as we have seen, by a reciprocity between Williamsburg and the plantations: the town gardeners were supplied by the plantations with plants, tools, fencing, and so on, while the planter-gardeners and their wives for their part could visit Williamsburg to see how town gardening, including that at the college and Palace, was progressing, talk to other planters about their gardens, share ideas and gardeners, and carry on plant exchanges among themselves. It is evident from his diaries that Byrd visited Williamsburg regularly with an appreciative eye for its architecture. Although he mentioned Custis's garden a few times, unfortunately he generally is silent regarding private gardens in town. Yet, living only twenty miles from the town, he delighted in visiting his friends at their homes, where there were gardens to see, and he took more than a passing interest in the landscaping of the Palace gardens during the Spotswood years. Byrd never says so, but we may wonder whether the civilizing coherence with which the growing capital began to endow colonial life encouraged him to garden more ambitiously, or whether—and there is some evidence for this—he consciously adopted a quasi-Horatian pose of the gentleman-gardener-farmer. That pose depended on the gentleman living in quiet semi-retirement near an urban center. Such a pose, with its strong gardening theme, was not beyond a man who read Horace and other Roman writers almost every day. Byrd was unique as a planter in many ways, but the type of country-city perspective that he illustrated grew stronger and more pervasive as the century wore on.

The third component of Custis's and Byrd's gardening was the pictorial. This principle of design appears in both town and plantation gardening throughout the century but is not well documented graphically in Virginia by plans and drawings until much later at Monticello and Mount Vernon. Yet Custis's rationale for choosing plants from England and Byrd's painter-like eye for landscape compositions is early evidence in the colony that both understood the value of the pictorial in planting and laying out grounds. Such evidence weighs against the prevailing thesis that American gardening in general did not become expressive, imaginative, or picturesque in either town or plantation until the end of the century.

. . .

John Custis (1678–1749) owned two Virginia plantations in 1717, Arlington on the Eastern Shore and Queen's Creek about one mile north of Williamsburg.[4] Nonetheless, he wanted to own a house in Williamsburg itself to partake of the growing refinement and civilized culture of the young town. He decided, therefore, to buy eight lots and build a house, which he did by 1717. Thus begins the story of a fine private Williamsburg garden in the early eighteenth century.

Custis's move to town in 1717 initiated a new period in his life. His sometimes turbulent marriage to Frances Parke had ended suddenly with her death in 1715, and he brought his two children to his new house. He resolved immediately to turn his four acres into a handsome and exceptionally well-planted garden. Eventually, the garden became for him a landscape of fulfillment. Although it did not, so far as we know, originate any innovative principles of garden design, it surely increased English botanical knowledge of southern colonial plants; it also helped to confirm for several English botanists and gardeners that progressive and energetic scientific gardening was going on in the southern colonies. Collinson, among others, saw to it that "Custis Square" was well known to botanists on both sides of the Atlantic.

Soon after moving into his house, Custis began writing to his London friends for plants for his new garden. These he desired to complement the native varieties, which he undoubtedly obtained from his own plantations and elsewhere. "I have lately got into the vein of gardening," he wrote to his London agent, Micajah Perry, about 1717, "and have made A handsome garden to my house; and desire you will lay out £5 for me in handsome striped hollys and yew trees, but most hollys, gett some one to chuse them that has judgment in such things, choose them with handsome body and not too big; and buy them as near the Waterside as you can [since] land Carriage will bee apt to shake and loosen them too much; let them be care[fully] put up in pots."[5]

Custis's delight over the arrival of plants was frequently matched by frustration and anger when he discovered the plants were dead. At such times he got very worked up, blaming the ship captains for their ignorance and indifference or the gardeners who inexpertly packed the boxes. "The box for my garden was all rotten as dirt," he complained in 1723; "I did not have one sprig; the gardener was either a fool or a knave . . . I had rather bin disappointed in any one thing else."[6] It was not until Collinson took over supervision of the shipments that Custis began more consistently to receive healthy specimens, although even then the seasons and ship captains' other priorities took their toll.

In spite of these obstacles, Custis was proud enough of his garden in 1725 to call it a "pretty little garden"; and Catesby complimented him for it in 1730. Catesby had known the garden only between 1717 and 1719, but apparently he heard more about it later. Custis's first surviving letter to him, in June 1730, alluded to the praise of his garden: "you are pleased to compliment me concerning my garden which I assure you no ways deserves it; my greens are come to perfection, which is the chief fruit of my assiduous endeavors." By 1734 he was calling himself "a great admirer" of plants and no longer indulged in such modesty as he had shown to Catesby, claiming that his garden was "inferior to few if any in Virg[ini]a in which . . . my whole delight is placed."[7]

Custis was not the only naturalist to whom Peter Collinson wrote in America.[8] The botanist knew others there either personally or through correspondence.[9] He had come to know Byrd II, for example, during the latter's long visits in England up until 1726; Byrd could have told him about Custis's garden in Williamsburg as well as about his own at Westover. Advising John Bartram in 1737 as to naturalists and gardeners he should visit on his anticipated trip from Philadelphia through parts of the South, especially along the Eastern Shore, Collinson remarked: "In Virginia, there is Colonel Custis and

Colonel Byrd, [who] are both curious men."[10] Collinson believed that if American botanists would help one another's researches, the increase in knowledge to the world of botany, and to himself in particular, would be significant. From England, therefore, he engineered the first meeting between Bartram and Custis in Williamsburg. "The Gardens of pensilvania are all furnish'd with European Rarities," Collinson wrote to Custis; "possibly He [Bartram] may assist you with plants that you want & you may Assist Them."[11]

After Bartram's successful visit in 1738, Collinson hoped to obtain from him an impartial judgment of Custis's garden. "Pray what didst thee see new in his garden?" he asked. This information he apparently received, for he told Custis a few months later that Bartram had been "Delighted with thy Garden which is the best Furnish'd & next John Claytons of any He Mett With—in all that Journey."[12] Custis need not have been offended by having his garden deemed second best to Clayton's. A clerk who lived and gardened in Gloucester County, Clayton was a highly regarded botanist and plant collector in Virginia at this time; his treatise, *Flora Virginica* (1739–1743, 1762), was published in London and had the reputation there of being the most reliable study of native American flora in the first half of the century.[13]

. . .

With Collinson's help over the years, Custis's garden eventually boasted one of the best collections of English plants in America. Custis highly prized a present of plants. When he received Collinson's first parcel in 1734, he confessed to his new friend that if he had sent him "20 times the weight of the seeds, etc. in gold it would not have bin the 20yeth part so acceptable to me."[14] His satisfaction derived both from his personal desire to stock his garden and from his scientific curiosities. Many of the plants the Quaker botanist sent were new not only to Williamsburg but also to the colonial South generally.[15]

In 1737 Custis drew up for Collinson a list of the trees and flowers that "at present are inhabi-

tants of my poor Garden."[16] Although this list sadly has not survived, the correspondence between the friends over eight or so years gives away a few of the secrets of the garden. Custis clearly wished to make his garden as colorful as possible with English plants. Again and again, it is the vivid colors of Collinson's shipments that both men emphasize, so that apart from the design and style of the garden the color especially must have been distinctive. Eventually, there took root tulips, chrysanthemums, foxgloves, Persian lilac (which Collinson described as a "Low plant so very ornamental in a Flower Garden"),[17] lilies, polyanthus, hyacinth, altheas, yellow asphodel, jessamine, narcissus, crocus, pinks, cyclamen, and many others such as Collinson believed were "not Very Common in your Gardens." The crown imperial lily, which usually rotted in passage, was one very colorful flower that tantalized and eluded Custis until 1739, when a lemon-colored one finally was brought to flower—the first in Williamsburg. It was "looked on as a great rarity," Custis exulted, but he also wanted the orange variety and especially the striped ones he recalled having seen in England thirty years earlier.[18]

More than any other flower, however, it was the rose that gave the garden its color and roused Custis's wonder (figure 27b). In 1735 Collinson sent him Italian tuberoses with the observation that "In South Carolina the Italian Tuberoses Increase prodegiously as no doubt They will with you." Somewhat miraculously, at least from Custis's point of view, these arrived "fresh and sound and sprouted." "I put them immediately in the ground under a south building and am in great hopes of their doing well." Custis surprised Collinson with the news that neither he nor anyone else he knew in Virginia had tuberoses in their gardens. "I admire you had them not," Collinson declared in November 1736, "when they are on both sides of you in South Carolina and Pensilvania, my friend [Bartram] from [the] Last place writt Mee he had last yeare 149 flowers on one single Flower Stalk. . . . I would have you try some of them in the Ground next year under a south wall or pale."

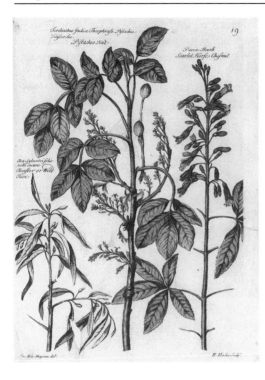

This exchange suggests that Custis may have gardened in some degree of isolation in Williamsburg until Collinson introduced him to Bartram the following year—he is not known to have traveled far afield to other gardens in pursuit of plants and ideas—but he then resolved to propagate in his garden as many different colored, but chiefly yellow, roses as Collinson could send him.[19]

. . .

Another prominent theme emerging from Custis's English plant acquisitions is his taste for evergreen bushes, boxwood, and hollies, the leaves of which he preferred either striped, variegated, or gilded. The cumulative effect of such ornamental planting along paths and around flower beds would have been, again, to enhance the pictorialism of the scene. One of Collinson's shipments, for example, contained "one striped box" that had "some life in it; I should have bin glad of it; being a great admirer of all the triple striped gilded and variegated plants; and especially trees." This taste, Custis acknowledges, is "out of fashion; but I do not mind that[.] I allways make my fancy my fashion." By "fancy" he meant simply his eye for the pictorial.[20]

In the meantime, however, a discouraged Custis was beginning to recognize the difficulties of introducing a diversity of flowers into his garden, especially herbaceous plants, which even then were the glory of an English garden. "I know not how it happens," he grumbled, "but the seeds in generall wee have from England very often never come up." And he had seized upon another scapegoat besides the ship captains: "I believe it is often the faults of the seeds men," who pack them inadequately for the jour-

27a (top) and b (bottom). Hand-colored engravings of plants in Catalogus Plantarum *(1730), 'A Catalogue of trees, shrubs . . . which are propagated for sale in the gardens near London . . . By a Society of Gardeners' (attributed to Philip Miller). Among the plants illustrated that Custis requested for his Williamsburg garden are the double yellow rose, Moss Provence rose, scarlet horse chestnut, and pistaccio tree.*

ney.[21] As time passed, however, he realized that the Virginia climate was mostly to blame. Many plants, seduced to bud by a forward spring, were nipped with demoralizing regularity by frosts in spite of Collinson's suggestions for retarding early blooming. It was either that or drought and heat. The climate's effects on his tender English flora began to evolve in Custis's mind into an allegory of the vicissitudes of human experience, which in turn suggests his close personal identification with his garden and the plants either thriving or struggling in it.

We know a great deal about the native flora in Custis's garden because he sent many specimens to Collinson. Frequently, Collinson desired that the Virginian should first cultivate them in his garden, and their correspondence consequently mentions in some detail the native species of trees, bushes, fruit, and vegetables that Custis was growing. Virginia trees particularly interested Collinson,[22] and especially the sorrel. Catesby had told him about it: "a very pretty plant that . . . Grows between Williamsburgh and York."[23] When Collinson asked for one, Custis, who had not thought much of its ornamental value, did not have a specimen in his garden. But finally, at Collinson's urging, he ended what turned out to be the saga of the sorrel tree by going himself, in spite of ill health, into a swamp to retrieve several specimens for his garden. He reported his success to his friend: "I went myself into the woods this last February and found a swamp w[h]ere a great plenty of sorrell trees grew and got fifty fine young trees! . . . now in my garden in full health and glory." He sent Collinson two boxes full of the seeds, which safely arrived in England.[24]

Collinson and Catesby, along with many other Englishmen in their day, longed for specimens of pink and white dogwoods. Custis was partial to the white; "as for dog woods," he remarked in 1735, "these in my garden are blossomd white which are much more beautiful than the other." Catesby suddenly in 1737–1738 became very concerned about a rare red- or peach-colored dogwood that he had planted in both his sister Elizabeth Cocke's and Custis's gardens before

leaving Williamsburg for England in 1719. Collinson relayed a message in January 1737—"Mr. Catesby Desires to know if you have the Red Flowering Dogwood"—and followed up one year later with this more definite and urgent enquiry:

Mr. Catesby Gives His Humble service and is und'r Great Concerne for fear the Race of that Curious peach colour'd Dogwood is Lost, without [that is, unless] you have One in your Garden. He says most of them that He had Transplanted from the Mother Tree into Mr Jones Garden was Destroyed by Fire, but He Thinks One or Two was saved & He brought and planted in your Garden. There is many flowers when In Decaye in particular the White thorn with us will Turn Redish but He says this open'd of a Red Colour att First.

Custis's curt reply must have distressed Catesby: "as for the peach [pink] colord Dogwood Mr. Catesby mentions; I had two in my garden, but they never bloomed." Besides, as he had told Collinson a couple of years before, he could not satisfy himself "if they bee not both the same; only some decay in those that look reddish which is but a small blush." Custis was wrong: the pink dogwood is in fact a different species. Nevertheless, it was in Williamsburg that Catesby managed to cultivate for the first time the pink dogwood that he discovered in the Virginia forests. He thought so much of the discovery that he immediately planted the tree in a garden and recorded the fact in his *Natural History* many years later, where he also provided an illustration (figure 28): "In *Virginia* I found one of these Dogwood Trees with Flowers of a rose-colour, which was luckily blown down, and many of its Branches had taken Root, which I transplanted into a Garden."[25]

Collinson also wanted the umbrella tree (American magnolia), which Custis valued as an ornamental plant. "It is a Thousand pities," Collinson wrote, "but that such Curious Gentlemen as you, Colonel Byrd, Mr. Clayton, and Doctor Mitchell[26] should annually sow seeds of the Umbrella Tree to preserve it from being Intirely Lost. Can any Tree from the particularity

28. *Watercolor painting of a dogwood taken from Mark Catesby's* Natural History of Carolina, Florida, and the Bahama Islands *(1731). Catesby hand colored each one of the plates for this work.*

of its Growth & Flower Deserve better place in a fine Garden then the New Early flowering Magnolia at Esquire Smiths."[27] By 1743 umbrella trees were thriving in Collinson's garden at Mill Hill, but a hard winter that year killed them all; he immediately asked Custis for more seeds and was still asking for them when his correspondence with Custis ended in February 1746.

A few rare Virginia flowers also interested Collinson. He was most curious about the Virginia tree primrose, Indian iris, the orange mountain cowslip or dogsbane, the wild passion flower, and the red or white moccasin flower or lady slipper.[28] One of Collinson's last requests was for the passion flower, which in 1745 he still did not have; "I presume [it] grows in your Garden," he wrote.[29]

. . .

An important segment of eighteenth-century Virginia garden history concerns the native plants sent to England by people like Custis. These influenced the appearance of English gardens; and their often exotic look, as well as their hardiness, made them generally popular by mid-century. When Collinson lost hundreds of roots and rare plants during a severe frost in 1741, he was delighted that his American species survived, with the exception of only one "fine sarsifrax" (sassafras). They did well relative to other imported plants, too: "your Americans stood it out better than Asians or Africans," he told Custis. As for their embellishment of gardens and general importance to English botany, Collinson observed in 1735:

> there is no Greater pleasure then to be Communicative & oblige others. . . . for Wee Brothers of the Spade find it very necessary to share amongst us the seeds that come annually from Abroad[.] It not only preserves a Friendly Society but secures our Collections, for if one doues not raise a seed perhaps another does & if one Looses a plant another can Supply him[;] by this Means our Gardens are wonderfully Improved In Variety to what they was Twenty Years agon.

Six years later Collinson looked out appreciatively at his own garden and felt sincerely grateful to Custis for the "pleasure & Delight" he had been given by Virginia flora. "Indeed you may Assure yourself of this satisfaction att least—that your pains & trouble has not been In Vain for I have had high Entertainment in makeing my Remarks and Observations on so many wonderful productions." On behalf of fellow English gardeners and botanists, he was commenting on a significant chapter of early American garden history in which Custis played an important part.[30]

Many plants, owing to the greater extremes of weather in the colony, normally fared less well at home than in England. During a quarter century of gardening in Williamsburg, Custis lived through vagaries of climate that would have been demoralizing for any gardener. For him in particular, it seems, the weather often brought on periods of personal crisis. His letters to Collinson tell of these, especially in 1737 and 1738.

The winter of 1736–1737 was one of the coldest and wettest Custis could remember, and it was by far the most harmful to his garden. He mourned the loss of many plants Collinson had sent to him over the preceding three years, especially the Dutch box edging that bordered his flower and vegetable beds, in spite of his taking all "the care immaginable to preserve them." It was also "the ruin of my poor tulips you sent," he told Collinson; "I should have been very proud of them because I have a few or no double ones." That severe winter began three or four years of abysmal weather for the Tidewater gardener, if Custis's experience is a reliable sign. The winter was followed by a summer drought, so that several English plants that had survived the freeze succumbed in the arid July and August. Custis wrote:

Wee have had the greatest dry season that ever was known in the memory of man; I was obliged for severall weeks to keep 2 lusty men all day long to draw water and put in tubs in the sun to water my garden and notwithstanding a great many things perishd. The dutch box edgeings that survived the sever[e] winter; perishd in spots in the borders which had been established many years.

In reply, Collinson advised Custis on how to protect his European plants from drought, even if it is doubtful whether the English gardener could have fully appreciated the exhausting extremes of a Virginia summer. He recommended "tall Hedges of Quick growing plants," behind which the European ones could be planted in rows; he suggested native cedar, phileria, laurel, and yaupon holly for the purpose, which would have provided the garden some shade as well as a clipped neatness.[31]

The heat and drought of 1738 were particularly devastating. Beginning in May, Custis kept "3 strong Nigros continually filling large tubs of water and put them in the sun and waterd plentifully every night, made shades and arbors all over the garden allmost." This did not help much. Many of the European plants burned up and left the garden too "native" for Custis; the whole garden was "much impaired." Even Collinson's tip about using moss as a protection for small herbaceous plants like polyanthus and auricula and green fern leaves for the taller plants apparently could not prevent much destruction.

Custis judged that his "poor country grows more unseasonable yearly."[32]

Pernicious weather drove Custis to adopt a philosophic turn of mind about gardening in Williamsburg, and he was forced to confront a trait he had in common with his garden: frailty. He told Collinson, "the greatest pleasure I find is in my garden, and sometimes even that is insipid." After another damaging winter in 1741, he could no longer rouse his gardening enthusiasm. In his mind his garden began to reflect his states of feeling and thought. "At present I have little taste for anything," he writes plaintively; "my garden is the chiefest pleasure I have besides reading," but the winter has killed many of its joys, causing "dreadful havock" in it. "But w[h]ilst I do live," he added, "[I] would amuse myself a little with my garden."[33]

Twenty-five years of keen gardening in Williamsburg had taught him a lesson: "If I were a young man I would never plant any trees that would not endure our winters because I would not make myself uneasy for the loss of them." Plants kept arriving, of course, as did tools, especially hoes, about whose strength he complained to Loyd & Co. in 1741 because "a strong man can break them." Collinson tried to rouse his flagging interest with colorful descriptions of plants and gardens. But Custis's era as a gardener was gradually ending. "I confess your charming description of the trees and flowers raises great desire in me," he wrote, but "they soon whither" and "tis all vanity."[34]

. . .

Custis's love of flowers and taste for evergreens and striped and variegated leaves suggest his alertness to compositions in the garden. He also believed in the pictorial and in perspective for and from his garden. The latter is evident from the position of his house, on the somewhat elevated corner of Francis and Nassau streets, and garden in relation to adjacent features of the town plan. He took pleasure, for example, in telling Dunbar Parke that the courthouse below on the corner of Francis and South England

29. *Robert Furber's oil painting of the flowers of "September," from* The Flower-Garden Displayed *(1732).*

streets was "in sight of my door."[35] Prospects from his garden complemented his inclination to arrange his garden pictorially.

In view of the value Custis placed on the pictorial as an aesthetic factor, it is interesting that he saw connections between gardening and painting. He used flower prints inside his house, for example, and alluded to painting in his letters. Several of his pictures he doubtless acquired when he was in England in 1716. Byrd II wrote to him in January of that year, telling him that the "prints and maps" for his new house had been put aboard ship. In 1723 he wrote to Byrd in England, asking for "two peices of as good painting as you can procure[;] it is to put in the summer before my Chimnys to hide the fire place[;] let them be some good flowers in potts of various kinds."[36] In 1725 he ordered glass from England for mezzotint prints; and in 1734 he was again acquiring prints of flowers "coloured to life," painted by the English nurseryman Robert Furber—the first collection (1732) of accurately represented flowers to be published in England (figure 29). Not surprisingly,

30. *Fragments of an earthenware urn with decorated arms found in the Custis well, Williamsburg.*

31. *Pedestal base from an eighteenth-century earthenware flower urn, covered with gray and pink paint, found at the site of the Custis gardens.*

Custis was one of the 450 prepublication subscribers to the thirteen prints. Also in 1736 he ordered from Jonathan Day in England "6 flower pots painted green to stand in a chimney to put flowers in the summer time with two handles in each pot" (see figures 30–31).[37] A hint of the iconographic value that flowers held for him appears in a portrait of Custis that the English painter Charles Bridges executed around 1725 (figure 32).[38] The painter added two details alluding to Custis's horticultural interests: the title of the book he holds is *Of the Tulip*, and a large cat tulip lies nearby.

Custis took his interest in painting one step further toward making a connection between it and gardening. The reciprocity between painting and poetry, a classical (Aristotelian) principle known as *ut pictura poesis*, also informed much English gardening near mid-century. Custis implied the same approach of seeing and designing gardens and landscapes as a painter might. His second letter to Collinson in 1735 opens with this allusion to an artist: "A curious painter may nicely delineate the features and air of a face, or the pleasant prospect of A Landscape." He tended to use the painting metaphor naturally, as in 1742, when, impatient over Collinson's medical advice, he declared it is "as impossible for the more learnd experienced Phisi[ci]an truly to take a case by information, without seeing the patient . . . as it is for the most expert limner truly to paint a face without seeing the originall." We can infer that Custis could have accepted the principle that one cannot design a garden without first consulting the "genius of the place"—a cardinal principle or tenet of the new English landscaping of the early eighteenth century, which held that in order to lay out a garden the gardener must first see and feel the spirit and character of a scene.[39]

Shapes, too, informed part of Custis's alertness to composition, although his taste here was perhaps a residue of the French and Dutch influence of the preceding century. His garden, like the gardens of the College of William and Mary, contained its share of topiary work. Some of the

32. *John Custis. Oil painting, artist unknown, ca. 1725. He is holding a book entitled* Of the Tulip.

yew, box, and privet he ordered from England during the first years of his gardening in Williamsburg he clipped into pyramids, balls, and other decorative shapes. In his last letter to Collinson, he explains that the havoc wrought in his garden by the drought was especially harsh on evergreens: "I had very fine yews balls and pyramids which were established for more than 20 years; and flourishd and were very fine[;] the south side of most of them are as it were burnt up and killd." He even ordered holly, yew, and privet already shaped, as he told Collinson in 1738, by way of arguing that such plants, if individually wrapped in baskets of earth, could arrive safely: "I have had silver and gold hollys yews philereus etc. come flourishing to me three feet high, the balls or standards having heads as big as a peck and the pyramids in full shape and are at this time flourishing in my garden." Custis may have asked Collinson how readily certain other species lend themselves to topiary because in April 1744 Collinson replied, "Neither Firr nor pine will bear Cutting in shapes but They Naturally grow in Conic Figures which looks Ornamental in a Garden."[40]

No plan or sketch of Custis's grounds has survived, if indeed one was ever drawn. According to the Frenchman's Map (1782; figure 14), the garden was large (eight lots, or four acres)—"You have Ground enough" for peach and nectarine trees, Collinson once remarked—and enclosed with trees or hedges.[41] The boundary is clearly marked with dots that elsewhere on the map almost certainly designate trees. That enclosure itself stands out as a prominent topographical feature on the map, and it suggests a separate, well-identified garden. Unfortunately, neither the Rochambeau nor the Desandrouins map (figure 8) indicates a garden in Custis Square, but both show outbuildings to the south; by then (1782) the garden had long been neglected and perhaps disappeared.[42] The Frenchman's Map shows three outbuildings in addition to the main house, two of which were located in the southeast corner of the property. The southern half of the lot afforded sufficient room for vines, vegetables, and orchards, with the vegetables, as was the custom, closest to the kitchen east of the house. The house stood a bit north of dead center in the property; it would have been most convenient to have had vehicular access to it off of Nassau Street from the west, since the ground slopes steeply to the north. In that event, the drive separated pleasure gardens north of it from orchards to the south and established at the same time the garden's principal east-west axis.[43]

• • •

If less is known about the layout of Custis's garden than about the plants in it, the reverse is true of Byrd's garden at Westover. His letters are not so communicative about his horticultural interests, but two plans of his garden have survived, showing its position and shape and a few of its features. Beyond that, Byrd's letters, essays, and diaries often provide glimpses of attitudes to landscape and autobiographical vignettes of a gardener. Moreover, as a contemporary of Custis's and his earnest brother of the spade as well as his brother-in-law, Byrd in his writings helps to illuminate the gardening world of his Williamsburg relative.

Custis got a head start on Byrd. While he was carrying on his gardening and plant exchanges in the early 1720s, Byrd (1674–1744) was still in England attempting to marry profitably so that he could afford to remain there. Most of his capital and extensive landholdings were in Virginia, but culturally he preferred England, where he had grown up and spent about half his time between 1705 and 1726. Finally, he gave up hope of living permanently in England, returned to Virginia in 1726, and took up gardening seriously at his Westover plantation. In letters to his English friends, several of whose gardens he much admired, Byrd promptly, reminiscent of Spotswood, began to make certain claims for Virginia gardening that seem like rationalizations. In a way recalling Spotswood's deployment of a gardening pose to satisfy his emotional as well as social need for the semblance of a civilized colonial life, Byrd represented Westover life with images of paradise, patriarchal bliss, ordered gardens, and leafy settings. He thereby hoped to make clear to his correspondents that he was not languishing away, isolated from the springs of his own cultural ambitions. As an apt symbol of the gentleman's leisure and recreation and of artistic inventiveness, the garden at Westover served him well in these claims. It is a pity we do not know whether his correspondents found his descriptions convincing and enticing.

If Byrd is taken to have been a prototypical Virginia plantation gardener in the second quarter of the century (figure 33), it is nevertheless accurate to see him as exceptional in many ways. To begin with, he came early to gardening. He was a force of transition between the original efforts of planters like his own father, Fitzhugh, Beverley, "King" Carter, and Ludwell and those of his successors at plantations up and down the major rivers of Tidewater Virginia.

He was exceptional also because he approached gardening and responded to open

lieu in England to a large estate on the banks of the James River. If ever Virginia gardening and changing English norms of taste discoursed with each other intimately in the early eighteenth century, it was in the mind and art of Byrd.

Byrd's life in England as a young man, before he inherited Westover in 1705, is not as well documented as the twelve years he spent there from 1714 to 1726, but his letters suggest that even then he possessed an inquiring intelligence regarding plants and gardens. In 1701, at the age of twenty-seven, he accompanied Sir John Perceval to Scotland.[44] The gardens they saw on this journey at the beginning of England's greatest century of gardening were mostly typical of the grand manner that George London and Henry Wise had been creating and planting through their successful partnership at the Brompton Park nurseries. Judging, however, from Byrd's first letter to Sir Robert Southwell in July 1701, what catches his interest appears to be well-planted parkland comprehending the houses and immediately adjacent gardens. He speaks of the trees and the impressive "scituations" [sic].[45] Rural or "extensive" gardening was chiefly what later caught Stephen Switzer's attention, too; in his authoritative and influential *Ichnographia Rustica* (1718) he cited classical authority for a more empirical English antidote to the imperial, wasteful, autocratic symmetry of the grand manner of European gardens.[46]

In the letter to Southwell, Byrd promises only "the skeleton of our travels." Even so, it is clear that the subjects that interest the young man include country houses and gardens. On seeing New Hall, the duke of Buckingham's estate near Harwich, he was struck by "a streight shady walk of a mile long, that leads from the entrance of the park to the house, but the view is intercepted by a riseing in the middle; there is besides this a grove of firrs the finest I have seen in England." He also alluded to Felix Hall, "finely scituated in the center of a good park," and to another "extraordinary park" supposedly once owned by the Southwell family. After viewing this, he and Perceval rode off to see the "pretty

33. William Byrd II. Oil painting by Sir Godfrey Kneller, early eighteenth century.

landscape from an English point of view. Years of rambling around English country estates had by 1726 schooled him not only in the increasingly outmoded French and Dutch traditions but also, more significantly, in the heightened landscape-oriented gardening. He was keenly aware of the tides of English taste. Even that great landscape gardener Thomas Jefferson, in the half century after 1770, did not live in England and discover its gardens from within the culture; he visited important gardens, but chiefly as a traveler, sizing them up in terms of strengthening turn-of-the century patriotic American values and attitudes. Byrd lived in England just at the time English landscaping was moving quickly in the direction of freer, more naturalized forms, propelled by new attitudes toward the natural world and a rejection of the luxury of French fashion at the same time that it sensitively invoked classical Italian notions of landscape variety and flexibility. He was fortunate, too, in being able to move directly from this miseat" belonging to Brackly Lodge, and later they admired the "prospect of Manningtree-River," which they crossed. As they passed northward, they intended to see Euston Hall, Suffolk, owned by the dukes of Grafton and visited by a steady stream of visitors for much of the century. It was one of the most admired seats in England, its park and gardens designed first by Sir John Evelyn and later modified by William Kent. The young travelers also visited Audley End (Essex), which was beautiful then but later took on added importance because of the work Charles Bridgeman did there.

From this appealing country house milieu Byrd was suddenly removed in 1705, when his father died and he had to leave promptly for Virginia. On his arrival at Westover he must have experienced a fresh wonder over the fecundity of nature in the landscape. There was so much unfamiliar flora to see, identify, record, and describe for his English friends. His first letter to Dr. Hans Sloane in April 1706 reveals an early interest in plants and declares his frustration over the infinite variety of that plant life, with scarcely anyone qualified and available to study it:

> The country where fortune has cast my lot, is a large feild [sic] for natural inquirys, and tis much to be lamented, that we have not some people of skil and curiosity amongst us. I know no body here capable of makeing very great discoverys, so that nature has thrown away a vast deal of her bounty upon us to no purpose. Here be some men indeed that are call'd doctors: but they are generally discarded surgeons of ships. . . . They are not acquainted enough with plants or the other parts of natural history, to do any service to the world, which makes me wish that we had some missionary philosopher, that might instruct us in the many usefull things which we now possess to no purpose.[47]

So Byrd began to develop his garden as a nursery of Virginia species, cultivating wild plants and then sending specimens to Sloane and others for identification. In his letters to Sloane,

Byrd often sounds as if he fancies he is telling much that the great naturalist did not know; but Sloane's replies put the record straight with an outpouring of scientific information about the plants Byrd had mentioned and sent. It was a case of the thorough professional writing to the enthusiastic amateur. Sloane even includes instructions, such as: "When you send any other herbs pray send their leaves and flowers dryed between papers and their seeds that they may be known & raised here."[48] In his reply, Byrd shows a loyal interest in the Royal Society, promises to send more "raritys," and reiterates his belief that Virginia is not well served by men "of skill in the works of nature."[49] In his own pseudo-scientific way during this first decade at Westover, he continued to serve the members of the Royal Society with botanical information; at the same time, he turned to the improvement and expansion of his father's gardens.

What scant knowledge we have of Byrd's gardening at Westover during his first ten years comes from the "secret diary" he kept in shorthand between 1709 and 1712. He was neither as introspective nor as descriptive as we might wish, so the light the diary shines on Westover's grounds is dim. Still, two facts are clear from the diary: Byrd loved to walk in his gardens, no matter what the season, and he had set about improving them with a good deal of energy, especially when Mark Catesby happened on the scene in 1712, the last year of the diary.[50]

By no means an armchair gardener, Byrd reveals in his diary that he constantly supervised improvements to the grounds. When he went to the orchards for a walk, he was likely to take pruning shears and saws with him. His fine library contained numbers of gardening books that doubtless instructed him on how to prune and perform other practical chores. On February 23, 1711, he was out there for a walk and "trimmed some trees"; about a year later, in January 1712, he "set his razor" and lingered in the "new orchard" until dark, pruning and trimming. He was angry with his gardener Tom in March 1712 for being lazy, so he "went into the garden and trimmed the vines"—a reference either to a separate vineyard or to ornamental vines in the pleasure gardens somewhere near the house. On June 23, 1712, he took a stroll through his plantation and then "trimmed some trees in the walk."

In addition to cherries, of which he was very fond, he had apples, pears, peaches, oranges (in his greenhouse), and probably a host of other native and English or European fruit, which he describes in his *Natural History of Virginia* (1st ed., 1737). There Byrd's partiality for fruit trees is clear, and he writes affectionately of this or that fruit being tasty, fragrant, and beautiful in Virginia gardens. Whenever the wild plum is in blossom, he writes, "it smells as beautiful as jasmine, and is as white as snow. They make a quite beautiful adornment around a house, or in a garden."[51] Significantly, in this account he always describes fruit in gardens, not orchards, although he writes little else about Virginia gardens. Either in his mind an orchard was itself part of the artifact he and his Virginia contemporaries conceived of as a garden, or he deliberately distinguished between the garden and orchard and discussed the fruit trees as ornamental features in the pleasure garden.

Byrd was off again to England in 1714, leaving the gardens in the care of Tom. They probably changed little until 1719, when Byrd returned for a brief period and set about making some alterations. During those intervening years in England he had acquired additional knowledge of the English garden.

He had felt he was coming home when he returned to England. Among other things, he made a point of visiting gardens. A number of the most imaginative, innovative, and grand ones that he saw adorned the Thames between Fulham and Twickenham: the second duke of Argyll's at Sudbrook House; the third duke of Argyll's at Whitton Park; and Lord Orkney's at Cliveden above the Thames near Windsor (figure 34).[52] For a glimpse of his enthusiasm for

34. *"A View of Cliefden [Cliveden] in Buckinghamshire,"* *by Luke Sullivan, 1759.*

rambling, consider this diary excerpt from May 10, 1719, which unfortunately mentions three gardens about which nothing is known. First, "after dinner we drank tea till 4 o'clock and then we went all hands to my Lady Dudley Fielding's park, which is very pretty and so is the house." By "pretty" Byrd must have meant pleasingly natural and unpretentious, not defiantly formal and imposing. He continued: "Then we went to my Lord Guildford's [Durdans in Epsom, Surrey], and walked in his garden and then to Mr. Diston's [Woodcote Grove, Surrey], and then to my Lord Baltimore's [who became governor of Maryland in 1732 and owned a country house called Woodcote Park], which is a place run to ruin." His travels ranged more widely, too. In July 1718, he visited Blenheim Palace and "saw the house and garden which was extremely fine. We then saw the [Vanbrugh] bridge which was also fine and remarkable for the middle arch and the engine to raise the water." (That bridge, incidentally, later offended Capability Brown, who in his naturalization of the park raised the Blenheim lake to hide half of it.) By "fine" in these remarks about Blenheim, Byrd meant something quite distinct from "pretty": he was registering his awe over the garden's elegance and extravagance, for Blenheim was laid out in the European grand manner, not in the more subtle, pictorial, expressionistic character of the later famous Lyttelton gardens at Hagley Park, which he judged "very pretty." As for the duke of Wharton's estate, Uborn, which Byrd saw but did not remark on in September 1718, John Macky judged in his *Journey Through England* (1724) that "with its garden, stables, and other offices" it was "inferior to very few in the kingdom."[53]

Byrd would have been happy to remain in England, even though he defended his Virginia wealth and holdings. "For Gods sake," he asked, "where's the difference between its lying in Virginia or in Berkshire as long as I receive the Profits of it in London?"[54] Having failed, however, to capture an English wife and her fortune, he was obliged to return to Virginia in 1719 for

35. *Westover plantation, Charles City County, Virginia.*

just over a year. He found he missed England: "I often cast a longing Eye towards England, and sigh'd," he once conceded, and he admitted to the earl of Orrery in March 1720 that he longed to return to "the joys of London."[55] In the meantime, the Westover gardens perhaps appeared less adequate than ever (figure 35). He seems to have set about some gardening promptly after his return on February 13, 1720. His "old gardener Tom Cross" was up from Williamsburg within a fortnight: "I walked about with the gardener and talked abundantly with him about the garden," he wrote in his diary.[56] By March 4 a bricklayer had been hired for some project, very likely the kitchen or some new garden walls. Apart from these random entries, however, the diary never specifies what he was up to in the gardens. Simply, on March 26 he "took a walk in the garden till twelve when George Walker came and I showed him everything with which he was well pleased." And on April 10 he led a party of guests into the garden and "showed them several rarities." When he and his guests were not admiring the plants, they were putting the grounds to good use with races and other English-sounding garden games.[57]

George Walker was at Westover admiring the gardens again in June, this time "much pleased with the seats" that Byrd had introduced into the garden. In the winter of 1720–1721, Byrd may have had more ambitious landscape projects under way; he mentions in February that he and Tom "marked out where I would have the 'ditch,'" a possible allusion to a ha-ha separating the gardens from adjacent ground. And on March 16 he says, "we began to turf the bowling-green."[58] This is the first known reference to a bowling green at Westover, although a man who liked to play bowls as much as Byrd did—he frequently played at Green Spring and in Williamsburg—might have laid one out before this. An entry from April 8 makes a further distinction about the gardens, alluding to the "main garden." Conceivably, this was the area of the main walled garden today, northwest of the present house; but since the new brick mansion house possibly was not built until the 1730s or 1740s, the walled garden may not have been created until then. The "main" garden was one of the two walled gardens that in August 1761 Byrd III's second wife, Maria Taylor, mentioned in a letter to her son: "I have let the Gardener have Five Pounds, which was the sum he asked. I have the Bricklayer now at work repairing the Walls of both Gardens."[59]

When Byrd finally returned to England in 1721, he stayed until 1726. Apart from his resumed search for a wife and some political skirmishing, though, his activities during these years are unknown, for no diary survives and his letters are few and not very revealing. We find him back in Virginia in 1726, whereupon his letters and the 1739–1741 secret diary begin again to show what he was up to. His writings at this point take on a ring of genuine satisfaction and pleasure about his sense of place in the Virginia landscape. His best writings in the 1730s, including his *Secret History of the Dividing Line*, demonstrate that he was by then at peace about living in Virginia. There is no mistaking his love affair with the landscape.

. . .

Byrd's appreciation of the pictorial complexity and variety of landscape clarifies and complements his delight in gardens. Color, shades of green, perspective, multiple elevations, prospects, water effects, plant life, rock formations, and the sounds of nature were all to him landscape features of Virginia that he relished. He liked to describe them in the 1720s and 1730s for his friends in England, whose scenery afforded bucolic beauties of meadows and purling streams but not the more sublime and wild prospects of untamed landscape. In the following passage, for example, from a 1729 letter to Charles Boyle, earl of Orrery, he reveals his sensitivity to landscape as he describes his crossing of the south branch of the Roanoke River on an expedition to survey the boundary line between Virginia and North Carolina:

> Since I last paid my respects to your Lordship I have ranged ten weeks more in the wild and uninhabited woods, in order to extend our dividing line to the Apalchian Mountains. . . . In our progress we forded several times over the most beautifull river I ever saw. It was near two hundred yards over, and it's bankes are edges with tall canes, that continue green all the winter, affording excellent forage for horses and cattle. The stream runs murmuring down with water clear as chrystal. The bottom is gravel spangled every where very thick with small flakes of mother of pearl, that almost dazzled our eyes, and the sand on either shoar sparkles with the same glittering substance. Here and there a rock rears it's head out of the water, to add to the variety of the prospect. The course of this delightfull river was generaly west, so that our line cross't it six several times, till at last it hides it's head in the mountains.[60]

That Byrd in passages like this was also playing up to the archetype of Virginia as an Edenic paradise is evident in the title, "Journey to the Land of Eden," of one of his prose accounts of an expedition he took in 1733 to some of his own lands in that same wilderness near the North Carolina border.

One of the ways of discovering Byrd's technique of description is to imagine him holding up his fingers to a natural scene as if to simulate a picture frame. In fact, he probably did not have to resort to his fingers but habitually viewed a scene in this way. This approach allowed him to isolate the features of a scene into a well-composed picture. It is no coincidence that he offered up most of these "framed" landscape sketches from campsites, where he had both the leisure and ordered comfort to indulge in them.

The point about comfort is especially relevant. A campsite in the wilderness is a source of order against which the wilderness scene may be contrasted and enhanced. A picture totally taken up with a rushing river is beautiful, Byrd thought; but if seen through the opening of a tent, let us say, which may also appear in the picture, the river is framed and thereby dramatized. A tablecloth, bench, window, or whatever would do just as well to control the scene—in a sense, taming it. This is what garden designers in England were beginning to do more commonly in the early eighteenth century: they created a varied pictorial scene with elements of open landscape, either duplicated within or visible from a garden, but controlled it all with innumerable garden features that would not allow an observer to forget he or she was in a garden and that the scene was not beyond the reach of art. Much of the pleasure came from this juxtaposition.

Another way to comprehend Byrd's imaginative response to this wild landscape is to read him as actually seeing what he wants to see: a landscape invested with art. This point is as relevant to Byrd's approach to gardening as is John Dixon Hunt's observation about Joseph Addison's perspectives on open landscape and his plea in the *Spectator* for more naturalized landscaping. Art and nature were not at war with one another in Addison's mind; rather, the former could be seen as bringing out the intrinsic character of the latter. For an observer with such an informed perspective, nature is especially pleasurable. As Hunt puts it, "natural objects may look artful to those who know their art." In a sense, Byrd was "colonizing" wild nature for

art.[61] And he had, it may be said, an advantage over Addison: he had at his doorstep a much wider, more "pure" or wild nature to colonize imaginatively with his artistic and literary habits of mind.

"In the front of our camp rose a very beautiful hill," Byrd wrote in *The Secret History of the Dividing Line*, "that bounded our view at about a mile's distance, and all the intermediate space was covered with canes."[62] What we get in this image is depth of field, a hill as a terminal focal point, and the color green. The following, more complete sketch shows Byrd ruralizing a beautiful perspective into what could pass for a view of an undulating garden scene beneath the front window of an imaginatively placed house, such as Nomini Hall or Mount Airy above the Rappahannock River:

> The tent was pitched on an eminence which overlooked a wide piece of low grounds, covered with trees and watered by a crystal stream gliding through the middle of it. On the other side of this delightful valley, which was about half a mile wide, rose a hill that terminated the view and in the figure of a semicircle closed in upon the opposite side of the valley. This had a most agreeable effect upon the eye and wanted nothing but cattle grazing in the meadow and sheep and goats feeding on the hill to make it a complete rural landscape.[63]

The cattle, sheep, and goats sound like a sentimental pastoralizing of the scene; but by thinking of livestock, Byrd is helped imaginatively to transform a wilderness into a scene resembling parkland. At one point he also describes a "beautiful range of hills, as level as a terrace walk."[64]

For pictorial brilliance, consider Byrd's rendering of the Dan River in October 1729: "it was . . . a most charming river, having the bottom spangled as before, with a limpid stream gently flowing and murmuring among the rocks, which were thinly scattered here and there to make up the variety of the prospect." Or there is this equally evocative vignette of a spot next to another river: "in the evening we encamped on a charming piece of ground that commanded the prospect of the reaches of the river, which were about fifty yards over and the banks adorned with canes. We pitched the tent at the bottom of a mount, which we called Mount Pleasant for the beauty of the prospect from thence."[65] His use of the word *adorned* in this passage reinforces the impression he wants to give that the landscape can be appreciated as a work of art to rival or exceed the beauty of a garden.

Byrd's depiction of water—cascades and rivers mostly—captures his joy at hearing it as well as its movements and appearance. The sound of water effects had long been a prized dimension of gardens. He alludes to garden water effects—while at the same time implying the incomparable beauty of Virginia's waters, which are natural, not contrived—when he uses such words and phrases as "crystal stream gliding," "limpid stream gently flowing and murmuring among the rocks," "full of shining particles," "a small cascade fed by a stream as clear as liquid crystal, and the murmur it made composed my senses into an agreeable tranquillity," "crystal stream serpentining."

Unlike much of Byrd's other writing, the *Secret History* was written for publication in London. Intended chiefly for English readers, its purpose was persuasion. Byrd wrote to influence his countrymen to cross the Atlantic and settle in the colony, ideally on his own "Land of Eden" along the James River. His descriptions of nature therefore are revealing in yet another way. English taste for the pictorial, expressive, and even wild landscape was in the ascendancy. His readers would not have been as responsive to his descriptions if he had written them in 1705, when he first arrived in Virginia. By the late 1730s, however, perspectives had opened up, and English gardeners had assimilated and were conversant with a broader spectrum of landscape effects.[66] A comparison of the *Secret History* with Robert Beverley's *History and Present State of Virginia*, written nearly forty years earlier, and with

John Lawson's *Description* and *Natural History of Carolina* (1709, 1714) demonstrates Byrd's more deliberately artistic and painter-like portrayal of nature. Although Lawson, an ardent and for his time innovative gardener, shows flashes of insight into garden-like images present in the wilderness, even he, compared to Byrd, seems muted and vague and keeps repeating a meaningless word like *delightful* to characterize attractive scenes.

Upon his return from England, Byrd also began to adopt a new pose. He liked to think of himself as a "patriarch" among his possessions. This metaphor had the effect of making him feel he had more roots at Westover than was the case, as well as more stability. He wrote to the earl of Orrery in July 1726: "Like one of the patriarchs, I have my flocks and my herds, my bondmen, and bond-women . . . we sit securely under our vines, and our fig-trees without any danger to our property."[67] Time passed, he built his new house, the gardens evolved with plants and ornamentation, and the 1730s carried him into new sensations of permanency. His relish for innocent diversions amid his newly designed paradise also increased, as he smugly told his sister-in-law Anne Taylor Otway in July 1736: "We jogg on soberly and peaceably in our state of innocence, enjoying all the blessings of a comfortable sun and a fertile soil. Our comforts like those of the good patriarchs are mostly domestique, observing with a partial delight how the flowers of our own planting improve."[68]

. . .

Plants for his garden were Byrd's first consuming interest after he returned to Westover. They would have suffered most during his absence, so that the numbers and varieties may have struck him as limited, especially after his exposure to the richness of English gardens. He had become well acquainted with Peter Collinson and Sir Hans Sloane, so it was to them he turned in the late 1720s as sources of English plants. His letters to naturalists in this period present him again in the role of the scientific enthusiast fancying himself as shining light on the dark wasteland of empirical and scientific colonial thinking. In his earliest known letter to Collinson, in June 1729, he thanks the naturalist for vines and cuttings of apple and pear trees, which he intends to graft immediately in order to strengthen their resistance to the hotter climate. He also asks for plums and advice on how to grow his nectarines and apricots so as to prevent their dropping off the trees unripe.[69] He remained for the rest of his life enthusiastic about his orchards, and in his vineyard he became something of a pioneer with his successful attempts to raise French grapes. Other scientific interests included the ginseng plant, which over the next few years he unsuccessfully attempted to promote to his English friends as a medicinal herb, and the snakeroot, a remedy for snake bite. In spite of his most energetic protestations, both causes seemed to some of his English contemporaries as examples of enthusiasm run wild.

In July 1728, Byrd wrote to another expert naturalist-gardener in England, John Warner, whose garden at Rotherhithe was celebrated especially for its vineyard and dwarf fruit trees. The letter illustrates Byrd's brainstorming approach to the planting of his garden. He is canvassing talented sources of information and advice and recalls in Warner's garden just the equation of art and nature that he wishes to emulate at Westover. Remembering his visit to Rotherhithe, Byrd tells Warner he had come "to see the curiositys in your garden, and indeed I never saw nature better assisted by art than I did there—you had corrected the rigour of that northern clymate and reconciled it to the productions of the south." Apparently Warner had applied himself to raising pineapples, a rare fruit in England at the time. "We saw other fruits," Byrd adds, "in great perfection, as well as exotick, as natives." He then tactfully mentions that Archibald Campbell, the third duke of Argyll, had sent him Rhenish vines from his well-known gardens at Whitton Park, also in Twickenham, and he wonders whether Warner could

oblige him similarly with "the choicest kinds of vines."[70]

. . .

Byrd's embellishments were not limited to plants. In a letter from the 1730s he sounds philosophical about all the improvements he had made in his gardens. He tells his wife's sister-in-law in England that continuous improvements to house and garden can easily lead to an insipid sufficiency and make one feel like King Solomon, "who, after he had built him stately palaces, and made beautifull gardens, grew sick of 'em soon, and pronounc't them vanity and vexation of spirit."[71] What these embellishments were precisely is not known, although John Bartram saw them on his visit to Virginia in 1738 and in a single sentence summarized what impressed him most: "Colonel Byrd is very prodigalle . . . [with] new Gates, gravel Walks, hedges, and cedars finely twined and a little green house with two or three orange trees with fruit on them; in short he hath the finest seat in Virginia."[72] Peter Collinson had told Bartram much the same thing in 1738: "I am told Colonel Byrd has the best garden in Virginia, and a pretty green-house well furnished with Orange Trees."[73]

Bartram mentioned new gates at Westover that struck him as extravagant. Presumably he would not have called them new if they were old, so doubtless Byrd had these built after 1726 and made them part of his new garden layout. But where were they and what did they look like? And what do they tell us about the garden? These were most likely the gates facing the land (or north) front of the house (figure 36), constituting the principal entrance to the grounds at the end of the long avenue pictured in the 1701 plan (figure 11). Normally, entrance gates to an estate do not reveal much about the gardens within, but these do.

Although in his diary Byrd mentions putting up some gates in May 1711, sometime in the late 1720s or 1730s he must have altered the arrangement of fences and gates, if not the iron gates themselves, which survive today from the

36. *Iron gate at Westover, eighteenth century. The gateway is one of the finest examples of English wrought iron work in America. Byrd's cypher appears in the center of the scrollwork of the overthrow. The iron railing on either side of the gateway is from the twentieth century.*

37. *Figure of a martlet on top of one of the main gate piers at Westover.*

eighteenth century. The wrought-iron gates are part of a large clairvoyée scheme, on which he would not have embarked unless he had been certain of the ultimate orientation of the house and therefore the relative position of the gardens.[74] As it happened, the house was probably built on the same axis and perhaps the same site as Byrd I's original dwelling, so Byrd II's undoubted conclusion was that topographical features such as the river and dominant avenue of trees to the north made the position of the original dwelling the right one. Having built his kitchen and decided on the orientation of house and gardens, Byrd then left for almost six years in England, hoping he would be able to live there permanently and forget entirely about ever building the house. Three years after returning from England, he still had not built his house, judging from his May 1729 letter to a Mr. Spencer, informing him that in "a year or 2 I intend to set about building a very good house."[75]

Byrd never applied the term *clairvoyée* to his walls and gates, but they certainly had that function. A clairvoyée was a French garden feature of the seventeenth century, usually an iron gate or grate placed strategically at the ends of walks in order to penetrate walls visually and extend views outward. They were a common, although old-fashioned, feature in late-seventeenth-century and early-eighteenth-century English gardens before other means of "calling in" the countryside were contrived. At Westover, Byrd built his clairvoyées facing the land front of the house so that from the gardens on that side one could see through the resulting "screen" into the adjacent landscape. But he did not stop there. He ornamented his gate piers or pedestals with elaborate finials and figures such as remained rare in the colonial South throughout the century (see figures 37–40). Sections of stone urns have been found along the line of the clairvoyée, resembling the ornamental garden urns found at Kingsmill plantation, nearer Williamsburg. The whole affair was imposing and elegant. It would seem to have been at least as sophisticated a treatment as the brick walls with finials and piers eventually built at the Palace in Williamsburg. To the approaching visitor along the avenue, the clairvoyée and iron gates initiated a theme regarding the house's garden setting that was continued elsewhere in the garden.

· · ·

No archaeological work such as has been done in the Palace gardens or in the Monticello gardens has been carried out at Westover. Nevertheless, a plan of a portion of the grounds has survived. The usefulness of the plan, drawn by a young William and Mary student, Thomas Lee Shippen, a kinsman of the Byrds, is limited because it dates from his visit there in 1783.[76] By that time, Byrd III and his wife could have altered the gardens according to late-century fashion or taste. But in fact, Byrd III showed little interest in plans or gardens, judging by his letters; and the improvidence that placed him un-

38–40. *Stone pier ornaments along the clairvoyée at Westover.*

39

40

der greater financial strain than ever his father experienced was likely an obstacle to major landscaping alterations, although he did modify the decorative fabric of the house itself.[77] As for his mother, who continued to live at Westover, and his wife, there is evidence that, apart from building some brick walls, they applied themselves chiefly to preventing the decline of the house and gardens. Thomas Anburey, for example, wrote in April 1779 that, while "the grounds around the house at Westover, are laid out in a most beautiful manner and with great taste, and from the river appear delightful," "the widow Byrd through good management has had to devote herself to rescuing the estate from the financial chaos left by her deceased husband."[78]

Shippen appended his plan of Westover (figure 41) to a letter to his parents in which he described the gardens, the house, the farmyard, and the lengthy approach to the house from the Williamsburg-Richmond road. Together with descriptions written two years earlier by Baron Ludwig Von Closen and the marquis de Chastellux, Shippen's contributions convey some feeling for and images of what the gardens may have looked like when Byrd II died in 1744. Shippen obviously was an appreciative witness, especially responsive to landscape beauty. It is appropriate, too, for a change, that a native American rather than a Frenchman or Englishman has passed on such a precise verbal and graphic record of an important colonial garden. His account reflects an awakened American, post-Revolution love for the native landscape.

Shippen opens the letter by asking his parents to imagine him sitting at his bedroom desk looking out of his riverfront window, "commanding a view of a prettily falling grass platt variegated with pedestals of many different kinds, about 300 by 100 yards in extent, an extensive prospect of James River and of all the Country and some gentlemen's seats on the other side." By "falling grass platt" he meant that this sizable turfed area sloped gently down to the river, not that it fell in terraces. In describing David Meade's splendid gardens almost directly across

the river at Maycox, the marquis de Chastellux does mention a terrace at Westover: "Only the river separates the two houses," he writes, "which are nevertheless more than a mile distant from each other. . . . Mr. Meade's garden, like the one at Westover, forms a terrace along the banks of the river."[79] Chastellux is perhaps describing only a terrace-like promenade buttressed by a river wall, a practical as well as pleasurable feature along the river. Shippen goes on to describe something of this sort at Westover: "the river is banked up by a wall of four feet high, and about 300 yards in length, and above this wall there is as you may suppose the most enchanting walk in the world. Nor are the prettiest trees wanting to compleat the beauty of the Scene."

It was in the area of this one-hundred-by-three-hundred-yard garden that much, perhaps most, of the ornamental gardening unfolded. Shippen mentions that this turfed area was "variegated," or picturesquely dotted with decorative pedestals. Von Closen, who accompanied the comte de Rochambeau on his visits to several plantations in the early 1780s and was overwhelmed by the affluence and beauty of Westover, which he thought "worthy of Paris," noted that the "completely beautiful" garden "is decorated with very lovely statues."[80] Some of these, as well as the finials mentioned earlier, must have sat on Shippen's pedestals. Byrd's riverside gardens were enclosed to the west and east by what Shippen shows as a row of trees with fencing or walls penetrated by two gates, although these gates may not have stood where they stand today. He mentions that from an adjacent "grove" to the east "one of the pretty gates leads to the improved grounds before the house."

In his self-consciously precocious way, Shippen describes the mile-and-a-half approach to the house from the public road. He sounds like a painter, passing first through "a most charming Wood," then through two gates and into "the improved grounds," by which he means the open cultivated fields. The fine, wide road beyond the second gate is spacious and level,

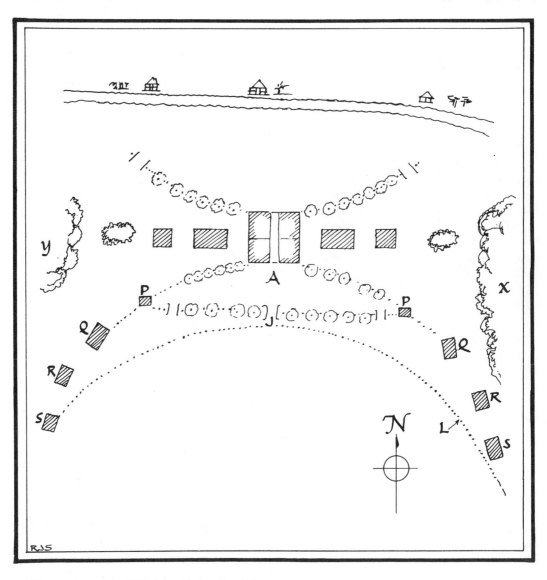

41. Westover landscape, 1783 (after Thomas Lee Shippen). FEATURES: *A, main house; J, main gate; L, road; P, "Temple of Cloacina"; Q, R, S, stables and coach houses; X, "The Garden"; Y, grove.*

bounded on either side by a "handsome ditch & fence"—a ha-ha—separating the road from "fine meadows whose extent is greater than the eye can reach." Through the trees to the right he sees the river. Every now and again an irrigation ca- nal crosses under the road, requiring a bridge with sets of twin gates. "You cannot easily con- ceive how fine an effect this has," he declares, especially with the thinly planted trees along both sides of the road. The road eventually swerves around and approaches the house (marked A in his sketch) in a large arc from the west (L), passing the stables and coach houses (Q, R, S) until it reaches the main gates (J). The gates are "made of iron curiously wrought" and are "exceedingly high, wide, and handsome."

In his sketch, Shippen shows two arcs of trees each on the land and river fronts of the house, with the main house positioned at the apex of both arcs and in between them. The clairvoyée, also lined with trees, closed the northern arc, with pride of place given to two privies or, as he felicitously termed them, "Temples of Cloacina" (P) at its corners. While in 1783 these arcs of trees were tall and stately, in Byrd II's days they would have been small and no impediment to the prospects through the clairvoyée.

Shippen mentions "the garden" and locates it with an X to the west within a wavy line indicating an enclosure. He says it is "very large and exceedingly beautiful indeed." This is roughly the area now enclosed by straight brick walls with Byrd's monument in the middle.[81] That Shippen refers to it as "the garden" suggests it was there that Byrd did most of his planting and may have had his vineyard. Chastellux, too, noted the walls of "the garden" and the masses of honeysuckle draped all over them. The beauty Shippen sees in it derived from the colors and shapes of plants and their arrangements, not from prospects and vistas.

To the west of the grass plat on the river side Shippen identifies an evocative area that he called a "pretty grove neatly kept" (Y). A faint wavy line indicates its position on the sketch. The phrase "neatly kept" does not necessarily suggest that the area was formally planted; it could mean instead that its paths were kept clear and that the decorative features within were well maintained. In fact, Von Closen possibly describes this grove when he says there were by the river "two ponds, and two little summer-houses, prettily arranged. It is admirably cared for and just as it had been described to us. . . . art and natural beauty are delightfully combined there."[82]

The house and its gardens became famous over the course of the century—pieces of colonial iconography—and travelers frequently stopped to see them during their journeys along the river. To many, as to Chastellux, Westover and other plantations made the river seem like "the garden of Virginia." Westover, he judged, "surpasses them all in the magnificence of the buildings, the beauty of its situation, and the pleasures of the society to be found there."[83] He, Von Closen, and Shippen all spoke from the point of view of a so-called high phase of Virginia plantation landscape gardening, and they saw Westover about forty years after Byrd II's death, so it is not possible to take their accounts of the gardens as certain evidence of his designs. Judging from what we know of Byrd III's interests and resources, however, it is likely that the outlines, arrangement, and shapes of the garden they saw, as well as the stone and fence ornaments, were not modified by the son and may therefore be taken as the father's handiwork.

. . .

It is as far as we can go to conclude that both Byrd and Custis, with their enthusiasm, botanical curiosity, English background and contacts, and eye for pictorial and pleasing compositions exerted a considerable influence on early-eighteenth-century colonial gardening in the Tidewater area. Their combined impact on botanical studies in Virginia and on methods of designing a garden with particular plants in mind must be judged their most important and best-documented contribution. That aspect of gardening is abundantly better documented for Custis than it is for Byrd. On the other hand, Custis's direct knowledge of and communication with the Royal Society was meager, whereas Byrd's varied contacts with English botanists has inclined one historian to see him as "the most constant link between the Royal Society and Virginia during the first half of the eighteenth century."[83] His several lengthy sojourns in England allowed Byrd to maintain direct contact with such eminent naturalists as Hans Sloane, James Petiver, and Leonard Plunkenett and thereby readily exchange horticultural and botanical information. His *Natural History of Virginia*, even if it is a surprisingly dull and unimaginative treatise, was a logical result of his desire to impart to these Londoners facts about the physical colonial environment. Custis might anguish over his experiments and the dearth of experts to help him with them, but it was Byrd who repeatedly urged his London contacts to send naturalists to Virginia to study the native flora and fauna. There is little reason to doubt that in his own way at Westover Byrd created with well-chosen plants as beautiful a garden as did Custis in Williamsburg.

These two men also contributed to colonial town and plantation gardening through their ability and desire to see gardens in terms of pictures or compositions. This pictorial ideal they approached through variety, whether of plants, elevation, prospect, water, color, or stone work.

The intensely personal element of Custis's gardening—and of Byrd's in a more cosmopolitan or European manner—suggests that gardens and landscapes were a significant part of their lives. In an area of history that is generally so poorly documented, they appear to have been unusual in this respect. In light of this personal element—and considering that they were related by marriage, lived not too far from each other, and saw each other in Williamsburg frequently—it is a special pity that we do not have more evidence of any exchanges between them about gardening. Perhaps because they saw each other often, they felt no need to write to each other about the subject. It seems inevitable, however, that they did collaborate and that, looked at in another way, this would have been a form of collaboration between town and plantation, with the resources of each helping the other. It is ironic that while traces of the Westover gardens have survived as a legacy of Byrd's efforts, Custis's famous garden had long since disappeared by the end of the century.

4

Williamsburg Gardens in the Second Half of the Eighteenth Century

By the 1740s, when both John Custis and William Byrd II died, Williamsburg had become a focus of colonial civilization and culture for plantation patriarchs, relatively well-established lawyers, doctors, and politicians, and a varied group of tradesmen and artisans who appreciated both the town's pleasant village character and its growing promise as an economic center. Francis Nicholson's ideas about town planning and Alexander Spotswood's leadership as a garden designer and architect had helped establish this ambience of the capital.[1] The horticultural enthusiasm of Custis and Byrd, as well as of John Clayton, had drawn the attention of America and England to both town and colony as places of significant gardening activity. And the traffic of ideas between Williamsburg and the surrounding plantations had encouraged a congenial gardening reciprocity that established a basis from which gardening possibilites could expand and become more expressive.

It is surprising that almost no descriptions of Williamsburg before 1750 have survived from the diaries and journals of visitors. In 1724 Hugh Jones found the town comfortable, genteel, and pleasant and noted that the building lots were "sufficient each for a house and garden."[2] But his remarks on the town's existing gardens were limited to the college and Palace, because by the early 1720s Custis's was, so far as we know, the only noteworthy private garden in the capital. Edward Kimber, in 1742, did not think much of the town, calling it "a most wretched contriv'd Affair for the Capital of a Country." "There is nothing considerable in it," he added, "but the College, the Governor's House, and one or two more, which are no bad Piles."[3]

Kimber rightly placed his main emphasis on the college and the Palace, and the pejorative "Piles" clearly refers to buildings. Still, could he have overlooked the handsome gardens? With the exception of a few private gardens, and notwithstanding some lapses at the Palace, the gardens of the college and Palace continued to provide the town's two principal emblems of culture in this vein up to mid-century. Thereafter, the social broadening of gardening practice in the town that resulted from the proliferation of imaginative private gardeners of some means appears, for whatever reason, to have coincided with the decline of these two public gardens.

After William Gooch and his wife left Williamsburg and the Palace in 1749 to return to their English "fair retreat," which by contrast to the Palace was a "snugg place not taken notice of,"[4] the House of Burgesses deplored the "ruinous condition" of the Palace gardens and buildings.[5] Gooch's somewhat straitened financial circumstances probably were partly responsible; but whatever the reasons, the gardens never regained the unrivaled supremacy in the town or colony, indeed in America, they had previously enjoyed during the successive governorships of Spotswood, Hugh Drysdale,[6] and Gooch. The same was true of the college gardens. The private gardens that began to appear after mid-century, because they were located all over the town, tended to determine the appearance of the capital much more than the public gardens ever could.

. . .

The evidence that is available about Williamsburg's private gardens in the second half of the century brings forth certain issues and themes. The themes are not so much new to the colony as they are new in emphasis. For example, until the Revolution and the removal of the capital to Richmond, the large public personalities in Williamsburg continued to dominate the gardening world. Like Custis, they did so in the sense that they spent the most money, established the largest gardens, and identified themselves most strongly with them. And it was these people who, after Williamsburg's era as the capital had ended and the Revolution had ruined much of its beauty, tended to vanish from the scene, with the result that their gardens soon became neglected and forlorn. On the other hand, people like St. George Tucker and Joseph Prentis, with relatively stronger local attachments, remained in town and gardened with unfailing energy and enthusiasm.

Also, it seems that, while not as many of the gardeners about whom there is evidence also owned plantations—Robert Carter of Nomini Hall and John Tayloe of Mount Airy are two who did—there was still an active interrelationship between plantation and town gardens. The nature of the relationship may have changed

slightly, however, in the second half of the century. With the decline of the college and Palace gardens and the absence of figures on the landscape like Custis and Spotswood, Williamsburg, so far as is known, held up fewer models to be emulated at plantations. The plantations, though, still supplied town gardeners with plants, tools, and other materials.

The second half of the century also saw a new dimension of Williamsburg gardening evolve along Francis and South England streets: landscape gardening. As we saw earlier, certain characteristics of what is known as landscape gardening in mid-century—the deliberate use of landscape either within or adjacent to gardens as an element of design—had been anticipated in town by Spotswood at the Palace. But not until gardens began to be laid out on the edge of the town along Francis and South England streets can landscape gardening be said to have become part of the townscape. This happened at Bassett Hall, Tazewell Hall, and Robert Carter Nicholas's house, and it was compatible with the appearance, if not the baroque principles, of Nicholson's and Spotswood's town planning.

Plant exchanges with England continued, as did the ordering of specimens and seeds from English agents, although the appearance of a plant nursery business in Williamsburg in 1790 suggests that both plantation and town gardeners increasingly turned to local sources. Significantly, neither St. George Tucker nor Joseph Prentis, two of Williamsburg's most distinguished gardeners late in the century, ordered plants or seeds from abroad. As for the planting of gardens, for the first time in the century there is graphic evidence that the ornamental use of fruit, vegetables, and nuts may have been quite common. Practical or kitchen gardening, of course, had always been crucial to household economy, whether in big or small gardens; but the discovery of garden plans for the Waller and George Wythe gardens reveals that vegetables were grown next to ornamental plantings. By way of some context, it is useful to cite a different type of graphic evidence and a few eye-witness accounts of what the town was beginning to look like during that period.

. . .

In 1759 or 1760, the Reverend Andrew Burnaby, an Englishman, thought the town's wooden buildings indifferent in character, but he nevertheless judged that "the whole makes a handsome appearance." He approved of the "handsome [Market] square in the center" and the town's agreeable sociability: "there are ten or twelve gentlemen's families constantly residing in it, besides merchants and tradesmen: and at times of the assemblies, and general courts, it is crowded with the gentry of the country: on those occasions there are balls and other amusements."[7]

An English officer and member of the aristocracy, Lord Adam Gordon, visited in 1765 and came away with the favorable impression that Williamsburg "resembles a good Country Town in England." "There are many good Houses in Town," he added.[8] Lord Gordon had the sort of credentials that would have gained him entrance into private homes and gardens, but he did not mention whom he visited. Travelers like Lord Gordon who had such entrées usually liked the town more than those who did not have introductions to the wealthier families and were therefore compelled to visit chiefly the public buildings and eye the private houses from the dusty streets.

Another clue to the evolution of the town in mid-century emerges from the journal of an anonymous French traveler in 1765. Approaching Williamsburg from Yorktown along "a fine road and pleasant Country," this Frenchman is first impressed by what appears to him in the distance as a large town; but he discovers that the town is "far from it." He seems to have been expecting the well-defined and extensive grid layout that he knew well in France because he finds the town "Irregular," with only one street "which Can be Called so."

Perhaps this traveler was not aware of them, or simply did not state them, but he has revealed two facts about the town in 1765 and its evolution to that date. The town seems large to him because of its comprehensive scale as laid out by Nicholson; it is, after all, more than one mile long. Coming in along the Yorktown Road, the traveler probably first looked down the wide and lengthy Duke of Gloucester Street and drew his initial conclusions. Inspecting it more closely, however, he discovers that the town does not have enough dwellings, except along the main street. There are open spaces all over. "It is very spacious," he observes, but it cannot claim to be much of a city.[9] Because the town was not yet built up, the sophisticated plan was not immediately perceptible. This Frenchman was looking for a town with a grid plan, but he found only individual streets with irregular-looking, perhaps leafy, promenades. Several travelers in the next twenty years, like Claude Blanchard in 1781, underline this point by mentioning that the town "consists of only a single street" or at the most two main parallel streets.[10]

As the years passed, visitors kept saying the same things. William Eddis from England did not think as much of Williamsburg's "situation" as he did of Yorktown's, nor did he like the buildings; but he was "greatly entertained by the variegated beautiful prospects, lofty woods, and highly cultivated plantations" in all directions.[11] As a "European," John Smyth was perplexed by the paradox of a long, wide avenue endowed not with stately and substantial dwellings and public buildings but with houses "detached from each other." He was distressed that the streets were not paved but covered with deep sand, which "is very disagreeable to walk in, especially in summer, when the rays of the sun are intensely hot, and not a little increased by the reflection of the white sand, wherein every step is almost above the shoe, and where there is no shade or shelter to walk under, unless you carry an umbrella."[12] This does not necessarily mean there were no trees along other streets. The Frenchman's Map (figure 14) and Jefferson's plan of the Palace show that the Palace Green was lined on both sides by trees; and along the side and back streets, too, very likely there were trees. A French officer, Chevalier de Bore, observed in 1777 that Williamsburg occupied "a charming situation" and that there was "a big lawn [Palace Green] extending to the second [Scotland] street," which "forms a pretty avenue."[13]

Nicholas Cresswell, another Englishman, felt that at Yorktown the "gentlemen's" gardens were "laid out with the greatest taste of any I have seen in America"; but he also believed that the capital was "the finest town I have seen in Virginia."[14] Unlike Byrd II, who used the word *fine* to describe English gardens at the start of the century, Cresswell reserved *finest* to mean pretty and charming, not elegant and large. Chevalier Dupleix de Cadignan in 1781, a bad time for Williamsburg, conceded that it answered his notion of "a very pretty town."[15]

A German mercenary soldier in the Yorktown campaign, Johann Doehla, bequeathed to us this sensitive account of the town: "While it is not, it is true, so very large, one may nevertheless count it among the beautiful cities of America"—and this after the ravages of war and after the town had been deserted as the seat of colonial government. Trees apparently helped to make it beautiful. "At Williamsburg I saw many trees, including the locust," he added, "which were as big and tall as the maples and elms are with us, and the pods on them were abundant and as long as one's hand." He also noted that from the courthouse in the Market Square one commanded a good prospect "over the whole city."[16] That point was also made by Johann David Schoepf in 1783. From the Powder Magazine, he wrote, "one has a view of the most important buildings and the finest part of the town."[17] Nicholson and Spotswood would have been gratified to learn that their designs of the square had been preserved and that trees and prospects enhanced garden elements in the townscape.

. . .

While visitors continued to be critical of Williamsburg precisely because of their frustrated expectations that it would be as large and popu-

lated as befitted the capital of the oldest British North American colony, its residents and plantation patrons would have seen it another way. The autocratically baroque themes implied by Nicholson's layout were not congenial to their views, mostly for aesthetic reasons, but also perhaps for ideological ones. They wanted neighborhoods with lanes and gardens; and wooden houses for the most part suited even the affluent residents' perceptions of and aspirations for the town. The eighteenth-century word for the kind of desirable neighborhood settings that were unfolding throughout the town was *situation*, a word used repeatedly in house sale advertisements in the *Virginia Gazette*.

The pride in gardens and landscape design that these advertisements reflect is further suggested by a group of mid-century vignettes (figure 42a-f) that editor William Rind used to accompany them. The vignettes appeared for only a short period, from 1766 to 1770, but nevertheless illustrate that prosperous citizens were looking for interesting "situations" and landscapes when they purchased property. The picturesque grounds laid out in these scenes were obviously meant to appeal to an existing taste for pleasant natural settings.

Rind used six different vignettes to entice purchasers. The most impressive is a tree-lined avenue leading to a house (figure 42f). There is also an idyllic little scene of a house at the bottom of a glade, with a screen of trees ascending a hill in the background and a prancing horse in the foreground (42e). Another shows a house crowned by a cupola resembling the Palace's, with an attached wing and a front garden enclosed by a high brick wall (42b); that house, too, sits at the base of a hill, and a tree outside the brick wall gives the scene a greater intimacy and less exposed look. Frequently, as we shall see, the advertisements themselves stressed the pleasant situations and neat gardens. Although most of these vignettes portray plantations, or at least houses in rural settings, the aesthetic sense to which they were meant to appeal relates no less to town properties and their owners.[18]

a

b

c

d

e

f

42a-f. Vignettes used by William Rind in his edition of the Virginia Gazette *(1766–1770) to advertise the sale of houses.*

By the 1740s, when Byrd and Custis died, the town had plenty of residents who desired to improve the grounds around their houses and enjoyed the leisure with which to do it. Terraces, fencing, hedges, flowers, herbs, imported as well as native vegetables, waterworks, garden pavilions, statuary, nurseries, and the right sorts of tools all came into play. But that lingering problem of too few gardening professionals who possessed some horticultural expertise complicated matters. Whether he owned a humble half-acre utilitarian garden in the capital, a larger garden combining ornament and utility in one of the town's choicer areas, or extensive grounds at a plantation, the Virginian normally had to learn to be his own gardener—that is, he needed to acquire a knowledge of plants and their propagation, as well as some skill in planning and designing garden spaces. Fortunately, the amateur could turn to gardening manuals, dictionaries, encyclopedias, and "Kalendars" from England, which were widely available in the colony. With some adaptations for the Virginia climate, these were indispensable, especially Philip Miller's *Gardener's Dictionary* (1st ed. 1724). Copies of Miller's work and others from time to time were sold at the printing office of the *Virginia Gazette*.[19] The libraries of Lord Botetourt, William Byrd II, and John Mercer, for example, contained among the best colonial collections of a few practical English and French gardening volumes. Many others in the colony could also turn to their own well-supplied shelves for gardening advice.

A garden owner's self-appointment as his own designer and nurseryman was another aspect of the independence and general knowledge required of him. Still, he would consider himself fortunate to snatch a gardener like the new immigrant in 1766 who advertised himself in the *Virginia Gazette* as "understanding both Flower and Kitchen garden, likewise grafting and budding."[20] The Englishman George Renney, who identified himself in 1769 as a gardener "from England" intending to settle in Williamsburg, advertised that he would "undertake by the Year, to keep in order a few GARDENS at a reasonable price." He would have had little difficulty finding work. Renney also remarked in his advertisement that, should he not find gardening work in Williamsburg, "he would be willing to engage with any Gentleman in the country." It is not known where exactly he finished up, but he must have succeeded in town. James Hubard of Williamsburg, who had a garden on Francis Street and, before that, one "next to Green Hill" closer to the Palace, took the step in 1774 of advertising for "a skillful gardener" who would "meet with good Encouragement."[21]

. . .

Close to Hubard's garden on Francis Street, Benjamin Waller laid out his garden around midcentury. Since Waller acquired that property in the 1740s and built his house immediately, his earliest gardening there may well have overlapped with Custis's latest.[22] What most attracts our attention to his garden is the surviving plan of it (figure 43), which shows an imaginative blending of the useful and the decorative within a small area. The plan was not drawn until after the end of the eighteenth century, so it is impossible to say how the garden had changed in the preceding half century. Nevertheless, the highlighting of the importance of the practical in the small space near the house that was available for planting matches the designs that appear in the surviving Wythe garden plan and, more generally, corresponds to what we know about how half-acre town lots were planted. Gardeners, both rich and poor, seem to have insisted on vegetables and fruit near their houses.

Waller's garden also records another link between town and plantation. The Waller correspondence with the Blow family is filled with plant exchanges between their Norfolk, Williamsburg, and Tower Hill plantation gardens. Indeed, the surviving garden plan is supposed to have been drawn so that the Williamsburg garden could be re-created at Tower Hill. A plausible local tradition has it that Waller's granddaughter, Eliza, loved her father's garden so

much that when she married George Blow and moved to his Tower Hill plantation in Sussex County, probably in the first decade of the nineteenth century, she drew the plan to facilitate her re-creation of it.[23]

Archaeologists have found Eliza Blow's drawing of the garden to fit remarkably well within the size and shape of the enclosure defined by fence lines and outbuildings in back of the house. It shows a garden composed of four main sections, with some blurring or overlapping, arranged in a balanced and symmetrical order: the flower garden; the fruit orchard; the vegetable garden ornamented with bushes and fruit; and the plain strawberry, corn, and potato patches. The central gravel walk leading from the yard to the enclosed family graveyard in the southwest corner (not shown on the plan) was verified through archaeological excavations, as was the entrance through a little gate from the yard area, with its kitchen and outbuildings, to the garden. Boxwood hedges were planted along the yard side and dwarf box along the garden side of the fence separating the two areas. The orchard to the east, with cherry, plum, pear, apple, and quince, perhaps grew between the gardens and the pasture. Strawberry, corn, and potato patches balanced the scheme to the west. The symmetrically arranged flowers, soft fruit, and vegetables in between were bordered by herbs and a terrace. Other embellishments included the grape arbor planted east-west in the center and the garden pavilion or "arbor" in the middle where the two axes intersect.[24]

Some perspective on the Blow garden plan and the Waller and Blow family gardening interests can be gleaned from a plan from about 1776 of the Norfolk house and garden belonging to Richard Blow, father-in-law of Eliza Blow (figure 44).[25] This is one of the very few extant eighteenth-century plans of both a house and garden. Richard Blow's corner lot in Norfolk embraced an area between two streets, one of them running parallel to and close by the Elizabeth River, and contained a town house with a garden perhaps the size of Waller's. A notation of un-

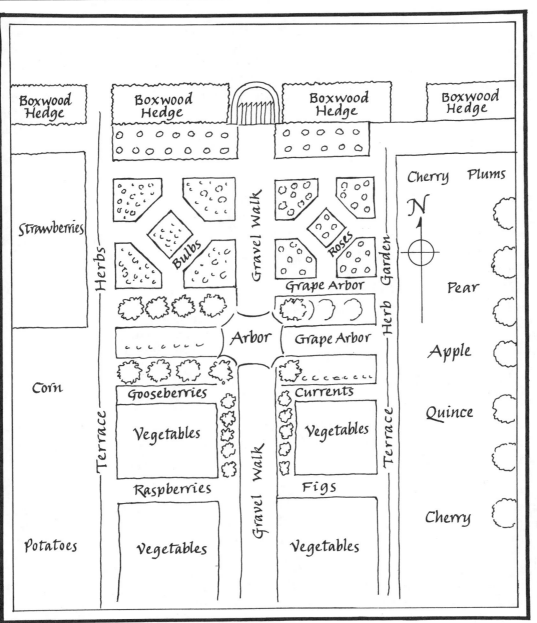

43. Waller garden in Williamsburg, ca. 1807 (after Luty Blow).

known date at the bottom of the sketch reads: "This is a very roughly drawn plan, but mother says it is exactly like it, only the garden walk ought to be in the middle of the gardens, on a line with the hall." This could be Eliza's writing, referring to her mother-in-law, years after Richard Blow had died and the property been sold.

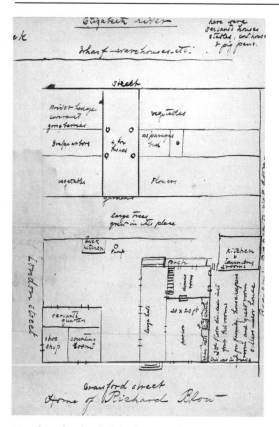

44. *Plan of Richard Blow's house and garden in Norfolk, Virginia, late eighteenth century.*

In addition to the pride in the garden that the plan obviously demonstrates, the layout resembles that in Eliza's plan. Blow's garden was separated from the yard by "large trees" instead of a boxwood hedge, but inside the garden a central path like Waller's ran the full length, dividing the garden into two halves. Blow had vegetables in the first area to the left, as well as in the last section on the right, whereas Waller relegated all his vegetables to the bottom of the garden beyond the arbor, where they would have been less conspicuous. And instead of an arbor, Blow had "4 box bushes" in the center. But the positions of a grape arbor, currants, and gooseberries are almost identical. Blow's grounds did not have Waller's sense of space, however, because his garden was rigidly bounded by streets and a

neighbor's lot, shutting it in and isolating it from adjacent land.

When Benjamin Waller died in 1786, the Francis Street house passed to his youngest son, Robert Hall Waller, who with his wife and daughter Eliza had been living there for several years. After Eliza's marriage to George Blow, the Williamsburg house and garden became, as it were, the third point in the triangle of domiciles embracing also George Blow's Tower Hill and Richard Blow's Norfolk home. It would be pure speculation to suggest that the Norfolk and Williamsburg gardens, so similar in layout, owed some aspects of design to each other; there is no such evidence, and, in any case, the dating of each is uncertain. But within a family like the Blows' this sort of exchange or transference of ideas would be perfectly plausible. It appears to have happened, at least, between the Williamsburg garden and Tower Hill. Moreover, the plans themselves and the occasional allusions to rural life that appear in the Blow papers enhance the possibility, since it is clear that this family loved gardening.

One charming passage occurs in a letter of May 28, 1809, from George Blow to his father-in-law in Williamsburg, inviting him to taste the pleasures of country life at Tower Hill and engage, for a change, in a life of reflection and meditation: "The Country—long rambles in shady woods—still streams of Meandering waters and all other rural charms, rouze the mind to inquiry, fire the soul with a noble ambition, inspire the Heart with godlike virtues, invite to Study, and promote reflection."[26] In 1812 George wrote to his father from Tower Hill, requesting numerous plants, presumably from the Norfolk garden, and asking for some box cuttings on behalf of his "mother," the now widowed Martha Hall Waller, in Williamsburg. The letter also implies Eliza's considerable horticultural interests:

Make Hercules [the gardener] send as many scions of Privy [privet] as can be spared without injuring the main Bushes. If he has any young

Box scions with Roots I would be glad of as many as he can possibly Beg, as well as what can be spared from the Garden. Make him also sett out (my mother says) a trench of young Twigs of Box for the purpose of taking Root to sett out next year. . . . Eliza begs from the garden some currant Bushes . . . English Raspberries, ditto a few bunches of Sweet Violet, and my mother wishes some of each Kind of the Garden Seed from New York.[27]

There is also an invoice dated 1814 from a Mrs. Norman for supplying certain shrubs to the Waller house: a bay tree, tuberoses, two blue plums, two "egg" plums, a rose of Malta, a capio rose, English gooseberries, and yellow raspberries.[28] Plants apparently traveled back and forth between the families, so that the Waller garden seems not to have been allowed to decline while Martha Hall Waller continued to live in Williamsburg.

After Martha Hall Waller died in 1816, Richard Blow had to decide what to do with the old family "mansion," as a Waller nephew called it. He was bound by her will to preserve the graveyard in the garden; beyond that, he was himself determined to "save the Enclosures and Garden from total Destruction" in "the good old City."[29] He was keeping up a garden then almost three-quarters of a century old. Only the Custis garden is known to have survived as long in Williamsburg within the same family.

. . .

It is critical that we use the two surviving plans that illustrate the gardening of the Waller and Blow families to draw certain conclusions about gardening in Virginia at the end of the century. First, the common practice in a small, half-acre town garden was still to arrange features symmetrically, with gravel or shell paths dividing areas into evenly balanced geometric parts. In the case of a more stylistically minded person like Waller, the wooden fences used to separate areas from one another inside a garden were likely to be fashioned in attractive designs. This was a particularly good idea in a small garden, where a concentration of fencing could otherwise look prosaic and dull. Box hedging was still popular as an alternative to wooden fencing. As for plantings, vegetables, herbs, and fruit often grew together in the same bed, although vegetables were more likely to be segregated in a less prominent part of the enclosure.

Second, the Blows were typical in obtaining their plants from sources within America or the colony; gardeners no longer felt the great urge to write to England for them, although a few of Williamsburg's prominent personalities still did so. One could conveniently purchase European plants from ever more nurseries in Charleston, Boston, Philadelphia, and New York—even from one in Williamsburg. There was also in the last quarter of the century a shift of sensibility: patriotism played a subtle role. It was part of a feeling, articulated most clearly by Thomas Jefferson, that the American landscape could sustain and improve itself without foreign assistance. Custis's and Byrd's desires for English plants with which to "civilize" their demesnes and make themselves feel more in touch with a culture they missed began to be replaced by pride in being an American. Also, the wonders of botanical discovery and experimentation that had stimulated Custis, Byrd, Clayton, and Bartram had faded, although far from disappeared. People generally knew which European plants could thrive in Virginia, and they were available in American nurseries.

. . .

Only one other detailed plan of a private town garden is known for this period in Virginia, that of George Wythe's garden in Williamsburg (figure 45), dating from sometime between 1837 and 1844. The plan was drawn by Kate Blankenship, daughter of the naturalist Dr. John Millington, who leased the property in 1835 and then purchased it in 1841.[30] Wythe may have begun to lay out his garden on the Palace Green as early as the 1750s—his house was built about 1750 by Richard Taliaferro of Powhatan plantation

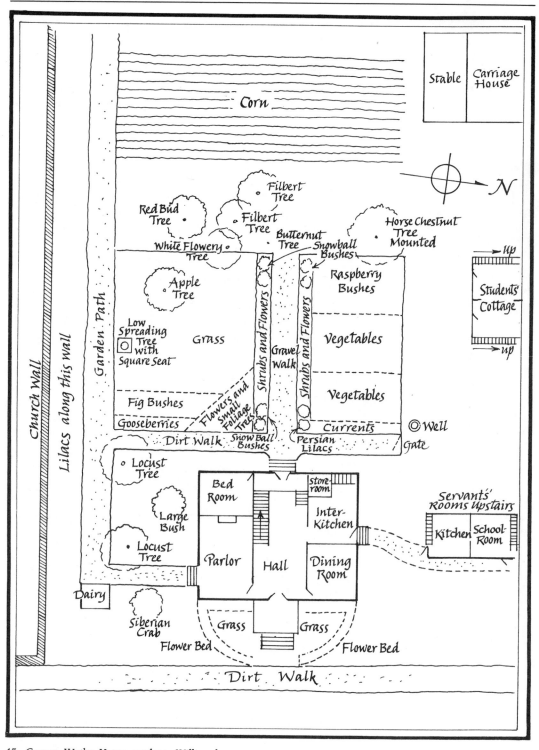

45. George Wythe House gardens, Williamsburg, ca.
1837–1844, after Kate Millington Blankenship.

just outside Williamsburg—so the plan probably does not entirely convey what Wythe himself designed. How the garden looked in his day or what he himself thought of it is unknown, although scraps of documentation, archaeological excavations, and aspects of the plan suggest not only a carefully conceived layout but also practical fruit and vegetable gardens, ornamentally designed, that proved to be serviceable to two or three governors, including Thomas Jefferson.

Wythe and his bride moved into the house soon after it was built.[31] Most of what is known about his gardening casts him firmly in the role of a practical gardener, although the prominent position of the house on the Palace Green at the head of Nicholson Street made it almost as visually important as the Palace in that part of town and, in a sense, demanded an ornamental as well as a useful garden.

The only surviving remark Wythe ever made about his gardens was in reply to a request from his former law student Thomas Jefferson. In March 1770 Jefferson sent a messenger from Monticello to bring back some Bantam pomegranates and nectarines from Wythe's Williamsburg garden. Just then beginning to plant his orchards and lay out his own gardens at Monticello, Jefferson apparently liked the quality of Wythe's fruit, which he would have known from his student days. Wythe replied promptly, as the planting season had arrived. "I send you some nectarines and apricot graffs [grafts] and grape vines, the best I had," he wrote on March 9, "and have directed your messenger to call upon Major Taliaferro for some of his. You will also receive two of Toulis' catalogues. Mrs. Wythe will send you some garden peas."[32]

Wythe was no novice at grafting fruit and raising an orchard. In 1814 Jefferson remarked in a letter to James Mease that Wythe had "grafted an orchard" from a splendidly delicious and juicy apple that his father-in-law had picked "in a large old field near Williamsburg where the seed had probably been dropped by some bird."[33] It became known as the Taliaferro apple. From such a slight remark we know that Wythe had an orchard somewhere in his garden. Whatever its size, it was most likely situated at the bottom (west end) of the garden, where perhaps it would not interfere with any ornamental garden patterns. As for soft fruit, Wythe was particularly fond of gooseberries and raspberries, which he liked to present now and then to Governors Fauquier and Botetourt. He also had a partiality for figs, which he probably raised. Jefferson wrote to him in 1794, after Wythe had moved to Richmond, the new capital, indicating as much: "I ever wish to have opportunity of enjoying your society, knowing your fondness for figs, I have daily wished you could have partaken of ours this year."[34]

That is the extent of the documentary clues to Wythe's garden. But there is more information in the Desandrouins Map and in the surviving plan. Around the perimeter of the garden on the Desandrouins Map are dots that doubtless represent trees or foliage of some sort; they appear elsewhere on the map only in the college and Tazewell Hall gardens. Within the dots, two clear garden areas show up, separated by a central path. Since Wythe owned only three of the four lots between the Palace Green and Nassau Street, it is also significant that the west end of the dotted enclosure excludes both the westernmost lot he did not own along Nassau Street and the westernmost lot he did own, in the middle of which sits a large structure. This map therefore suggests that the enclosed garden included only two lots, with a third very likely reserved for the orchard and whatever other crop Wythe may have been inclined to grow.

As most of these hints are corroborated by the surviving detailed plan of the garden, it is likely that the plan shows the garden much as it was when Wythe left it in 1791. When tested against archaeological and documentary evidence, it holds up well.[35] It shows fairly correctly the positions of a few of the outbuildings discovered through excavations and, most important of all, the location of two of the three major east-west paths (of undetermined date) leading from the house along the length of the garden.[36] Beyond

46. *The restored George Wythe House gardens.*

that, it affords a glimpse of a late-colonial garden with a large area relegated to grass and with skillfully arranged decorative features interspersed with vegetables and soft fruit. In front of the house, fronting the Palace Green, a little forecourt garden treatment around the steps—a semicircular plat of grass bordered by flower beds—could easily have survived from Wythe's day. It was a more humble, but equally decorative, version of the oval beds that had once existed in the Palace forecourt.

More revealing is the treatment on either side of the central "gravel walk." Since the proportions of the areas on both sides of this path resemble those suggested by excavations, the gar-

dens here offer an idea of the sorts of designs Wythe could have laid out (figure 46). Most prominent is the large grass lawn in the south garden. At both ends of the central path, in particular, Persian lilacs and snowball bushes provided shape and color.[37] These, plus the flowers along the path, must have created a colorful scene heightened by the contrasting grass lawn and the generally axial pattern. Still more flowers were introduced into the northeast corner of the grass plat, near the garden steps leading from the house, next to "small foliage trees." At the east end of the grass plat there were fig bushes and gooseberries, perhaps a legacy of Wythe. Standing at the south perimeter of the grass plat, midway along the southern path, was a "low spreading tree with square seat"—a point of visual importance since from it one could see up and down the garden easily and enjoy the openness and flatness of the grass.

North of the central walk, the narrower garden close to the outbuildings and the well was used for vegetables and soft fruit (raspberries and currants).[38] The currants bordered the east end of the north garden just as the gooseberries did the south garden. The vegetables could have been pushed to the bottom of the garden near the stable, although Wythe undoubtedly used most of that section for his orchards. On the plan the collection of horse chestnut, butternut, filbert, redbud, and other trees west of the gardens tends to argue that Wythe had an orchard at that end, one that extended further to include what is marked on the plan as an area for corn.

Wythe's advantage may be said to have been the flatness of his garden, enabling him to cultivate and plant most of the space. Nor was he without vistas from the garden. From the front garden he enjoyed the view down Nicholson Street, while the spire of Bruton Parish Church and its tranquil churchyard not only provided perspectives but also enhanced the setting with mild associations of the meditative. If such associations did not translate consciously into the theme of *et in arcadia ego* or emotive versions thereof, they surely at least affected the sense of place in the garden. A man of Wythe's intellect and philosophical character, and one with his roots in the town, could have been expected to be sensitive to such ideas in the manner later displayed by his former students, the avid gardeners St. George Tucker and Joseph Prentis.

The Wythe garden plan, unlike the Waller and Blow plans, was drawn far enough into the next century to inhibit or make less credible any conclusions we might draw from it about late-eighteenth-century town gardening. It is useful, however, to summarize the contrasts in design between this garden and the others. The Wythe plan illustrates less symmetry and axial dominance. The large grass area, ornamented with a spreading tree and a square seat beneath it, conveys more a feeling of leisure and recreation. There are no curving lines except in the grass forecourt, but the entire scene appears more relaxed. The vegetable beds are placed in a surprisingly prominent position for a garden with such an ambience, but their utilitarian aspect would have been minimized by the chief delight of the place: the colors of its flowers, shrubs, and trees. Plants provide lots of color everywhere, especially along the central gravel walk leading directly to sensibly placed trees that in hot weather must have offered welcome shade. The plan in general portrays a more festive garden than Waller's, one reflecting the rising nineteenth-century desire to arrange gardens in order to display flowers more than to feature shapes.

. . .

Notwithstanding the plan of his garden, Wythe's apparent interest in plants is not at all adequately documented. If he had kept a journal of his planting, either practical or ornamental, as did Custis or his friend Thomas Jefferson, his garden today would be more comprehensible. Extant diaries or journals of that kind are scarce, however, though a man who lived down Nicholson Street from Wythe did keep such a journal. Joseph Hornsby purchased Peyton Randolph's house in 1783 and lived there until 1796, when he moved to Kentucky.[39] His journal starts in 1798, after he had left town, but it records the plants he grew in Randolph's former garden.[40] Kitchen gardening interested him most in Williamsburg, and apparently he highly prized his specimens there. After he sold his house, he fastidiously gathered up seeds from the various beds, sorted them into different bags, labeled them, and carried them to Kentucky. On March 6, 1798, for example, he planted "2 Rows fine Cabbage Lettuce seed . . . saved in Wmsburg 1795"—rather like a vintage wine. The "next 2 Rows," he adds, he planted with "Cress seed saved in Wmsburg [bag] No. 6." On the sixteenth he "Planted the North Asparagus Bed East side the main walk with 4 Rows planted at 1 foot distant in the Row, the Seed came from my Garden in Wmsburg, sow'd here last Spring and the plants were the best I did ever see."

Another diarist who recorded a few observations on plants was John Blair, president of the Governor's Council. Only his journal for 1751 survives to convey something of the excitement that plants and excursions into gardens and orchards could still hold for such a man of culture. At the time, Blair was living in a house on Duke of Gloucester Street. Dining at Carter's Grove on February 7, he notes that the "fine Greens" for dinner "were planted about 1st September"— rather late in the season. Then a visitor to his house on March 16 expressed surprise over his "Garden, and Pictures." Not very helpfully, he provides no hint as to why either his garden or pictures should surprise a guest. On the eighteenth he and his family went off to Green Spring, where, in the greenhouse or orangery, "we gather'd oranges"; and on the twentieth he served guests asparagus from his garden. The diary goes on to mention other aspects of his family gardening, including an entry for planting flowers on November 26 and three vague allusions to his gardener. One sign of his neighborliness, if not his sensitivity to his chattels, appears in an entry for May 25, when he loaned his gardener to Peyton Randolph, of whom "Mrs. Randolph gave a fine account."[41]

. . .

In the search for good plants, Williamsburg gardeners after 1790 were fortunate to have a commercial nursery, Bellett's, in town. For most of the century, until Bellett moved there, no nursery is known to have been in business. Rather, the function was performed from time to time by professional gardeners like Thomas Crease, Christopher Ayscough,[42] James Nicholson, James Wilson, and John Farquharson at the Palace or college and by nearby plantations like Green Spring and Westover. These people were chiefly gardeners, however, and their supply of plants and seeds was not part of any professionally developed commercial venture. Bellett, on the other hand, was among the more successful of a new breed of entrepeneurial nurserymen who flourished after the Revolution, when the by then rapid ascendancy of the middle class in the gardening world of the new nation made it imperative that plants and seeds be much more readily and widely available. More people than ever were laying out ornamental gardens and required flowers and decorative bushes and trees to embellish them. Bellett specialized in the ornamental and had huge stocks in his Williamsburg nursery to draw upon.[43]

Bellett's career not only illustrates a dramatic growth of ornamental gardening in the Chesapeake but also suggests that to a professional like him Virginia represented an attractive market. His choice of Williamsburg indicates that he thought the old capital was an appropriately quiet, clean, and generally pleasant center for his business, where the present and past gardening ambience—irrespective of the town's lost political importance—was compatible with his trade. It was good business to have a Williamsburg address.

A Frenchman, Bellet began his career in the 1780s as a seed merchant in Philadelphia, developed as a commercial nurseryman in Baltimore—where he appears to have been the first to sell plants for gardens directly to the public— and eventually moved to Williamsburg, whence he carried on a vast business, selling his stock all over the Chesapeake region. From his base in Baltimore, he had at times toured Virginia on business and discovered a promising market there. Calling himself a florist as well as a gardener, botanist, and seedsman, he must have had little doubt of his chances of success in Williamsburg. He could still appeal to gardeners with advertisements stating that much of his ornamental stock, especially flowers, was imported from Europe, especially London; but once in Williamsburg he used his own land extensively to grow and collect seeds of all sorts of plants, ornamental as well as utilitarian, which he advertised widely. In the *Virginia Gazette and Weekly Advertiser* for January 25 and 30, 1793, for example, he announced he was selling, among other things, topiary ("fifteen sorts of very curious Pyramids") and "American Flowerings, trees and shrubs" to "any part of Europe." On January 8, 1799, in the same paper, he advertised "a variety of flowerings, shrubs, and ornamental trees" in addition to an extensive line of fruit and vegetables. By the turn of the century, he had built up a most extraordinary stock of fruit trees on his premises along Capitol Landing Road (see figures 8 and 16), as he proudly announced on January 21, 1803, in the *Petersburg Intelligencer*: "*Twenty Thousand Grafted* Fruit Trees, *From one to four years old, for Sale at my Nursery*, in Williamsburg . . . of which eighty sorts I imported myself from London, in the year 1799, which I have vastly propagated."[44]

Once established, the nursery achieved a wide reputation for reliability. Thomas Jefferson bought plants there, as did Joseph Prentis. Prentis's kinsman, Peter Bowdoin, wrote to him from his plantation Hungars around 1790, asking for plants from a Mr. Bellett, the owner of a new nursery in town: "My Boat will go up to Capital Landing for the purpose of bringing a number of Trees from Belletts. Dr. Lyon requested me to write you and ask the favor of you to select such trees as you would recommend for him sending four of each kind"—for twenty dollars, he adds. Bowdoin then asks Prentis for plants from the latter's garden, but "if you have not as many to spare as will make fine beds, supply the deficiency from Belletts." On the back of the letter he lists the plants and trees he wants from Bellett.[45]

Bowdoin was fortunate to have such a skilled horticulturist as Prentis to choose plants for him. Others needed to see for themselves, and for them Bellett followed a new nursery practice for selling flowers: he allowed his customers to mark with notched sticks the varieties of blooms they wished to buy once the flowers' seasons were over. The traffic to his nursery at particular times of the year must therefore have been considerable. Indeed, it is a historical irony that there should have been such a late-century attraction to Williamsburg after the seat of government had been removed in 1780 and the town's chief raison d'être thereby eliminated. It is as if Williamsburg's *genius loci* had whispered in Bellett's ear and urged him to reassert the town's gardening past. There is an element of symmetry to this: Bellett may be said to have kept Williamsburg on the gardening map of early America well into the nineteenth century, just as Nicholson and Spotswood in a sense put it on that map almost a century earlier.

In the late-eighteenth-century world of Williamsburg plants, and their propagation, it is astonishing that no American book had yet been published as a type of supplement to Philip Miller's *Dictionary*. Doubtless, handwritten "calendars" were circulated, or gardeners kept notes taken from their own experiences or from Miller year after year. But a considerable degree of uncertainty and inconsistency must have resulted, especially as Miller did not write chiefly for American colonial gardeners. In the mid-1760s, John Randolph, who lived in a large house with a sizable garden at the south end of South England Street, wrote a manual designed to guide American gardeners through the steps of profitable kitchen gardening. Whether or not he wrote it for publication is a mystery; and indeed, "Randolph's Culinary Gardener" appears not to have been published until 1816.[46]

Although Randolph occasionally took his methods and advice from Miller and sometimes plagiarized him, his distinctive achievement was to adapt Miller's English system to the Virginia climate. He knew whereof he wrote, because most everything he recommended he had tried out himself in his Williamsburg garden. Although Randolph's prose does not rival the spicy style of Thomas Tusser's sixteenth-century work, *Five Hundred Points of Good Huswifery*, its gardening counsel is not infrequently relieved by a metaphoric and humorous turn of phrase.

A reader turning to Randolph's book for information on Virginia ornamental gardening will be disappointed, though hints of the ornamental occasionally appear. When Randolph identifies varieties of honeysuckle, he slips in the remark, "They may be removed in bloom for the sake of a prospect, and replaced when out of bloom." Or when directing the reader how to grow chamomile, he observes that it is used "in making green walks or edgings." He also advises about the garden cultivation of ranunculus, with its lovely and fashionably yellow, orange, and red flowers. In the monthly calendar of gardening duties at the end of the book, he includes a few tips for the ornamental. For March he writes, "you may begin to mow your grass walks [both in between the vegetable beds and in the pleasure garden], and continue so to do every morning, and roll them; turf this month; plant Box." In November it is time to "prune your trees and vines, plant out every thing of the tree or shrub kind, that has a root to it . . . plant Box; turf early." Regarding the grass walks among the vegetables, he has some advice for keeping the beds pretty as well as convenient: "I would recommend your beds to be about four feet wide, that the grass may be cut without treading on the beds, which often hardens the earth so much that the grass cannot come up, and must of course perish."[47]

This little book represented a new genre for colonial literature. It is analogous to an almanac; hence it partakes of the same homespun and aphoristic style. "If you are scanty with regard to your land," Randolph tells his poorer and less fortunate readers, "you must cut your coat according to your cloth." He is inclined to wax metaphoric when pointing out the effects a few plants have on digestion, as in the case of Jerusalem artichokes, which, he says, "are of a flatulent nature, and are apt to cause commotions in the belly." Asparagus are delicate, and he cautions the need to use a fork when digging around them, because "a spade is a very prejudicial in-

strument to them." At times he is moved by a philosophical impulse. Although cauliflowers are not promising material for would-be philosophers, he does his best: "Cauliflowers, must be sown *critically to a day*, or else there is no dependence on the success of them. I cannot, nor do I find any one else capable of assigning a good reason for this, but the experience of this country, as well as England, verifies the proposition. We must therefore receive this fact as we do many others, and rest ourselves satisfied, that the thing certainly exists, though the mode of existence is an impenetrable secret to us." If cauliflower is a source of wonder and mystery, parsley seems to be of the devil's party without knowing it. "The gardeners," he observes, "have an advantage as to this plant, that the seed goes nine times to the devil before it comes up, alluding to the length of time it lies in the ground before it germinates, which is generally six weeks."[48]

Randolph's own garden at what later was called Tazewell Hall (for John Tazewell, who purchased the property in 1778) was notable in Williamsburg's townscape because, like others privileged in their location at the edge of town where there was adjacent open landscape, it was laid out at the southern perimeter of the town and therefore could not only be larger than most but also command views south toward field and woods. So far as we know, the term *landscape garden* was never applied to any property in eighteenth-century Williamsburg, although the concept was familiar to at least a few plantation gardeners in the last quarter of the century. Still, these gardens at the southern edge of town, notably including those of Bassett Hall and the Robert Carter Nicholas house, possessed one—perhaps the major—characteristic associated with the landscape garden: landscape views. Not enough is known about them to enable us to discover whether they reflected any other ingredients of the landscape garden, such as a taste for the picturesque, the emotive, and even freedom.[49] But the sense of space and freedom allowed into these gardens via the adjacent landscape represented a type of relaxation from the rigidity inherent in Nicholson and Spotswood's original town planning.

The tract of land belonging to Tazewell Hall originally totaled ninety acres.[50] Ten acres around the house had been annexed to the town in 1762, four years after Randolph took possession, and were described at the time as "fronting England Street" and bounded on the east and west by two ravines or water courses. That same year the property was described as "lately built" with "considerable improvements thereon."[51] The Desandrouins Map (figure 8) indicates just how large the garden had become by 1781; it also reveals two "faces," as it were, of the property: the position of the house in relation to South England Street (figure 47), where the building serves as a terminal focus to the view down the street from the Powder Magazine and therefore supports the baroque spirit of Williamsburg's town plan; and the more expansive southern aspect, where garden and open landscape are in proximity to one another.[52]

According to the Desandrouins Map, Robert Carter Nicholas's garden was also very large, about the largest in town, in fact, although the draftsman must have erred in picturing it as larger than the Palace garden. The property consisted of ten lots, which Nicholas purchased in 1770. Large as it was, it must have been given over partly to orchards and a large kitchen garden and partly to areas of grass and flowers. Today, much of the garden lies under the Williamsburg Lodge, and, unfortunately, the only extant descriptions of it are several sale advertisements. "The square . . . contains about 8 lots," began one advertisement in 1777, "great part of which constitute a very large garden, well enclosed and very well cropped. . . . An exceeding fine spring is very convenient to the house. Also a very large and valuable pasture adjoining the city, and under good enclosure. It includes several fine springs, and a valuable piece of meadow pretty well reclaimed."[53] This reads like a summary description of a miniature landscape garden. Running water was of course not only a good selling

47. *Tazewell Hall, Williamsburg, with South England Street running up to it. John Randolph's gardens were laid out on the other side (south) of the house. The photograph dates from the 1920s, shortly before the house was removed.*

point but also vital for a well-maintained garden and for livestock grazing in the pastures and meadows. Just where the pastures were is unclear in the Desandrouins Map or any other source; if they adjoined the lots, they must have been to the south, perhaps adjacent to and west of Randolph's lots.

Wherever the meadows were, they may have afforded Nicholas some pleasant views from his garden. A hint that he valued such vistas and perspectives of the landscape crops up in a letter of 1772 to John Norton in which he asks for six large prints of "Gentlemens Seats" and six "Landskips."[54] He was not indifferent to the view from his front door, either, if it was he who wrote another sale advertisement in 1778: the view took in the "square which is surrounded with streets and a fine green in front for fifty yards to the main [Duke of Gloucester] street."[56]

Nicholas, whose large garden on South England Street faced Market Square, went to the trouble of ordering his seeds and plants from England because there was nobody like Bellett

48. Bassett Hall, Williamsburg.

yet in the colony when he began gardening in earnest in the 1770s.[56] In September 1771, Nicholas wrote to the English merchant John Norton, complaining about the quality and price of seeds he had received in the past and ordering a good many more. "The Seedsman I can't but complain of," he remarked, "for sending such a Parcel of Trumpery, several of the Articles are Weeds in this Country, & many of the Seeds not good."[57] Here are echoes of John Custis. So late in the century, Nicholas seems out of step with the times in ordering so extensively from abroad and in denigrating native sources.

Over at the east end of Francis Street, next to the Waller house and a stone's throw from the Capitol building, there was in the last quarter of the century another large garden that appears on the Desandrouins Map and may be interpreted as a type of landscape garden. Bassett Hall (figure 48) was built in the 1750s by Colonel Philip Johnson, who owned it when the Desandrouins Map was drawn. Doubtless it was he who sited the house a few hundred feet south of the street. His attitude toward his little estate is reflected in a 1755 *Gazette* advertisement, where he calls it a "plantation . . . near the Capitol in Williamsburg."[58] Burwell Bassett, from whom the house took its present name, purchased it in 1796. The property then comprised two lots on the streeet and extensive pasture land and woods south of them.

When the Irish poet Thomas Moore visited Williamsburg in 1804, so the legend goes, he was struck by the "beautiful lawn at Bassett Hall" and inspired to write a poem, "To the Firefly"— not great poetry, but full of the sort of nostalgia that the old town was by then likely to invoke.[59] A glimpse of this lawn, identified as two acres in size, is provided by a plan of the Bassett Hall grounds (figure 49). Of uncertain date and origin, but probably dating from the mid-nineteenth century, the plan also shows the disposition of gardens and landscape. If the layout had not altered much in half a century, this map offers clues to its late-eighteenth-century appearance. It shows the rather grand entrance through the lawn, with the drive winding south beside the house and along the garden and orchard down to the barn and beyond. A few other features dotting the landscape also suggest that the acreage had been landscaped. The barn, an icehouse, a couple of springs (over one of which a springhouse previously may have stood[60]), an "inside fence" curving picturesquely from in front of the orchard outward in the direction of the woodland, the "old burying ground," and an assortment of fencing indicate a pleasant farm-like setting. Indeed, the farm road and the extended avenue southward both may have helped create a version of the *ferme ornée* here: a farm ornamented with sundry prospects, trees, and buildings.

Two elements of the Bassett Hall landscape stand out in this plan. The first is the practical, encompassing the orchard and "garden"—presumably a vegetable garden. Immediately in back (south) of the house and squeezed within a long rectangular area extending several hundred feet from Francis Street, these are functional and straightforward in shape and location. Near the house, bordered by the main drive or avenue into the property from the street, and regularly shaped, they are entirely consistent with prevailing eighteenth-century plantation and town practices of simply enclosing with fences or hedges areas close to the house in order to grow

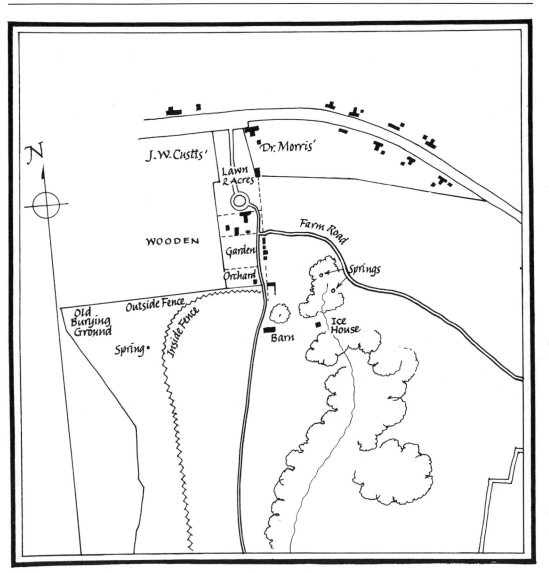

49. *Bassett Hall plantation environs on the outskirts of Williamsburg, mid-nineteenth century (after an anonymous drawing).*

produce needed for the household economy. It is a pity that the garden shown on this plan is not drawn with more detail; but, given its shape, there is little reason to suppose that in the eighteenth century it was much different from the Waller garden, combining vegetables with soft fruit, herbs, and perhaps even flowers. It is also important to note that the orchard is, as we conjectured in the Wythe garden, beyond the garden. If a town garden contained enough space—that is, more than half an acre—this pattern recommends itself as the most likely arrangement of principal features, one that recurred throughout the century from Custis onward. In this, Bassett Hall holds no surprises.

As for the second element in the Bassett Hall grounds, there can be no doubt that this plan portrays the most sophisticated deployment of landscape gardening features in Williamsburg, or any Virginia town, in the late eighteenth and early nineteenth centuries. Such a design was possible, of course, because of the expanse of terrain south of the house, an advantage shared by other properties on Francis and South England streets and also by the Palace itself to the north. For this reason, it is likely that toward the end of the century others who owned houses on the edge of the town with extra acreage in one way or another became landscape gardeners. The result is a plantation-like estate within the town. The appeal of such landscaping possibilities is not difficult to imagine. If a potential landowner entertained ideas of adopting aspects of the life of a planter without the constraints imposed by small building lots, but was disinclined to isolate himself from town life on some remote plantation, what better way to realize his ambition than to acquire a place like Bassett Hall?

The Bassett Hall plan illustrates only the possibilites. It cannot prove that others engaged in this sort of landscaping elsewhere on the town's southern perimeter, although other types of evidence argue strongly that they did. Nor does this plan, like the Wythe plan, picture an eighteenth-century landscape scheme. But we know that the Bassett Hall estate in the second half of the eighteenth century did include this extra acreage, as well as certain features shown on the plan, such as the fencing, roads, icehouse, and front lawn and avenue. It was there to be landscaped. Virginia plantations had been providing numerous examples of landscape gardening at least since the 1780s, so it was not beyond the early owners of Bassett Hall and other large town properties to adopt the appropriate consciousness and approach and turn their landscapes into something of beauty as well as use. Ironically, this activity would have occurred just as the town was de-

clining in importance and prosperity. On the other hand, it provides another instance of how plantations and the town were linked.

. . .

What other general conclusions may be drawn from Williamsburg about the progress of urban Virginia gardening in the second half of the eighteenth century? To begin with, there is reason to think that kitchen or vegetable gardening for the most part proceeded much as it had in the first half of the century. John Randolph's *Treatise* suggests that planting beds of varying sizes, either dug deeply for good drainage or raised slightly, were still commonly used for vegetables and herbs. It is difficult to make a relative judgment about the ornamental uses to which kitchen gardens were put in the second, as distinct from the first, half of the century; except for the planting beds excavated in back of the Peyton Randolph house and the example of John Custis, there is little reliable evidence available from the earlier period. But if the plans of the Waller and Wythe gardens and certain phrases in Randolph's *Treatise* are credible guides, it is plausible to suggest that in the later decades there was a greater taste for planting and siting kitchen gardens with a touch of the ornamental. Fruit, vegetables, herbs, and nuts could all be brought into play.

Whatever type of gardening a person decided to undertake, he or she needed to be his or her own expert. Good professional gardeners still were difficult to come by. One factor that made gardening easier, however, was the presence of nurseries like Bellett's within the community, augmenting the supply of plants from nearby plantations. Seeds and specimens thereby became more accessible to the average person, and as a consequence there was much less ordering from nurseries in neighboring colonies or in England.

As for garden design, the common garden plots accommodated within half-acre, acre, or two-acre town lots were still laid out in regimented and balanced fashion, the straightforward character of it all conducive to efficient maintenance and household economy. Larger properties of three or more acres—especially on the edge of town—offered greater possibilities for more expressive design. The Wythe garden plan, although from the early nineteenth century, and hints from other sources suggest that asymmetry, the use of more grass, the colorful mingling of fruit, flower, vegetable, and herb, and varieties of shape and texture may well have become more prevalent. And, finally, the emergence of a gardening style in the town that brought into play landscape views and prospects presented an interesting urban counterpart to the flourishing of landscape gardening at the plantations in the second half of the century.

5

The Plantations

*I*t was the great plantation owner-gardeners who tended to exert the most significant influence on colonial gardening. They did this through their examples of designs and patterns and their self-conscious emulation of the country house mentality as they imagined or knew it to exist in England. Although the southern colonial climate and soil prevented even the most eager elite planter-gardeners from creating parterres and landscape gardens believably recalling English practice, a few of them made a good try at it.[1] In the process, they helped generate on American soil the sense of an art.

At least until the 1780s, even at the larger plantations, gardens were limited in the main to geometrically shaped areas enclosed by fences of various kinds or, more rarely, by walls. Naturally, these enclosed areas were larger than those laid out by town gardeners and could accommodate garden features—bowling greens, orangeries, terraces, and so on—near the main house that would not have fit into town gardens. Notwithstanding the considerable expense involved in carving out terraces and establishing geometric parterres, however, the visual effect within the uncompromising fences and boundaries most likely came across as somewhat dull and

artificial—as if nature was somewhere else but not there. Exotic and varied plantings, with diversity of color, texture, and shape—especially cascading down terraces—helped considerably to alleviate this visual impression, but only a handful of planters indulged in that sort of thing.

In the prevalent, prosaic pattern, the enclosure featured fruit and vegetables rather than stylized ornamental elements. This is not to say that the former was never combined with the latter in attractive ways. A few of the best-documented gardens combined pleasure with profit and represented a late-eighteenth-century Virginia version of *in utile dulce*. One characteristic in particular distinguished this classical idea as practiced in Virginia. Whereas the English country house owner may have fashionably posed as a farmer-gardener—as one interested in and directly concerned with agriculture and planting—the Virginia planter had to be a legitimate farmer familiar with agriculture and how to make it pay. The produce in the gardens, even if much of it was decoratively arranged, was a vital part of the household economy. Thus Landon Carter, for example, was punctilious about recording the growth of his vegetables and fruit at Sabine Hall.

It was not within rigid garden enclosures, however, that natural effects were chiefly sought or realized. Practical considerations most often governed the choice of elevated ground for many plantation houses, but frequently so did the aesthetics deriving from prospects that could take in forests, rivers, fields, and hills. If one could command such views from a garden enclosure that itself may not have been varied or interesting, then the effect could be visually and pictorially pleasing. Indeed, contrasts between a garden that was geometrical, regular, and enclosed and the landscape views surrounding it could heighten the beauty of grounds around the main house. A few houses, including Carter's Grove, Kingsmill, and Nomini Hall, were deliberately positioned so as to obtain the most desirable views of a river, for example, or a certain range of hills. Gardens needed to be protected by fences and shaped as squares or rectangles, but there was no reason the orientation of such spaces could not enhance their appearance.

John Robinson, Speaker in the House of Burgesses, spent vast amounts on his "manor Plantation," Pleasant Hill, overlooking the Mattaponi River. There he created gardens within an enclosing brick wall and prominent terraces; but it is the vistas from these gardens that are emphasized in a sale advertisement of 1770: "The manor Plantation is beautifully situated, commanding a fine view of the river and marshes for many miles. There is on it a large genteel two story brick house . . . and a large falling garden enclosed with a good brick wall." An advertisement for Pleasant Hill run in 1777 by John Custis's son stated: "No situation can exceed this in beauty and few in Conveniences."[2]

Terraces, usually turfed, proliferated in plantation gardens. In the Renaissance Italian tradition, as mediated by the English garden, they performed a type of theatrical function, a stage set from which to look out on the drama either in the landscape or evident elsewhere in the gardens. Early in the nineteenth century, Bernard McMahon, a friend of Jefferson and possibly the

first American garden historian, acknowledged the prominence and theatricality of terraces in American gardens in his *American Gardener's Calendar* (1806): they "ranged singly, others double, treble, or several, one above another, on the side of some considerable rising ground in theatrical arrangement."[3]

When contemporary travelers wrote in their accounts of plantation gardens that Virginians by the 1780s were still not practicing pleasure or flower gardening, they actually were saying that it was not yet pervasively practiced by planters, either large or small. "Horticulture is not generally in vogue," observed the Reverend John Spooner in 1793, "though there are [in Virginia] some gardens that do not yield to the best in the United States."[4] And David Meade, formerly of Maycox plantation, wrote from Kentucky in 1797 to Joseph Prentis that, "considered as a fine art," landscape gardening was "even less practiced [in Kentucky] . . . than in Virginia."[5] The art was indeed practiced in Virginia; but as an art of the amateur, gardening, and what we may call landscaping, remained firmly the province of the wealthy planter well into the nineteenth century. There simply were few people who did it in the way Meade meant or in the way Meade himself had done it at Maycox on the James River.

. . .

For some background to the taste for pleasure gardening on the plantations and the ascendancy of open landscape in the aesthetics of garden design, it is useful to record how, toward the end of the eighteenth century, a few commentators responded to the scenery and gardens they found in the colony.[6] Their observations on both general landscape and specific gardens came for the most part in the last quarter of the century, long after the initial layouts of several gardens examined in this chapter. They nevertheless suggest earlier activity.

In the course of his travels through the colony in 1759 and 1760, the Reverend Andrew

50. Belvidere, Richmond. Watercolor by Benjamin Latrobe, late 1790s.

Burnaby specifically related what he called the pomp of plantation life to garden embellishment. He thought it was all a rather decadent pursuit of materialism. From his clerical viewpoint, the "extravagance, ostentation, and disregard of œconomy" in Virginia plantations derived from indolence and an excessive fondness of "society" and "convivial pleasures."[7] Among these pleasures were those of ornamental gardening, which struck Burnaby as frivolous and akin to the worship of mammon. He was not incapable of appreciating Virginia's open landscape, however, and the evidence he saw of its incorporation into garden settings. He was responsive to the picturesque and romantic in scenery. Charmed by Belvidere, for example, William Byrd III's seat on a hill above the falls in Richmond (figure 50), he judged it as romantic and elegant as anything he had ever seen: "It is situated very high, and commands a high prospect of the river." From it "no country ever appeared with greater elegance or beauty," he concluded.[8]

Except for Belvidere and a handful of other plantations, the Reverend Burnaby had little opportunity to see the great plantations. Neither did the German Johann David Schoepf in 1783 and 1784. Schoepf traveled widely in the colonies but perhaps not too well. Gardens were "purely utilitarian," he announced; "pleasure-

gardens have not yet come in and if perspectives are wanted one must be content with those offered by the landscape, not very various, what with the still immense forests." Although he said he had seen virtually no landscape gardens, he allowed that "perhaps a few of the most considerable families have made attempts" to design them. Perhaps someone had told him this; as for himself, the closest he could get to the larger estates was by river: "Whoever will see Virginia in its greatest pomp must travel by stream."[9]

The marquis de Chastellux went about his visits differently. Before he embarked on a three-year expedition to America in 1780, he arranged visits to the leading gentlemen and institutions from Boston to Charleston; and as he proceeded in his travels, he scheduled still more. He therefore saw a good many plantation gardens and described a few of them, especially along the James River, which he called "the garden of Virginia." Coming to Virginia with the object of seeing such places, and culturally equipped to evaluate them in terms of what he knew about English and European fashion, Chastellux is one of the more reliable witnesses.

He saw William Byrd II's Westover, as well as David Meade's Maycox directly across the river, both of which he felt had been laid out in imitation of the *jardin anglais*—a favorite phrase of his. He was also enchanted by the irregular and secretive style of Thomas Jones's Spring Garden on the Pamunkey River, laid out conceivably as early as the 1740s. "The country through which I passed is one of the most agreeable of lower Virginia," he announced; "one sees many well-cultivated estates and handsome houses, among others, one belonging to Mr. Jones." He was surprised to see evidence of the so-called English style in Virginia; he says it was "uncommon" in America. But, as he saw three gardens in this style on the James and Pamunkey rivers alone, one may well wonder what "uncommon" meant. This is what he wrote about Spring Garden: "What is more uncommon in America . . . it was further embellished with a garden laid out in the

English style. It is even said that this kind of a park, which is bounded in part by the river, yields not in beauty to those English models which we [in France] are now imitating with much success."[10]

Chastellux also admired Maycox for its "delightful prospect" and because it was "charmingly situated" with its terraces fronting the James River. The Reverend John Spooner wrote a superb description of the plantation in 1793, after David Meade had been living there for more than twenty years. The writer adopts a somewhat "poetic" or fanciful tone, especially in his hint of an enchanting or suggestive mood in the gardens, but there is no reason to doubt that the mood was palpable enough. Meade had lived in England until 1761, when he was seventeen, so that he probably was not unfamiliar with the mid-century English adoption of the picturesque when he began to lay out Maycox in 1772. Writing about gardening only generally, Spooner nonetheless focuses on Maycox:

> In connection with this may be mentioned the pleasure grounds of David Meade, Esq., of Maycox, in this [Prince George] county. These grounds contain about twelve acres, laid out on the banks of James river, in a most beautiful and enchanting manner. Forest and fruit trees are here arranged, as if nature and art had conspired together to strike the eye most agreeably. Beautiful vistas, which open as many pleasing views of the river; the land thrown into many artificial hollows of gentle swellings, with the pleasing verdure of the earth; and the complete order in which the whole is preserved; altogether tend to form it one of the most delightful rural seats that is to be met with in the United States, and do honour to the taste and skill of the proprietor, who was also the architect.[11]

Spooner thought that this was a garden where, to quote James Thomson's poem "Autumn," "simple Nature reigns; and every View Diffusive."[12] The views from near the house were crucial to the overall effect of variety—the "View Diffusive." Spooner suggests that Meade may even have controlled and multiplied the vistas by converting a single, unbroken view of the river into many glimpses of the scene through the planting of trees.

Maycox's gardens were well known in the area at least by 1781. Visitors like Chastellux, William Feltman,[13] and Baron Ludwig Von Closen made a point of seeing them during and just after the Revolution. Their interest reflects the growing taste for landscape gardens with views, moods, natural variety, and contrasts between geometric planting arrangements next to a house and the distant woods, rivers, and fields.[14] Although Von Closen did not describe Maycox except to say that it "provides a charming view," he did remark on Tuckahoe plantation, Thomas Jefferson's boyhood home on the north bank of the James River a few miles above Richmond. With its maze, the place struck him as possessing some of the character of a naturalized garden: "We walked in the garden, at the foot of which is a maze that led us to the James River. This stream is lined on both banks with very thick willows, in which the birds love to sing."[15]

In fact, all along the James River Von Closen found "the banks . . . embellished with plantations, one more beautiful than the other, and inhabited by the aristocracy of the country; all, such as the *Carter, Randolph, Harrison, Byrd,* etc. families live in very comfortable circumstances, have many connections, & get along very well together." He found the view at Monticello "very picturesque" but apparently no more remarkable than the others he mentioned. At Hornquarter, one of Thomas Nelson's seats on the Mattaponi River, he was struck by the garden and enticing walks along the river: "The house is not remarkable; the garden is rather pretty. But the walks along the Mattaponi, which flows one-quarter of a mile behind the house, are charming." At Scotchtown, he approved of an "English garden below [that] adds a great deal to the charm of this estate." On another visit there in July 1782, when the oppressive heat would have made him glad of any available shady walks, he observed:

> The grounds around Scotchtown are very pretty, and there are little woods in the shade of which we took some country walks. The garden is an attractive sight. There are several rather pretty flower-beds, although these are still rather neglected in this country. There are very few flower-gardeners, and it may be observed, in general, that nature is very beautiful, but art and education have not yet attained the degree of perfection to be found in Europe.

As we shall see later, he liked Mount Vernon, too.[16]

Another observer who traveled widely in the realms of gardens was Thomas Lee Shippen, who, it will be recalled, supplied the most detailed description of Westover toward the end of the century. Shippen's sensitivity to gardens is evident in a letter to his father in September 1790 after a visit to one of Virginia's most stately plantation homes, Stratford Hall, built by Thomas Lee. When Shippen wrote the letter, the H-shaped house was already more than fifty years old and the gardens were well established. The gardens have been restored in recent times, but all the documentary evidence about them and the adjacent landscape in the eighteenth century may be found succinctly put in Shippen's letter. The letter also illustrates the importance to Shippen of the prospects from the house and gardens. He praised the "venerable magnificence of its buildings, the happy disposition of its grounds, . . . the extent and variety of its prospects." He wrote of stepping out "to look at the gardens, vineyards, orangeries, and lawns which surround the House." He was even more struck by the views from another Lee plantation, Chantilly, which enjoyed an enviable setting above the Potomac River. The house, he wrote, "commands a much finer view than Stratford by reason of a large bay into which the Potowmac forms itself opposite to Chantilly, and a charming little creek whose windings spread across and water the space which lies be-

tween Chantilly and the river. Besides these, a fine island called Blackstone's adds a finish to the landscape."[17]

. . .

Little is known about plantation gardens, or about the people who gardened them, in the first half of the eighteenth century. William Byrd II at Westover is one of the exceptions, although most of what is known about his garden dates from the second half of the century. In the Tidewater area of Virginia, however, there were two other gardens whose histories began in the 1730s and 1740s and about which enough is known to suggest they were impressive: Kingsmill and Carter's Grove. They are useful in an effort to judge how plantation gardening progressed throughout the eighteenth century and into the next.

A fine Georgian house that has now disappeared, Kingsmill overlooked the James River about three miles from Williamsburg. The views from this location near the little College Creek, which flowed into the James (figure 51), surely were a factor in the choice of the house's site. When Lewis Burwell, grandson of Lewis Burwell III, who built the house, advertised the plantation for sale in 1781, he pointed out that "the situation is equal to any on the James River."[18] Archaeological excavations have revealed ornamental gardening around the house and a deliberate orientation of the house to command the distant views of river and landscape. As an early plantation garden with such prospects, Kingsmill anticipates some of the regular and irregular, or natural, features of the more resourceful landscaping at Virginia plantations in the second half of the century.[19]

Except for the occasional item of expense in an account book, there is no documentary evidence of what Kingsmill's gardens looked like. All that is known was found by archaeologists, who discovered the outlines of what seem to have been large and even lavishly decorated gardens.[20] The house itself, with its two surviving flanking buildings partially enclosing a fore-

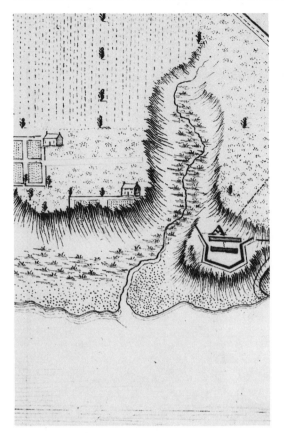

51. *Simcoe Map (1781–1782), showing the position and gardens of Kingsmill plantation (top left corner) above the James River.*

52. *Kingsmill garden archaeological excavations.*

court, brings to mind the forecourt treatment at the Palace and has been cited as one of the earliest instances of the Palace's influence on the building of Georgian houses in the colony. This forecourt enclosure matched the apparent elegance of the buildings and general layout of the grounds. It was endowed with some additional grace early in its history through the building of a perimeter wall consisting of square brick pillars connected perhaps with wooden paling or even some sort of ironwork laid out in symmetrical ogee curves.[21] The softness of the curves was augmented by a similarly curving line of plantings between the marl walks and the wall (see figure 52). A gate lined up with the house, and

a central axis pathway completed the forecourt, which turned out to be larger than that of the Palace.

Kingsmill topped a fairly steep slope, from the edge of which Burwell could look over some terraces and down to his main garden enclosure, an ornamental affair including regularly and symmetrically arranged features. Excavations have revealed the precise dimensions of such a paled-in area—a long rectangular garden (figure 53), including three broad terraces, extending almost 500 feet to the south, with a constant width of 220 feet. It must have been a beautiful sight, with the thick woodland and river in the distance providing dramatic contrasts of art and nature, regularity and wildness. Although we do not know what grew within the enclosed garden, it is clear that the area was divided by a central axis and a main cross-axis into four quadrants.[22] Given the affluence of the Burwells and the elegance of the forecourt, it is conceivable that this rectangular garden contained some formal planting, in the style of the diamond-shaped beds at the Palace.

Burwell also decorated his garden with some quality stonework. Three flights of stone steps up the three terraces are still in place. The stone is a type of granite common to Wales and north-

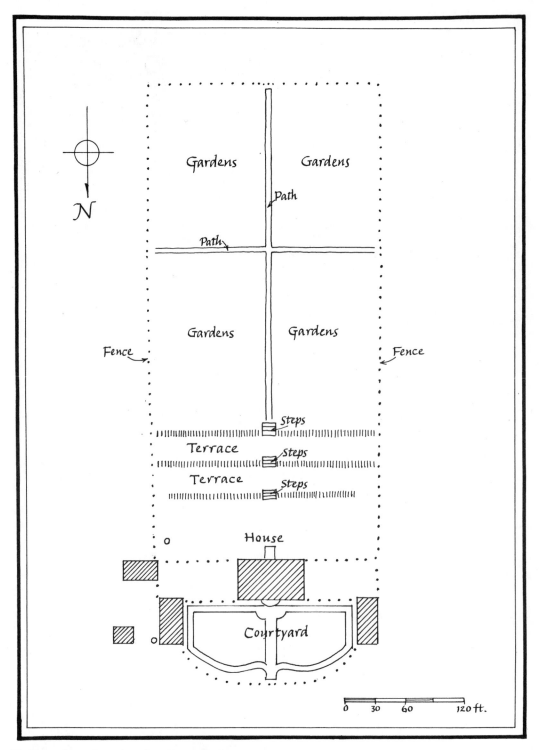

53. *House lot and garden plan, Kingsmill plantation, James City County, Virginia. Based on archaeological excavations (after Fraser Neiman, 1975).*

54. *Excavated terrace steps at Kingsmill.*

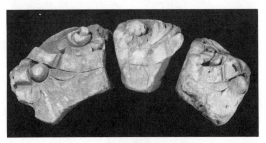

55. *Excavated volute from the river-front steps at Kingsmill.*

56. *Excavated fragments of carved sandstone at Kingsmill, evidently part of a decorative arc displaying bunches of flowers.*

ern England, suggesting that Burwell went to some trouble to obtain it.[23] The steps are also sufficiently broad to be both elegant and imposing (figure 54). Fragments of carved sandstone garden sculpture and finials were found as well (figures 55 and 56), proving that Burwell was not modest in the way he went about decorating his gardens. Perhaps he meant in this way, at least, to rival the architectural primacy of the Palace.

. . .

Just two miles from Kingsmill and also on the north bank of the James River, Lewis Burwell III's cousin, Carter Burwell, began in 1751 to build a large and elegant house on a plantation called Carter's Grove.[24] Circumstantial evidence suggests he was determined to build a beautiful and expensive house set in ornamented and well-ordered gardens.[25] According to graphic, documentary, and archaeological evidence, the gardens, with their terraces and prospects, were worthy of the house, which was extremely well built at great expense. These gardens also illustrate the thesis that in mid-century Virginia planters with the means and inclination could be single-minded in creating beautiful landscape settings for their homes and that these settings could also include the obligatory, starkly fenced geometric garden enclosures without appearing overly arid, monotonous, and practical.

Although Carter Burwell inherited this considerable tract of land, and several others, in 1732 and came into possession of them in 1737 at the age of twenty-one, a legal technicality kept him from building at Carter's Grove immedi-

57. *View of the James River from the restored gardens of Carter's Grove.*

ately. The legacy, which came from Robert "King" Carter, one of the largest landowners in the colony, specified that Burwell had to preserve the labor force at the plantation and could not transfer any of the slaves to other tracts. The intention was to ensure that the place would be maintained as an important income-producing tobacco and grain plantation. A landscape of tobacco plants and fields dotted with slave quarters surrounding an expensive house and overlooking a lovely river does not appear to have been consistent with Burwell's ideas for his home. Apparently more to his taste was a landscape of woods and improved fields of wheat, barley, oats, and peas, naturally disposed around the house's immediate grounds. In order to achieve the latter at Carter's Grove, he needed to abandon ideas of making the plantation a major source of tobacco income, move many of his slaves to others of his tracts, and then transform the plantation into a type of country house where rural pleasures could be pursued in a more civilized setting. To this end in 1749 he managed to have the entail broken by an act of the assembly, so that by 1751 he had begun in earnest to site, build, and landscape his house. He thereby set in motion a process that very likely was repeated in other major home plantations in Virginia and one that was sustained by his son Nathaniel's guardian and uncle, William Nelson of Yorktown, and then by Nathaniel himself after he came of age.[26]

Why did Burwell choose Carter's Grove as his home? In the absence of any statements on the

58. *Restored gardens at Carter's Grove.*

subject by Burwell himself, we can only speculate. The plantation was near Kingsmill, the gardens of which may well have inspired Burwell and given him a few ideas for his own. It is also about eight miles from Williamsburg, so that the family could easily visit the capital and receive friends and acquaintances who wished to partake of the pleasures of the estate. Perhaps most important, the site contained elevated land near the river (figure 57), ideal for an owner who desired beautiful prospects.

In fact, the orientation of the house illustrates a thoughtful decision by Burwell to take the greatest possible advantage of the vista down river. Because of its position in relation to a particular turn of the river, the house looked directly down the length of it.[27] This siting opened up much more varied and picturesque views than would have been the case if the house squarely faced the river. It is likely that the prospect from the land side of the house was also extensive, dominated by a winding approach avenue through pastures where livestock grazed. Woodlands serving as a background would have terminated the views in the distance. This type of landscape or park treatment was not simply nature's doing. It resulted partly from Burwell's elimination of cultivated land, except for sixty acres or so reserved for the needs of Carter's Grove itself, and his decision not to cut down woodland to create space for agriculture.[28]

As for the gardens near the house, archaeological excavations have demonstrated that, as at Kingsmill, terraces descended from the house to a large, fenced-in, rectangular garden (figure 58).[29] These findings make it clear that the gar-

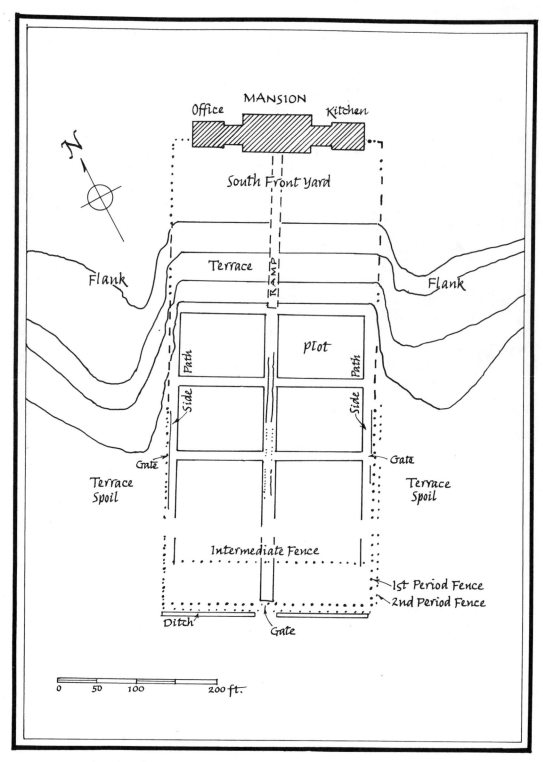

59. *Reconstructed garden plan, Carter's Grove, James City County, Virginia, based on archaeological excavations (after William Kelso, 1972).*

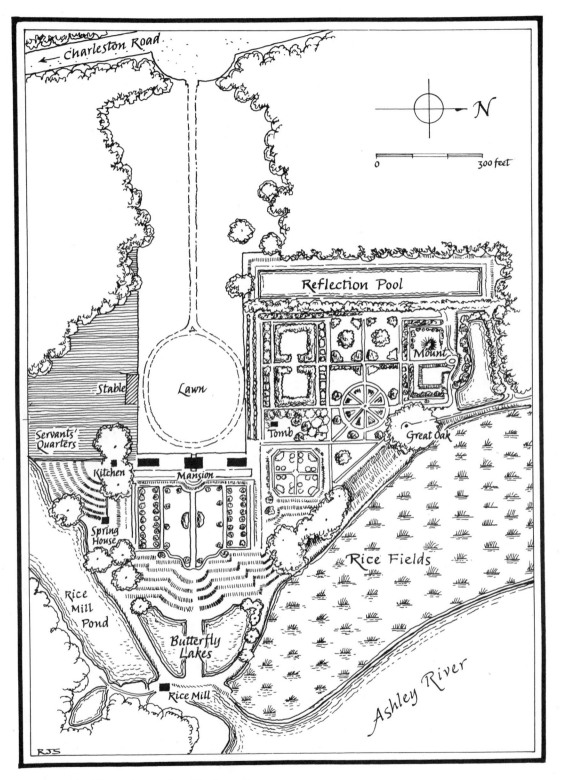

60. Plan of Middleton Place garden, Charleston County,
South Carolina (after Samuel Stoney).

dens evolved gradually, becoming throughout the second half of the century more elaborate, well-defined, and sophisticated.[30]

In their shape and position, the Carter's Grove terraces resembled those of Kingsmill, but Carter Burwell's imaginative use of the displaced earth from their construction went beyond Kingsmill's example. Archaeologists have determined that as he carved out his terraces Burwell piled the earth into what became flanking terraces and mounds. These terraces extended to the southeast and southwest and then curved to the northeast and northwest. A plan of the gardens based on the excavations illustrates how beautifully and irregularly this idea must have enhanced the natural contours of the ground (figure 59).

In a way, the flanking terraces and the straight terraces together bring to mind the elaborate terracing at Middleton Place on the Ashley River outside of Charleston (figure 60), except that Burwell's looked more natural and were not so geometrically severe. As restored, they also have a look of the "green theater" about them, a seventeenth-century Italian innovation that found its way into English gardens, as at Claremont, Surrey, in the early eighteenth century. The west flanking terrace included a mound constructed from the displaced earth—a platform of sorts from which people could gaze out at the view and also over to the straight terraces and enclosed gardens below.

The proportions, scale, and shape of Burwell's gardens are evident from the plan based on excavations (figure 59). As at Kingsmill, there was a flat garden space adjacent to the river front of the house, probably planted with parterres of some kind. Descending from this level were the terraces. The excavations uncovered no central terrace steps, however, so that today a rather steep turfed ramp has been restored.[31] Originally, these terraces overlooked a simple central pathway extending southward for an undetermined distance toward the river. Later, Burwell put up a substantial and tall wooden fence on either side of the straight terraces, enclosing not only the flat garden at the top but also a garden stretching 540 feet from the house and maintaining a width of about 242 feet. A central path of marl ran the entire length, 13 feet wide and narrowing to a 6-foot path of crushed shell across the top flat garden from the highest terrace to the house. The fencing had to be sandwiched in between the flanking terraces and created, at the bottom, what has been called the "sunken garden." This was itself divided by an east-west cross-path, which, like at least one of the other two cross-paths, was 10 feet wide and also covered with marl. Inside and along the length of the fences, from the lowest terrace to the so-called intermediate fence (built after the southernmost fence to contain an area 55 by 245 feet, doubtless for separate planting), there were two long marl paths 6 to 8 feet wide. Six smaller rectangular gardens, therefore, were laid out symmetrically, with two more beyond the intermediate fence after it was installed. How they were planted and what was their comprehensive visual effect as seen from the house and terraces are subjects wide open for speculation, although more archaeological and some documentary evidence helps.

The soil in those six beds had been carefully prepared: the hard subsoil on that plain was dug to a depth of two feet and then filled in with a rich brown loam. Although one archaeologist believes that no decorative shrubs or trees could have been planted within the enclosure—no separate large plant holes or root "molds" were found there—most shrubs do not require holes deeper than two feet and so they could easily have adorned the borders along all the paths. In any case, excavations sufficiently deep to ascertain whether such plant holes are there were not done. It is at least possible to suggest that the planting beds at Carter's Grove, notwithstanding their symmetrical layout, very likely were beautifully ornamented, even if they contained vegetables.[32]

An idea of what the enclosed garden at Carter's Grove could have looked like may be obtained from descriptions of a similarly enclosed garden in Maryland with almost identical rectangular beds on either side of a central pathway. Lewis Beebe's account of Henry Routh Pratt's garden in 1800 ignores the adjacent landscape, which at Carter's Grove was vital to the total effect, but it does depict the variety and beauty that could be achieved in a symmetrical, balanced, and fenced garden. Beebe makes no apology for the garden's formality: "The Garden for beauty and elegance, exceeds any thing of the kind, that I ever saw," he declared. "The main alley, 13 feet wide, and 20 rods long, is upon each side graced with flowers of every kind and colours. The prospect captivates the eye, and affects the heart." He continues in a later letter with more detail:

61. *Mid-nineteenth-century watercolor of Carter's Grove and its terraces. Artist unknown.*

> An ally of 13 feet wide runs the length of the garden thro' the centre —. Two others of 10 feet wide equally distant run parallel with the main alley. These are intersected at right angles, by 4 other alleys of 8 feet wide—Another alley of 5 feet wide goes around the whole garden, leaving a border of 3 feet wide next to the pales. This lays the garden into 20 squares, each square has a border around it of 3 feet wide. The border of the main alley, is ornamented with flowers of every description. Likewise the border of every square, is decorated with pinks and a thousand other flowers, which it [is] impossible for me to describe. The remaining part of each square, within the border, is planted with beans, pease, cabbage, onions, Bettes, carrots, Parsnips, Lettuce, Radishes, Strawberries, cucumbers, Potatoes, and many other articles. Without [outside] the pales stand a row of trees upon three sides of the garden. These consist of Pears, Peach, Apple, cherry, & mulberry trees. Within the pales, on the out border, one planted, Quince, snowball, Laylock, and various other small trees, producing the most beautiful flowers. The beauty, taste, and elegance which attends it, is perfectly indescribable. . . . It is an enchanting prospect.[33]

Pratt's garden was roughly of the same size and proportions as the one at Carter's Grove, and all of his ornamentation would have worked in the latter—or at Kingsmill, for that matter, or in any plantation garden with large rectangular enclosures. The garden was a riot of color and scents. Its otherwise monotonous symmetry was relieved by shrubs and smaller trees along the fence, while the entire enclosure was embraced on three sides by larger fruit trees, the effect of which would have been to soften the contours of the perimeter and prevent the enclosure from looking so exposed and stark in its setting.[34]

A mid-nineteenth-century painting of Carter's Grove (figure 61) depicts even the terraces as likely sites for ornamental plantings, provided the latter were not tall enough to obscure the prospects of the garden and distant countryside from the house. In fact, excavations discovered two late-eighteenth-century planting holes for bushes or small trees on either side of the central walk. In England terraces frequently were planted with small trees. So the gardens of Carter's Grove facing the river front of the house could reasonably have been colorfully and decoratively planted.

The painting may suggest that the plantation had become well known as a graceful place of beauty in the nineteenth century, but it had already won a reputation as a pleasant house and park at least by the time Nathaniel Burwell owned it. In 1787 and 1788, when Burwell was living there with his new wife, a French traveler, Helene-Louise de Chastenay Maussion, visited and was impressed by what she thought was "one of the most elegant habitations in Virginia." Apparently, she had seen other beautiful plantations in Virginia, for she added: "It is really a beautiful house. I have tried to make a little sketch of it, which I here enclose for you to see how well-to-do people live over here."[35] Sadly, that sketch has not survived.

. . .

When in 1726 "King" Carter bequeathed the plantation to his daughter and son-in-law, Carter Burwell's father, he named it "Carter's Grove." In so doing, he was impelled by a sense of identification with his lands generally, to which he hoped his large family would be similarly attached. Unfortunately, Carter Burwell left no diary and scarcely any correspondence, so the early history of Carter's Grove is a blank from the point of view of what its master thought of it or hoped for it. For two other plantations, however, both belonging to Carter families, there is more of this type of personal evidence. Neither Sabine Hall nor Nomini Hall bears its owner's name, but the owners of both felt the type of identification with their estates, and the gardens on them, that "King" Carter apparently did. Also, for the gardens of both these plantations there is enough evidence to warrant a closer look.

Soon after his father died in 1732, Landon Carter (figure 62), a younger son of "King" Carter, built his house on the north side of the Rappahannock River, on land that his father had given to him. He was a well-read man with an extensive library, which included Philip Miller's ubiquitous *Gardener's Dictionary*, Richard Bradley's *Experimental Husbandman and Gardner* (1726), and Stephen Switzer's *Practical Husbandman*. His particular love was the classics, so it is not surprising that he named his own estate Sabine Hall, after Horace's villa outside Rome, Sabine Farm.[36]

There must have been more in this allusion than a merely dilettantish desire to display his knowledge of Horace. For the next fifty years Landon Carter took seriously the world of agri-

62. *Landon Carter. Oil painting, artist unknown, late eighteenth century.*

culture and plants, and his gardens reflected his self-conscious pose as a Virginian embodiment of Horace's *beatus ille*—the virtuous figure who has left the city and the "busie companie of men" to study the ways of agriculture in a rural retreat. The measure of his success may be borne out by William Byrd II's gift to him of Abraham Cowley's collected poems when Carter married in 1742. Cowley's poems and essays were readily identifiable in the late seventeenth and eighteenth centuries with retirement literature and an awakening to classical models for treasuring agriculture and rural living as symbols of the ideal life. Carter's copy of Cowley included the poem "Plantarum" (1661) and the essay "Of Agriculture." The essay concludes with a translation of Virgil's portrait of a husbandman, which Carter may in passing have been tempted to adopt as his recipe for happiness and fulfillment:

> Mean while, the prudent Husbandman
>   is found,
> In mutual duties striving with his ground,

And half the year he care of that does take,
That half the year grateful returns does make.
  Each fertil month does some new gifts
      present,
And with new work his industry content.
This, the young Lamb, that the soft Fleece
    doth yield,
This, loads with Hay, and that, with Corn
    the Field:
All sorts of Fruit crown the rich *Autumns* Pride:
And on a swelling Hill's warm stony side,
The powerful Princely Purple of the Vine,
Twice dy'd with the redoubled Sun,
    does Shine.[37]

Implicit in the Horatian pose of the *beatus ille* is the notion that in the countryside a man is purer because he is less pretentious and ready, even aspiring, to live in a humble dwelling. In this way he is more sensitive to the cycles of nature. Carter appears to recall his own early years on his land, before he built Sabine Hall, when in his diary for August 9, 1777, he writes of having "contentedly thought I ought to build my self [a house] and took an old brick building tore down in many places and . . . repaired it."[38] Byrd II, of course, knew Carter's mode of life at Sabine Hall, so that he likely saw his gift of Cowley's poems as especially apt.

It is important to note that although Landon Carter had a sustained classical allusion in mind as he named and lived at Sabine Hall, it was a literary allusion, not one that derived from actually having seen Italian Renaissance gardens. The supposed classical features of plantation gardens like his—the terraces, piazzas, groves, and statuary—could certainly have been borrowed from firsthand observation in Italy. But it is far more likely that they were transmitted to Virginia and the Chesapeake region through their appearance in English gardens in the late seventeenth and early eighteenth centuries. Thus, to remark, as one writer has done, that the classical element in the Chesapeake garden is further evidence that the latter was affected "only slightly by the English natural grounds movement" of the eighteenth century is to miss the point.[39] In terms

of influence, the classicism of the English garden was English, not Italian. Carter may have seen himself gardening in the classical tradition, but it was a tradition mediated by the English example.

Carter also regarded Sabine Hall as a refuge from unsatisfactory personal relationships and, for him, unhappy political realities. He tended to withdraw within himself and does not appear to have been as emotionally and intellectually stable as Horace, his model. Richard Bland put a good face on it in a poem describing Carter's first retirement from the "Pomp" and "Luxury" of the House of Burgesses in 1758:

  . . . bless'd with all that Heav'n below can give
  A mind contented and a taste to live,
  [He'd] . . . smile superior on their empty show,
  Their seeming pleasure and their real woe
  At Sabine Hall, retir'd from public praise,
  [He'd] . . . spend in learned ease . . .
      future days.[40]

Carter's diary, while illustrating his commitment to agriculture, is short on gardening detail. He did not tire of mentioning that he had sown various vegetables or that he maintained several orchards. On one occasion he even planted turnips in a flower bed. He blamed dry weather for that decision, but it sounds as if his once youthful enthusiasm for pleasure gardening may have faded by 1777. He remarks that in his old age he could not get around as well to tend to his flowers:

  As the weather was so dry last year as to kill nearly all my bulbous flower roots in my river front garden, I thought of turning that ground to advantage in the way of my cows to be fed in the winter, and had it all pricked off in lines about a foot asunder and sown with turnips. It proved a very fine crop, and answered its Proposed end much. . . . This makes me, as an old man, think it an excellent scheme, especially as my Colic will not let me, as I used to do, walk out and injoy the pleasure of flowers. I shall therefore order the ground to be new dunged, and intend to continue this turnip Project.[41]

63. Sabine Hall, Richmond County, Virginia. View of the house, gardens, and terraces.

His concern about his age also puts an interesting light on an earlier complaint, in February 1764, that his hip was "almost . . . disjointed by walking in my garden."[42] The cause is not difficult to imagine, given the steep slopes of the garden on the river side of his house.

The "river front garden" Carter mentioned consisted of six deep terraces that spanned the width of the house (see figure 63). These terraces still survive. He also mentioned his "bowling green," a fashionable element of English gardens by the mid-seventeenth century. While it provided recreational activity at Sabine Hall, the green also functioned as a convenient grass plat on which to walk. He may have been referring to it when he recalled on April 2, 1770, "I . . .

remember some time in my second wife's days a covering of snow that whitened the houses and grass plats in the month of June."[43] It is difficult to say where the bowling green was located; the most likely spot seems to have been the top terrace, where it would have been easily accessible and, as an ornamental grass plat or lawn, within view from inside the house. Carter kept it closely cut one way or another: "Talbot set to work yesterday to shave the bowling green," he wrote on April 25, 1772; "he seems to do it well, but he is very slow."[44] On another occasion, in March 1770, he used a less tidy but perhaps equally effective means of cropping it: "I had my Ewes first on my bowling green yesterday and then on the hill sides."[45] Presumably, the green was very dry; otherwise the ewes' hooves would have ruined it. He had trouble of this sort in April 1776, when a vindictive servant named Parker "ordered the boy who held the mare on the bowling green to carry her into the Garden like a simpleton or possibly a revengeful fellow. I beleive [*sic*] the latter with a design that the Colt should run about and trample all my beds."[46] Having reseeded the bowling green in November 1770, he covered it and "other grass in the garden" with flax to protect it from the cold and birds.[47]

Each of the terraces must have looked different from the others. Some commentators have suggested that the lowest were relegated to vegetables in order to conceal the kitchen gardening as much as possible; this is doubtful, since such gardens normally were kept close to the kitchens. Deep terraces like these at Sabine Hall could easily have accommodated fruit trees; if this were the case, the lower terraces would have been the place for them, since trees can interrupt the desirable cascade effect of "falling gardens."

The terraced garden at Mount Clare plantation, overlooking the Patapsco River about two miles from Baltimore, can shed some light on Sabine Hall's garden design. Mount Clare was laid out beginning in 1756.[48] A painting of the house by Charles Wilson Peale in 1775 features the terraces and adjacent gardens and shows a scheme resembling that of Sabine Hall. The five or six terraces probably had grass ramps, as at Sabine Hall today, instead of steps between them. On either side of the terraces were orchards and vegetable gardens, with pastures and a snake rail fence in the foreground. When Mary Ambler visited Mount Clare in October 1770, she was struck by the beautiful arrangement of the bowling green and terraces and by the planting on the latter. She took

> a great deal of Pleasure in looking at the Bowling Green & also at the Garden which is a very large Falling Garden[;] there is a Green House with a good many Orange & Lemon Trees just ready to bear besides which he is now buildg a Pinery where the Gardr expects to raise about an 100 Pine Apples a Year. . . . The House where this

Gentn & his Lady reside in the Sumer stands upon a very High Hill & has a fine View of Petapsico River[.] You Step out of the Door into the Bowlg Green from which the Garden Falls & when You stand on the Top of it there is such an Uniformity of Each side that the whole Plantn seems to be laid out like a Garden[;] there is also a Handsome Court Yard on the other Side of the House.[49]

As at Sabine Hall, there were splendid views over the river from the bowling green near the house and overlooking the terraces. No less a personage than John Adams saw Mount Clare's gardens in 1777 and felt the same way about the terraces and prospects: "it stands fronting looking down the river into the harbor; it is one mile from the water. There is a most beautiful walk from the house down to the water; there is a descent not far from the house; you have a fine garden, then you descend a few steps and have another fine garden; you go down a few more and have another." In the spring and summer, he mused, "this scene must be very pretty."[50]

• • •

Another Carter family garden for which more documentary evidence exists is Nomini Hall, owned by "Councilor" Robert Carter, a grandson of "King" Carter, who lived on the Palace Green in Williamsburg for about ten years before the Revolutionary War. Unlike Sabine Hall, nothing remains of either Nomini Hall or its gardens, but one can pick up more nearly their late-eighteenth-century character from Philip Fithian's journal from 1773 and 1774.[51] Fithian was hired by Robert Carter to tutor his children at Nomini Hall shortly after he and his family moved back to his plantation from Williamsburg. A romantic young man from New Jersey who was especially fond of Mrs. Carter, Fithian had a knack for descriptive prose and managed to record many details about Nomini Hall's buildings and gardens. Two general impressions emerge from his descriptions of the gardens and their setting above the Potomac River: the prospects and views from the gardens were at least as important to him as any other single feature of the plantation layout, and he associated the gardens chiefly with Carter's wife, Frances Anne Tasker Carter, with whom he frequently found himself walking in them.

He was particularly impressed by Frances Carter's authority and competence in gardening matters. He was aware of her sentiments about the superiority of country living, especially after ten years in the capital. She told him, he noted on December 16, 1773, that "to live in the Country, and take no pleasure at all in Groves, Fields, or Meadows; nor in Cattle, Horses, and domestic Poultry, would be a manner of life too tedious to endure." Later that month, a time of year when gardening projects live in the imagination and fancy, she told Fithian that she would not feel settled at Nomini Hall until her husband "made her a park and stock'd it." On the last day of the year, Fithian records a few pleasing moments in the garden as he almost hung on her every word:

> I took a walk in the Garden; When I had gone round two or three Platts Mrs Carter entered and walked towards me, I then immediately turn'd and met Her; I bowed—Remarked on the pleasantness of the Day—And began to ask her some questions upon a Row of small slips—To all which she made polite and full answers; As we walked along she would move the Ground at the Root of some plant; or prop up with small sticks the bended *scions*—We took two whole turns through all the several Walks, & had such conversation as the *Place* and *Objects* naturally excited . . . we walked out into the *Area* viewed some Plumb-Trees, when we saw Mr Carter and Miss Prissy returning—We then repaired to the Slope before the front-Door where they dismounted.

In another season, they "gathered two or three Cowslips in full-Bloom; and as many violets—The English Honey Suckle is all out in green and tender Leaves . . . Mrs Carter shewed me her Apricot-Grafts; Asparagus Beds &c." Here, then, was a prominent planter's wife casting herself, to use an eighteenth-century term, in the role of

"farmeress"—a lively and fashionable female pose in the English tradition of that century.[52]

In the spring of 1774, a few months after he arrived at Nomini Hall, Fithian recorded his feelings about the view of the house at the end of the long poplar avenue-entrance: it was "most romantic, [and] at the same time . . . truly elegant." The house's position struck him as felicitous, with its "exceedingly beautiful Prospect of the high craggy Banks of the River Nominy!" He described this prospect poetically:

> Some of those huge Hills are cover'd thick with *Cedar,* & Pine Shrubs; A vast quantity of which seems to be in almost every part of this Province, Others are naked, & when the Sun Shines look beautiful! At the Distance of about 5 Miles is the River Potowmack over which I can see the smoky Woods of Maryland; . . . Between my window and the Potowmack, is Nominy Church, it stands close on the Bank of the River Nominy, in a pleasant agreeable place.

Eight months later, the views still thrilled him. In a June letter to his future wife he celebrated "the charming Landskips, & long delightsome Prospects of our winding River which we have from the high Hills! . . . I should take these Walks & Arbours [at Nomini] to be a verdant flowery Elysium!"[53]

Rarely has anyone better evoked this sensitivity to picturesque scenery from that period in America. It demonstrates the importance to these people of situation, perspective, hilly landscape, and pictorial scenes in which the sun, haze, forests, a little church, shades of green, and meadows "composed" prospects. As Fithian observed, the gardens themselves were both natural (an "Elysium") and regular or formal, so that there was variety and contrast within the gardens as well as between them and the landscape.

Fithian promised on December 31 to "describe the great-House . . . the *Area, Poplar-Walk, Garden,* & *Pasture*: In the mean time I shall only say, they discover a delicate and Just Tast[e], and are the effect of great *Invention* & *Industry* & *Expence*."[54] Details about the gardens are not as extensive as one might wish, but he did describe some select features. He also was fairly precise about the orientation of the house.

To the north, about a quarter of a mile distant, there was a fork in the Nomini River, a tributary of the Potomac. Beyond that was Nomini Bay, and beyond that the great Potomac. In what appears to have been the style of Stratford Hall, four corner buildings, the schoolhouse, stable, coach house, and wash house or laundry stood about one hundred yards from the corners of the main house, making "a Square of which the Great-House is the Center." Fithian continues: "The Area of the Triangle made by the Wash-House, Stable, & School-House is perfectly levil, & designed for a bowling-Green, laid out in rectangular Walks which are paved with Brick, & covered over with burnt Oyster-Shells."[55] It would appear that the level grass area or bowling green extended the length of both the north and east fronts of the house—or along the two sides of the triangle. Fithian does not say what lay beyond the bowling green on the north front, but the area may have looked like the garden enclosure shown in the background of a painting of Mrs. Charles Carter of Cleve Plantation on the Rappahannock (figure 64). This painting, dating roughly from 1745–1749, shows the gardens fronting Cleve, with a substantial wall enclosing a flat, terraced, rectangular (or square) garden.

The main approach to Nomini Hall was from the east along an avenue bounded by "two Rows of tall, flourishing, beautiful, Poplars . . . these Rows are something wider than the House, & are about 300 yards Long, at the Easternmost end of which is the great Road leading through Westmorland to Richmond. These Rows of Poplars form an extremeely pleasant avenue." Fithian mentions one terrace, but it does not appear to have been near the bowling green: "From the front yard of the Great House, to the Wash-House is a curious *Terrace*, covered finely with Green turf, & about five foot high with a slope of eight feet, . . . before the Front-Doors is a broad flight of steps of the same Height, & slope of the *Terrace*." He adds that the terrace "is produced along the Front of the House, and ends by the Kitchen." The reference to the yard and kitchen,

64. *Mrs. Charles Carter of Cleve plantation. Oil portrait attributed to William Dering, ca. 1745–1749.*

and the location of the kitchen either on the west or the south side, indicates that the terrace must have crossed along the south front of the house, which, although not the main entrance front, was also elegant and decorative: "There is a beautiful Jutt, on the South side, eighteen feet long, & eight Feet deep from the wall which is supported by three tall pillars." Fithian thought the terrace "curious": rather than falling vertically, it sloped in the manner of the terraces that exist today behind Robert Carter's house in Williamsburg. This slope could be planted, of course, whereas a vertical drop could not. It "appears exceeding well," he wrote, "to persons coming to the front of the House."[56]

Fithian's distinctions of "*Area, Poplar-Walk, Garden* and *Pasture*" are also significant. By "Area" he meant the orchard, whereas by "Garden" he was thinking of the pleasure grounds. As for the pasture, it was obviously beyond the gardens, in some unknown direction. Some distance down the poplar avenue there were figs and persimmons and a large orchard, where

65. Nomini Hall, Westmoreland County, Virginia. Mid-nineteeth-century watercolor by E. Mound.

Fithian picked fruit on a walk one day. A mid-nineteenth-century watercolor sketch of Nomini Hall is no help whatever in clarifying the arrangement of the gardens (figure 65), but it does show the fields adjacent to the house.

One final point concerns Robert Carter's own attachment to his estate and how he felt about that attachment in relation to the garden. Fithian records that late one winter night, thinking in a meditative vein about his own grave, Carter observed that "no Stone, nor Inscription [ought] to be put over him—And that he would choose to be laid under a shady Tree where he might be undisturbed, & sleep in peace & obscurity—He told us, that with his own hands he planted, & is with great diligence raising a *Catalpa*-Tree at the Head of his Father who lies in his Garden."[57] Here again are overtones of the *beatus ille* who declines fame and monuments in favor of the

sanctuary of his garden's green shades. Carter feels he would be honoring himself by simply providing for his unnoticed grave within his own garden in the same manner that he honors his father in the garden with a catalpa tree as a monument or memorial. Carter's remark, even if he never fulfilled his wish, implies his desire to establish a form of family iconography whereby the garden takes on subtler meanings from its owner's emotional link with it. Indeed, throughout Fithian's journal the theme of the integrity, closeness, and beauty of the family is inseparably linked to descriptions of the house and its garden and landscape settings.

· · ·

Traveling with the Carter family in April 1774 to John Tayloe's mansion, Mount Airy, further down the Rappahannock, Fithian was overwhelmed by the beauty of the gardens there: "Here is an elegant Seat! . . . He [Tayloe] has . . . a large well formed, beautiful Garden, as fine in every Respect as any I have seen in *Virginia*. In it stand four large beautiful Marble Statues—From this House there is a good prospect of the River *Rapahannock*."[58] In December 1785, not a good month in which to see a garden, Robert Hunter offered this further testimony: "Mr. Taylor's [Tayloe's] at Mount Airy is one of the most elegant in Virginia—something in the style of Mr. Beverley's at Blandfield."[59] He must have thought Mount Airy recalled an English country seat because he went on to use such an image when he described Blandfield as "one of the handsomest and largest houses in America, and beautifully situated on the Rappahannock. It looks like an elegant nobleman's-seat in England."[60]

On the basis of eighteenth-century evidence and modern clues in the surviving garden, it appears that Mount Airy's was an exceptionally luxurious garden even among the grand plantations we have been discussing. It had in common with a few of the others some delightful prospects of surrounding countryside, but it also possessed some features that were not at all common: marble statuary; other forms of stonework such as urns (figure 66); an orangery; and elaborately carved terraces, sunken gardens, and banks. Fithian's notice of the four marble statues is particularly indicative of opulence; it is one of the few extant contemporary references to garden statuary in Virginia, much less to examples fashioned out of marble. Tayloe had set up other statuary in the garden at least eight years before Fithian saw the marble ones. One piece provided an amusing note in the *Virginia Gazette* in 1766: "September 5. On Saturday the 9th of last Month, Col. Tayloe's Gardener, being very sensible of the intense Heat, by Way of Experiment, put an Egg on the Freestone Pedestal of a Statue in the Garden, which, in four Hours, was sufficiently roasted, and he ate it."[61]

The gardens matched the house in their elegance and scale, as is evident from the layout that has survived (see figure 67),[62] from the sub-

66. *Urns in the Mount Airy gardens.*

stantial orangery (the ruins remain), and from a few notes kept about the gardeners and their maintenance of the garden features. Very likely, most of those features had been laid out and established well before Fithian saw them. Tayloe built the house in the 1750s and was in residence by 1758. But the earliest mention we have of the garden's features is in a "Minute Book" kept by John Tayloe III in 1805, which details the gardeners' work for that entire year. Not just a list of plants cultivated and when they blossomed and ripened, this little book—which as a genre must have been commonly kept by planters who from year to year needed to keep track of their elaborate agricultural and horticultural schemes—mentions terraces and "banks," a

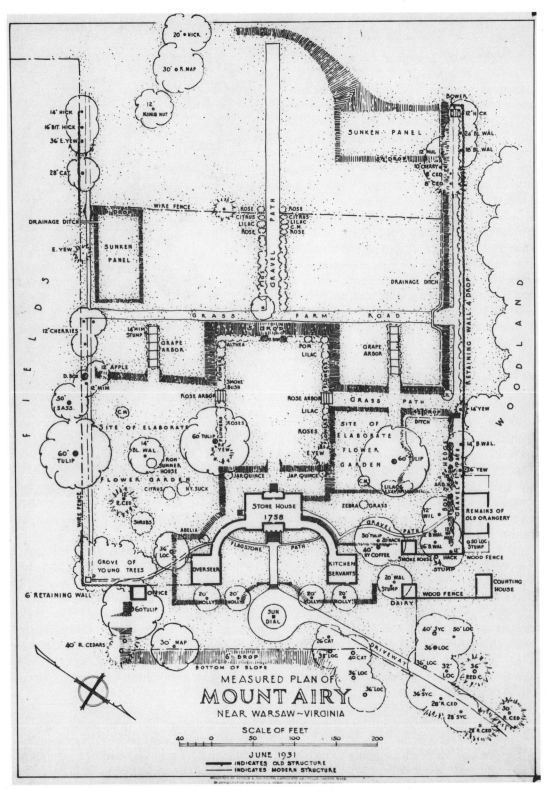

67. *Measured drawing of the Mount Airy gardens, Rich-mond County, Virginia, by Arthur Shurcliff (1931).*

bowling green edged with decorative borders and planted round with "a row of different kinds of shrubs," an elaborate greenhouse (built around 1790), a neat and ornamental courtyard laid out with grass, lawns, extensive gravel walks or paths, hothouses attached to the ends of the greenhouse, and a separate tree nursery. (The precision of the "Minute Book" regarding garden features brings to mind Jefferson's own garden book at Monticello, which is a remarkably full source.) Tayloe's list goes on: flower and shrub borders, a kitchen garden interlaced with gravel and grass paths and set out in squares, a deer park planted with cedars and locust trees, orchards, hot beds for melons, numerous flower plots, a serpentine walk that was shaded by carefully planted and tended trees, a grove of pine trees, trimmed hedges, a sunken garden with banks that needed regular "mowing," a garden cistern for collecting water that may also have had an ornamental function, a "fruitery" (probably for soft fruit like raspberries), an area at the "Bottom [end] of Garden" for plum and apricot trees, and an icehouse.[63] There are few colonial gardens, either town or plantation, about which such detail is known today, and it all delineates a complex, even extravagant landscape garden. What the "Minute Book" does not state is the location of these various garden features.

The "Minute Book" also mentions the numerous vegetables and fruit grown at Mount Airy. Manure was constantly applied; greenhouses, hothouses, and all plants were continually watered and "dressed"; lawns were regularly "picked," mowed, raked, and weeded; vegetable "squares" were punctually dug, manured, edged, and weeded; fruit trees were grafted; hedges were trimmed; the nursery was kept stocked with trees; grass and walks were frequently rolled; gravel paths were hoed and weeded and the grass cut; flower borders were "dressed" and hoed; and the trees were trimmed. The place must have been bustling with gardening activity.[64]

The man who built these magnificent gardens, John Tayloe I, left nothing in writing about his landscaping skills and interests. Nor did he keep a diary or journal that might have reflected this interest. And no one else, not even Shippen, is known to have paused long enough to describe the gardens at length. This is a pity, for such a description would have been of considerable importance for the garden history of America.

. . .

Overlooking the Potomac, not far from Nomini Hall and George Washington's Mount Vernon, George Mason built himself a plantation in the 1750s on the south bank of a little inlet known as Gunston Cove. The gardens that Mason laid out at Gunston Hall in the ensuing years embodied all the features of plantation gardens that have thus far been discussed (see the plan of the restored gardens, figure 68). The views of river, woodland, and fields were exquisite, and they were "improved" in a sense by the positioning of the house and the arrangement of garden features from which they could be enjoyed. Sloping away from the house and garden were adjacent fields or pastures for livestock, also planted artfully with groups of trees. These, as well as a carefully fenced deer park, were meant to be seen clearly from within a regularly shaped garden[65] on a level platform squarely facing and immediately next to the south front of the house. In other words, Mason deliberately opened up this garden, which was probably symmetrically planted, to adjacent grounds below that were managed to look as if nature there was allowed to have its own way.

Unlike Carter's Grove, however, no prominent wooden fence is known to have enclosed the main southern garden, so that formality and naturalness felt in closer proximity to one another and provided a more subtle interplay. Little is known of the planting around the garden that Mason used to naturalize the setting and smooth the transitions from the regular to the irregular, although there was a spacious walk at the southern end of the garden that sloped naturally and steeply east and west into the fields below.

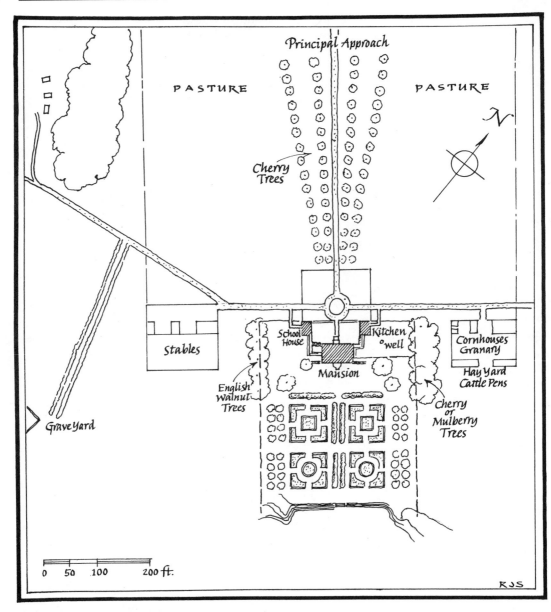

68. House lot and garden plan, Gunston Hall, Fairfax County, Virginia. Hypothetical reconstruction after the recollections of General George Mason, 1832 (after Fiske Kimball and Erling Pederson, 1949).

Mason was well served by his library in his garden designs at Gunston Hall. He had inherited a good selection of English and French gardening books from John Mercer, an avid gardener under whose guardianship he had grown up at Marlborough plantation, also on the Potomac and not far from Gunston Hall.[66] In light of the geometric, flat platform garden that Mason positioned centrally in front of his house, it is interesting that most of his gardening books had been published in the seventeeth century and reflected the dominant European baroque and autocratic taste then fashionable. These included John Gerard's *Herball* (1597), John Evelyn's *Acetaria, a Discourse of Sallets* (1699) and *Sylva, or a Discourse of Forest-Trees* (1664), John Woolridge's *The Art of Gardening* (1677), and de la Quintinie's *The Compleat Gard'ner* (1693). On the other hand, he also owned Stephen Switzer's pioneering *Nobleman, Gentleman, and Gardener's Recreation* (1718, 1742), which regarded the European fashion as outdated, un-English, and uneconomical. Switzer, it will be recalled, boldly advised English gardeners to integrate their gardens visually with surrounding scenery and turn landscaping to more agriculturally productive directions. The influence of that book, in addition to Richard Bradley's *General Treatise of Husbandry and Gardening* (1726) and *New Improvements of Planting and Gardening*, may be evident in Mason's later contrivance that the fields and pastures below, with their livestock and deer, could be seen from the platform garden and the terrace at its southernmost end. And there were, too, the sloping paths that led picturesquely down from the back of the terrace to the pastures below, with their orchards to the southeast.[67]

Mason also possessed in *Britannia illustrata* a fine set of views by John Kip and Leonard Knyff of seventeenth-century English estates, whereby he could picture clearly the splendor of the grand manner. This he balanced with Jacques Rigaud's fine views of Stowe gardens (1739), an important early-eighteenth-century garden that elegantly demonstrated the new English principles of design.

The dates of Mason's major landscaping schemes are not known exactly, although the late 1750s and early 1760s sound plausible. Nor is there much more than the details already mentioned on which to base the descriptions that follow. But it would appear from Mason's library that at Gunston Hall he tried to implement two gardening traditions.[68] Most of what is known about the appearance of the Gunston Hall gardens is found in a description by Mason's son, John, in 1834. Although written rather late, this account is one of the more complete surviving descriptions of an eighteenth-century Virginia garden. It is long, but worth citing in its entirety for the feeling as well as design of the gardens it sketches:

> Gunston Hall is situated on a height on the right bank of the Potomac river within a short walk of the shores, and commanding a full view of it, about five miles above the mouth of that branch of it on the same side called the Occoquan. When I can first remember it, it was in a state of high improvement and carefully kept. The south front looked to the river; from an elevated little portico on this front you descended directly into an extensive garden, touching the house on one side and reduced from the natural irregularity of the hill top to a perfect level platform, the southern extremity of which was bounded by a spacious walk running eastwardly and westwardly, from which there was by the natural and sudden declivity of the hill a rapid descent to the plain considerably below it. On this plain adjoining the margin of the hill, opposite to and in full view from the garden, was a deer park, studded with trees, kept well fenced and stocked with native deer domesticated.[69]

The prospect of the adjacent fields and river also impressed William Loughton Smith, a South Carolinian who visited Gunston Hall in 1790 after a night at Mount Vernon. In his journal Smith approved of the "ancient brick building, with a neat garden, at the end of which is a high natural terrace which commands the Potomac."[70] Perhaps Smith knew that a few of the trees with which the deer park was studded and which he could see from the terrace had provided Washington with cuttings and seedlings. In his diary for March 29, 1764, Washington refers to having grafted fruit trees and acquired cuttings from Gunston Hall.[71]

Turning his attention to the north front of the house, John Mason continues:

> On the north front by which was the principal approach, was an extensive lawn kept closely pastured, through the midst of which led a spacious avenue, girded by long double ranges of that hardy and stately cherry tree, the common black heart, raised from the stone, and so the more fair and uniform in their growth, commencing at about two hundred feet from the house and extending thence for about twelve hundred feet; the carriage way being in the centre and the footways on either side, between the two rows, forming each double range of trees, and under their shade.

This main avenue-approach, flanked by double rows of cherry trees twelve hundred feet long, was (on a smaller scale) reminiscent of the noble avenues of European gardens in the seventeenth century and of the copper engravings of English estates to which Mason could refer in his copy of *Brittania illustrata*. Moreover, his clever method of planting it suggests he greatly valued its role in the landscape scheme. His son remembered the treatment precisely:

> But what was remarkable and most imposing in this avenue was that the four rows of trees . . . [were] so alligned as to counteract that deception in our vision which, in looking down long parallel lines makes them seem to approach as they recede; advantage was taken of the circumstance and another very pleasant delusion was effected.[72]

The "delusion" his son described was achieved by planting the rows of trees so that they diverged or radiated slightly away from the house: "and so carefully and accurately had they been planted, and trained and dressed in accordance each with the others, as they progressed in their growth, that from the point . . . as taken for the common centre [in front of the house], and when they had got to a great size, only the first four trees were visible." John Mason tells of the delight his father would take in leading unsuspecting visitors to that "common centre" and asking them how many trees they saw. When they replied, "Four," he would ask them to take a few steps to the side, whereupon they could see, "as if by magic, four long, and apparently close walls of wood made up of the bodies of the trees." This element of surprise was part of the wit of Mason's landscape, where half the skill was to conceal and not leave all open to view at once. Mason surely understood this principle of early-eighteenth-century English garden design if he read the books of gardening and literature on his shelves.

As for the adjacent landscape, the young Mason mentions that "adjoining the enclosed grounds on which stood the mansion . . . on the eastern side was an extensive pasture for stock of all kinds running down to the river, through which led the road to the Landing."[73] The description has a soft rural sound, as though the area had the look of the ferme ornée, an idea that Switzer had promoted.

· · ·

Perhaps the most remarkable garden known to have been planted, and perhaps designed, by a woman in eighteenth-century Virginia was Lady Jean Skipwith's at Prestwould plantation in Mecklenburg County, on a high knoll overlooking the Dan and Staunton rivers just half a mile west of where they flow into the Roanoke. Considerable manuscript material in Lady Skipwith's own hand has survived to show her for over twenty years to have been a great lover of fruit and flowers and a highly systematic recorder of what she grew in her gardens (as well as of when certain plants bloomed) and what she wished to

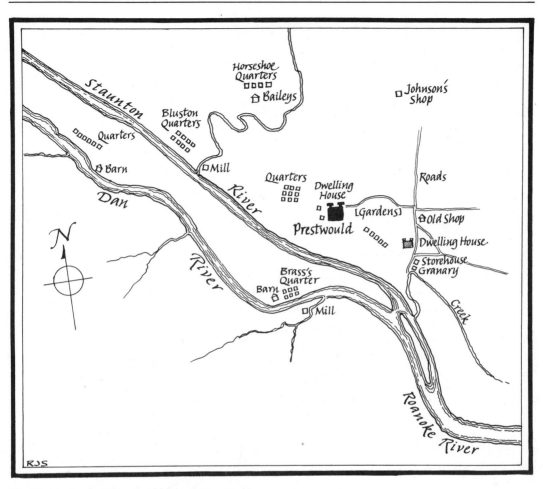

69. *Neighborhood of Prestwould plantation, Mecklenburg County, Virginia, 1798 (after John Hill).*

introduce. Though born in Virginia, she, like Byrd II, lived in Britain for many years (from age twelve to about thirty-eight), where she appears to have been equally interested in gardening. Her relatively modest circumstances there, however, did not allow her to indulge in the pastime as freely as she did after she moved back to Virginia and married Sir Peyton Skipwith, seventh baronet, in 1788. Her manuscripts suggest that her most active period of gardening began at her childhood home of Elm Hill (twenty-five miles from Prestwould), where she and her husband first lived, then at the couple's elegant new home

at Prestwould after 1797.[74] Following her husband's death in 1805, she does not appear to have gardened so intensely, but she continued at Prestwould for another twenty-one years, until her death in 1826.

Apart from Lady Skipwith's copious notes on her plants, the evidence of what Prestwould looked like in the late eighteenth and early nineteenth centuries is lamentably limited to two items, one graphic and one verbal. A plan of the house and surrounding terrain drawn in 1798 by John Hill (figure 69) shows the proximity of the house to the two rivers well below it and certain quarters and outbuildings, but nothing at all of the gardens. Then there is a brief but appreciative description of the house and grounds in a letter from Sir Peyton's friend Wade Hampton to Aaron Burr on October 25, 1800:

> This edifice and its appendages stand on a very commanding h[e]ight, half a mile from the Roanoke which is formed opposite the door by a junction of the Dan and the Staunton. . . . The ground to the river is sloping, wavy and highly improved to a great extent up and down, which affords a fine view of the rivers and of an Island between the two latter of upwards of 1,000 acres in which that of cultivation—upon the whole—except New York or up the North River I have never seen anything so handsome.[75]

Among the Skipwith Papers at the College of William and Mary are two garden plans (figure 70), drawn presumably by Lady Skipwith, showing two ornamental flower beds. These may have been sketches of ideas for the Prestwould gardens that she never executed.

Even though Hill drew his plan only a year or two after the Skipwiths moved to Prestwould, it is surprising that he did not indicate where the gardens were located in relation to the house. Nevertheless, his drawing presents the enviable position of the house, so close to two rivers, and it shows clearly the so-called island between the rivers that Hampton mentioned as being so beautifully cultivated. Hampton's description is in fact more helpful because it conveys something of the ambience of the place: the house's high position and the ground sloping down from it, "wavy and highly improved," to the junction of the rivers. The word "improved" in this context must mean landscaped in a deliberately naturalized (or "wavy") manner, probably with bushes, trees, and paths. In this, Prestwould appears to have been unique: although most of the plantation gardens discussed in this chapter are similarly positioned well above rivers, this is the only known example of a carefully designed landscape between house and river. Clearly it suggests that the Skipwiths especially

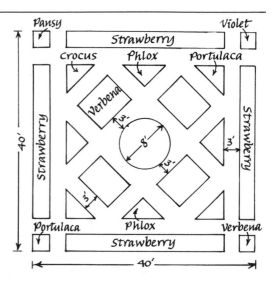

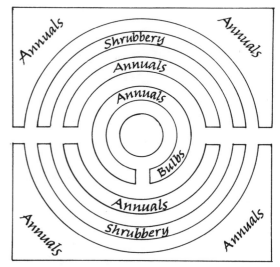

70. *Garden plans of Prestwould plantation, ca. 1790 (after plans attributed to Lady Jean Skipwith).*

valued the visual and physical relationship between their demesne and the rivers.

Apart from the aesthetic value of improving that sloping ground, there was the practical need of getting down to the rivers conveniently for access to the island between them. Hampton described this island as an area of one thousand acres given over to general cultivation. But it was in this area, undoubtedly due south of the house and adjacent to the juncture of the two rivers, that Lady Skipwith introduced her own version of an island paradise: a garden of orchards and native wildflowers that could be seen from the house above. Among her manuscript notes, she several times refers to her "Island" and what she had either discovered or planted there. On a separate "Island map list" of wildflowers, for example, she included:

> Dog's Tooth Violet. What we call Island Martagon. . . . * Solomon's Seal (our Jacobs Ladder). Two sorts, one with the red, the other purple berries and I believe a third sort in the point of the island. * . . . Campanula pyramidalis. What we here call Bear grass * Claytonia, the little narrow-leafed black-rooted flower from the foot of the garden * Ixia Bermudiana, perhaps the blackberry lily in the garden * Bastard Lychnis (see Phlox). What we here call Woods Pink. . . .[76]

Lady Skipwith's appreciation and enhancement of the island as a natural "cabinet of curiosities," as it were—an indigenous setting for the exhibition of native species—bespeaks a complex of values that, though it might not have occurred to her, could be traced back to Renaissance Italy but that nonetheless was part of her heritage as a gardener: the nurture of a careful balance of art and nature; the setting aside of an area some distance from the house and its immediate gardens that could function as a type of vigna containing native plants and fruits in a farm-like setting and that was regarded as part of the landscape garden; and the appropriation of the area as a type of botanical garden where experimentation with fruit culture could be carried on. There is no explicit evidence that Lady Skipwith recognized any classical precedents for her island or that she idealized the area with a classical perspective. But volumes in her extensive library, such as a copy of the *Spectator* that she brought with her from Scotland, could have put her in mind of such associations; and through her stepdaughter and niece, Lelia, who married St. George Tucker, she had access to a number of classical works in Tucker's library in Williamsburg. In any case, the assimilation of agricultural appendages within landscape gardens both practically and symbolically—the congruence of garden and farm—which did have classical sources, had become by then part of many educated men's and women's cast of thought. At the very least, in her attitude toward the island Lady Skipwith luxuriated in a sense of the unspoiled wildness of the American landscape. This last theme, as we shall see, is one that emerges particularly strongly in Jefferson's gardening.

Even more suggestive than wildflowers of the evocative fecundity of the post-Revolutionary American landscape was the fruit that obviously fascinated Lady Skipwith. Her notes elaborately document her propagation of fruit, chiefly (but not exclusively) on the island. In the early stages of landscaping at Prestwould, even while she and her husband were still living at Elm Hill, she appears to have been collecting from friends and nurseries a variety of specimens of pear, peach, apple, cherry, nectarine, plum, and quince. She also kept a record of where she had obtained the specimens. Her earliest notes, for example, followed the heading, "List of grafted fruit Trees of different kinds grafted, or, planted, at Prestwould, 16th March 1792." Here is a sample:

1. Large . . . Dukes Cherry from Princes Garden [nurseries]
2. Black Heart Cherrys from Do.
3. Carnation Cherrys, Do.
4. White Heart Cherry, Do.
5. Cluster Cherry . . . from Mr. Eppes
6. Quinces from Do.
7. Green Gage plumbs from St. G: Tucker
8. Cloptons hangfast from Benedict Crump
9. Esopins Spitzenburg [sic]—a very large red apple—reckoned the finest eating apple in America next to the Newton pippin. St. G. T.
10. Doctor Apple—a fine eating apple. S.G.T.
11. A very fine white Clinston peach. S.G.T.

Another list is labeled "Peach Stones burried [sic] at Prestwould Octo. 1791" but includes sundry other fruit as well. Later, in 1805, the gardener—probably Samuel Dedmans, who was mentioned on April 24, 1808, as having been paid "Twenty two dollars . . . for services in building a Garden"—wrote a "Memo of Pear Trees in Sir Peyton Skipwith's Island" that included, among other types, "a large rough looking pear, but when ripe the finest in the Orchard— . . . Lady Skipwith's favourite." The memo later adds that Lady Skipwith "will find a name for these pears." A "Memo: of the Season when the different fruits at this place are ripe, or fit to gather," dated "Prestwould 1807," includes strawberries, raspberries, and red and black currants in addition to the other varieties already mentioned.[77]

Plants for her island represented only one category of Lady Skipwith's notes on plants; the others she designated included: "My House plants"; "Shrubs to be got when I can"; "Wild flowers in the garden" (figure 71); "Flowering shrubs"; and a general list under the heading "Plants." A brief selection from that general list will illustrate her analytical and inquisitive approach to gardening:

> Purple cupped statice or thrift, dried—it retains its colour which renders it ornamental for a Mantel-piece in Winter—a biennial yet often increased by parting its roots, but more advantageously from seeds * Candytuft * Anemone * Cortusa—or Bear's Ear Sanicle—can be raised from seed or roots—the purple is the finest * . . . Fraxinella (see Dictamnus M.) raised from seed, sown soon after they are ripe, very ornamental with little trouble—valuable * . . . American cowslip (see Miller) * . . . Medeola the Lilly or Little Martagon—perhaps what we got by the Branch at Elm Hill with the whorled leaves. . . .

There are also sundry pages of transcriptions taken from Lady Skipwith's copy of Miller's *Gardener's Dictionary*, mostly the details of propagation of plants. Not infrequently, she failed to find a native plant listed in Miller, whereupon she would indicate as much in her notes and name the plant herself. It is clear from these

71. *Manuscript page of notes headed "Wild Flowers in the garden," by Lady Jean Skipwith.*

notes, incidentally, that while she may have been exceedingly methodical and intelligent in her collection and study of plants, her reading about them, if her library inventory is a reliable guide, was limited mainly to Miller.[78]

Lady Skipwith's notes make her the best-known woman gardener in eighteenth- and early-nineteenth-century America, and her personal library reveals her as one of the best read; but there can be no doubt that numerous other women in this period took a scientific and designing interest, as well as a culinary one, in their gardens. Frances Carter at Nomini Hall is a good example, as is Lelia Skipwith Tucker. If there is only a handful for whom we have documented hints of such interests and skills, there must nonetheless have been many more whose presence in the garden was felt palpably in a creative and empirical vein.

. . .

Isolated pieces of gardening information and description have survived for many colonial Virginia plantations, but these details are too fragmentary to allow informed conclusions about the appearance and styles of the gardens. Scotchtown, Pleasant Hill, Chantilly, Marlborough, Corotoman, Maycox, Belvidere, Spring Garden, Rosewell, Shirley, Tuckahoe, Matoax, and several others apparently were the scenes of ambitious landscape gardening in the second half of the century. It is a great pity that these gardens, vanished now so long, do not live even in description except for the occasional and suggestive glimpses revealed in this or that letter, journal, travel account, and memorandum book.

Still, from the evidence at hand, certain recurring features in the large plantation gardens do emerge. Several of these are descended in one form or another from English landscaping, although several of them are modified by the American temper, as well as by the Virginia climate and the much greater sense of space present in the native landscape.

Except at places like Mount Airy, Mount Vernon, Monticello, and perhaps Blandfield in the last two decades or so of the century, planters who could afford to go in for ambitious landscape schemes generally did not abandon the central motif of a large rectangular, rigidly fenced, and symmetrically planted enclosure lined up axially with the house. From Bacon's Castle to Carter's Grove, that was the pattern. Although the interior spaces of such enclosures were also laid out in a rigidly geometrical style, the planters apparently did not find this utilitarian and convenient arrangement, in which vegetables and herbs were most commonly grown, incompatible with their landscaping efforts to achieve variety and even a touch of the romantic around their houses.

This reluctance to part with the dominant symmetrically aligned rectangular enclosure was one legacy of what might be termed the colonial paradigm of the wilderness and the habitual need to keep the immanence of wild and uncharted nature clearly distinguished or away from the improved grounds near the main house. In the colonial South there was little of the abandonment to nature not infrequently involved in the elimination of such formal separations between house and landscape in English landscape gardens. That is why a landscape garden like the one at Carter's Grove may appear today somewhat dull and conservative, or chiefly utilitarian. That huge rectangular garden was wonderfully sited, but its prosaic geometry somewhat impedes the modern taste for imaginative flight.

In other respects the efforts of Virginia planters to achieve variety and a measure of the romantic had much of the English picturesque about them. This was manifested in the artful orientation of houses to command the best possible prospects of surrounding countryside; terraces that could turn awkward slopes into commanding and attractive vantage points; the carving of banks, hollows, and sunken gardens to lend visual interest to scenes and help frame perspectives; deliberate contrasts between the regular and irregular; the presence of bowling greens (although it is doubtful that they were widely used for bowls, the grass generally not being fine or thick enough); and a taste for flower gardening, in spite of what several travelers toward the end of the century said was its undeveloped state. There were also hints of the *jardin anglais* in the deployment of winding paths through thick verdure down to rivers and up hillsides. Even so, notwithstanding the Reverend Andrew Burnaby's declamations, Virginia in the eighteenth century never saw the kind of extravagance in pleasure gardening that was displayed in England. There was not the money for it, but neither was there the inclination. It seemed out of character with the landscape to introduce all sorts of rich embellishments.

Coloring all of this landscaping was the fact that planters saw themselves enjoying it as one of the principal pleasures of country life. This is a more prevalent theme in the second half of the century, although Custis embodied it earlier in Williamsburg: a type of self-conscious posing as a Virginian "Cincinnatus," a "farmeress," a benevolent and retired figure in the country landscape. In the eighteenth century this attitude surfaces only occasionally in a hint or phrase from a diary, description, or letter. We have to wait for Jefferson and Washington for it to be given a more explicit statement.

England offered plenty of precedents for this style of emblematic or associative gardening in the eighteenth century—indeed, it represented one of the strong themes in the new English gardening. If a new dimension was added in Virginia, it was that the planter saw himself gardening against a wider and more limitless background, one that encouraged him to feel more like a discoverer, an image maker in realms where such art had never before existed. There was also the feeling that the landscaper's medium was nature—nature that was truly natural and replete with uniquely grand American possibilities. In the English landscape, one's partner in landscaping ventures, the "genius of the place," reigned over acreage that was relatively well known, cultivated, and improved. The "genius" of the American landscape waited for a partnership that would be more ambitious.[79]

The most distinctive theme characterizing the plantations along Tidewater rivers is that they were deliberately, even artistically, poised high enough above the rivers to command prospects of them and the surrounding countryside. Contemporary commentators and travelers frequently alluded to these prospects in the context of gardens by way of suggesting or implying that the former enhanced the latter. The English in the eighteenth century found much to praise in prospects and views, so the taste for them as expressed in Virginia plantations was not in itself new. What was different was the scale of it all and the majesty of wide rivers flowing through vast territories. It was the seemingly endless space that was striking and added aspects of the sublime to what otherwise would have remained essentially picturesque.

Aesthetically, the appeal of these views was similar to that of the village of Yorktown throughout the eighteenth century. Not much is known of Yorktown's gardens, but its picturesque position on a bluff overlooking the York River did not go unremarked by appreciative travelers, even early in the century, in language reminiscent of English landscape gardening accounts from that period.[80] Just as Yorktown's position was in this way superior to Williamsburg's, which offered no elevation relative to any natural feature, the elevated "situation" of Carter's Grove, Gunston Hall, and Stratford Hall, to name just a few, was superior to Westover's or Maycox's essentially flat terrain next to and on the same level as the James River. This was a large and valued advantage, and it played its part in ideas about landscaping possibilities. Moreover, if parts of gardens were laid out on a slope, they could be terraced most attractively, successive terraces providing their own small and distinctive garden spaces with distant views.

Another theme that emerges is that the major plantation gardens were transitional. For practical as well as ornamental reasons they continued, in their enclosed areas near the house, seventeenth- and early-eighteenth-century European traditions of symmetry and balance, with the adjacent gardens lined up axially with the house. But during the later half of the century many also increasingly demonstrated their owners' inclinations to comprehend within their demesnes landscape gardens where the total area around the house, including middle and distant prospects as well as immediate garden areas, contributed toward a conscious design. Pictorial effects, the contrast between formality and landscape freedom, variety of elevation, perspective, the appearance of decorative stonework and walls, and diverse planting successfully varied the scene.

As with Williamburg gardens, most of what is

known concerning these so-called transitional gardens has to do with plants—plants that were cultivated and raised in nurseries on the plantations—chiefly because they generated data that had to be recorded if it was not to be forgotten. Yet the excitement of experimentation and discovery concerning plants that motivated the first half of the century does not seem to have continued in either Williamsburg or the plantations. Jefferson and Washington were exceptions because they were not only landscape garden designers but also scientific farmers, husbandmen, and horticulturists. Generally, planters were interested in plants as either ornaments for their gardens or as produce for their tables and the markets that existed in nearby towns. For decades before and after the Revolution, for example, Kingsmill and Carter's Grove profitably supplied Williamsburg with vegetables and fruit.

Whether an interest in botanical gardens continued, we cannot say from the evidence. There was then enough variety of plants to satisfy planters' needs and tastes. Scientific curiosity had declined. The spirit of plant exchanges that characterized a Custis, Byrd, Ludwell, or Beverley had given way somewhat to the spirit of the "improver," that is, the landscaper intent on perpetuating his image of himself as successful and in control by carving out of his grounds emblems of pleasure and pride. In this sense, there is more of a Spotswood than a Custis in the landscaping approach of a John Tayloe or a Nathaniel Burwell.

In a personal vein, however, these plantation gardens could evoke a lively family pride and encourage a family's identification with its landscape. A commentator like Fithian at Nomini Hall or Shippen at Westover could be quick to detect and respond to these personal and emotional overtones. Robert Carter thinking of memorializing his father with a tree, Frances Carter guiding Fithian through the gardens, and Landon Carter seeking a refuge at Sabine Hall all hint at such personal colorings of their landscapes. Again, both Washington and Jefferson realized this sense of place even more, the former styling himself as a Virginian Cincinnatus. So far as it is possible today to draw conclusions from the surviving evidence, they took the principles of landscape gardening much farther, grasped the distinguishing features of the American landscape gardening tradition, and thereby helped bring in a new era of taste and practice in the art.

6

Landscape Gardening at Mount Vernon and Monticello

Thomas Jefferson wrote to George Washington on April 25, 1794, in a contented tone. He had just resigned as secretary of state and retired to his plantation at Monticello: "The difference of my present & past situation is such as to leave me nothing to regret, but that my retirement has been postponed four years too long. The principles on which I calculate the value of life, are entirely in favor of my present course. I return to farming with an ardor which I scarcely knew in my youth."[1] Although Washington had resisted Jefferson's resignation, he himself during his presidency felt the same profound desire to return to his plantation permanently and get on with his farming and gardening. Each man's intense identification with his home and landscape is, on the face of it, a remarkable historical coincidence: at roughly the same time, these two leaders of a new nation created in Virginia two of the most famous landscape gardens in America.

No other eighteenth-century or early nineteenth-century American gardens are so well documented. This happy circumstance may be explained by the stature of the two men. Their letters and papers were carefully preserved by family, friends, and acquaintances; moreover, many curious travelers came to visit their plantations, a few of whom recorded or drew or painted what they saw. Jefferson himself sketched all manner of plans for the Monticello gardens. Both men, from youth, also had an abiding love of agriculture and plants and were fortunate to have inherited at young ages gloriously situated plantations. Jefferson wrote to Charles Wilson Peale on August 20, 1811: "I have often thought that if heaven had given me choice of my position and calling, it should have been on a rich spot of earth, well watered, and near a good market for the productions of the garden. No occupation is so delightful to me as the culture of the earth."[2] The opportunities were there, and both men started their landscaping early—Washington when he was about twenty-eight and Jefferson around age twenty-five.

Most important about Mount Vernon and Monticello, however, is that they were the two most successful and comprehensive landscape gardens in Virginia. Both Washington and Jefferson set out to create landscape gardens that would use extensive acreage as part of a large, well-considered artistic plan. These acres were not, as in the case of most of the plantations already discussed, merely to be enjoyed as elements of vistas or prospects from the main house and garden. They were arranged or "improved" so as to be walked through. Washington and Jefferson acknowledged, either directly or by implication, that much of their inspiration was European, mainly English. Julian Niemcewicz, a Polish visitor to Mount Vernon in 1798, observed, "The Gl. [General] has never left America. After seeing his house and his gardens one would say that he had seen the most beautiful examples in England of this style."[3] The two Virginians had the additional advantage of being able to look back on the gardening of their colony, in Williamsburg and on the plantations, and respond accordingly; and both felt that the landscape of the new nation possessed heightened meaning for them as they proceeded to turn their acres into landscape gardens. Ahead in

the nineteenth century was to come the era of the professional landscaper; Washington and Jefferson were the two last great eighteenth-century amateur practitioners of the art.

. . .

Washington's considerable agricultural interests, farming talents, and horticultural competence are better known than his skills as a garden designer, notwithstanding the beautifully restored Mount Vernon gardens (figure 72), which bear witness to these skills. It so happened that when in his journals, diaries, and letters Washington wrote about Mount Vernon, it was chiefly the farming that preoccupied him, and for good reason: between 1759, when he moved into the house with his wife, and his death in 1799 he was compelled to be away from home for fully half the time and needed to run the plantation

72. *Aerial view of the restored gardens at Mount Vernon.*

through correspondence. He also kept notes in his diary to remind himself of practical plantation matters that had been resolved or needed attention. The gardens could more easily wait for his concentrated attention until after he "retired" to his home after the Revolution; the farms could not.

The great exception to this pattern was his interest in plants. From an early age he showed a love for them; and even before settling in to design his landscape garden, he wrote to fellow gardeners in the colonies and other countries asking for various specimens of trees, shrubs, flowers, and vegetables.[4] When he obtained them, or even when he did not, he frequently recorded the fact in his diary.

Garden design, however, is not a subject about which Washington expressed himself much at all in his diary or in his correspondence, except when he wrote to his overseer, Anthony Whiting, instructing him to see to various tasks in the garden. At such times he occasionally slipped in an observation or two on the visual effects he intended. Although his writings misleadingly suggest a lack of interest in the aesthetics of landscaping, his frequent allusions in the 1780s and 1790s to the different areas of his gardens—allusions mostly in the context of plants that he had earmarked for certain areas—leave no doubt that he considered carefully and deeply the styles and arrangements he desired.

The restoration of the Mount Vernon gardens has been soundly based on these references in Washington's papers, as well as on contemporary graphic evidence and descriptions. Washington may not have been as articulate as Jefferson about his gardening ideas or have traveled through England, as Jefferson did, with a copy of Thomas Whately's *Observations on Modern Gardening* (1770) in hand, evaluating the designs of gardens, but the available facts give us a firm foundation for estimating his approach to this "little amusement," as he called the art of gardening.[5]

Washington's longest and least interrupted period of residence at Mount Vernon began in

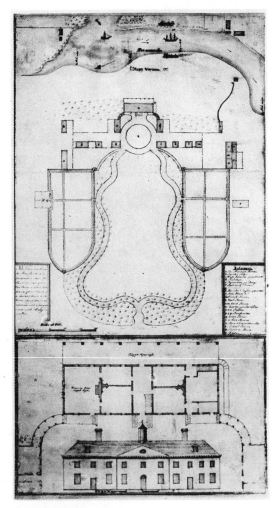

73. *Plan of the Mount Vernon gardens by Samuel Vaughan (1787).*

1783 and lasted until he was called away to the presidency of the new nation in 1789. Most of his initial garden and landscape layout dates from this period, although before the Revolution he had established certain features that essentially never changed. As early as 1783, for example, Baron Ludwig Von Closen saw the gardens in a developed and cultivated state: "There is an immense, extremely well-cultivated garden behind the right wing [as you look at the west front of the house], containing the choicest fruits in

74. *"View to the North from the Lawn at Mount Vernon."*
Watercolor by Benjamin Latrobe (1796).

the country."[6] Von Closen mentioned no other garden areas, however. A 1787 plan of the gardens by Washington's English friend and admirer Samuel Vaughan (figure 73) shows how much Washington had done in the following three or four years. Not only did the house enjoy glorious views of the Potomac River to the east—as seen in Benjamin Latrobe's paintings in 1796 (figures 74 and 75) and a view by Alexander Robertson and Francis Jukes of the east lawn and front dating from 1800 (figure 76)—but the gardens were full of curving lines (see the modern plan of the gardens, figure 77[7]): soft contours, a pear-shaped bowling green, shady walks, serpentine paths, an elegantly disposed greenhouse, flower and kitchen gardens enclosed by curving brick walls topped with wooden palings, thickly planted "wildernesses" and groves, two artificial mounds, an attractive circular courtyard (see figures 78 and 79), and even a curving ha-ha. Together, these features presented a bold statement of naturalized gardening. The only apparent concessions to traditional formality or regularity were the square or rectangular beds within the Upper Garden and Lower Garden on either side of the bowling green.

Vaughan gave his plan to Washington as a present. The general was not totally pleased. In his letter of thanks, Washington quickly pointed out that the plan described "with accuracy the houses, walks and shrubberies etc. except in the front of the Lawn, west of the Ct. yard. There the plan differs from the original; in the former you have closed the prospect with trees along the walk to the gate; whereas in the latter the trees terminate with the two mounds of earth on each side of which grow Weeping Willows leaving an open and full view of the distant woods."[8] He said he mentioned this only because the plan was otherwise remarkably accurate; but in fact, Vaughan's mistake was a serious one, and Washington had to put the record straight on a crucial element of his landscape design. According to Vaughan's plan, the pear-shaped bowling green was completely cut off visually from any view of the woods and fields to the west. In his enthusiasm for putting in the trees of the "wilderness," as Washington called it, around the bowling green, Vaughan had encroached on the western gate and thus sealed off the area. In this way he obscured a feature that the whole scheme of the "wilderness" and bowling green depended upon for its ultimate effect: the means by which the area was opened up to western prospects. It is surprising that a plantation garden in Virginia sitting high up on a hill overlooking such spectacular scenery should be so extensively screened from the views by its own trees. Compared with Mount Vernon, most other known plantation gardens were more exposed. Washington clearly succeeded in creating a feeling of concealment and privacy in a natural way with groves cut through with twisting paths. But the effect was heightened by the surprise of coming out of the shade to the opening at the gate and gazing out on the scenery. From the house itself and the bowling green the opening was like the lens of a camera letting in a variety of images from the distance.[9]

Numbers of other travelers in the 1780s and 1790s described the gardens, notably Benjamin Latrobe, who also sketched the view of the river from the house. He wrote in his journal in 1796:

The ground on the West front of the house is laid out in a level lawn bounded on each side with a wide but extremely formal serpentine

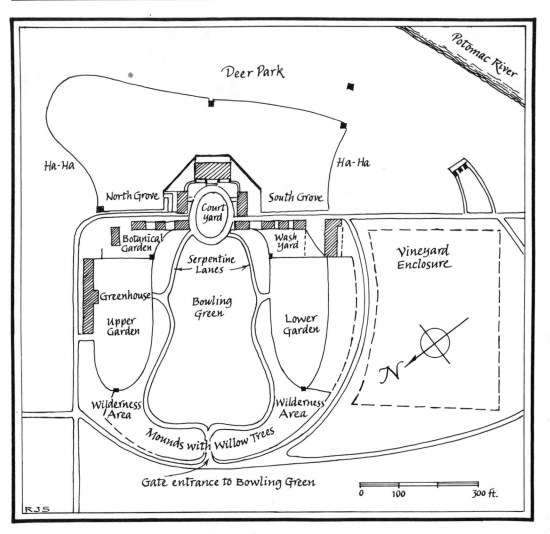

Deer Park

Potomac River

Ha-Ha

Ha-Ha

North Grove

South Grove

Court Yard

Botanical Garden

Wash Yard

Vineyard Enclosure

Serpentine Lanes

Greenhouse

Bowling Green

Upper Garden

Lower Garden

N

Wilderness Area

Wilderness Area

Mounds with Willow Trees

Gate entrance to Bowling Green

0   100   300 ft.

RJS

77. *Plan of the restored gardens at Mount Vernon (after Samuel Vaughan, 1787, and Elizabeth Kellam de Forest, 1982).*

75 (opposite, top). *"View of Mount Vernon looking to the North. July 17th 1796." Watercolor by Benjamin Latrobe.*

76 (opposite, bottom). *Robertson-Jukes view of the east lawn and front of Mount Vernon (1800).*

78. *Courtyard garden at Mount Vernon. Anonymous oil painting (1792).*

79. *View of Mount Vernon from the northwest. Aquatint by George Parkyns (1798).*

walk, shaded by weeping Willows, a tree which in this country grows very well upon high dry land.[10] On one side of this lawn is a plain Kitchen garden, on the other a neat flower garden laid out in squares, and boxed with great precission.[11]

Vaughan's plan was apparently correct enough, then, even in the way he drew the flower garden—what Washington also called the Upper or North Garden to distinguish it from the Lower or South Garden (for vegetables and fruit) on the south side of the bowling green.

According to Latrobe, the Upper Garden at least was laid out in symmetrically arranged "squares" edged with box. But this "precission" did not please him much: "For the first time again since I left Germany, I saw here a parterre, chipped [i.e., clipped] and trimmed with infinite care into the form of a richly flourished Fleur-de-Lis: The expiring groans I hope of our Grandfather's pedantry."[12] If there is one garden feature that Latrobe generally disliked, it was the outdated European taste for topiary. He apparently thought he would never find samples of it in America, certainly not in the gardens of a modern thinker like Washington.

Julian Niemcewicz, the Polish visitor whom Washington personally escorted around the

gardens and plantation over a period of several days in June 1798, is more precise than Latrobe in his description of certain details. After noting that engravings by the Italian landscape master Claude Lorrain—whose paintings have often been credited with inspiring eighteenth-century English landscaping—hung on Washington's walls, Niemcewicz mentions (among other things) a ha-ha surrounding the west garden:

It is surrounded by a ditch in brick with very pretty little turrets at the corners; these are nothing but outhouses. Two bowling greens, a circular one near the house, the other very large and irregular, form the courtyard in front of the house. All kinds of trees, bushes, flowering plants, ornament the two sides of the court. . . . Near the two ends of the house are planted two groves of acacia, called here *locust,* a charming tree. . . . The ground where they are planted is a green carpet of the most beautiful velvet. . . . There were also a few catalpa and tulip trees there. . . . The path which runs all around the bowling green is planted with a thousand kind[s] of trees, plants and bushes; crowning them are two immense Spanish chestnuts that Gl. Wash planted himself. . . . A thousand other bushes, for the most part species of laurel and thorn, all covered with flowers of different colors, all planted in a manner to produce the most beautiful hues.[13]

Whether or not, as Latrobe wrote, Washington was guilty of gardening pedantry in the west gardens, the rest of the landscape to the east, or facing the river front, of the house delighted the architect most. His painter's eye, always on the lookout for picturesque and sublime scenery, rested agreeably on the view from the east portico: the locust groves, mentioned by Niemcewicz, in the foreground framing the house on its north and south sides; trees and shrubs were strategically planted on the slope toward the river and in the deer park; and the hills and river terminated the view. Latrobe observed that in this part of the landscape, art has played a useful but unobtrusive role:

> Towards the East [of the Mansion] Nature has lavished magnificence, nor has Art interfered but to exhibit her to advantage. Before the portico a lawn extends on each hand from the front of the house and of a Grove of Locust trees on each side, to the edge of the bank. Down the steep slope trees and shrubs are thickly planted. They are kept so low as not to interrupt the view but merely to furnish an agreeable border to the extensive prospect beyond. The mighty *Potowmac* runs close under this bank the elevation of which must be perhaps 250. feet. . . . Beyond this Sheet of verdure the country rises into bold woody hills, sometimes enriched by open plantations, which mount gently above one another till they vanish into the purple distance of the highest ridge 20 miles distant.[14]

Niemcewicz, too, was delighted with the views from the portico. Several evenings during his stay he sat with the Washingtons in the portico, savoring the panoramic scenery, which for the moment did not include Washington's deer:

> On the opposite [east] side is an immense portico supported by eight pillars. It is from there that one looks out on perhaps the most beautiful view in the world. One sees there the waters of the Potowmak rolling majestically over a distance of 4 to 5 miles. A lawn of the most beautiful green leads to a steep slope, covered as far as the bank by a very thick wood where formerly there were deer and roebuck, but a short time ago they broke the enclosure and escaped. . . . The opposite bank, the course of the river, the dense woods all combined to enhance this sweet illusion. What a remembrance![15]

Notice that Niemcewicz mentions the classical portico in connection with this view; it was from there, he was careful to point out, that the view might be enjoyed to great advantage. He does not elaborate, but this portico, with its pillared and elevated elegance, provided a contrast to the open landscape. It was a stage, in effect, a framing artifact, from which the scene could be leisurely contemplated. The contrast enhanced the views in somewhat the same way that a rectangular, flat, symmetrical, and enclosed garden area near a house and overlooking a natural landscape could do. The view from the portico also recalls William Byrd II's appreciation of the wild scenes along the Virginia–North Carolina boundary line from the sanctuary and perspective of his camp sites. One is not really in the landscape but rather is an observer from an artificially arranged vantage point. In the English landscape garden of mid-century and later, such vantage points occasionally were formally established and identified with numbers, so that as one progressed through the scene along the prearranged route a succession of set views would open up. William Shenstone's Leasowes and Philip Southcote's Woburn Park (Farm) were two of the finest and best known examples of the *ferme ornée*.

William Loughton Smith, an English traveler who saw a number of plantations in Virginia in 1791, also visited Mount Vernon. In his journal he could scarcely contain his enthusiasm for the picturesque view commanded from the gardens and portico. There are so few extant descriptions of landscapes such as this one that it is eye-opening to cite it here at length:

The house at Mount Vernon is most magnificently situated; I hardly remember to have been so struck with a prospect. It stands on a small plain near the river, which is 200 feet below; the view extends up and down the river a considerable distance, the river is about two miles wide, and the opposite shore is beautiful, as is the country along the river; there is a verdant lawn between the house and the river, and a rapid descent, wooded, down to the river. From the grand portico which fronts the river, the assemblage of objects is grand beyond description, embracing the magnificence of the river with the vessels sailing about; the verdant fields, woods, and parks.

The river traffic, the verdant—he uses that word twice—fields and lawn, the woodland, the parkland, and the sloping ground all compose a grand picturesque composition of wood, water, and green expanses. At the end of his account, Smith adds that there were also "two pretty gardens, separated by a gravel serpentine walk edged with willows and other trees; a circular lawn back of the house; the grounds well cultivated and improved."[16]

From these descriptions it is clear that Washington made a comprehensive effort over the years to design his surrounding acres so as to create a landscape garden. He never writes about this effort in his social correspondence with friends, but there are a few hints worth citing in his lengthy letters to Whiting about gardening matters. In 1792 and 1793, for example, he seemed particularly occupied with creating distant "pleasing effects." In a letter to Whiting in October 1792, he took note of a particular vista: "The . . . Visto which I mentioned to you is but a secondary object, and yet I am anxious to know over what ground it will pass." On January 13, 1793, he tells Whiting: "My object in clearing the grounds *out side* of the pasture . . . was that you might see the Mansion house as soon as you should enter the little old field beyond it."[17] Here is a specific instance of Washington's aim

to have the house itself serve as the terminal focus for a set view from somewhere out in the landscape. Further evidence of such contrivance is wanting; but if Washington set out to multiply such scenes, he would have been attempting much the same effect as his English contemporaries in their country house landscapes.

Although Latrobe was particularly fond of the grounds and views east of the house and had mixed feelings about the gardens to the west, it is those gardens that recommend Washington as one of the two or three most imaginative and innovative landscape gardeners in eighteenth-century Virginia. Surprisingly, Latrobe superficially and puzzlingly dismissed the serpentine paths leading to the "wilderness" as "wide but extremely formal." Perhaps he thought that the path itself, although it wound through the trees in a natural fashion and helped determine the pear shape of the bowling green, was too broad and well edged. Little was formal, though, about Washington's management of these areas on either side of the bowling green, which he began to lay out in 1785.

Washington's greatest pride, judging from his letters and diaries, was in the variety of trees in the gardens. The different species of trees and shrubs he planted along the paths were irregularly placed and of varying height, forming a sort of thin natural screen between the paths and the bowling green and between the paths and the walls of the Upper and Lower gardens. He began by looking over his own land "in search of the sort of Trees I shall want for my walks, groves, & Wildernesses." He found crab apple, poplar, locust, pine, maple, dogwood, the fringe tree, and several others, all of which he introduced into his gardens. On January 19, 1785, on a bright day, he was "Employed until dinner in laying out my Serpentine road & Shrubberies adjoining."[18]

As part of that same scheme, Washington planted the two wildernesses at the west end of the bowling green, and by March he had completed the planting and the paths on both sides.

In the weeks of intense planting that followed, he continued to add other specimens of trees and shrubs, many of which he obtained from distant friends—all designed to "diversify the scene," as he told Colonel William Grayson in Scotland on January 22, 1785.[19] They included maple, black gum, ash, elm, holly, mulberry, hemlock, magnolia, laurel, willow, sassafras, linden, arbor vitae, and aspen. But he still found the planting thin. Toward the end of March he decided in favor of more pine trees and, carting three wagon loads full from another of his plantations, "planted every other hole round the Walks" in the wildernesses. He was still at it on March 24: "Finding the Trees round the Walks in my wilderness rather too thin I doubled them by putting (other Pine) trees between each." Six years later he referred to the area as his "Pine Labyrinths."[20]

It was always Washington's intention to enclose completely the Upper or North Garden and the Lower or South Garden. He did not want what was planted inside these enclosures to relate visually to the other features of the gardens in the way, for example, the formal gardens at Gunston Hall related to the adjacent grounds and fields. So far as we know, he never states a reason for this preference; but the principal explanation must be that he thought the symmetrical and geometrical planting arrangements inside the walls were incompatible with the looser and more natural style of the gardens outside the walls. The latter would be compromised by the former. Other, more practical reasons were the need to keep animals of one kind or another out and the desire to provide certain plants, especially near the greenhouse, with additional warmth and protection from wind. And by curving the walls somewhat, he could also augment the natural look of the route of the serpentine paths and the wildernesses. Initially designed as straightforward rectangles, these gardens were extended in 1785 and their walls made to curve slightly at their western ends. The curves of the walls also allowed extra space for the wildernesses, which were shaped as triangles with curving sides.

Especially interesting because of improvements there after Vaughan's visit in 1787 was the Upper Garden, where in the customary colonial fashion vegetables composed part of an ornamental pattern together with flowers, box and flowering shrubbery, and small trees.[21] This thickly planted garden, laid out in squares and rectangles intersected by gravel paths, possessed a feeling of seclusion. Like the Lower Garden, but more elegantly,[22] it was entered through a wooden gate off the serpentine path. Three years after Latrobe complained of this "flower garden" laid out and "boxed with precission," the Reverend John E. Latta recorded a different point of view: "The garden is very handsomely laid out in squares and flower knots and contains a great variety of trees, flowers and plants of foreign growth collected from almost every part of the world."[23]

Since Washington was acquiring so many exotic and tender plants, he set about building a greenhouse in 1784. As one walked into the Upper Garden, this graceful brick building, with its tall windows, stood directly ahead and provided an elegant focus. Washington's design for the building appears to have been based somewhat on the greenhouse at Mount Clare, which he probably saw, for he asked for its measurements that year.[24] Vaughan saw Mount Vernon's greenhouse in 1787 and described it as "a stately hot house,"[25] but to Latrobe in July 1797 it was "a plain Greenhouse" containing "nothing very rare."[26] The more enthusiastic Reverend Latta saw it the year of Washington's death and was delighted by the "foreign plants and trees," which "at the approach of winter, [are] carried into a large greenhouse built of brick, which stands at one side of the garden. That they may be portable they are all planted in large wooden boxes filled with earth."[27]

From the surviving papers concerning Mount Vernon, it is evident that as a landscape gardener Washington was not as ambitious as Jefferson.

As far as we can tell, it seems that he drew no plans for his gardens, whereas one of Jefferson's pastimes was drawing plans for his. Except for his greenhouse, neither did Washington conceive and design any ornamental buildings, temples, or obelisks, whereas Jefferson designed (although he did not build) several for Monticello. What is particularly disappointing is that he did not write much about what gardening and gardens meant to him or, more specifically, what the Mount Vernon gardens meant to him. From Jefferson we have more on this subject.

Yet Washington's achievements as a landscaper from the 1760s to the end of his life were considerable. Three of them stand out especially: his insistence on curving lines in walls, paths, and green spaces; his deliberate opening up of short vistas within the gardens themselves and of distant views to and from the house; and his careful choice of native and foreign trees and shrubs with which to provide variety of shape and color and to screen certain garden features. Finally, no other landscape garden in Virginia, not even Jefferson's, is as fortunate as Mount Vernon to have been the subject of such particular contemporary descriptions as those that have been cited. They bear witness to Washington's elegance and control, resistance to bizarre schemes and effects, intelligent ability to combine beautifully the regular and irregular, and love of the countryside in his corner of Virginia. The modern restoration is a tasteful and restrained tribute to his landscaping skills.

. . .

Jefferson would have been quick to agree with a remark Washington made in a letter of April 1787 to Sir Edmund Newenham at Bell Champ in England. The pleasures of gardening, Washington observed, lie in seeing "the work of ones own hands, fostered by care and attention, rising to maturity in a beautiful display of those advantages and ornaments which by the Combination of Nature and taste of the projector in the disposal of them is always regaling to the eye."[28] But Jefferson would also have gone further in articulating just what composed that "beautiful display" and the ideal "Combination of Nature and taste." Like Mount Vernon, Monticello is an ambitious statement of landscape gardening ideas in Virginia near the end of the century. Jefferson, however, left behind him not only more writing on the subject but also several plans that help to trace his thinking about gardens. Jefferson found it pleasurable and convenient to put his ideas down on paper. Many of these ideas he never used, but he did express himself clearly with them. It is a pity that Washington and Jefferson did not write more to each other about gardening or visit each other's gardens, for they thought very much alike about the subject.

Jefferson's enthusiasm for landscape gardening at Monticello was fired partially by patriotic sentiments about the American landscape, a theme apparently absent in Washington's ideas about gardening. Jefferson invoked the patriotic sentiment that a landscape garden patterned on American soil symbolized values that were outworn or dying in Europe. An American landscape garden, so this line of thought went, therefore could delineate and satisfy emotional and intellectual demands concerning liberty and democracy that the English landscape garden could never do so well, in spite of its exquisitely gentle beauty.[29] In America, Jefferson wrote in 1788, "we have only to cut out the superabundant plants."[30] The climate helped too, he thought, to make Virginia the gardener's ideal, although it was the Piedmont, not the Tidewater, to which he was referring when he wrote to his daughter Martha Jefferson Randolph in May 1791 with an enthusiasm for his native land that seems unbounded:

> On the whole I find nothing any where else in point of climate which Virginia need envy to any part of the world. . . . When we consider how much climate contributes to the happiness of our condition, by the fine sensations it excites, and the [natural] productions it is the parent of, we have reason to value highly the accident of birth in such a one as that of Virginia.[31]

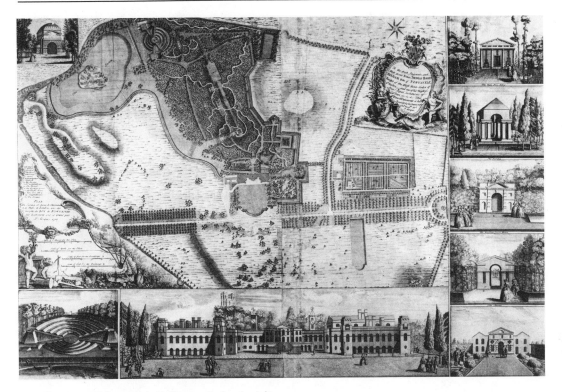

80. *Claremont (Esher, Surrey). Engraved plan by John Rocque (ca. 1739).*

Nonetheless, Jefferson thought it was important for an American who would design gardens to see English landscape gardens in person. Writing from Paris in May 1786, just after he had methodically visited a number of famous English gardens, Jefferson observed to John Page, the owner of Rosewell plantation, that the "gardening in that country is the article in which it surpasses all the earth. I mean their pleasure gardening. This indeed went far beyond my ideas."[32]

But he was not completely impressed. When he visited English gardens in 1786, in the company of John Adams and with Thomas Whately's *Observations on Modern Gardening* (1770) as a guide, he had already been landscaping his grounds at Monticello for about seventeen years and had established the first stage of his garden's layout. By then, he had firm ideas about how to design a garden, ideas reflected in his remarks about what he saw. A few of the gardens—older ones designed in the early eighteenth century or parts of more recent landscape gardens that still showed signs of too many straight lines—struck him forcibly as outdated, or autocratic, or insipid. For Lord Burlington's famous gardens at Chiswick House, which Alexander Pope and William Kent helped to design, he had little time: "the garden shows still too much of art. An obelisk of very ill effect; another in the middle of a pond useless." Of Charles Bridgeman's and Kent's fine work at Claremont, in Surrey (figure 80), he wrote simply, "Nothing remarkable." A straight, broad, gravel walk in front of the house at Caversham, Surrey, had "an ill effect," even though it terminated with a Doric temple. The straight approach to Stowe, in Buckinghamshire, was "very ill"; and the Corinthian arch

81. Esher Place (Esher, Surrey). Engraved view by Luke Sullivan (1759).

"has a very useless appearance," especially because "it is an obstacle to a very pleasing distant prospect." At William Shenstone's Leasowes, he thought the ferme ornée idea scheme poorly conceived because the landscape made only a pretense of being a farm: "This is not even an ornamented farm—it is only a grazing farm with a path round it, here and there a seat of board, rarely anything better. Architecture has contributed nothing." Philip Southcote's ferme ornée at Woburn Farm, Surrey, was not convincing either; it is "merely a highly-ornamented walk through and round the divisions of the farm and kitchen garden." The ostentatiousness of Blenheim disturbed him, and he had to note that it took two hundred people to keep the estate, with its two hundred acres of garden, in order: "art appears too much."[33]

What Jefferson liked very much in a few English gardens, and what he later would try to create at Monticello—but not, as he acknowledged, with very great success—was the soft and pastoral "variety of hill & dale," which he called "the first beauty in gardening."[34] At Esher Place, for example, less than a mile down the road from Claremont, he was taken with the romantic hill on which the gardens were laid out above the River Mole (figure 81). It was a scene that reminded him of his own hillside at Monticello and illustrated its landscaping possibilities:

> The house in a bottom near the river; on the other side the ground rises pretty much. The road by which we come to the house forms a dividing line in the middle of the front; on the right are heights, rising one beyond and above another, with clumps of trees; on farthest a temple. A hollow filled up with a clump of trees, the tallest in the bottom, so that the top is quite flat. On the left the ground descends. Clumps of trees, the clumps on each hand balance finely— a most lovely mixture of concave and convex.

Water effects often added to the picturesque charm of such scenes. At Leasowes, where a series of prospects was numbered, Jefferson was pleased by the cascades: "The first and second cascades are beautiful. The landscape at number eighteen, and prospect at thirty-two, are fine. The walk through the wood is umbrageous and pleasing." At Wotton he liked a gentle walk that circumscribed the grounds: "A walk goes round the whole, three miles in circumference, and containing within it about three hundred acres: sometimes it passes close to the water, sometimes so far off as to leave large pasture grounds between it and the water." At Hagley, in Worcestershire, so well blended were the gardens and parkland that there seemed to be no separation at all: "no distinction between park and garden—both blended, but more of the character of the garden."[35]

In several ways, Jefferson desired to create the feeling and style of such natural settings in his own gardens but judged that the Virginia climate would not allow him much scope to do so. In a letter to William Hamilton, however, he expressed certain ideas of what he could do at home in this English vein. They are a bit fanciful, as were many of his plans and proposals for future garden projects, but worth citing here as examples of his efforts to accommodate English landscape garden fashion to Virginia's requirements:

Their sunless climate has permitted them to adopt what is certainly a beauty of the very first order in landscape. Their canvas is of open ground, variegated with clumps of trees distributed with taste. They need no more of wood than will serve to embrace a lawn or a glade. But under the beaming, constant and almost vertical sun of Virginia, shade is our Elysium. In the absence of this no beauty of the eye can be enjoyed. This organ must yield it's gratification to that of the other senses; without the hope of any equivalent to the beauty relinquished. The only substitute I have been able to imagine is this. Let your ground be covered with trees of the loftiest stature. Trim up their bodies as high as the constitution and form of the tree will bear, but so as that their tops shall still unite and yield dense

shade. A wood so open below will have nearly the appearance of open grounds. Then, when in the open ground you would plant a clump of trees, place a thicket of shrubs presenting a hemisphere the crown of which shall distinctly show itself under the branches of the trees. This may be effected by a due selection and arrangement of the shrubs, and will I think offer a group not much inferior to that of trees.[36]

Here, then, is an early meditation on how the American landscape garden needed to be different from the English. It must cultivate shade, not necessarily through comprehensive planting schemes, but through the propitious pruning of what umbrage the landscape already possessed. As Jefferson put it in his "Hints to Americans Travelling in Europe" (1788), under the subheading "Objects of Attention for an American," English gardens and garden making were peculiarly "worth the attention of an American, because it is the country of all others where the noblest gardens may be made without expence. We have only to cut out the super-abundant plants."[37]

Like Latrobe, Jefferson and Adams—perhaps partly as a result of their immersion in the luxury of the gardens they saw—felt that the English taste for expensive temples, statuary, obelisks, and other furnishings was unsuitable for either the American landscape or the new national mood of liberty and equality. Although he admitted that at Stowe, Woburn Farm, Hagley, Leasowes, Painshill, Esher Place, and other famous gardens he learned "such practical things as might enable me to estimate the expense of making and maintaining a garden in that style," Jefferson still felt that an American counterpart of that natural style would bring better or more sublime results.[38] For his part, Adams noted wryly that "a national debt of two hundred and seventy-four millions sterling accumulated by jobs, contracts, salaries, and pensions, in the course of a century might easily produce all this magnificence of architecture and landscaping." He underlined this perspective with a rousing patriotic call to American gardening: "It will be long, I hope, before ridings, parks, pleasure grounds, gardens, and ornamented farms, grow so much in fashion in America; but nature has done greater things and furnished nobler materials there; the oceans, islands, rivers, mountains, valleys, are all laid out upon a larger scale." On a more botanical note, he observed proudly on July 24, 1786, that one garden he saw was "full of rare shrubs and trees, to which collection America has furnished her full share."[39]

Jefferson doubtlessly would have approved the spirit of such remarks. To his way of thinking, nature had endowed Virginia with superior natural resources, but there was room in the colony for parks, pleasure grounds, and ornamented farms. Two years after seeing the English gardens, he wrote to Angelica Church about God's "improved plan" or "new creation" in Virginia and how it was more conducive to the ideal landscape garden:

> I remember you told me when we parted, you would come to see me at Monticello. and tho' I believe this to be impossible, I have been planning what I would shew you: a flower here, a tree there; yonder a grove, near it a fountain; on this side a hill, on that a river. indeed madam, I know nothing so charming as our own country. the learned say it is a new creation; and I believe them; not for their reasons, but because it is made on an improved plan. Europe is a first idea, a crude production, before the maker knew his trade, or had made up his mind as to what he wanted.[40]

The concept of a ferme ornée especially appealed to Jefferson because he believed that the culture of the earth, something not abused by a properly managed ornamental farm, was the proper labor of "the chosen people of God"— "the focus in which he [the farmer] keeps alive that sacred fire, which otherwise might escape from the face of the earth."[41] The ferme ornée later became a favorite and central feature of his plans for Monticello's grounds: it exhibited his valued ideal of *in utile dulce*. On a visit to Nervi, Italy, in 1787 to see the gardens of Count Du-

razzo, he said they ought to be studied by Americans because they contained "as rich a mixture of the Utile dulci as I ever saw."[42]

. . .

It is important to bear in mind that during his forty to fifty years of landscaping at Monticello, Jefferson never laid out and executed the majority of the plans, diagrams, and proposals that are sprinkled throughout his surviving papers. This is not surprising in view of the highly fanciful and imaginative nature of many of his ideas. What he knew of English styles lies at the root of much of this type of creativity. Even before his 1786 visit, it was his reading of English literature and about English gardening taste and practice that drew out of him projects, sometimes featuring an elaborate iconography, that for Virginia were extravagant. The tour with Adams promoted what in a small way may be seen as his indulgence in a gardening fantasy. In addition, his familiarity with French architecture and classical literature tempted him to plan some garden temples, most of which he never built.[43] In the middle of the second stage of his landscaping, in 1809, he was brimming with new ideas, so much so that a visiting friend, Margaret Bayard Smith, was bewildered:

> Mr. J. explained to me all his plans for improvement, where the roads, the walks, the seats, the little temples were to be placed. There are two springs gushing from the mountain side; he took me to one which might be made very pictur-

82 (opposite). Monticello landscape (after a study-plan by William L. Beiswanger, 1990).

FEATURES: *1, graveyard; 2, site of grotto proposed in 1771; 3, terraced vegetable garden, laid out in 1774 and later extended; 4, lawn on west front bordered by serpentine path; 5, Mulberry Row; 6, garden pavilion; 7, ha-ha; 8, orchard; 9, first or upper roundabout; 10, second roundabout; 11, third roundabout; 12, grove; 13, site of wilderness or labyrinth of broom, in a pinwheel design; 14, layout of "articles of husbandry" conceived as a ferme ornée.*

esque. As we passed the graveyard, which is about half way down the mountain, in a sequestered spot, he told me he there meant to place a small gothic building. . . . I looked on him with wonder as I heard him describe the improvements he designed in his grounds, they seemed to require a whole life to carry into effect, and a young man might doubt of ever completing or enjoying them.[44]

Even before 1809, Jefferson had thought of placing a little gothic temple "of antique appearance" in the graveyard. When he was a young man, in 1771, he had formulated elaborate ideas for that spot that could well have taken him much of his life to execute. These ideas represent the most comprehensive landscaping project to have been put down on paper in Virginia by that date.[45] Already he had been laying out some of the grounds at Monticello for two or three years and apparently felt inspired by his reading to in-

troduce a little gothic atmosphere and iconography into his scheme with evocative allusions to literature and sacred allusions to his family.[46]

His idea was to level an area about sixty feet in diameter on a hillside to the west of the upper gardens near the house (no. 1 in figure 82),[47] among "antient and venerable oaks" and interspersed with "gloomy evergreens." "Encircled with an untrimmed hedge of cedar, or of stone wall with a holly hedge on it," the area would contain, in addition to the gothic temple, "pedestals with urns, etc., and proper inscriptions." On the grave of a faithful servant there might be a "pyramid erected of the rough rock stone." The provision for servants as well as family suggests how seriously Jefferson took his role as a responsible country house owner, which recalls the country house English literary tradition.[48] In the middle of the temple he would place a rather bizarre "altar, the sides of turf, the top of plain stone." The entire scene would be dark to en-

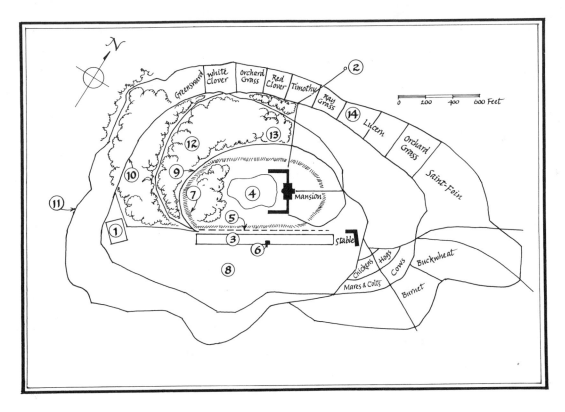

courage the proper mood: "very little light, perhaps none at all, save only the feeble ray of an half extinguished lamp."

As if this would not have been enough at that early stage, Jefferson also projected a temple next to a natural spring on a rather steep slope northeast of the house (figure 82, no. 2). Again, a few feet below the spring the ground would have to be leveled to about forty or fifty feet square. According to his description, the potential for romantic water effects was dramatic: "let the water fall from the spring in the upper level over a terrace in the form of a cascade. then conduct it along the foot of the terrace to the Western side of the level, where it may fall into a cistern under a temple from which it may go off by the western border till it falls over another terrace at the Northern or lower side."[49] A statue of a reclining nymph on a marble slab just next to the spring, with an appropriate Latin inscription alluding to her function as custodian of the sacred scene, would serve as a useful emblem.[50] The emblem would be more complete, he thought, if a separate inscription alluding to the image of the *beatus ille* could be written on a metal plate and posted to a tree. The latter device seems artificial, dilettantish in the young designer, but it does point to his role-playing as the blessed rustic who has escaped from "the contentious forum" and "shuns the insolent thresholds of the great."[51]

Alternatively, and involving less earth moving, Jefferson also considered an elaborate grotto beneath the spring, replete with classical echoes and including another nymph, this time with Pope's famous inscription, a version of a popular Latin epigram:

> Nymph of the grot, these sacred springs, I keep
> And to the murmur of these waters sleep;
> Ah! spare my slumbers! gently tread the cave!
> And drink in silence, or in silence lave![52]

The grotto would be dug into the hill, its walls covered with clay and moss, its floor paved with pebbles, and the interior spangled with shells and translucent pebbles. The water from the spring would be guided into the grotto, empty into a basin, and then run off down the hill.

Jefferson did not put any of these ideas into practice. Only a simple graveyard found its way into the landscape. But the 1771 description concluded with rather more practical, and realizable, suggestions under the heading of "The ground in General." Since it was very early in the first stage of his landscaping, he specifies numbers of trees, shrubs, and flowers, and he mentions the need for much clearing and digging out of old stumps and undergrowth; but even here his eye for the pictorial and taste for the illusion of the natural is evident as he notes, "except where they may look well." He also wants to encourage animals and birds to his land: "court them to it, by laying food for them in proper places." He desires a "buck-elk" as "monarch of the wood" but seriously warns that the animal must be kept shy so as not to "lose its effect by too much familiarity." He concludes with a proposal that would turn his woods into re-creations of the literary pastoral: "inscriptions in various places, on the bark of trees or metal plates, suited to the character or expression of the particular spot. benches or seats of rock or turf."

What he needed perhaps was a witty and unsentimental Rosalind to play opposite his own version of the pedantic and romantic Orlando, the "defamer" of trees. While there is an admirable inventiveness in many of his landscaping projects, there is also a comically eccentric, even (by European standards) decadent, streak in them. The elk that had to be kept apart from good society is unhappily analogous to Charles Hamilton's hired hermit at Painshill Park in Cobham, Surrey, who had to sign a contract promising, among other things, that he would not be seen talking to people. He lasted two weeks on the job. Perhaps the elk would have lasted longer, but both ideas are equally absurd. Jefferson seems at times almost like a Dr. Syntax,[53] going to pedantic extremes in imagining this or that picturesque effect.

Something is known of what Jefferson planned for his landscape gardens before he departed for

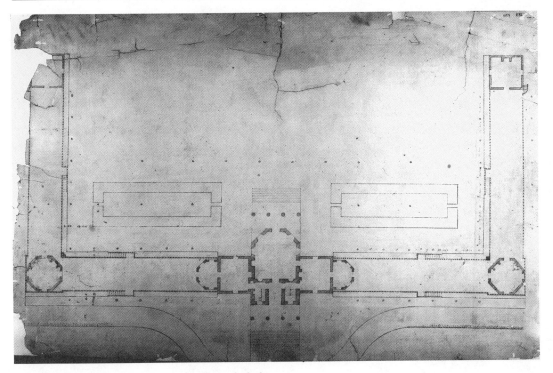

83. *Jefferson's sketch of two rectangular flower beds for Monticello (ca. 1772).*

Europe in 1784; less is known of what he actually laid out during that first stage. For example, in 1772 or before, he drew two sketches of the house, its innovative wings, rectangular flower beds, and a prominent semicircle of shrubs and trees facing the east front (see figures 83 and 84); but he appears not to have created the rectangular beds or introduced the trees and shrubs into the semicircle until the second stage of landscaping around 1808. He must have laid out flower beds somewhere, probably near the house, because his Garden Book indicates that he had been planting lots of trees and flowers in his gardens.[54]

Most of his attention was focused on building, especially the two L-shaped wings to the house. Because of the slope of the ground next to the house, these wings could be entered from the outside of the L but were underground on the inside. This clever design meant that the wings,

the roofs of which inside the L were at the same level as the main floor of the house and could be used as a promenade, did not narrow and obscure the view of the landscape from the house.[55] Jefferson's papers also contain occasional references to "roundabouts" he was laying out to circumscribe the small mountain on which his house sat. Even in this earlier stage of the landscape Jefferson must have been thinking of using them to create a ferme ornée out of his grounds and to exploit the views from the mountain. In the second stage of his plans for the grounds, the roundabouts were to become crucial to the ferme ornée and more generally to his conception of a landscape garden.

The landscape views to the west from the house were well served in 1771, when Jefferson took an important step toward improving and preserving them. In exchange for legal services he had rendered Edward Carter, he acquired "as

84. *Jefferson's sketch of the house and adjacent grounds at Monticello (ca. 1772–1808[9]).*

much of his [Carter's] nearest mountain as can be seen from mine, and 100 yds beyond the line of sight."[56] This mountain, which was four hundred feet higher than Monticello and directly opposite it, he called Montalto (figure 85). He planned to build a five-story tower or observatory on Montalto, to be clearly visible from Monticello, but this was one of several decorative buildings for his landscape that he never built.[57]

One landscape feature he did begin to establish was the long platform, terraced vegetable garden (figure 82, no. 3) south of the central lawn (no. 4) and along an approach road or path he called Mulberry Row (no. 5). His sketch of it around 1774 (figure 86) shows that he planned nine beds, which would be bordered along the northeast side with a number of functional wooden buildings.[58] Archaeological excavations on the site have verified the existence of an early version of this garden as well as its extended, second stage laid out sometime between 1807 and 1809.[59]

When Jefferson retired from the presidency and set about the second stage of his landscape in earnest, he considerably enlarged the existing terraced platform area to about one thousand feet long by eighty feet wide. Obviously, he wished to transform it into a garden more attractive than it had been with those functional buildings between itself and the west lawn in front of the house—a feature that he could confidently open to view from the lawn above. Excavations have shown that he did this by eliminating a few of the wooden buildings, erecting a garden pavilion (figure 82, no. 6) "at the center of the long walk" in the vegetable garden (figure 87),[60] and introducing a ha-ha (no. 7) between the vegetable garden and the lawn and pleasure grounds above (see the aerial view of the grounds, figure 88).[61]

The orchard south of the vegetable garden (figure 82, no. 8) is another feature of the landscape in its first stage about which we know a good deal, thanks to archaeology and a surviving plan. Jefferson drew the first plan for the orchard

(figure 89) in 1778, on which he recorded exact positions for trees planted in squares and rectangles. In this and another plan of 1811 he specified what trees went into what holes, leaving nothing to chance. Excavations on the site uncovered the tree holes arranged just as the plans suggested.[62]

Apart from Jefferson's seemingly endless pursuit of plants during these early years, that is all we know about the first stage of the gardens. He returned from Europe in 1789, eager to try out all sorts of new landscaping ideas, but he was unable to make any immediate, significant alterations to his initial design because he accepted the post of secretary of state in Washington's cabinet, became vice president in 1796, and then from 1801 to 1809 served as America's third president. According to his papers, he did a good deal of farming and planting in the 1790s, but not much designing. In 1794 he embarked on the remodeling of his house, a project that was not completed until his retirement in 1809. When the duc de La Rochefoucault-Liancourt visited Monticello in 1796, what he recorded in his journal for the most part concerned the prospects from the gardens, not the gardens themselves, which may mean there was not yet much noteworthy in the pleasure gardens. La Rochefoucault was particularly impressed by the contrived view of Montalto:

in the back [west] part the prospect is soon interrupted by a mountain more elevated than that on which the house is seated. The bounds of the view on this point, at so small a distance, form a pleasant resting-place, as the immensity of prospect it enjoys [to the east] is perhaps already too vast. A considerable number of cultivated fields, houses, and barns, enliven and variegate the extensive landscape, still more embellished by the beautiful and diversified forms of mountains. . . .[63]

In 1804, Jefferson began again to sketch plans for landscape improvements. A period of creativity ensued, illustrated by the plans and his corre-

85. View of Montalto from the vegetable garden at Monticello.

spondence, but it is likely that he waited until his retirement in 1809 before really getting on with the second stage.

The first substantial sign of renewed activity is a memorandum from about 1804, "General ideas for the improvement of Monticello" (figure 90), in which Jefferson projected some detailed alterations to both the landscape and the pleasure grounds.[64] A primary objective was to loosen the garden design so as to open up and improve the views from near the house and up and down the mountainsides. He achieved that with the ha-ha and the elimination of the wooden outbuildings along Mulberry Row. On the hillsides he would lay out "the ground between the upper & lower roundabouts [figure 82, nos. 9 and 10] in lawns and clumps of trees, the lawns opening so as to give advantageous catches of prospect to the upper roundabout. Vistas from the lower roundabout to good portions of prospect." From the lower roundabout upward on all sides of the mountain he proposed straight walks in a criss-cross fashion, presumably passing through the trees and shrubs as if the mountainside were a type of "wilderness."

For prospects of water, he liked the idea of using a natural spring on Montalto to create a cascading waterfall down its slopes; the water would then be brought up to Monticello by pipes. There is no evidence that he ever proceeded with that plan. He mentions also a "fish pond to be visible from the house"; such a pond near the South Pavilion, a decorative part of the flower garden, was not built until 1808.[65]

A third roundabout further down the mountain, to lead from the "thoroughfare," would "circumscribe the garden grounds." Beneath this he planned a "park and riding grounds" that would take in the ground beneath the third roundabout and all of Montalto; a bridge over the thoroughfare would prevent the two sections of the park from being cut off from one another. In order to translate the outlying farms into more bucolic-looking orchards, all visible from the house, he thought of turning the farms into orchards "of

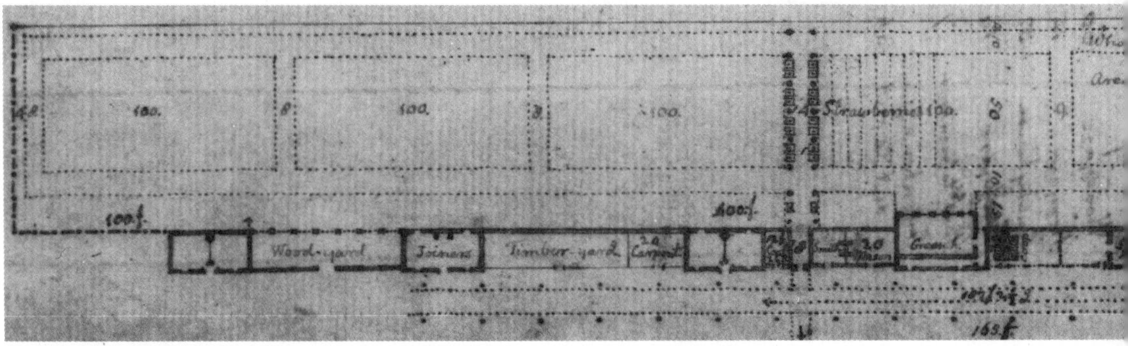

86. Jefferson's sketch of the first vegetable garden proposed along Mulberry Row, Monticello (ca. 1774).

cyder apple & peach trees," with orchard grass beneath them. For the vegetable garden, the levels of which were to be planted with hedgethorn and privet, he first had in mind ornamental placements of "boxes" along its lower edge in various styles such as gothic, Chinese, and classical; but then he reconsidered and noted, "but after all, the kitchen garden is not the place for ornaments of this kind. bowers & treillages suit that better, & these temples will be better disposed in the pleasure grounds."

It is not clear what he meant by the pleasure grounds in 1804, but it appears that he included in that category the huge grove west and northwest of the house (figure 82, no. 12). Writing as a painter might, he began by choosing his trees for that area and specifying the style of their planting: "The canvas at large must be Grove, of the largest trees, (poplar, oak, elm, maple, ash, hickory, chestnut, Linden, Weymouth pine, sycamore) trimmed very high, so as to give it the appearance of open ground, yet not so far apart but that they may cover the ground with close shade." More interesting is his delineation of the clumps of thickets that must be planted beneath this high canopy of trees, for which he cites English precedent as his guide: "This must be broken by clumps of thicket, as the open grounds of the English are broken by clumps of trees." Broom, althea, gelder rose, magnolia, oralea, fringe tree, dogwood, red bud, wild crab, euony-

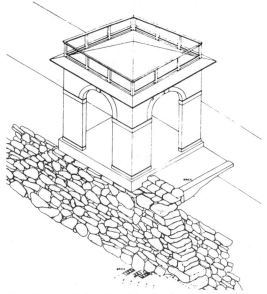

87. *Conjectural drawing of the Garden Pavilion at Monticello, based on archaeological excavations.*

mous, rhododendron, oleander, lilac, honeysuckle, and bramble are among the plants to be used for the thickets. And then, with an idea for a baroque-styled maze-like spiral pattern, he suggested how the thickets might be used to command vistas by "putting the tallest plants in the center & lowering gradation to the external termination. A Temple or seat may be in the center, thus leaving space enough between the rows to

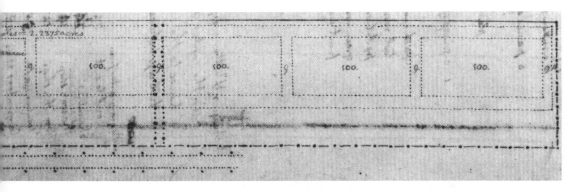

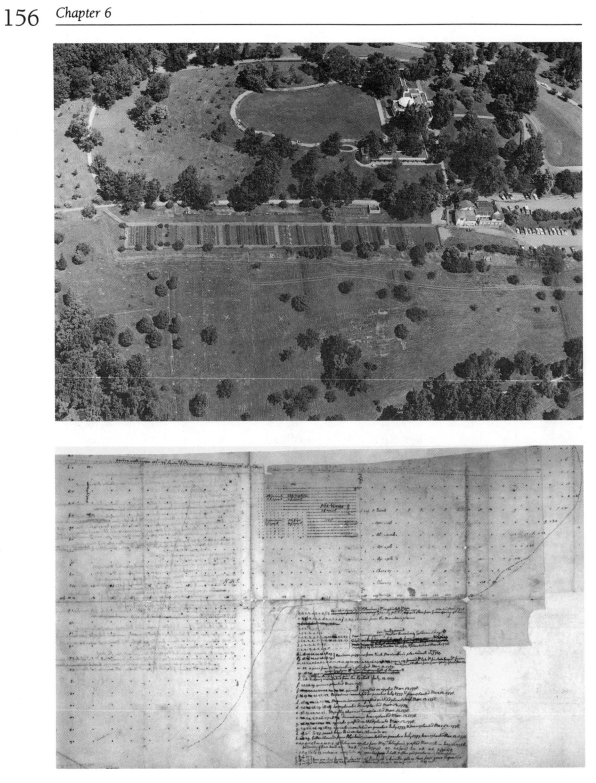

90. Jefferson's "General ideas for the improvement of Monticello" (ca. 1804).

PAGE 1: *These general ideas mainly addressed opening up the landscape for better views, strategic planting of clumps of trees, layout of walks, deployment of natural springs to create water effects, development of the round-about scheme, and creation of orchards and the vegetable garden.*

PAGE 2: *These proposals for the pleasure grounds focused mainly on forming thickets, groves, and undergrowth and establishing walks throughout them, ornamented with sundry temples.*

88 (opposite, top). *Aerial photograph of the Monticello grounds.*

89 (opposite, bottom). *Jefferson's sketch for the orchards at Monticello (1778).*

walk." As for temples and seats elsewhere, they should be placed in "those spots on the walks most interesting either for prospect or the immediate scenery." Somewhere on "the South ride" he already had laid out a "Broom Wilderness," which he would improve, among other ways, by introducing "chambers with seats" sheltered from the wind and open to the sun. Another structure that might do nicely for the Broom Wilderness, he thought, was a temple with yellow glass that would give the illusion of sun on a cloudy day.

All of this was so very contrived and precious, with its layers of intended gothic, rustic, and classical effects, that it is no wonder little of it was ever realized at Monticello. It seems a paradox that Jefferson, who in England resolved with some arrogance and disdain not to indulge in such artifices at home, where nature would do most of the work, should twenty years later be playing in his imagination with all those temples, classical and hermitage-like seats, pedestals, straight walks, labyrinths, and so on. Surely this is a case of the excesses of the English landscape garden run wild in one American's imagination.[66]

As Jefferson began to focus more attention on the second stage of his landscaping, he naturally also thought much about gardening as an art. In a letter to his granddaughter Ellen Randolph in July 1805, responding to her question about the fine arts, he argues on behalf of landscape gardening as the seventh fine art: "not horticulture, but the art of embellishing grounds by fancy. I think Ld. Kaims [Kames] has justly proved this to be entitled to the appellation of a fine art. It is nearly allied to landscape painting, and accordingly we generally find the landscape painter the best designer of a garden."[67] This was not an original idea, but then Jefferson did not mean it to be. Writing in July 1806 to William Hamilton, whose gardens at Woodlands,[68] near Philadelphia, he much admired and after which he wished to model his own, Jefferson confessed that to do justice to the landscape at Monticello "analogous to its character would require much

more of the genius of the landscape painter & gardener than I pretend to."[69]

In that letter to Hamilton, Jefferson fortunately detailed the present state of the garden and his gardening plans, although in this and other letters he wrote between 1806 and his retirement there is a strong theme of frustration, even resentment, that the presidency prevented him from proceeding with them. He tells Hamilton plainly that what he wants is a landscape garden in the English style, featuring a mount with walks up to the top. The mount was very popular in the eighteenth-century garden. The difference, however, between the English mount and the one Jefferson planned was that the former were generally artificial or small, whereas Jefferson's Montalto was huge—indeed, a high hill:

> The grounds which I destine to improve in the style of the English gardens are in a form very difficult to be managed. They compose the northern quadrant of a mountain for about 2/3 of its height & then spread for the upper third over its whole crown. They contain about three hundred acres, washed at the foot for about a mile, by a river of the size of the Schuylkill. The hill is generally too steep for direct ascent, but we make level walks successively along it's side, which in it's upper part encircle the hill & intersect these again by others of easy ascent in various parts. They are chiefly still in their native woods, which are majestic, and very generally a close undergrowth, which I have not suffered to be touched, knowing how much easier it is to cut away than to fill up. The upper third is chiefly open, but to the South is covered with a dense thicket of Scotch broom (Spartium scoparium Lin.). . . .

He adds that he hoped once to consult the Scottish gardener George Isham Parkyns when he was in Philadelphia but that he was "disappointed."[70] Perhaps Hamilton, he wonders, would care to come to Monticello to advise him, or he himself could go to Woodlands: "Should I be there you will have an opportunity of indulging on a new field some of the taste which has

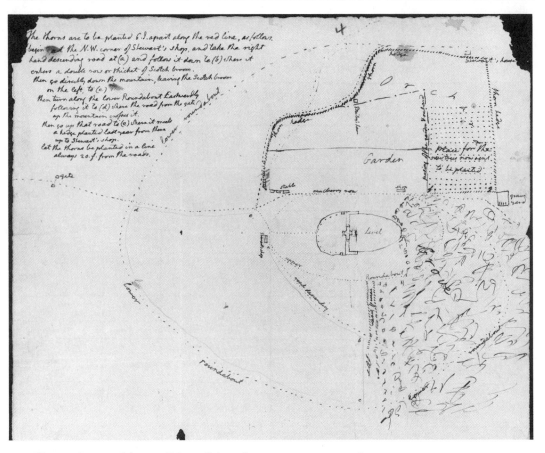

91. Jefferson's drawing of the top of Monticello's gardens, showing the groves, vegetable "Garden," and "Level" or lawn not yet with the serpentine walk of flower beds (1806).

made the Woodlands the only rival which I have known in America to what may be seen in England."[71]

In 1806 Jefferson drew a plan of the top of the Monticello gardens (figure 91), which included the grove to the northwest, the semicircular planting facing the east front, the orchard, the "Garden" or terraced vegetable garden, and, most interesting of all, the "Level" or oval-shaped lawn on the west front. The latter is not yet shown with the serpentine walk around its perimeter, and neither the west nor the east lawn has any flower beds. It was not until the next two years that Jefferson set about sketching, laying out, and planting the oval and round flower beds in those areas (see figure 92). As he told another granddaughter, Anne Randolph, on June 7, 1807, this project was part of a general plan for the lawn:

I find that the limited number of our flower beds will too much restrain the variety of flowers in which we might wish to indulge, & therefore I have resumed an idea, which I had formerly entertained, but had laid by, of a winding walk surrounding the lawn before the house, with a nar-

1807. Apr. 15. 16. 18. 30. planted & sowed flower beds as above.
April. 16. planted as follows.

	N.E. clump	S.E. clump	S.W. clump	N.W. clump
13. Paper mulberries	2.	2.	5.	4
6. Horse chesnuts	3	3		
2. Taccamahac poplars	1	1		
4. purple beach			2	2
2. Robinia hispida	1	1		
2. Choak cherries	1	1		
3. mountain ash. Sorbus aucuparia			1	2
2. Xanthoxylon			1	1
1. Red bud	1			

the above were from Maine except 5 horse chesnuts from nursery & the Red bud
planted same day 1. Fraxinella in center of N.W. shrub circle
    * 1. Gelder rose in do. of N.E. do.   } from Maine's
    1. do.   in do. S.E. do.
         1. Laurodendron in margin of S.W. do. from the nursery
planted also 10. willow oaks in N.W. brow the slope, to wit from the N. Pavilion
         round to near the setting stones at S.W. end of level
    and 12. Wild crabs from the S. to the N. pavilion near the brow of the slope
    * Viburnum opulus rosea.
Apr. 17. planted 2. Robinia hispida & 2. choak cherries on the S.W. slope.
    20. Weymouth pines on the slope by the Aspen thicket.
In the Nursery. began at the N.W. corner & extended rows from N.W. to N.E. & planted
    1st row, at 2.f. from the pales
    2d. do. 18 f. from that   } 100. paccans.
    3d. do. . . . . Gloucester hiccory nut from Roanoke.
    4th do.   do. from Roanoke. 79 in all. 6. do. from Osages. 2. scarlet beans.
    5th a bed of 4 f wide, 3 drills. globe artichoke. red.
    6th a do. do.   green
Apr. 18. . . 7th a bed. Cooper's pale green asparagus. 5. rows   feet long. a seed every 6.I.
    8th   at N.E. end of same bed 14. Ricara beans very forward.
        a bed 26 f. long. 2. rows & about 8 f. of a 3d. say 60 f. Missouri great Solsafia. 120 seed. 6.I. apart

92. Jefferson's sketch of the planned oval flower beds for
the east and west lawns at Monticello (1807).

row border of flowers on each side. this would give us abundant room for a great variety. I enclose you a sketch [figure 93] of my idea, where the dotted lines on each side of the black line shew the border on each side of the walk. the hollows of the walk would give room for oval beds of flowering shrubs.[72]

The serpentine path recalls Washington's treatment of his main lawn, except that at Mount Vernon the lawn was embraced by a thick planting of trees and shrubs so that the serpentine was a shady walk leading to the equally shady wilderness; the prospect was framed by and limited to the opening at the west end. Jefferson's lawn and serpentine, with flower beds, was open to views in every direction except to the east; his wildernesses and shady thickets were located down the sides of the mountain, away from the house.

Apart from his mounting interest in his flower beds, Jefferson's principal gardening project over the last fifteen years of his life was to develop his *ferme ornée*. Over the years he had played with the idea of an ornamented farm through his disposition of the roundabouts and paths up and down the mountainsides. In 1808 he planted various crops between the second and third roundabouts north of and not far from the house, possibly as shown on a plan he sketched in the 1790s (figure 94).[73] It was in connection with the *ferme ornée* that he planned that year an experimental garden: "in all the open grounds on both sides of the 3d. & 4th. Roundabouts, lay off lots for the minor articles of husbandry, and for experimental culture, disposing them into a *ferme ornée* by interspersing occasionally the attributes of a garden."[74] It will be recalled that he censured several examples of the ferme ornée he had seen in England because they only pretended to be farms. Undoubtedly he justified his own ferme ornée by insisting that he had indeed laid out a farm. Walking along the roundabouts or along the northern path from the house on the way to the spring, a person would see signs of agriculture that, according to a few English examples Jefferson well remembered and Ste-

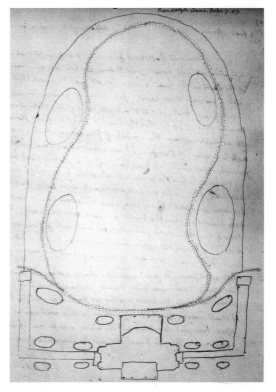

93. *Jefferson's rough sketch of the proposed serpentine walk around his west lawn at Monticello, with oval flower beds (1807).*

phen Switzer's books on the subject, which he owned, illustrated how a landscape garden could combine pleasure with profit. He might, as he said, have entertained the idea of becoming a florist, but he never abandoned his commitment to the principle of *in utile dulce*.

After 1809, when Jefferson retired, most of his garden designing consisted of seeing to completion the plans and proposals he had drawn up in the preceding four or five years. Except for the extension of the long vegetable terraced garden, he began no major gardening projects after this year, although there was much to do by way of planting. In his absence the grounds had inevitably been neglected, notwithstanding the overseer's best efforts. His orchards were doing well, having just been enlarged and stocked with new

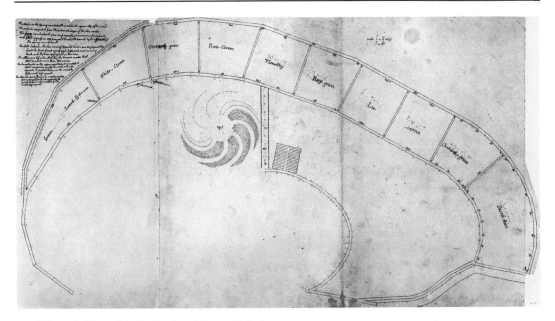

94. *Jefferson's "Plan of the Spring Roundabout at Monticello" (1790s).*

varieties of fruit. Either the gardens looked relatively bare of plants or Mrs. Samuel Harrison Smith was simply not a good observer. In the summer of 1809 Mrs. Smith, who was guided through the grounds by Jefferson, was not much impressed by what had been done. She liked best the view:

> He took us first to the garden he has commenced since his retirement. It is on the south side of the mountain and commands a most noble view. Little is as yet done. A terrace of 70 or 80 feet long and about 40 wide is already made and in cultivation. A broad grass walk leads along the outer edge; the inner part is laid off in beds for vegetables. This terrace is to be extended in length and another to be made below it. The view it commands, is at present its greatest beauty.[75]

Jefferson would not have argued with what she said about the views. He told Benjamin Latrobe a few months later, "what nature has done for us is sublime & beautiful and unique."[76] Still, Mrs.

Smith presumably would have been additionally disappointed by what he told her the following year: "I have made no progress this year in my works of ornament: having been obliged to attend first to the utile. my farms occupy me much, and require much to get them underway."[77]

That would be the pattern for the rest of his life. Architectural garden projects were a thing of the past. From then on, his farms, and his desire to make a profit out of them, took up most of his time. "I talk of ploughs and harrows, of seeding and harvesting, with my neighbors," he wrote in 1810.[78] In addition to his farms, plants were his abiding interest. His flowers perpetually delighted him, as he told a friend: "Nothing new has happened in our neighborhood since you left us; the houses and the trees stand where they did; the flowers come forth like the belles of the day, have their short reign of beauty and splendor, and retire, like them, to the more interesting office of reproducing their like."[79] On April 8, 1811, he wrote to the naturalist Bernard

McMahon: "I have an extensive flower border, in which I am fond of placing *handsome* plants or *fragrant.* those of mere curiosity I do not aim at, having too many other cares to bestow more than a moderate attention to them."[80] Nonetheless, he corresponded with countless individuals on both sides of the Atlantic about plants, soliciting help and sharing discoveries. In his final ten years, illnesses sapped him of much of his gardening energy. He found he could walk little further than a turn through his gardens. In 1816 he turned over the management of both the gardens and the farms to his grandson, Francis Eppes. His gardening life, in effect, was over.

After Jefferson's death in 1825, Edmund Bacon, who had served as overseer at Monticello since 1806, described the gardens nostalgically but doubtless accurately:

The grounds around the house were most beautifully ornamented with flowers and shrubbery. There were walks, and borders, and bowers, that I have never seen or heard of anywhere else. Some of them were in bloom from early in the spring until late in the winter. A good many of them were foreign. Back of the house was a beautiful lawn of two or three acres, where his grandchildren used to play a great deal.[81]

A watercolor of the house and west lawn, painted around 1825 by Jane Bradick (Peticoles), perhaps just before Jefferson died, shows the abundance of flowers there (figure 95).

. . .

Without question, Mount Vernon and Monticello represented the fullest and finest statements of landscape gardening in the colony. One can say this because there is plenty of extant material, much of it graphic, to suggest as much. Even so, it seems unlikely that any other landscape garden in the eighteenth century could rival them. Nevertheless, Jefferson's death ended a

95. *View of the west front and lawn at Monticello. Watercolor by Jane Bradick (Peticoles), 1825.*

century in Virginia during which the great plantations played major roles in the development of landscaping.

Jefferson himself did not really see it that way. He did not think that the landscape garden in Virginia, or in America as a whole, had emerged as a distinguishable art form until the last quarter of the eighteenth century. He would have disagreed with the thesis that pleasure gardening with landscape as a primary feature of design began to appear in colonial gardens before then. The traditional view is that Jefferson, really for the first time, allowed open landscape to play an important part in the creation of a Virginia garden. This view derives somewhat from the claims he made for Monticello at the same time he called for a new American brand of landscaping. Retrospectively, the great plantation gardens before the Revolution are made by this teleology to look hopelessly imitative and even un-American—merely English, if even that.

There is a parallel here to Horace Walpole's Whiggish assertions in his *History of the Modern Taste of Gardening* (1785), that the value and importance of early-eighteenth-century English landscaping was confirmed in the process of naturalization that it began, a process that culminated in the landscape or "picturesque" movement of the second half of the century. The gardening of Pope and Kent, Walpole implied, was fulfilled in the landscaping of Capability Brown and others.[82] As for Jefferson, his writings do not credit Virginia gardening, in town or plantation, during the first three-quarters of the century as a prelude to his own ideas, although he once in 1769 vaguely praised Williamsburg's gardens over Annapolis's.[83] He could have cited several examples, from the 1730s to the Revolutionary War, of Virginia landscape gardens, or at least of gardens that possessed features reflecting their designers' alertness and responsiveness to prospects, variety of elevation, associations, iconography, and generally the pictorial. These are apart from gardens that displayed extensive ornamental gardening in the more traditionally geometric and formal vein—gardens that, in his enthusiasm for the landscape garden, Jefferson presumably thought were outdated.

Toward the end of the eighteenth century Jefferson contributed greatly to American landscaping by popularizing and accelerating a departure from the regular, geometric, and predominantly axial garden design that had prevailed for much of the century. But, notwithstanding the impression given by his extensive writing on gardening, he did not begin that movement of taste, nor was he the first in Virginia to think in a sustained artistic way about the subject. Contemporary descriptions of Westover, Mount Airy, Gunston Hall, and Mount Vernon, among others, suggest otherwise, that at least by the 1760s appreciation of open landscape had begun to be linked to the layout of a plantation garden. After the Revolution, the association of landscape gardening with a sense of the American landscape's unique beauty and with a patriotic political theme, especially in the minds of Jefferson and John Adams, carried large-scale American gardening rapidly forward into the era of Andrew Jackson Downing and the professional landscaper of the nineteenth century.

7

Two Gardeners in Williamsburg after the War: Joseph Prentis and St. George Tucker

*T*homas Jefferson had mixed feelings about his election in 1779 as governor of Virginia. On the one hand, it wrenched him away from Monticello to Williamsburg for long periods. The quick progress he had been making on his landscaping inevitably slowed. On the other hand, for more than a decade after he graduated from the College of William and Mary and left Williamsburg, he kept returning to the capital to taste its cultural pleasures as well as to transact business. Now these pleasures were close at hand. He particularly liked listening to the parish church organ, attending the playhouse, and visiting old friends like George Wythe. And as we know from a comment he made in 1769, he preferred the town's gardens, although not its houses, to those at Annapolis. It is ironic that he, perhaps more than anyone else, was responsible in April 1780 for the removal of the colony's seat of government from Williamsburg to Richmond. His feelings about the move were somewhat self-serving. It might be said that Williamsburg's loss in this instance was Monticello's gain, because at Richmond Jefferson was much closer to his estate and could more conveniently run it. Once Williamsburg lost its favored status as the colonial capital, however, it began to decline as the center of culture, especially for Virginians living in the Tidewater area.

But not everyone was disappointed that the political focus of the colony had turned elsewhere. St. George Tucker, for example, remarked with approval that the town increasingly began to feel and look like a village. Joseph Prentis appears to have liked it that way, too, for it was beginning to suit more nearly his own ideas of the domestic pleasures that residential life in the old capital could or ought to offer. Unlike George Wythe, for example, who left his house and garden on the Palace Green and moved to the new capital, these men anticipated their future lives in Williamsburg almost as semiretired and their homes and gardens as places to which they could retreat and recover from professional and political responsibilities. One of Tucker's friends good-naturedly called him a "Hermit" who hobbled about in his "Cave" and gardens. Of course, this attitude toward their dwellings involved some role-playing, perhaps an acting out of certain classical values, notably the *beatus ille* figure, with which they would have been familiar from their reading. They by no means isolated themselves from family and friends. Indeed, their families became especially crucial emblems of their identification with home and generated much of the emotive quality of their attachments to the places where they had chosen to live.

For both Prentis and Tucker in the last two decades of the century the removal of the capital to Richmond and the increased urbanization of Virginia life of which this was a portent—it must be remembered that Virginians generally had been content to live without cities or large towns—induced them to embrace the village-like character of their own town with renewed vigor and a heightened nostalgia. In this way they could, as it were, exclude any signs of change or progress from the garden and ward off what they saw as the fresh threats to the styles of old colonial life symbolized for them by the development of Richmond and other cities. Even more broadly, the westward movement of the population after the Revolution, as well as the decline of plantation life, encouraged people like Prentis and Tucker to turn to their own landscapes for reassurance. David Meade, an ardent gardener after he moved from Williamsburg to Kentucky in the 1790s, understood this about his old friend St. George Tucker and in his letters sympathetically articulated what his friend must have been feeling back in the old town. It was not only a place, but a way or condition of life—the general character of living together in a village—that was so appealing about Williamsburg.

Such local attachment accounted in particular for the conspicuous energy that Prentis and Tucker brought to their gardening. They carried on, aware of two facts. One concerned the past as well as present: the gardening history of the old capital. Although in decline, the Palace and college gardens continued to allude to that history and its exciting beginning. In a more practical vein, the examples of Joseph Hornsby, John Custis, and John Randolph, among others, provided a precedent for Prentis's interest in kitchen gardening and his methodical way of proceeding with and recording it. Custis's garden had by then all but disappeared, but Prentis and Tucker would have been well aware of its earlier fame and Custis's contributions to American horticulture. And a few of the larger gardens—those of Wythe, Nicholas, Bassett Hall, and Tazewell

Hall—illustrated in Prentis's and Tucker's own time what could be done to create pleasure gardens in the town with a few half-acre lots joined together. There was also the unexpected arrival in town of Peter Bellett soon after 1790, who proceeded to develop one of the most successful commercial nurseries in America. Bellett's fame certainly was heartening, for it returned a measure of practical attention to the old capital that it had lost in 1780; and the Bellett nurseries were a godsend to local gardeners like Prentis and Tucker.

The other fact that guided Prentis and Tucker concerned the present and future: landscape gardening showed signs of becoming more pervasive. Even in Williamsburg, where gardens on the edge of town could command views of surrounding fields and woods, landscaping was in evidence, and since mid-century it had been done on a larger scale at several plantations. By the 1780s Washington and Jefferson had already begun to demonstrate the beautiful effects attainable through the integration of garden and landscape in the laying out of grounds. Tucker, a friend of Jefferson's, possibly had seen Monticello; he surely had by the time Jefferson completed most of the second stage of his landscaping. Tucker definitely liked open landscape views, which at times he described in his journals. Within the limited space of their Williamsburg gardens, of course, and without woods and open fields and meadows to view from their gardens, neither Tucker nor Prentis could entertain landscaping projects on the scale of Monticello or Mount Vernon. Nevertheless, they could create smaller natural and pictorial effects that were sympathetic with the new ideas. Prentis, as it turned out, had more scope for such variety because his garden at Green Hill possessed a natural spring and uneven, sloping ground, whereas Tucker's gardens were flat and smaller. Tucker, though, enjoyed the advantage of laying out his garden next to the Palace Green and the perspectives it offered.

Another current of taste that near the end of the century began to flow alongside the course of landscape gardening came to be known as the "gardenesque." Inevitably, it influenced Jefferson and Washington as well as Prentis and Tucker. More horticultural in emphasis, it featured the profuse display of flower beds, shrubs, and colorful trees in irregular and asymmetrical arrangements, either close to or somewhat distant from the main house. We have seen how both Jefferson and Washington, with flower beds, various flowering trees, and exquisitely delicate variety of foliage, included this element of design in their large gardens next to their houses. But the style was equally appealing and practical in smaller town gardens like those of Prentis and Tucker, both of whom were extremely fond of flower beds and grateful for the immediate diversity of color and texture that flowers could introduce into a scene.

The gardenesque contrasted with the earlier landscape gardening emphasis on large-scale perspectives achieved through shades of green, light and dark, and the placement of water and groups of trees. Humphry Repton, in the last two decades of the eighteenth century, was one of the earliest English landscape gardeners to employ the gardenesque style in his designs; conceivably, since his books were in the libraries of several colonial gardeners, it was from him that American gardeners first learned of it, although there is no firm evidence.

The gardenesque was most successfully popularized in England by John Claudius Loudon in the first decade of the nineteenth century as a reaction against what he saw as the facile and decadent methods of late-century landscape gardeners who were not practicing what he regarded as the genuine picturesque principles of Uvedale Price and Henry Payne Knight. Both Price and Knight were keen horticulturists, and Loudon followed their example. He was a prolific professional gardener and writer as well. One of his influential works, *Observations on the Formation and Management of Useful and Ornamental Plantations* (1804)[1] set out, among other themes, the proper uses of flower beds. He felt that, with their large and idealizing brushstrokes

across vast acreage, landscape gardeners like Capability Brown and Repton, who had held center stage for many years and whose influence had long since reached America, had ignored sources of the picturesque that were more practical and rational, more comprehensible, natural, and immediate. He advocated softer and more colorful shapes through the planting of trees, shrubs, and flowers—especially flowers—all disposed naturally and without rigid symmetrical constraints. In an early essay, he urged on gardeners advice that Prentis and Tucker would have heartily accepted, if they had read it; he told them to learn from the display of infinite variety that was continuously unfolding before them in nature, which there was no need to idealize:

> We see in natural Forests that in one place the *Oak* is the principal tree, the *Hazel* the principal shrub, and the *Cowslip* the principal flower; next succeeds the *Beech* as the principal tree, the *Box* as the principal shrub, and the *Violet* as the principal flower; and so on, according to the nature of the soil: which at once produces the most interesting variety, and the largest timber. Let us then derive our principles in the arrangement of shrubberies, plantations, and even flower-gardens, from the scenery of Nature.[2]

Loudon's books were widely read in America during the first half of the nineteenth century and could be found in several personal libraries in Virginia. Although flowers and botanical interests had always accounted for much of the energy and impetus in eighteenth-century Virginia gardening, his particular attention to them took advantage of a rising fashion for the display of plants in gardens in America and England. In both countries, in fact, horticultural curiosity became the dominant influence in garden design during the nineteenth century.

One early-nineteenth-century American nurseryman and garden designer who did much to link horticulture and landscaping was the Irishman Bernard McMahon, who emigrated to Philadelphia in 1796 and in 1806 published the first book on horticulture and gardening in America,

The American Gardener's Calendar. He immediately sent a copy to Jefferson and from then until his death in 1816 (at the age of forty-one) corresponded with the former president frequently about plants for Monticello. McMahon's book was widely read and much appreciated; it is astonishing that this was the first book published in America that specifically treated native plants growing in native conditions. Prentis owned a copy, and, although neither he nor Tucker mentioned it in correspondence or journals, both must certainly have used it extensively. What is especially interesting about this book is that it combines horticulture with garden design and follows Repton's principles closely.

Because we know so little about what Prentis's and Tucker's gardens actually looked like, it is impossible to say to what extent they were influenced by McMahon's Reptonian landscaping ideas. It is worth mentioning, however, that McMahon rejected signs of formality, such as geometrical shapes and straight walks, and urged the use of "rural open spaces," such as softly contoured grassy areas embellished with winding walks, irregularly shaped flower beds, and clumps of trees and shrubs arranged so that through them one could glimpse the adjacent landscape or scene beyond. Grass lawns next to the house ought as well to be abundantly surrounded with flowers. And if there were any natural water in the garden, in the form of streams, springs, or ponds, it should be incorporated as part of the comprehensive garden plan. Prentis, it will be seen, had opportunities along these lines.[3]

. . .

There were, then, plenty of new ideas to see Virginia gardening through the end of one century and into the next.[4] Prentis and Tucker are fitting gardeners to turn to at this point, not only because they bring us back to Williamsburg, but also because they reflected many of the crosscurrents of gardening that had appeared in colony and town for more than a century and because they looked to the future with new ideas and impressions. They combined the practical with the pleasurable. They exhibited an appreciation of the aesthetics of open landscape, while at the same time they used their gardens to cultivate and display a wide variety of flowers, bushes, and trees—at least partly within regularly shaped and paled areas. Both were enthusiastic horticulturists. For both, gardening was a deeply personal activity, and their gardens expressed their values. It was crucial for them both that they gardened in Williamsburg. In Tucker's case, gardening revealed a way he could relate plantation and town in his own experience, for he gardened both in town and at his wife's plantation, Matoax. It is a coincidence that he, the last great gardener in the old capital, and Jefferson, the last and greatest landscape gardener in eighteenth-century America, both began their legal careers in Williamsburg and died at the end of the first quarter of the next century, having gardened into a new era in their respective and private ways.

. . .

Prentis's house and gardens at Green Hill represented a strong theme in his life from young adulthood to the end of his days. A hint of this appears in one of the books from his surviving library, the third volume of the London periodical *The Adventurer* (1770), in which he scribbled the following: "22 yrs 8 mo. 12 Days I have lived at Green Hill as a married man ought to live. 'Sleep on in peace; obey thy makers Will / Then rise unchanged; and be an angel still.' "[5] The remark, which was induced by grief over his wife's death, is dated August 27, 1801, which means that he moved to Green Hill in mid-December 1778—about four years earlier than the available records have suggested. The remark also underlines the strong sense of place he felt about the town when he moved there at the age of twenty-five.[6]

The Prentis correspondence bears out the importance of Green Hill's garden to the Prentis family.[7] On April 23, 1799, Prentis wrote one of the typically warm and moral letters he sent home to his son Joseph Jr. while he was away, as he frequently was, on his legal circuit. He longs for a sight of his garden: "I hope the Weather with you has been more favourable [than in Charlottesville], and that the Sun has been sufficiently warm to bring forward vegetation. . . . How are the Gardens? is the Asparagus plenty . . . ?" Father and son shared a deep attachment to the "peaceful dwelling of your Friend and Father," as Joseph Sr. put it on November 8, 1802, as well as a love for the garden. In that November letter to his son, Prentis also refers proudly to his flowers, especially to his collianthus, and to the large demands made by friends for flower bulbs and roots. A poignant interlude to the story of this garden involves Prentis's wife, Margaret, who in 1801 was seriously ill in Richmond and unable to join her family at Green Hill. She asks her husband on April 27 to "tell Joe [Jr.] allways to put sweet flowers in all my letters." Then, on May 1, she asks, "How does the garden come on, very pretty I suppose." On the sixth she reminds them about the "sweet flowers" and adds, "I must really be at home when all that good frute is ripe."[8] Sadly, she never returned home and died later that year.

When he traveled in his capacity as judge of the general court, Prentis took his garden with him in thought and often wrote home to ask how plants were growing and to direct his gardener in this or that task. Consequently, except for the evidence from the Bodleian Plate for the Palace and college gardens, or the horticultural detail from Custis's letters, Judge Prentis's is one of the best-documented gardens, in personal terms, of eighteenth-century Williamsburg. People knew and respected him as a gardener. "I wish I could see my old Friend contemplating in his rural Flower Garden," wrote his relative Robert Prentis from Trinidad in December 1800; "I have no doubt of its striking Beauties, as I well know his Taste" and his "old Attachment, that of repairing and Embellishing old Crazy Houses." From his friend David Meade in Kentucky, too, Prentis received nostalgic letters about their gardening times in Williamsburg. In

a letter of August 1796, when Meade was struggling in Kentucky to create a home and garden amid unsettled land, he remembers wistfully his friend's "skill in Gardening." Almost one year and much gardening and building later, Meade can speak about his first successes in a manner he knows will appeal to his old gardening companion:

> You may be sure I have yielded liberally to the Garden. . . . the idea of Yourself and flowers are intimately connected in my mind—which must seem natural enough—as I am so well acquainted with Your taste for the culture of them. All the Country has been for several weeks past Natures flower Garden—I wish you had been here to make a collection of such as best merits the Florists attention—I have thought of saving the seed of somewhat that best pleased me to send to You—and have marked several for that purpose.[9]

In 1795, in one of his recurring poetic moods, St. George Tucker, a good friend of Prentis's, dashed off some verses briefly describing the gardens of Green Hill. The verses suggest the reputation and importance of those gardens as well as anticipate their owner's chagrin when a summer storm damaged them somewhat. Tucker writes in a light vein, but his lines allude to both the ornamental and the utilitarian nature of the gardens:

> Elms, Willows, and Poplars, Catalpa's and all
> Our Apples and Peaches and Pears got a fall,
> That bruis'd them so sorely, they only were fit
> For Pigs in a stye, or starv'd oxen to eat.
> . . . . . .
> Neighbor Prentis' pales were blown down from his garden
> And let in the Cows, which no mortal could pardon,
> To eat up his Cabbages, trample his flowers,
> And destroy his hot beds, and his Jessamine Bowers.

Tucker rather implies the fine reputation of Green Hill's gardens and Prentis's pride in them when he reports that cows, taking advantage of the moment, have committed a crime against Williamsburg gardens that "no mortal could pardon."[10]

As early as 1775, Prentis exhibited his more than passing interest in plants and gardens when he began a "Monthly Kalendar" of garden activity, which ran for four years.[11] As he kept this before his Green Hill days, it was probably a record of the gardening he did at the family home on Duke of Gloucester Street, where his elder brother, John, had just died. In 1784, at Green Hill, he began his "Garden Book," in which he kept track of his plantings and composed a set of directions on how to perform certain gardening tasks.[12]

For most of its history Green Hill had large and well-kept gardens.[13] Indications that it was recognized in the town for its gardens emerge from time to time through sale particulars and other sources. For some reason, perhaps financial since he had spent large sums improving the house and building brick stables and a carriage house on top of the expense of the gardens, Prentis tried to sell the property in 1790. Either he did not succeed or he thought better of it. His sale advertisement is revealing for this sentence about the gardens: "A considerable part of these lots are well enclosed, being laid off into two gardens; and a sufficiency of good timber provided for enclosing the remaining lots. There are several springs of very good water on these lots."[14] When Prentis died twenty years later, in 1809, St. George Tucker tried to convince Fulwar Skipwith to buy Green Hill, with "Garden and lot which including the Garden contains about 4 acres on which there is a very good spring and spring house all in *excellent* and *neat* repair."[15] The property was up for sale again in 1828, and the advertisement provides another glimpse of the house's landscape: "the situation of this property is doubtless the most eligible and agreeable in the old city; it has a delightful and never failing spring of water upon the lot, protected by a spring house . . . and a very large kitchen and flower garden."[16]

In his recollections of the old town during the Civil War, John Charles underlined the point, singling out some of Prentis's old trees and the arrangement of a few of the garden's features and areas. There was, he remembered,

> a spacious lawn in front of the house, on one side of which was an attractive flower plot. Shade was afforded by several huge mahogany trees and a row of fine apricot trees on the east. A vegetable garden containing at least an acre was on the east side. The southern half of the square contained an orchard and the spring lot. In the latter was a large spring flowing from under a marl bank that furnished fine drinking water.[17]

What Charles remembered existed half a century after Prentis died and therefore is not reliable regarding the flower plots and vegetable garden. But probably he is accurate about the "situation" of the garden, its division into several sections, the position of the orchard, and the feeling of a tranquil spot watered by a natural and flowing spring.

Prentis therefore possessed at Green Hill several of the ingredients required for effective practical, ornamental, and even landscape gardening. His garden was as large as Custis's; it possessed a "situation" consisting of uneven ground watered by springs; it was conveniently flanked by his separate acreage across the street, which he farmed and which doubtless endowed his corner of the town with a rural ambience; and it contained extensive vegetable and flower beds.

The farming he did on his ten acres or more north of Scotland Street seems to have been more than simply a pose adopted by a lawyer desiring a hobby. Two "Milch Cows" and two horses were mentioned in the July 1809 sale notice of his property. More suggestive was a letter Prentis wrote to his son from Charlottesville in March 1803, asking, "How goes on the Garden and the Farm?" On March 3, 1803, he alludes to "the Lot to the North" as needing to be "ploughed up and cropped." "I wish you would direct . . . Charles to have the wheat rolled," he adds, thinking of another field, "and inform me if the Rails are brought in." One month later he received "Herds Grass," rye grass, two bay trees (for the garden), and three pounds of Irish potatoes for planting in those farm areas and elsewhere.[18]

Another strong presence in the gardens of Green Hill, mentioned repeatedly in the family's correspondence, is Prentis's competent gardener, Ellick. In those times when good gardeners were scarce, Ellick must have been a highly valued employee. Perhaps he was trained by Prentis himself. "Tell Ellick," Prentis wrote from Northampton, Virginia, in October 1802, "that I expect the Gardens will be in very nice order, the Asparagus Beds both the young and old done up neatly, and the Walks in [the] small Garden and in the Yard gravelled. Those in the Yard to be [raked with] rounding at the top, and that in the small Garden perfectly flat, and level, but filled pretty high with gravel."[19] Prentis relied on Ellick for the cultivation and maintenance of his ornamental gardens, but he also had Pompey and Charles, Ellick's assistants, on his garden staff for extra work during busy times of the year.[20] Prentis's friends valued Ellick, too. A fellow lawyer, John Wickman, was happy to take Ellick's advice on a few specimens he wanted: "When in *Wms*Burg last spring I saw several Bay Trees that had thrown out a number of suckers and your gardener told me some of them might be taken off without Injury to the Trees and that he would send me some this Fall."[21] Wickman also asked for some "pomegranate Slips"— George Wythe, it will be recalled, also grew pomegranates in his garden. Peter Bowdoin, never reluctant to ask Prentis, his brother-in-law, for plants from Green Hill, benefited from Ellick's services on at least one occasion, although he hoped especially to have gardening advice from the master of Green Hill himself: "if you come over I think you can give me directions."[22] Jefferson, too, may have depended on Ellick when he lived at the Palace in 1779–1780; his account book for that year notes that he "hired" Prentis's gardener, something he would not have done had the gardener not been fully competent.[23]

The scattered evidence of Prentis's plantings at Green Hill suggests the active horticultural interests on his part, as well as among his friends, that helped promote the gardenesque approach in the new century. Hydrangea was not widely grown in Virginia gardens, at least until the last quarter of the century, when William Bartram, John's son, discovered the oakleaf variety in Georgia in 1773. Prentis's first specimens were those he received in 1809 from John Wickman, who described the plant as "very beautiful shrubs and well grown." Wickman promised to send them to Green Hill along with two varieties of oleander and other "tender plants" he was raising in his greenhouse.[24] Peter Bowdoin, who was busy ordering plants for his plantation, Hungars, from Bellett's very active nursery in 1807, also received his share from Green Hill, including, as he told Prentis, "Calianthus and Sweet Bay [that] you were so good as to promise me and Leak. . . . and if you have any flower Roots or Seed to spare."[25] Another beneficiary of Prentis's horticulture was a Mr. Stratton, who "shall have his callianthus."[26]

In his "Garden Book," under the heading "Directions about Gardeng," Prentis indulged himself in the role of horticultural teacher, perhaps merely for his own future edification but also not improbably with a view to having his expertise published for the use of others.[27] Most interesting about this "Garden Book" are the clues it gives us about how Prentis arranged the plants and areas in his garden. It will be recalled that in letters to his son he referred to the "small Garden" as distinct from the "Yard." He had specified in 1802 that whereas Ellick had to grade the walks in the yard with "rounding at the top," the gardener was to see to it that the small garden's walks were "filled pretty high with gravel" but kept "flat, and level."[28] The latter method was more suitable for sociable walking and was associated with more ornamental treatment of paths, while the former, a very common and practical way in Virginia of allowing rain to run off into beds, would more likely have been used in kitchen gardens. If this conjecture is valid, the "small Garden" may well have been a pleasure garden with flowers, shrubs, and perhaps a decorative use of fruit bushes and trees. Such a garden would have been adjacent to the house, which the records suggest stood at the northwest corner of the large block, facing south. Since the kitchen and an office, and perhaps another dependency as well, stood north and west of the house, it is likely that the yard was in that area, so that nothing interrupted the views of the gardens south and southeast from the house down the line of the sloping ground toward the ravine near which the spring and springhouse were located.[29]

Prentis's entries for 1786 mention other garden areas at Green Hill. He writes of a "large Garden," north paling, and "squares" in the "East Garden," from which it is clear that the east garden was his large vegetable garden. Since he owned all the lots along Scotland Street extending to Nassau Street, as well as all except the two easternmost lots along Prince George Street, his eastern garden conceivably extended all the way to Nassau Street. At the northeastern corner of the east garden he saved a small space for a family graveyard. He himself would be buried there next to his wife. The 1810 deed of sale, which cited "the Gardens both on the east and west side of the yard," also required the purchaser of Green Hill to preserve "the square of ground in the north East Corner of the Easternmost Garden" as a graveyard.[30]

If there was any constraint on Prentis's garden layout, it was the ravine and stream that ran obliquely southwest-northeast across the block and cut off the southeast corner from the rest of the land. Although the shallow ravine created a natural impediment to even more extensive gardens that Prentis laid out, it created an effect of hilliness within the block that accounted for the name Green Hill. It was a hill-like setting, however, only if one looked south and east from the house, not north or west. If Prentis wished to take advantage of prospects, he would have had

to concentrate on the undulating terrain south of the house. A further inducement to do so was the natural spring. His springhouse was also to the south and down in the ravine. During a severe drought in the summer of 1805, even the spring was affected, or so Prentis lamented, with echoes of John Custis, in an August letter to his son: "Our Grass [is] perfectly burnt up, and the Streams of Water very much reduced my Spring runs as they formerly were [and] are now quite dry."[31]

It must have been painful for Joseph Jr. eventually to have to part with the family "mansion" in 1810: "My residence and circumstances in life forbid that I should keep the establishment."[32] In a memorandum Joseph Jr. noted in 1811 that "my brother and self have accordingly sold Green Hill, and the Gardener Ellick, to Henry Skipwith."[33]

If Joseph Prentis ever thought and designed like a landscape gardener at Green Hill, there are few enough hints to that effect, much less hard evidence. As with most Williamsburg gardens, no graphic evidence remains of the grounds at Green Hill, not even in the Rochambeau and Desandrouins maps, which show a good many gardens in the town. The garden's psychological value to Prentis and his family are clear enough, as are its sections and a few of its plants. That evidence and his writing on the subject point up his considerable horticultural authority, both on the practical and the ornamental. Tucker's little poem bears that out, too. But there is little else to go on regarding his thinking about gardens and landscapes. What did it all mean to him? How did he respond to open landscape? These are questions that will never be answered because Prentis left behind him little in the way of descriptive writing. St. George Tucker, on the other hand, has left us more writing about landscape, although not as much about his garden specifically.

• • •

Tucker, whose residence and gardening life in Williamsburg lasted a quarter of a century longer than Prentis's and was almost exactly contemporary with Jefferson's time at Monticello, began his long love affair with the town when he left his family in Bermuda at the age of twenty to begin his studies at William and Mary in 1771. His Williamsburg garden on the Palace Green, across the street from George Wythe's, is better known than most in town (figure 96); but it was not only his gardening there that made him a significant figure in Virginia's garden history. He was a man who thought about gardens and landscapes a good deal and kept a record of what he saw. Even before he came to Williamsburg, he was well versed on the subject because of the informed interest he had taken in his parents' garden in Port Royal, Bermuda. When he traveled, he kept journals recording gardens he visited. He also described open landscape with the eye of a painter, or at least of someone who knew what he liked in the larger canvases of natural scenery. His descriptions before the Revolution evidence an appreciation of open landscape that had nothing to do with nationalism or patriotism. He was simply able to recognize painterly compositions in scenery such as those he appreciated in gardens. In this sense, as well as in his poetry about landscape, he anticipated the romantic landscape sensibilities of the nineteenth century.

Tucker's life is reminiscent of Prentis's as well because of the rival claims on him of legal duties and the pleasures of his "Hermitage," as he called his house. His home was a retreat, and he was its *vir bonus* ("happy man"). He even retired from a legal position of considerable stature and responsibility because it kept him too much away from his house and garden. Unlike Jefferson, he was not willing to put up with this kind of self-exile.

The Tuckers of Port Royal, Bermuda, had been a closely knit family, but by the beginning of the 1770s the three sons, St. George, Nathaniel, and Thomas, had all left the island to study law and medicine in Williamsburg and Edinburgh. Nathaniel's great ambition was to become a poet, an avocation at which he did not distinguish himself. His poem "The Bermudian," however, includes a few lines on the

96. *View of St. George Tucker House, Williamsburg, from the Wythe House across the Palace Green.*

Tucker garden that St. George must have especially enjoyed:

> Far in the front the level Lawn extends,
> The Zephyrs play, the nodding Cypress bends.
> A little Hillock stands on either Side
> O'erspread with Evergreens, the Garden's Pride.
> Promiscuous here appears the blushing Rose,
> The Guava flourishes, the Myrtle grows.
> The Earth-born Woodbines on the surface creep,
> O'er the green Beds the red Carnations peep,
> Aloft their Arms triumphant Lilacks bear
> And Jessamines perfume the ambient Air.[34]

So far as English poetry is concerned, this flower passage offers many conventional sentiments and images; but beyond that, it celebrates the garden as an important feature of Tucker domestic life on the island. It also anticipates the comparable later importance of gardens to St. George's domestic life in Williamsburg and at his first wife's plantation. It is natural that he, like Eliza Waller, in addition to creating a garden as an important part of his own adult family life, would have wanted to reify the imaginative and emotional value of his childhood gardens in the Virginia landscape.

Although Tucker's correspondence and notes tell us nothing about his experience, if any, as a garden designer in Bermuda, they do offer hints of his interest in plants. He had been in Williamsburg for about one year when his father wrote to him on August 1, 1772, responding to questions about the plants at home: "The Palmeto Royals are now in fine bloom . . . one of the tree's before the Green have two flowers and look beautifully and almost all the trees are putting out so that we shall in a few days make a Gay appearance. . . . I wish if you cou'd get me any seeds you would send some." Native Virginia plants were much sought after in Bermuda, just as English plants were; but that the father would ask his twenty-year-old son for seeds is the more important clue to St. George's horticultural background. Tucker's mother also liked to think of him in relation to their garden. She missed her son mightily and on one occasion wrote sadly, "I sometimes walk out or look into the garden, as if I was to see you, according to your usual way, busying over some plant, and then from one to another, to see which thrives best"[35]

As early as July 1768, when St. George was seventeen, he had set out to supply his brother Thomas in Edinburgh with seeds from Bermuda. "I thank you for the Seeds you intended sending me," his brother wrote, "tho' by mistake they were left behind." Later from Williamsburg, St. George was going to send some seeds to his Aunt Campbell in Norfolk but apparently put off doing so and was gently reminded about it by his good-natured cousin Archibald Campbell in January 1772: "You have milord a list of some Garden seeds which your Aunt desires you to gett and send down [the James River] by the packett." He was also receiving plants in those early years, probably for Williamsburg friends because he had no garden of his own to plant. In August 1772 his cousin Donald Campbell wrote that there had just arrived for him "from Bermuda two boxes with Plants in them"; and in August 1775 he heard from a Thomas Davis, again from Norfolk, that he was about to receive some "sprigs . . . green and flourishing."[36] These are all small matters, but they point to the young

man's foundation in horticulture, which served him well in later years.

His preparation as a gardener, however, was broader, or deeper, than that. Well-equipped with a romantic sensibility, he could be genuinely moved by lovely landscape images. He was, on the whole, given to emotional responses, whether to landscape, love, or institutions and people he respected, so that his enthusiasm for open landscape is partly understandable in those terms; but he appears also to have had an informed, keen aesthetic eye that could pick out pleasing compositions from a scene. One thinks back to William Byrd II, who similarly combined a curiosity about horticulture with a taste for beautiful natural images in open terrain. Byrd was urbane, however; Tucker was romantic and looked forward to liberal nineteenth-century ideas about nature in which emotion as well as aesthetics played a part. He kept a few brief journals over the years where he recorded such feelings about the natural world.

It did not take him long to develop a liking for Virginia's countryside, fields, orchards, and gardens. Journeying back to Bermuda for two months in August 1773, he kept a descriptive journal, "A Voyage to Bermuda," in which he apostrophized his new homeland in youthful and stylized, but genuinely felt, language: "Adieu, Virginia! . . . May Ceres still smile on thy verdant Fields, and Pomona deck thy blushing Orchards—with the most delicious Fruits, while Bacchus crown the rich Vines with purple Clusters." The next year he took a short trip to northern Virginia and scribbled in his 1774 "Almanack," "Beautiful Country. Number of Farms, Orchards, and Meadows with Haycocks." He was struck by the picturesque images along the way.[37]

In March 1777 he journeyed south to Charleston to see his brother Thomas, who had recently moved there to begin his medical practice. Along the way, he appreciatively took in the landscape, first at the Dismal Swamp, where his eye caught the pictorial compositions that had appealed to Byrd half a century earlier:

The Water is of a beautiful brown tincture with red. The stillness of the Evening left the Face of it utterly unruffled. Every object from above was represented in the most beautiful Manner imaginable. The lofty Cypresses invested with its venerable Beard of Moss represented a most delightful Image in this extensive looking Glass. . . . The brown tincture of the water mellowed the Colours and produced a pleasing Effect. A few Bays and other Evergreens which are found in those parts added agreeable variety to the scene.

Near Dorchester, North Carolina, he felt the fullness and luxuriance of nature: "The beauty of every surrounding Object at this Season of vernal Delight—the rich meadows, luxuriant Shrubs, and Vines which wreathed themselves in a fantastic Manner about the stately oaks and other Trees." As for Charleston itself, he wrote of "the rich meadows, luxuriant Woods, variegated surfaces, and exquisite variety of flowering Shrubs and Vines."[38] What emerges from these sketches is a sense of nature's personality, as if Tucker is responding to the *genius loci*, a resident force or genius that gives the landscape its character.

Tucker liked to use color images and words like *luxuriant* and *variegated* to depict the richness of a landscape. For him, open landscape offered endless displays of changing visual effects, and he was ready to compare them to descriptions in verse he had read. And others, including his brother, his sister-in-law Martha Dangerfield Bland, and his friend James Madison, appear to have recognized this sensitivity on his part.[39] As an example, consider his account of Morristown, New Jersey, in 1777, in which again he senses a willingness on nature's part to please: "the farmes between the mountains are the most rural sweet spots in nature, their meadows of a fine luxuriant grass which looks like a bed of velvet interspersed with yellow, blue, and white flowers[;] they represent us with just such scenes as the poets paint Arcadia, purling rills, mossy beds, &c but not dying swains and lovely nymphs."[40] There is something youthfully poetic

about such accounts, with their somewhat labored and florid imagery, but they also contain the perspectives of the gardener.

As of 1777, Tucker, so far as we know, had not yet designed or planted any gardens. In 1778 he married Frances Bland Randolph, the widowed mistress of Matoax plantation, and thereby acquired a garden that he took to planting immediately, especially with trees. By 1786, when he and his wife embarked on a tour to New York, Tucker's commentary on the gardens and landscapes he saw on that trip demonstrates a sharper and more confident critical judgment—the judgment of a landscape gardener—than those effusive entries about landscape in the earlier journal.

The Tuckers traveled between July and August, embarking from Portsmouth, where they were entertained the first night "very politely" by Richard Blow, Eliza Waller's father-in-law. It is a pity that Tucker did not jot down an account of Blow's garden. As his travel journal proceeds, it becomes evident that he was especially alert to prospects of river scenes with country seats dotted about, vessels passing up and down the river, and (after he arrived in New York) gardens such as Baron Friedrich von Steuben's. "From one part of his Garden," Tucker wrote, "there is a kind of Gallery shaded by trees, which projects over the extreme Bank of the [East] river—from four in the Evening until sunset this must be a most charming retreat from the heat." The views from such a gallery were doubtless dramatic and unexpected.

As Tucker proceeded along the East River, he savored the "delightful Prospects of Long Island"; and when he arrived at "the very delightful village of Jamaica," he felt compelled to record another scene of hills, farms, and trees: "on the left hand for about eight Miles of this road is a range of little hills which over look a number of delightful farms which fill the whole plain on the right hand of the road." He was struck with the spectacle of how agrarian industriousness was assisting nature and improving the inherent beauty of the landscape:

The soil is not in appearance very rich—but good management supplies what nature scantily affords. The size of the Farms is inconsiderable if compared with most of our plantations, but they are equally productive as some of ours of ten times their extent. The streets of Jamaica have a row of locust trees on each side which render the houses extremely cool, and have a very pleasing effect on the Eye.[41]

Tucker's comment on the tree-lined streets of Jamaica, New York, may imply some criticism of Williamsburg's hot streets, for it is not known whether the town's streets, apart from Palace Street, were lined by trees in this way.

Then the travelers were off to Fort Washington, where Tucker saw a sight that would perhaps surprise present residents of that area. To him, the view from a cliff above the river was a perfect composition, worthy of recording, and he generously uses words denoting variety and alluding to nature's designing genius:

The prospect from hence is infinitely varied. On the one side the lofty Cliffs of the North river, which sometimes appear to project over the river, give a Grandeur to the prospect far superior to any that I have seen—the beautiful plain of Haerlem, the meanderings of that little river, with the various interspersions of the Waters of the East-river beyond which is an extensive view of Long Island form a striking Contrast to the bold and noble view which I have just described.[42]

Unfortunately, he did not describe gardens on this tour in any detail, although he and his wife made a point of seeing quite a few.[43]

They rambled to various seats, including a house owned by a Mr. Apthorpe, where they were "civilly permitted to take a view of his Garden and Improvements." (In one of his almanacs, Tucker later noted he had obtained "a beautiful Shrubb" from Mr. Apthorpe's garden.) Then they were directed to the home of an "honest Dutch Brewer whose Garden we also visited." From there it was not far to New York City, the appearance of which did not please him at all: "Their houses are ill constructed; the rooms are very small. They have not an Inch of Garden, nay, hardly of a yard in most parts of the Town. The streets in general are very narrow—illy paved, and crooked." The city was not as attractive, presumably, as Williamsburg, nor were its gardens as memorable. He returned to Matoax in late August more convinced of the old capital's unique charms and more determined than ever to take up residence there.

Six years earlier, on an extended visit to Williamsburg, where he was recovering from an illness, Tucker had written to his wife at Matoax with a thought that had been on his mind for some time. "I wish more ardently than ever," he declared, "for a decent house in Wmsburg, and a small farm contiguous to the town—What say You? Can you resign Matoax and the Gayeties of it's unparallel'd Neighbourhood for the prospect of enjoying health, and less pleasure (that is to say frolick) in this little Village." In the past, Fanny had not taken to this idea enthusiastically. "I wish you liked the Spot," he continued, "as well as I do, I verily believe I should be tempted to do something conclusive before my return." By doing "something conclusive" he meant buying a house or lot in town. He had been licensed to practice law in Virginia for several years already and was confident of his ability to succeed, especially if he could live most of the time where the majority of his business originated. The town was having its problems, however.[44]

Although Jefferson and the General Assembly soon saw to it that the seat of government was transferred to Richmond, Tucker's feelings about Williamsburg did not change. What infuriated him were the ravages suffered by the town at the hands of the British Army in 1781, just before the Battle of Yorktown. Not entirely fairly, he laid the blame for most of the ills of "this unhappy Spot" on the British, from outbreaks of smallpox to plagues of flies. "As the British plundered all that they could," he complained in a letter to Fanny in July, "you will conceive how great an Appearance of wretchedness this place must exhibit."[45] He tucked away the idea of a Williamsburg home for better times and pleased his wife by focusing his energies on Matoax.[46]

Before Fanny died in late January 1788, Tucker had convinced her to move to Williamsburg, at least for part of the year. "I am at length an Inhabitant of W*m*sburg, if having a house without knowing what is in it can make me so," he joyfully wrote to John Page of Rosewell on January 13, 1788.[47] His joy was tempered by Fanny's death, however, just before they moved in as a family.

Described in 1782 as having "a good garden well paled in" and a "situation" which was "pleasant and healthy,"[49] the house, in Tucker's opinion, nevertheless had one drawback. Although it was on a parcel of land comprising three lots on the corner of Palace and Nicholson streets, just across Palace Street from George Wythe's imposing brick house, it faced Palace Street rather than Nicholson Street and the Market Square, which Tucker liked to think resembled an English village green. So he moved the house to face "Courthouse Green." With the house in its new position, the grounds in back of it could be gardened along Palace Street rather than along Nicholson Street and beside the Market Square. The house would thereby shield the gardens from the traffic and public nature of the square, while at the same time Palace Street would provide a more elegant, promenade-like boundary to the greater length of the garden.[49] In the short autobiography that he wrote about thirty years later, Tucker justified this ambitious project with the simple comment, "I was . . . extremely partial to a place where I had spent many very happy days."[50]

Gardening came along quickly in the new year. Old outbuildings were removed to make way for it. Father, sons, and the housekeeper, Maria Rind, moved into the house in January; 800 garden pales and 126 cedar posts were delivered in March; 132 garden rails in April and May; and 600 more garden pales in June. Tucker

had to decide fairly quickly where to locate his orchards so that he could position this paling accordingly and know where to plant the numbers of fruit trees he brought to the new garden from Matoax early in 1790. An interesting entry from his 1790 "Almanack" reads: "To be sent from Matoax: 1 Newtown pippin, 1 Esopus Spitzemburgs, 1 large early apple, 1 Doctor apple, 1 Early Bow apple, 1 Bergamot pear, 1 Bury de Roi pear, 1 Vergalieu pear, 1 Large fine apple, Clings peaches, 6 Seedling Cherries, 1 Green nectarine. Planted the above in my Garden in Williamsburg, February 1790."[51] Indeed, he was fortunate to have a well-established orchard and garden at Matoax to draw on rather as he might a nursery. He also could call upon his ten years' experience of gardening and fruit culture.

Until he remarried in 1791, Tucker kept up the gardens at Matoax and assisted with the administration of that plantation, enabling him to continue the transference of plants to his Williamsburg garden. After his marriage to the intelligent and witty widow Lelia Skipwith Carter, who had lived at Corotoman plantation, was the daughter of Sir Peyton Skipwith of Prestwould, and had emulated the gardening talents of her aunt, Lady Jean Skipwith, Tucker severed his connection with Matoax and turned all his attention to his own "Hermitage" in Williamsburg. A "Memo" in his 1792 "Almanack" (figure 97) therefore relates exclusively to that garden. The notes show that, with his Matoax source gone, he was relying heavily on friends from far and wide for plants, chiefly for fruit.[52] While he carried on with his fruit gardening, Tucker extended his house to include two new wings and a kitchen, turning a small house into a sizable family dwelling, although perhaps not a "Castle," as his good friend Dr. Philip Barraud of Williamsburg called it.[53]

As Tucker moved into the 1790s, he added natural history to his other considerable interests, which ranged from astronomy to early-eighteenth-century English literature. In October 1795, for example, he wrote a lengthy letter to Mathew Cary of Philadelphia, a collector and

97. Manuscript memorandum in an almanac belonging to St. George Tucker (1792).

founder of a new museum of local "specimens of earths, fossils, Plants, minerals &c." Tucker endorsed Cary's new enterprise but also recommended works by naturalists Mark Catesby and John Clayton in Virginia as worthy of study. Stating the by then commonplace theme that the study of Virginia's natural history was still deplorably undeveloped, he praises Cary as a man who possesses enough "spirit of Philosophy" to collect and examine "every different flower, shrub, tree, or blade of Grass that he meets." Then follows an account of what he calls "the Infancy of Authorship" regarding Virginia natu-

ral history, attempts at which "have heretofore been . . . either superficial—immensely costly—or consigned to oblivion":

> I have before me a Description of South Carolina printed in 1761 . . . which amounts to little more than a nomenclature—yet I deem it valuable, because it contains what I have not met with elsewhere. Catesby's natural history of which there is a copy in our College library, could not have cost less than twelve or fifteen guineas—being printed in two volumes of Atlas paper, with highly finished engravings, coloured, of every plant, bird, animal & fish that he describes. Doctor Clayton's flora virginica is only known to those who possess Gronovius's Works at large, being published by him.[54]

He goes on to summarize the abbreviated and frustrated scientific efforts of certain Virginians in recent years, especially "a Doctor Greenway of Dinwiddie County . . . said to have been engaged many years in the preparation of an hortus siccus."[55] For these reasons, he told Cary, he would like to encourage him both with his museum and with his publication of a serial to be titled *The American Museum*.[56]

There is no evidence that Tucker ever turned over a part of his own garden for the study of botany. His greatest and sustained love was fruit culture, and he and his wife concentrated on the ornamental uses of their grounds. One of the sources, however slight, of facts about their garden is Dr. Barraud, to whom Tucker in 1795 addressed the poem in which he mentioned Green Hill after the storm. Barraud's letters to Tucker in the late 1790s at times take on a bemused and detached view of his friend's enthusiastic gardening. Writing to Tucker in October 1796 about Tucker's family, whom in his absence Barraud often looked after, the doctor offers a tongue-in-cheek description of the Tucker household and its master's submersion in "village" life: "The world is alike a wilderness to him [Tucker], save this dear enchanting village. He calls it the terrestrial Paradise, the Seat of all joy and Delight, the Habitation of Angels and the

Society of God's chosen people. . . . Your Folks and the Castle are in Status-quo." He then added, "The Air is full of delicious odors—all nature seems cheerful. . . . There is nothing wanting to give us Paradise on Earth but a soaking Rain." In July 1800, a year after he moved to Norfolk, Barraud recalls the cooling effect of Tucker's garden in previous hot spells: "I hope your grass and Trees have soften'd the scortching [sic] sun beams about you." He greatly admired the garden. "The Pears begin to look tempting at your garden and the grapes too," he reported in August 1798, although he added that some nocturnal thief had made off with much of the fruit: "The peaches have been pillaged half ripe and God only knows how the Case may be with the pears and grapes." On another occasion, in May 1814, he praised the view of the garden, probably from the back doorway: "I am now beholding the Lawn from your door, so beautifully green and so richly bespangled with the yellow Flower—it is beautiful and serene."[57]

In that last letter Barraud even admired either his friend's own paintings or his collection of landscape and garden paintings, which offered, as he put it, "a full perspective of your groups, grottos, and waterfalls and the finest Imagery of your mind." This is a most interesting allusion to paintings as iconographic clues to Tucker's perception of gardens and landscapes. The identity of these paintings is unknown, but apparently they occupied a place in the complex of Tucker's values regarding housekeeping, alluding to a correspondence in his mind between image and fact, idea and reality, in which landscaping played no little part.

At the turn of the century, Tucker had been residing in Williamsburg for twelve years and had become its greatest apologist. He grew so warmly attached to his home life that after he resigned his William and Mary professorship of law in 1804 to take up the post of judge of the high court of appeals, he began to rue the legal duties that took him away from home. His absence made his gardening life appear that much more intense and desirable. In 1810, a year before Tucker gave up the judgeship, his understanding daughter, Fanny, wrote to her husband about her father's reluctance to leave the garden in the beauty of a sunny April: "It seems hard at his time of life to leave such a home as this and at this season too, when spring is putting forth all her charms. The double blossoms are beginning to look beautiful and the garden will soon exhibit many sweet and ornamental shrubs in perfection."[58]

It must have been a superbly colorful garden; there was at least plenty of yellow in it, judging by Barraud's remark about the yellow flower. The flowers were mainly under the care of Tucker's wife, whom he affectionately called the "Matron of the Green."[59] In a letter to his children in 1810, he praised her spirit and efforts in the garden: "Your Mama is in the Garden, planting, laying out, etc. etc. and even I have been trying my hand at grafting and making an Espalier of a peach tree. Next year perhaps may afford me no other employment so I may as well take a lesson or two before hand." Lelia had adopted the pose of the genteel "farmeress." "Will you believe," she asked her stepdaughter Fanny, "that I make every day a good plate of butter from my two cows, who have lately had calves and give me . . . between 3 and 4 gallons of milk a day."[60] She was as emotionally tied to the scene as her husband, fully responsive, as she put it, to "the sweet appearance of our House and everything around me." "I tear myself from the Garden this first real Spring day," she told Fanny, in order to write.[61]

We are able, then, to imagine somewhat the gardening lives the Tuckers led next to the Palace Green, although little is known about the garden itself other than that it consisted of orchards, flowers, and ornamental shrubs. Only a few details, mostly from Tucker's almanacs, add to this knowledge. The gardens consisted of slightly more than one acre laid out most likely in relation to a main north-south axis created by a central gravel walk (which Tucker mentioned in his poem "Riddle") leading from the main rear doorway of the house. Doubtless there was more than one north-south path, as in the Wythe garden, in addition to one or two cross-paths. Tucker also mentioned setting out some fruit stones at the corner of the stable; this stable, according to an 1815 insurance policy, stood due west of the house along the Palace Green. Garden pales probably ran along Nicholson Street and joined to the house; in the 1793 almanac Tucker scribbled that he had planted peach stones "at the Corner of the house on the south of the pales, East End." Two other almanac entries mention willow trees at the south and east sides of the stables.[62] In the poem that Tucker wrote about the great storm in 1795, he mentions that his garden included elms, willows, poplars, and catalpas, as well as apples, peaches, and pears.

To illustrate the variety of color and plants in the garden as well as the enthusiasm Tucker maintained for it through the years, consider two accounts from the almanacs that describe what was blooming. The first entry is from March 1794:

> In the course of the last week, peaches, nectarines, Cherries, and plumbs bloom. Blossoms of Apples and pears appear. Leaves of the Locust appear. Poplar buds appear. Lombardy poplar begins to shew its leaf. Ashen buds swelled. Green willow party—yellow willow more generally, and weeping willows in full, leaf. Flowering almond bloom. Double blossom peach begins to bloom.

And this is what he wrote for February 26, 1820: "Apricots in Bloom: a young Peach partly in blossom. Lilacks, willows, Aspen, Rose bushes & other shrubs in Leaf. Pears & Peaches with Blossoms much swell'd & Spring fast approaching."[63]

It would have taken more than gentle persuasion to rouse Tucker out of retirement in 1814. No less a personage than Jefferson tried to do it by suggesting him for the post of judge of the federal court for Virginia. John Coalter, his son-in-law, was at a loss when people asked why Tucker continually declined the appointment.

At last he thought of perhaps the most plausible answer: "to all this," he wrote in a jocular letter to Tucker, "I am obliged to confess that he is gardening, scraping his fruit trees, nursing his flowers, etc."[64] This was a reply that Jefferson, for one, would have acknowledged as believable and worthy. Tucker summed it all up in a tender poem, "On Domestic Happiness" (1809):

> Be this my Lot, beneath the rural Shade,
> Where peace, and comfort, and Contentment
>   dwell.[65]

The garden was for him a symbol of contentment. It was also his way of articulating the meaning of the town for him: he did not need the world of the busy company of men in Richmond, Washington, or anywhere else. He could renounce all that with a show of Horatian independence and indifference.

When the time comes for Colonial Williamsburg Foundation to restore Tucker's garden, its privacy, intimacy, and beauty will suggest the type of meaning both Tucker and Prentis added to Williamsburg's gardening history. Of all the town gardeners who have been the subjects of this study, none appear to have depended on their gardens so deeply and introspectively as these two lawyers. They sought privacy, fulfillment, contentment, and domestic peace in them. They luxuriated in the pleasures of horticulture and landscape. Twice Dr. Barraud applied the term *paradise* to Tucker's own sense of his landscape; a relative of Prentis's spoke of his "rural" town garden and of his "Attachment" to the place. David Meade wrote of the involuntary connection in his mind of Prentis and flowers; "no mortal could pardon" damage to them, remarked Tucker, perhaps invoking again the image of a terrestrial paradise.

• • •

Images of paradise applied to the American landscape had always been commonplace, but not until the late eighteenth and early nineteenth centuries did they come to be linked in American thought and literature with national identity or patriotism and Romantic sensibilities about the sublimity of wild or open landscape and the individual's place in it. Washington Irving eloquently described the prevailing self-conscious American attitude toward the American landscape in 1819:

> on no country have the charms of nature been more prodigally lavished. Her mighty lakes, like oceans of liquid silver; her mountains, with their bright aerial tints; her valleys, teeming with wild fertility; her tremendous cataracts, thundering in their solitudes; her boundless plains, waving with spontaneous verdure; her broad deep rivers, rolling in solemn silence to the ocean; her trackless forests, where vegetation puts forth all its magnificence; her skies, kindling with the magic of summer clouds and glorious sunshine: —no, never need an American look beyond his own country for the sublime and beautiful of natural scenery.[66]

There was more to the attitude toward landscape than that, however. Americans were not long behind the British in responding to Romantic poets such as Wordsworth and Keats and "the beauteous forms" of nature that they celebrated. But they felt especially well endowed by the Creator in possessing a majestic landscape that they believed could, much more readily than the pastoral and picturesque English landscape, inspire elevated moods and, as Wordsworth put it,

> a sense sublime
> Of something far more deeply interfused,
> Whose dwelling is the light of setting suns,
> And the round ocean and the living air,
> And the blue sky. . . .[67]

Jefferson had felt the specialness of the American landscape, but his mind was more on practical landscaping possibilities than on poetic sensibilities. He was no poet. The lawyer-poet Tucker, on the other hand, often felt how landscape could, again in Wordsworth's words, "flash upon that inward eye / Which is the bliss of solitude."[68] Tucker's moods and impulses composed a sort of prelude to the Romantic American dream or vision, although he localized them in Williamsburg and certain plantations he liked to visit. Philip Freneau, the American poet who bridged the classicism of the eighteenth century and the romanticism of the nineteenth, and who was a contemporary of Tucker's, articulated movingly the power of landscapes and gardens to induce moods and attitudes in ways that Tucker must surely have known and appreciated, although Freneau had in mind his native New England landscape. Describing in "House of Night" (1779) a neglected garden next to a domed house—a type of setting in which Tucker occasionally had pleasing and evocative picnics with his friends—Freneau generates feelings worthy of the so-called pre-Romantic gothic, graveyard school of English poetry:

> And by that light around the dome appear'd
> A mournful garden of autumnal hue,
> Its lately pleasing flowers all drooping stood
> Amidst high weeds that in rank plenty grew.
> . . . . . .
> No pleasant fruit or blossom gaily smil'd.
> Naught but unhappy plants and trees were
> seen,
> The yew, the myrtle, and the church-yard elm,
> The cypress, with its melancholy green.[69]

Tucker's and Prentis's gardens reflected complexes of values, attitudes, and emotions that explain their particular attraction and force, even as they also, ironically, reflected an increasing neglect of the old capital. The gardens thrived because the individual personas thrived; but the town declined. There was an unmistakable air of melancholy about it all.

Conclusion

Most Virginians who struggled with the "culture of the earth," as Thomas Jefferson put it, limited their efforts to productive gardening in order to sustain their household economies. They did not leave much evidence of their efforts. But from the late seventeenth century, across the eighteenth century, and into the nineteenth—from Alexander Spotswood and John Custis to Thomas Jefferson and St. George Tucker—Virginia also produced a remarkable diversity of creative gardening personalities who looked upon gardening not merely as a source of food but also as a form of self-expression and art. For many of them it was a science, too, that they strove to understand more clearly in the New World. Their horticultural discoveries made their gardens more productive, varied, and beautiful and were of immense interest to European botanists.

Several elements characterized Virginia garden history from the late seventeenth to the early nineteenth century. A few of the more important were botanical searches and experimentation, political rivalry, social pride and ambition, personal ego, feelings about local attachment, a strong sense of place, appreciation of open landscape, ideas about civilized and cultured living,

the interrelation of town and plantation gardening, family identity, literary allusion, the combination of the beautiful and useful, the ferme ornée, dependence upon European gardening books and ideas, the search for variety, the opening up of prospects within garden layouts, and a growing sense of the native landscape as a canvas upon which something of the new nation's ideals and hopes might be traced.

From the perspectives of Prentis and Tucker in Williamsburg, it is particularly clear how the mood and character of gardening throughout the eighteenth century had altered. As a pair of contemporary gardeners at the end of the century, they invite comparison to another pair in the first quarter of the century, Spotswood and Custis. Unlike Custis, neither Prentis nor Tucker adopted horticulture as a scientific pursuit, a matter for botanical experimentation. Custis clearly wished to lay out and plant a lovely garden, and the garden turned out to be a source of intensely personal gratification and disappointment; but his overwhelming interest was in the pursuit—one might almost say mad pursuit—of plants, mostly from England. That accounts for his ultimate frustration as well as achievement. One imagines from his letters that he was seldom content enough with his creation to be at peace with it and simply appreciate it. Always there was the search for more specimens, with endless questions about what could or could not thrive. Fellow botanists were immensely grateful to him, but it seems he had little time for the simple pleasures and profound personal appreciation of the art of gardening that we have glimpsed in Prentis, Tucker, Washington, and Jefferson. The affection and warmth of imagination with which these four invested their gardens was obvious and remarked upon by friends and relatives. Custis, with his egocentric sense of a botanical mission, failed to endow his garden with these ingredients. Jefferson had his own ideas of a landscaping mission to perform, but Prentis and Tucker did not. Tucker's plea for a Virginia natural history did not relate, really, to his garden. It was an intellectual sentiment, not so much a philosophical or personal one. His and Prentis's attitudes reflected an acceptance of the town as it had become. They had no desire to change it. Even their relative lack of interest in acquiring foreign plants bespoke an acceptance of the conditions under which they gardened.

Custis sought to use his garden as a source of credibility for the civilization and culture of his town. Spotswood, through his gardening, pursued a similar goal, although in a more psychologically complex way. His own personal well-being and self-serving came into it heavily. He hoped for growth and cultural development for Williamsburg at a time when the town sorely needed it. On top of that, he himself needed cultural reassurance. With his designing abilities, he obtained it vainly and with some defiance of the House of Burgesses and contemporaries like Custis and Byrd. Even politics entered the gardening picture. Such a gardening scene was not, therefore, exactly peaceful and idyllic; there were tensions and not always a great deal of charity. But that tension reflects the uncertain and early stages of both colonial and town culture, just as Prentis and Tucker's gardening milieu reflects a less pretentious and ambitious

town. Especially with the college and Palace gardens deteriorating, there was at the end of the century a sense that the town's gardening was coming to an end. Instead of using their gardens as signals of their own distinction, Prentis and Tucker resorted to them to escape, as a way to lose themselves in their village.

To put these differences in another, more general way, it can be said that as the century wore on and drew to a close, gardeners and landscapers such as Washington, Jefferson, Prentis, and Tucker allowed themselves, as Robert Frost put it, to be possessed by the native landscape. They no longer desired, as had Spotswood, Custis, Byrd, and others, to be possessed by European culture—"Possessed by what we now no more possessed." Paradoxically, they "found salvation in surrender." The note of harmony in Prentis's and Tucker's gardening sprang essentially from this surrender. Frost's lines are very apt as a postscript to this history:

> The land was ours before we were the land's.
> She was our land more than a hundred years
> Before we were her people. She was ours
> In Massachusetts, in Virginia,
> But we were England's, still colonials,
> Possessing what we still were unpossessed by,
> Possessed by what we now no more possessed.
> Something we were withholding made us weak
> Until we found it was ourselves
> We were withholding from our land of living,
> And forthwith found salvation in surrender.[1]

Whereas during the first half of the eighteenth century aspiring garden designers were preoccupied with European models and precedents, both scientific and artistic, and even cited them as evidence of their cosmopolitanism and expertise, toward the end of the century and into the next the theme increasingly was independence. This was true even though in practice late-century European landscaping ideas, especially English, exerted a fresh influence. Joseph Prentis's old friend, David Meade of Maycox, reflects this independence with a hint of defiance in a letter of June 13, 1797, written from the relative wilderness of Kentucky, where he had been landscape gardening. Flushed with an enthusiasm derived from working in what seemed to him an untouched landscape, and somewhat smugly looking back east to Virginia as a landscape he had outgrown, Meade declared: "there is nothing wanting but the hand of art—which . . . would form the productive farm—or the delightful Garden." In Kentucky, he told Prentis, he found even more scope than in Virginia for that "species of horticulture tending more to pleasure than profit," and he announced confidently that his garden at Chaumiere, "containing forty acres including ten acres of dressed native wood—is more extensive than any other in the United States which is said by all foreigners and eastern Americans who have visited them." He could not avoid censuring the more established and famous gardens in "the vicinity of the Eastern Cities" for what he construed as the prodigality of their owners. They had only one-quarter of the garden space he landscaped, yet they had been spending one hundred times as much as he, mainly on pompous ornamentation. He exaggerated their use of "gravel walks, marble basons with gold and silver fish, urns, statues, iron gates, and expensive green and hot houses, but little of nature."[2] The bias of his remarks notwithstanding, he points to a new mood at the end of the century.

With a transatlantic perspective, Horace Walpole struck a prophetic note in 1775 just before the outbreak of war. He imagined a declaration of gardening independence when he predicted that "some American will . . . revive the true taste in gardening. . . . I love to skip into futurity and imagine what will be done on the giant scale of a new hemisphere."[3] Walpole did not base his statement on any knowledge of American gardens. He simply lamented what he perceived to be the incipient stages of a reaction against the idealizing landscape gardening of Capability Brown in favor of an affected variety and intricacy that he thought characterized the picturesque school. The rising interest in horticulture

and uses of gardens as places to display flowers and flowering shrubs struck him, even in a manmade landscape, as out of tune with the sublimity of open landscape. For him, the best seemed over by 1770. Perhaps there was hope for a revival in America, where huge expanses of unspoiled and panoramic landscape offered endless opportunities to invoke "ideal beauty," with its natural harmony and continuity.

Many of the beauties of Monticello and Mount Vernon, as well as those of other plantations considered in this book, would have pleased Walpole—especially the distant prospects of uncultivated or "unimproved" countryside that seemed never to end. Indeed, Jefferson said much the same as Walpole about the potential of the American landscape gardener to approximate the large brushstrokes of sublime nature in the landscape garden. The American landscape garden, however, never realized that vision.

In America, as in England, the direction in the new century was toward the picturesque display of plants in gardens, a development promoted by the proliferation of nurseries and seed houses all over the East and by plant-hunting expeditions to all parts of the world. This horticultural emphasis, which was apparent early in the gardening spirit of Jefferson, Washington, Prentis, and Tucker, was not at all what Walpole had in mind. This was the picturesque and gardenesque again. Would he not have read such gardening as Americans' betrayal of their own landscape?

Yet the stunted growth of the American landscape garden resulted from a more significant cause. Bernard McMahon was not blind to the problem, but he seemed confused about the causes: America "has not yet made that rapid progress in Gardening, ornamental planting, and fanciful rural designs, which might naturally be expected from an intelligent, happy, and independent people, possessed so universally of landed property, unoppressed by taxation or tithes, and blessed with consequent comfort and affluence."[4] One reason for this lack of progress was hinted at in Meade's censure of the extravagance of some American landscapers: the liberal spirit of freedom and equality did not tend in that direction. John Loudon put the case clearly in his popular *Encyclopedia of Gardening* (1834):

> Landscape gardening is practiced in the United States on a comparatively limited scale; because in a country where all men have equal rights, and where every man, however humble, has a house and garden of his own, it is not likely that there should be many large parks [that is, private landscape gardens]. The only splendid examples of park and hot-house gardening that, we trust, will ever be found in the United States, and ultimately in every country are such that will be formed by towns, villages, or other communities, for the joint use and enjoyment of all inhabitants or members.[5]

He was perfectly correct. Americans in the nineteenth century, led by the likes of Andrew Jackson Downing and Frederick Law Olmsted, would put their energies chiefly into public gardens and parks. In retrospect, the eighteenth-century garden history of America would seem like a promise unfulfilled: a private world to some extent inspired by English examples and ideas, symbolic of hopes in the New World, tempered by economics and the climate, and ultimately dimmed by the ascendancy of the park movement and the economic and democratic realities of the nineteenth century. It would not really have its renaissance until the colonial revival movement in the twentieth century.

Notes

Abbreviations

CWF   Colonial Williamsburg Foundation
CWFL   Colonial Williamsburg Foundation Library,
       Special Collections
EJC   *Executive Journals of the Council of Colonial*
       Virginia, 6 vols. (Richmond, 1925)
JHB   *Journals of the House of Burgesses of Virginia*,
       13 vols., edited by H. R. McIlwaine (Rich-
       mond, 1915)
LJC   *Legislative Journals of the Council of Colonial*
       Virginia, 3 vols., edited by H. R. McIlwaine
       (Richmond, 1918)
VMHB   *Virginia Magazine of History and Biography*
WMQ   *William and Mary Quarterly*

Introduction

1. Nicholas Purcell, in his essay, "Town in Country and Country in Town," in *Ancient Roman Villa Gardens*, ed. Elisabeth B. MacDougall, Dumbarton Oaks Colloquium on the History of Landscape Architecture, 10 (Washington, D.C., 1987), observes that in Roman gardens (both in and out of town or city) "*both* town and country and their mutual connections were part of the total landscape into which the house of the wealthy man was inserted" (p. 195). Judith Kinnard has illustrated how at the Renaissance Villa Gamberaia in Settignano, outside Florence, the house and garden together projected and reinterpreted urban images in which gardens and garden-like settings played a part; see her essay, "The Villa Gamberaia in Settignano: The Street in the Garden," *Journal of Garden History* 6, no. 1 (1986): 1–18. In his overview of Dutch gardens, John Dixon Hunt also presents this theme: "Given the small and compartmentalized nature of many Dutch gardens, especially before the French style found favour and sometimes even when it had, it is not wholly strange that visitors to the Low Countries saw their towns as gardens, too. . . . The exchangeable effect of town and garden, noticed by so many more travellers, suggests, then, something of the latter's scale and effect." Hunt, "Reckoning with Dutch Gardens," *Journal of Garden History* 8, nos. 2 and 3 (1988): 52. For some time, garden historians have, in one way or another, interpreted eighteenth-century English country and city gardens in terms of each other.

2. A provocative and historically useful study of the opposition of country and city in English thought, as manifest in literature, is Raymond Williams, *The Country and the City* (London, 1973).

3. *Gnomologia: Adagies and Proverbs, Wise Sentences and Witty Sayings, Ancient and Modern, Foreign and British* (London, 1732), no. 701.

4. See, for example, Karen Ordahl Kupperman's fascinating article, "The Puzzle of the American Climate in the Early Colonial Period," *American His-*

torical Review 87 (December 1982): 1262–89. I am indebted to this article for my explanation of the problem that climate posed for Virginia gardeners. See also the Spring 1980 issue of *The Journal of Interdisciplinary History*, which is devoted to the history of climate.

5. *Brothers of the Spade: Correspondence of Peter Collinson, of London, and John Custis, of Williamsburg, Virginia, 1734–46*, ed. Earl G. Swem (Barre, Mass., 1957), p. 73.

6. December 4, 1736; *Brothers of the Spade*, p. 38.

7. October 20, 1741; *Brothers of the Spade*, p. 77. On February 6, 1743, Collinson again is perplexed by what he hears of the Virginia climate: "I would never have Imagined but by your Information that In your Latitude you should have such severe Weather as to make such Havock amongst Hardy Vegitables" (p. 82).

8. John R. Stilgoe, *Common Landscape of America, 1580 to 1845* (New Haven and London, 1982), p. 142.

9. January 31, 1740; *Brothers of the Spade*, p. 67.

10. Barbara Sarudy has argued in a special issue of the *Journal of Garden History* devoted to "Eighteenth-Century Gardens of the Chesapeake" (9, nos. 3 and 4 [July–September 1989]) that the naturalized English garden of the early eighteenth century had a negligible effect on Chesapeake gardening during the whole of the century. See especially "A Late Eighteenth-Century Tour of Baltimore Gardens" (pp. 125–40). Although I confirm her observations that the "traditional" geometric patterns of gardens in the Chesapeake remained dominant throughout the century, I disagree with her position that there was negligible movement toward the natural, especially in the last half of the century.

11. Joseph Spence, *Observations, Anecdotes, and Characters of Books and Men*, ed. James M. Osborn (Oxford, 1966), 1:252.

Chapter 1

1. *Observations Gathered Out of 'A Discourse of the Plantation of the Southerne Colonie in Virginia by the English,' 1606. Written by that honorable gentleman, Master George Percy*, ed. David B. Quinn (Charlottesville, 1967), p. 17.

2. See "Correspondence of Alexander Spotswood

with John Spotswood of Edinburgh," ed. Lester J. Cappon, *VMHB* 60 (April 1952): 229.

3. For an analysis of seventeenth-century perspectives on the Tidewater landscape, see John R. Stilgoe, *Common Landscape of America, 1580 to 1845* (New Haven and London, 1982), pp. 58–77.

4. Thomas Hariot attempted this type of description for the early settlement on Roanoke Island in North Carolina about twenty years before Percy. See Thomas Hariot, *A brief and true report . . .* (1588). A facsimile edition of the 1588 quarto was edited by R. G. Adams and published by the William L. Clements Library (Ann Arbor, 1931).

5. *Newes from Virginia: The Lost Flocke Triumphant* (1610), ed. W. F. Craven (New York, 1937), lines 113–17, 150–51.

6. Robert Beverley, *The History and Present State of Virginia*, ed. Louis B. Wright (Chapel Hill, 1947), pp. 16, 297, 298–99, 316. Beverley revised and enlarged his 1705 *History* for a new edition in 1722; citations here are taken from the 1722 edition, but unless otherwise stated the passages are part of the 1705 edition. For an analysis of the seventeenth-century English phrase "garden of the world," as applied chiefly to Italy, see John Dixon Hunt's provocative book, *Garden and Grove: The Italian Renaissance Garden in the English Imagination, 1600–1750* (Princeton and London, 1986), pt. 1, esp. pp. 80–81.

7. James D. Kornwolf, "The Picturesque in the American Garden and Landscape before 1800," in *British and American Gardens in the Eighteenth Century*, ed. Peter Martin and Robert P. Maccubbin (Charlottesville, 1984), pp. 94–95.

8. Edmund S. Morgan, *American Slavery, American Freedom: The Ordeal of Colonial Virginia* (New York, 1975), bk. 2.

9. Archaeological excavations at seventeenth-century 'sites like the Clifts plantation at Stratford, Virginia, have revealed that plantation grounds were work-oriented and generally prosaic in appearance. Gardens were areas for food crops that were enclosed by simple paling or with worm fences (split rails stacked in zig-zag fashion on the ground). See Fraser D. Neiman, *The 'Manner House' Before Stratford* (Stratford, Va., 1980).

10. For an account of the nature of immigrant elitism in Virginia at the end of the seventeenth century, see Carole Shammas, "English-Born and Creole Elites in Turn-of-the-Century Virginia," in *The*

Chesapeake in the Seventeenth Century: Essays on Anglo-American Society, ed. Thad W. Tate and David L. Ammerman (Chapel Hill, 1979), p. 278.

11. Lawson's letters from 1701–1711 are appended (pp. 267–73) to his *Description of North-Carolina* (1718); see *A New Voyage to Carolina*, ed. H. T. Lefler (Chapel Hill, 1967).

12. *Carolina, or a Description of the Present State of that Country*, reprinted in *Narratives of Early Carolina, 1650–1708*, ed. Alexander S. Salley Jr. (New York, 1911), p. 145.

13. Francis Nicholson Papers, Special Collections, CWFL. For a useful summary of the abortive efforts in the seventeenth century to establish an alternative to Jamestown as the capital of Virginia, see John Reps, *Tidewater Towns: City Planning in Colonial Virginia and Maryland* (Charlottesville, 1972), chap. 3.

14. *JHB*, I, p. 38. In an optimistic effort to establish silk and wine as consumer products, the 1624 act also required the planting of four mulberry trees and twenty vines for each male over age twenty in a household.

15. Ralph Hamor, *A True Discourse of the Present Estate of Virginia* (1615), ed. A. L. Rowse (Richmond, 1957), p. 23. In a 1623 "Letter of the Governor, Council, and Assembly of *Virginia* to the King," the following passage describes the relative roles of use and ornament in private houses in the colony: "Our Houses, for the most Part, are rather built for Use than Ornament; yet not a few for both, and fit to give Entertainment to Men of good Quality" (*JHB*, I, p. 24).

16. Letter to John Ferrar, April 8, 1623, cited in R. B. Davis, *George Sandys: Poet-Adventurer* (London and New York, 1955), p. 153. Pierce's wife later boasted "she hath a garden at Jamestown containing three or four acres, where in one year she hath gathered near a hundred bushels of excellent figs and that she can keep a better house in Virginia for three or four hundred pounds than in London, yet went there with little or nothing." *Works of Captain John Smith*, ed. A. Arber (Birmingham, Eng., 1884), p. 887; cited in Edward Neill, *Virginia Carolarum* (Albany, N.Y., 1886), p. 61.

17. See Richard Beale Davis, *Intellectual Life in the Colonial South 1585–1763*, 3 vols. (Knoxville, 1978), 3:1209–10.

18. See Peter Force, ed., *Tracts and Other Papers, Relating Principally to the Origins, Settlement, and Progress of the Colonies in North America . . . to the Year 1776*, 4 vols. (1836–1846), 2: viii, p. 4. The writing on seventeenth-century southern gardening, including Jamestown, has been highly romantic. In the absence of documentary evidence and thorough garden archaeology, of course, it is also highly speculative. See, for example, Alice B. Lockwood, *Gardens of Colony and State: Gardens and Gardeners of the American Colonies and of the Republic Before 1840*, 2 vols. (New York, 1934), 2:37–47; and Henry C. Forman, *Jamestown and St. Mary's: Buried Cities of Romance* (Baltimore, 1938) and *Tidewater Maryland Architecture and Gardens* (New York, 1956).

19. Earlier interpretation of the brick wall as the remains of the north wall of a house ignored the following evidence suggesting a terraced garden wall: brick work is finished on the south face and unfinished on the north face; the ends of the walls are finished with closers; there is no sign of broken brick or mortar fragments in the east and west boundary ditches; the brick wall is higher and narrower than those that usually supported large frame buildings; and, most important, the area enclosed by the wall and ditches is the wrong shape and size for a seventeenth-century building without evidence of internal divisions. There is also a wooden upright set into the wall cavity at the top of the steps on which a garden gate could have been mounted. The area is aligned with, and may have belonged to, a structure identified as S44-59-138. See the report on this brick wall, identified as Structure 100, in CWFL.

20. The plan is a surveyor's plat showing the Charles County, Maryland, courthouse. It is taken from Margaret Brown Klapthor and Paul Dennis Brown, *A History of Charles County, Maryland, Written in Its Tercentenary Year of 1958* (La Plata, Md., 1958), facing p. 22.

21. In his journal for August 3, 1797, Benjamin Latrobe, Ludwell's reluctant architect, wrote: "He [Ludwell] has entirely pulled down his old mansion, and he wanted me for the 3d time to give him a *new* design to proceed upon. I did so, but as his meannness seemed to grow upon him daily, I found it impossible for me to bend my ideas. . . . I therefore declined any further connection with him" (*The Virginia Journals of Benjamin Henry Latrobe 1795–1798*, ed. Edward C. Carter II [New Haven and London, 1977],

1:247). Louis B. Wright has written briefly about Berkeley in *First Gentlemen of Virginia* (San Marino, Calif., 1940), pp. 76–77. Louis R. Caywood directed the archaeology on the site of Green Spring in the early 1950s; see his report, "Excavations at Green Spring Plantation" (Yorktown, Va., 1955); and "Green Spring Plantation," *VMHB* 65 (1957): 67–83. See also Jesse Demmick, "Green Spring," *WMQ* 2d ser., 9 (1929): 129–30; and Jane Carson, "Green Spring Plantation in the Seventeenth-Century" (December 1954), Research Report, Special Collections, CWFL.

22. Berkeley recorded many of his observations on Virginia in his "Discourse and View of Virginia," British Library, Egerton MS 2395, ff. 354–59.

23. Appended to Berkeley's *Perfect Description of Virginia*; Force, ed., *Tracts*, 2: viii, p. 14.

24. Thomas Povey to Edward Digges, 1661, *WMQ* 2d ser., 1 (1921): 66. Povey's letter book (1655–1659), dealing with the West Indies and America, is in the British Library, Add. Ms. 11411.

25. Lady Berkeley's letter, the Cunliff-Lister Muniments, Bradford, Yorkshire, Bundle 69, Section 11.

26. After the Restoration, Berkeley had about seventeen years left to him to develop the gardens and landscape at Green Spring. It is likely that his mansion and gardens received a major stimulus from his marriage in 1670, at the age of sixty-four, to the thirty-six-year-old Frances Culpeper Stevens. Alternatively, Philip Ludwell, who married the widowed Lady Berkeley in 1678 and thereby became the master of the place, may have supervised the alterations.

27. See the entries for 1711–1712 especially, in *The Secret Diary of William Byrd of Westover 1709–12*, ed. Louis B. Wright and Marion Tinling (Richmond, 1941).

28. This letter was published in *VMHB* 23 (1915): 358.

29. See Blathwayt to Col. Philip Ludwell, December 10, 1710, William Blathwayt Papers, CWFL.

30. For a summary of the archaeological findings in the gardens at Bacon's Castle, see "Bacon's Castle," ed. Stephenson B. Andrews, Research Bulletin 3, Association for the Preservation of Virginia Antiquities (Richmond, 1984), pp. 30–32; and Nicholas Luccketti, "Archaeological Excavations at Bacon's Castle Garden, Surry County, Virginia," Interim Report, James River Institute for Archaeology, Inc., June 1987. The garden details that follow are taken from the Luccketti report.

31. For a lucid discussion of the diffusion of culture in the colonies, see Richard Bushman, "American High-Style and Vernacular Cultures," in *Colonial British America: Essays in the New History of the Early Modern Era*, ed. Jack P. Greene and J. R. Pole (Baltimore and London, 1984), pp. 345–83. I am indebted to this article for my remarks on this subject. Bushman's main point is that this diffusion of culture resulted not merely from the emulation of distant English society but also from the "strivings" of provincial Americans for an ideal that "had power of its own apart from the repetition of English behavior" (p. 352). Even so, as Bushman points out, this broadening of culture had to await the construction of stylish houses for the English middle class in the second and third decades of the century. On the spread of culture throughout the English middle classes, see J. H. Plumb, *The Commercialization of Leisure in Eighteenth-Century England* (Reading, 1973).

32. The social ambitions of these "gentleman" planters are analyzed and documented thoroughly by Louis B. Wright in *First Gentlemen of Virginia*. See also Richard Beale Davis, *William Fitzhugh and His Chesapeake World, 1676–1701: The Fitzhugh Letters and Other Documents* (Chapel Hill, 1963), pp. 3–55; and Thomas J. Wertenbaker, *The Planters of Colonial Virginia* (Princeton, 1922).

33. Edmund S. Morgan has explained the growth of slavery in the late seventeenth century and analyzed its influences in *American Slavery, American Freedom*, pp. 295–315. See also Wright, *First Gentlemen of Virginia*, p. 45. Wright observed that slavery in the late seventeenth century created "an economic situation conducive to the growth of an aristocratic order." On the growth of slavery, see also Lois Green Carr and Russell R. Menard, "Immigration and Opportunity: The Freedman in Early Colonial Maryland," in *The Chesapeake in the Seventeenth Century*, pp. 238–39.

34. Wertenbaker, *Planters of Colonial Virginia*, pp. 157–58.

35. Much of Fitzhugh and Byrd I's correspondence has survived. Fitzhugh's letters have been edited by Richard Beale Davis in *William Fitzhugh and His Chesapeake World*, and Byrd I's by Marion Tinling in *The Correspondence of the Three William Byrds of Westover, Virginia, 1684–1776*, 2 vols.

(Charlottesville, 1977), 1: pt. 1 (hereafter cited as *Byrd Correspondence*). Carole Shammas has explained that the English immigrant elite in seventeenth-century Virginia somewhat doubted, and were made to doubt by the English, their own legitimacy as rich gentlemen with accompanying social graces. See her essay, "English-Born and Creole Elites," pp. 274–96.

36. Shammas, "English-Born and Creole Elites," p. 279. Shammas points out that Virginia was not even the first choice of Englishmen emigrating to plantation colonies. In a letter to Nicholas Hayward, dated January 30, 1687, Fitzhugh observes that he certainly wishes well to any of his family and friends contemplating immigration to Virginia and hopes "they may sit safely under their own Vines & fig trees, & pray God to continue the same," but that they ought at the same time to be modest in their expectations. He acknowledges that he is well off: "I desire neither to be better seated, & am plentifully provided," he writes, in "a Country that agrees well with my constitution & desire, being of a melancholly constitution, & desire privacy & retirement." He adds, however, "I am for a Remove to take off that strangeness. . . . Our Estates here depend altogether upon Contingencys, & to prepare against that, causes me to exceed my Inclinations in worldly affairs, & Society that is good & ingenious is very scarce, & seldom to be come at except in books" (Davis, *William Fitzhugh and His Chesapeake World*, p. 205).

37. Davis, *William Fitzhugh and His Chesapeake World*, p. 173. On the metaphor of planters as patriarchs—a self-image that Byrd II especially would nourish in the 1720s and 1730s—see Rhys Isaac, *The Transformation of Virginia, 1740–1790* (Chapel Hill, 1982), pp. 21, 39–42, 301, 344–49. See also Julia C. Spruill, *Women's Life and Work in the Southern Colonies* (New York, 1972), p. 44.

38. Fitzhugh to Dr. Ralph Smith, April 22, 1686. See Davis, *William Fitzhugh and His Chesapeake World*, pp. 175–76; see also pp. 178, 189–90, and 203–4.

39. Wright, *First Gentlemen of Virginia*, p. 161.

40. *A Huguenot in Exile: or Voyages of a Frenchman exiled for his Religion with a description of Virginia & Maryland*, ed. Gilbert Chinard (New York, 1934), p. 151. Later Durand found himself "ex-tolling upon the beauty of the place we had just seen, the same lovely hills whence flow fountains and brooks, & broad meadows below, always covered with wild grapevines" (p. 154). Ralph Wormeley's landscaping at Rosegill, if indeed there was much in the ornamental sense to speak of, is illuminated somewhat by the books we know were in his library. He appears to have been receptive to French ideas. He owned two copies, for example, of *Maison Rustique; or, The Country Farm* (1616) by Charles Estienne and Jean Liebault, a French work that was prepared for English readership by Gervase Markham. It contained advice on ornamental planting and garden design as well as on agriculture. The seventeenth-century library at the Carter plantation, Corotoman, also contained this book. Significantly, Wormeley possessed a work by the eminent horticulturist and garden designer Sir John Evelyn: *The French Gardiner* (1658) is a useful guide to orchard and other utilitarian planting and how it all could be made to look elegant. See Wright, *First Gentlemen of Virginia*, pp. 207, 244.

41. Even Fitzhugh's interest in plants appears to have been essentially practical and scientific. For example, he asked his brother Henry to send him "raritys" like olives with directions on how to grow them to see if they "would not thrive in this country" (Davis, *William Fitzhugh and His Chesapeake World*, p. 216). Whether the "choice Plants" he was expecting from an English friend in January 1687 were ornamental or practical is not so clear, but he did exhibit an appreciation of the scarcity of cultivated specimens: "I thankfully take notice & longingly expect those choice Plants, mentioned in your letter, & when they arrive shall take great care to plant them in proper places, & at seasonable times, & doubt not their thriving" (ibid., p. 204).

42. See Donald Worster, *Nature's Economy: The Roots of Ecology* (San Francisco, 1982), pp. 3–55.

43. Beverley, *History*, p. 128.

44. Ibid., pp. 127–28.

45. This kind of allusion to the sublime or picturesque in landscape was rare in England at the time, especially in connection with gardens. Beverley may not have fully realized it, but English gardeners generally were far from ready—aesthetically, philosophically, or personally—for this kind of gardening. In fact, Thomas Burnet's

Sacred Theory of the Earth (1684), a volume that was in the libraries of Fitzhugh, Wormeley, and Byrd I (see Wright, *First Gentlemen of Virginia*, pp. 180, 204, 318), pseudo-scientifically announced that God had created the world flat but that the sinning of man had caused upheavals rendering it hilly and mountainous. With that sort of moral discourse coloring people's sensibilities about landscape configuration, it is not surprising that the seventeenth century on the whole found mountainous scenery less pleasing than did the eighteenth century. See Basil Willey, *The Eighteenth Century Background: Studies on the Idea of Nature in the Thought of the Period* (London, 1940), pp. 27–75.

46. Beverley, *History*, p. 140.
47. Ibid., p. 298.
48. Ibid., p. 316.
49. Ibid., pp. 293, 298.
50. Ibid., p. 139.
51. Ibid., p. 233.
52. One hesitates to call them botanical gardens at this early date. The earliest known, John Bartram's botanical gardens on the Schuylkill River outside Philadelphia, which he started in the 1730s, were the first so designated for commercial purposes in colonial America. The only available printed source of Bartram's letters is *Memorials of John Bartram and Humphry Marshall*, ed. William Darlington (New York and London, 1967). See also the biography by Ernest Earnest, *John and William Bartram: Botanists and Explorers 1699–1777, 1739–1823* (Philadelphia, 1940). For an excellent survey of research and writings on natural history during the colonial period, see U. P. Hedrick, *A History of Horticulture in America to 1860* (New York, 1950), esp. chap. 5.
53. This is not the so-called second John Clayton who wrote *Flora Virginica* in the eighteenth century.
54. The most complete biography of Clayton is by Walter T. Layton, *The Discoverer of Gas Lighting, Notes on the Life and Work of the Reverend John Clayton, D.D., 1657–1725* (London, 1926). See also Edmund Berkeley and Dorothy Berkeley, *The Reverend John Clayton, A Parson with a Scientific Mind* (Charlottesville, 1965). For Banister, see Joseph Ewan and Nesta Ewan, *John Banister and His Natural History of Virginia* (Urbana, Ill., 1970).
55. See Force, ed., *Tracts*, 3: xii. John Lawson did the same thing for North Carolina in the first decade

of the new century; along with Clayton's work, his survey complements, even more scientifically and methodically, Beverley's references to plants. Fortunately, Lawson completed the manuscript of his natural history, *A Description of North-Carolina* (1714), shortly before he was tortured and killed by the Tuscarora Indians in 1711. This work first appeared in Lawson's *A History of Carolina; Containing the Exact Description and Natural History of that Country . . .* There is a modern edition in *A New Voyage to Carolina*, ed. H. T. Lefler (Chapel Hill, 1967); Lawson's letters from 1701–1711 are appended (pp. 267–73). Lawson kept in close touch with James Petiver, as R. P. Stearns explains in "James Petiver, Promoter of Natural Science, c. 1663–1718," *Proceedings of the American Antiquarian Society* 62 (April 16, 1952–October 15, 1952). On December 30, 1710, Lawson wrote about North Carolina's good soil for orchards and gardens, vines, and exotic plants in (for that period) a "romantic" botanical vein: "If a man be a Botanist, here is a plentiful Field of Plants to divert him in; If he be a Gardner, and delight in that pleasant and happy Life, he will meet with a Climate and Soil, that will further and promote his Designs, in as great a Measure, as any Man can wish for" (ed. Lefler, p. 169).
56. Hedrick, *History of Horticulture in America*, pp. 111–12.
57. Lawson, "Description of North-Carolina," in *Lawson's History of North Carolina*, ed. Frances Latham Harriss, 2d ed. (Richmond, 1952), p. 79.
58. Beverley, *History*, pp. 140, 299.
59. Lawson, "Description of North-Carolina," p. 80.
60. Pliny's letters on the architecture of Roman villas were translated, edited, and illustrated in the eighteenth century by Robert Castell in *Villas of the Ancients* (London, 1728).
61. Beverley, *History*, p. 291.
62. Beverley listed the following "better Sorts of the wild Fruits," many of which by 1705 were thriving in Virginia gardens and orchards: cherries, plums, persimmons, peaches, apples, apricots, nectarines, pomegranates, mulberries, red and black currants, huckleberries, cranberries, raspberries, strawberries, and a variety of melons. Grapes were wild and ubiquitous, of course, and Beverley was hardly unique in recommending their cultivation toward a wine industry that never materialized in Virginia. In a 1686 "Cata-

logue" (in Latin) of Virginia plants, published by John Ray as an addendum to his *Historia Plantarum* (3 vols., 1686–1704), Banister gave most of his attention to fruit (2:1926–1928). On John Ray, see Charles E. Raven, *John Ray, Naturalist, His Life and Works* (Cambridge, 1942).

63. Glover's *Account* was originally published in the *Philosophical Transactions* of the Royal Society on June 20, 1676 (rpt. Oxford, 1904).

64. William Bullock, *Virginia Impartially Examined* . . . (London, 1649).

65. Force, ed., *Tracts*, 3: xii, p. 20. See Pierre Marambaud, *William Byrd of Westover, 1674–1744* (Charlottesville, 1971), pp. 15–24.

66. *Byrd Correspondence*, 1:18; see also p. 78.

67. Ibid., 1:71, 74, 83, 171. Byrd sent the following botanical notes to Sloane in 1694: "The Cypresses of another kind then that sent last year and a more beautifull Tree. There is one head of colocassia or the Aegyptian Beane of Parkinson. It grows plentifully here in marshes and bears a beautifull flower about July. The Euonimus with Scarlett-seed-vessells grows here near water, as also the Lauras Tulip-fera. The spinning yucca with the Rest grow freely on any ground." British Library, Sloane MSS 3343, f. 274. See Byrd's letter to Sloane, *Byrd Correspondence*, 1:259. See also the letter to Sloane, September 1708, 1:266–67; Sloane's reply on December 7, 1709, 1:272–73; and Byrd again to Sloane in June 1710, 1:274–75.

68. *Byrd Correspondence*, 1:18.

69. Ibid., p. 73.

70. The library included Gerard's *Herball* (first published in 1597; Byrd probably had the most recent edition, 1636, Sir Francis Bacon's *Sylva sylvarum* (first published in 1627), Lister's *De Cochleis* (1685), John Ogilby's *America* (1670), Robert Plot's natural history of Oxfordshire and Staffordshire (1677, 1686), Ray's *Historia Plantarum*, and the Royal Society's *Philosophical Transactions* (1679–1685). See Edwin Wolf II, "More Books from the Library of Westover," *Proceedings of the American Antiquarian Society* 88, pt. 1 (April 1978): 51–88. Another book of Banister's, with his name inscribed in it, that may have belonged to Byrd was John Parkinson's *Theatrum Botanicum* (1640); it is now owned by the Burlington County Historical Society, New Jersey.

71. Between 1697 and 1701 Sloane received from Sir Robert Southwell and others a number of trees, flowers, and bushes that Byrd I had sent. In April 1697, for example, he received: "Virginian Honeysuckle; Acer Florescens [maples]; pearl Tree; Fine flower'd tree like Sassafras; Virginia Pine; Spining Yucca; Sassafras; Parsimmons; Trumpet Flower . . . Fine flower'd Juy; Laourus Tulipfera; Myrtles winter green; with some others whose names are wanting" (British Library, Sloane MSS 3343, f. 58; see also ff. 95–96, 101, 102, 105, 106, 167, 201). On June 21, 1701, Sloane received a shipment of trees from Virginia "by the Governors [Nicholson's] order" (f. 204). This manuscript volume in the Sloane Collection also contains lists of plant shipments from, among other places, Maryland, Barbados, and China.

72. See Gertrude Ann Jacobsen, *William Blathwayt: A Late Seventeenth-Century Administrator* (New Haven, 1932).

73. These included "flowering shrubs, Virginia wild Bassill; Judas Tree; Locust; water Mellon, Plane tree"; he also sent the sweet bay magnolia or, as Beverley described it, "the fine Tulip-bearing Lawrel-Tree, which has the pleasantest Smell in the World" (Beverley, *History*, p. 140). See British Library, Sloane MSS 3342, ff. 150–218.

74. The Evelyn MSS are at Christ Church, Oxford; see the letter book for 1679–1699, f. 176.

75. Governor Edmund Andros, like many before and after him, was sending plants to people like Blathwayt to curry political favor and leverage.

76. The letters between Evelyn and Walker cited in this paragraph are in the Evelyn MSS, Box 1313–1375, 1376–1432, T-W No. 1338. Evelyn's relationship to the Parke family has been chronicled by Ruth Bourne in "John Evelyn, the Diarist, and his Cousin Daniel Parke II," *VMHB* 78 (January 1970): 3–33.

77. Francis Nicholson Papers, Special Collections, CWFL. For a biography of Blair, see Parke Rouse, *James Blair of Virginia* (Chapel Hill, 1971).

78. For a cogent assessment of Locke's and Evelyn's roles in the founding of William and Mary, see Glenn Patton, "The College of William and Mary, Williamsburg, and the Enlightenment," *Journal for the Society of Architectural Historians* 24 (March 1970): 24–32.

79. Hugh Jones, *The Present State of Virginia, From Whence Is Inferred a Short View of Maryland and North Carolina*, ed. Richard L. Morton (Chapel

Hill, 1956), p. 67. It is possible, but unlikely, that the piazzas Beverley saw were on the east side of the Wren building and that after its devastating fire of 1705 they and the orientation of the gardens were moved to the west side.

80. For a fascinating study of Italian sources of the interpenetration of garden and theater in seventeenth- and eighteenth-century English gardens, see John Dixon Hunt's *Garden and Grove*, chaps. 5 and 6. I am indebted to this study for several of my observations on Renaissance classical Italian garden styles.

81. The considerable similarities between these two maps suggest that one was copied or borrowed from the other. Both are extremely valuable because they show clearly a few of the larger gardens in town at the end of the Revolutionary War.

82. The piazzas and nearby garden were first mentioned by Beverley on April 15, 1704 (PRO, CO 5/1314).

83. John Dixon Hunt suggests a few of the political implications of Dutch gardening in England in "Reckoning with Dutch Gardens," *Journal of Garden History* 8, nos. 2 and 3 (1988): 56–59.

84. Cited by Hunt, *Garden and Grove*, p. 81. See his discussion of the emergence of the English botanical garden and Evelyn's role in it, pp. 79–82.

85. On the role of the botanical in this context, see John Prest, *The Garden of Eden: The Botanic Garden and the Re-Creation of Paradise* (New Haven and London, 1981).

86. Michel wrote that three stands for spectators were "drawn up before the college in a threefold formation, in such a way that the college building formed one side." In describing the chaotic fireworks, Michel noted that the first rocket "was to pass along a string to the *arbor*," where prominent ladies were seated, but he does not say what this "arbor" looked like. See his "Report of the Journey . . . from Berne, Switzerland, to Virginia, October 2, 1701–December 1, 1702, translated and edited by William J. Hinke, *VMHB* 24 (1916): 1–43, 113–51, 275–88.

87. See Hunt, *Garden and Grove*, pp. 110–26, for an account of the use of English gardens as court entertainments.

88. This copper plate is among at least eight plates that were given to the Bodleian Library, Oxford, by Richard Rawlinson in 1755. It dates from about the late 1730s and shows the public build-

ings of Williamsburg: the College of William and Mary, the Capitol, and the Palace. One theory about its origin is that it was intended for a book on natural history by an English naturalist. The plate is discussed by Luis Marden in "The Adventure of the Copper Plates," *Colonial Williamsburg: The Journal of the Colonial Williamsburg Foundation* 9 (Summer 1987): 5–18. It was discovered in the Bodleian in 1930 and given to CWF. Since its discovery, it has served as a basis for some of the restoration work done at Colonial Williamsburg.

89. Beverley, *History*, p. 105.

90. P. 67.

91. The 1701 plan was published in *VMHB* 47 (1939): facing p. 274.

92. Beverley, *History*, p. 299.

93. Ibid.

94. On the response to Virginia's landscape and a comparison of Beverley's and Jones's writing about it, see Rhys Isaac, *Transformation of Virginia*, pp. 13–17. See also Davis, *Intellectual Life*, 1:3–52, 3:1208; Peter A. Fritzell, "The Wilderness and the Garden: Metaphors of the American Landscape," *Forest History* 12 (1968): 16–22; Roderick Nash, *Wilderness and the American Mind* (New Haven, 1967); Lewis Simpson, *The Dispossessed Garden* (Athens, Ga., 1975); and Bernard W. Sheehan, *Savagism and Civility* (Cambridge, 1980). On the relation of seventeenth-century English verse to gardening and to ways of seeing gardens, see John Dixon Hunt, *The Figure in the Landscape: Poetry, Painting, and Gardening during the Eighteenth Century* (Baltimore, 1976) and *Garden and Grove*, pp. 173–74.

95. *The Transformation of Virginia*, p. 11.

Chapter 2

1. The governor's house began to be called the Palace only later in the century, but the term is applied to the residence at the beginning of its history as well as for the sake of convenience and clarity.

2. "The Correspondence of Alexander Spotswood with John Spotswood of Edinburgh," ed. Lester J. Cappon, *VMHB* 60 (April 1952): 229.

3. Jones, *The Present State of Virginia, From Whence Is Inferred a Short View of Maryland and North Car-*

olina, ed. Richard L. Morton (Chapel Hill, 1956), p. 71.

4. See Leo Marx, *The Machine in the Garden* (Oxford and New York, 1964), esp. chaps. 1–3, for a lucid and evocative introduction to views of landscape opened up to colonists in the New World.

5. Francis Nicholson Papers, Folder 1, Special Collections, CWFL.

6. On Nicholson's interest in town planning and probable exposure to the ideas of Wren and Sir John Evelyn, if not to those gentlemen themselves, see John Reps, *Tidewater Towns: City Planning in Colonial Virginia and Maryland* (Charlottesville, 1972), pp. 125ff.

7. Nicholson's library testified to his expertise in several facets of gardening, from the horticultural to the aesthetic. His volumes, which he catalogued in 1695 and gave to the college library before he left Virginia in 1705, included (in addition to *The Compleat Gard'ner*) Evelyn's *Sylva* (2d expanded ed., 1670); Leonard Meager's *English Gardener* (1670); John Worlidge's *Systema Agriculturae* (3d ed., 1681); Moses Cook's *The Manner of Raising, Ordering, and Improving Forrest-Trees* (1676) . . . ; Sir William Temple's *Works*, containing the influential essay "The Gardens of Epicurus or the State of Gardening in 1685"; and an anonymous piece on the "Anatomie of the Elder Tree." The catalogue of the Nicholson library may be found in the appendix to J. M. Jennings, "Notes on the Original Library of the College of William and Mary in Virginia," *Papers of the Bibliographical Society of America* 41 (1947): 258–67.

8. In addition to his literary interest in gardens, Nicholson was a promoter of plant exchanges and himself sent many plants to England. Later, as governor of South Carolina, he provided Carolina plants to William Popple, John Locke's friend and the first secretary of the Board of Trade (although Nicholson did so in part to curry favor and support from the Board). Nicholson wrote to Popple on July 20, 1721: "I have already agreed with a gardener to gett me some flowers plants . . . and according to your desire some shall be sent for your parradice at Hampstead" (PRO, CO 5, 358, ff. 137–38). Nicholson also facilitated Mark Catesby's botanical research in the Carolinas.

9. See Purcell, "Town in Country and Country in Town," in *Ancient Roman Villa Gardens*, ed. Elisabeth B. MacDougall, Dumbarton Oaks Colloquium

on the History of Landscape Architecture, 10 (Washington, D.C., 1987), p. 195.

10. Judith A. Kinnard, "The Villa Gamberaia in Settignano: The Street in the Garden," *Journal of Garden History* 6, no. 1 (1986): 14. Kinnard cites the definitive study on this subject: H. Rosenau, *The Ideal City in Its Architectural Evolution* (London, 1959).

11. From Evelyn's *Diary*, cited in *The Genius of the Place: The English Landscape Garden, 1620–1820*, ed. John Dixon Hunt and Peter Willis (London, 1975), p. 62.

12. This passage from Misson's *A New Voyage to Italy* . . . (1664) is cited by John Dixon Hunt in "Reckoning with Dutch Gardens," *Journal of Garden History* 8, nos. 2 and 3 (1988): 52.

13. "Epistle to Burlington" (1731), ll. 47–50, 191–94, 203–4 (*Twickenham Edition of the Poems of Alexander Pope*, vol. 3, pt. 2, ed. F. W. Bateson).

14. In *Tidewater Towns* (chap. 6), Reps explains tentatively how Nicholson laid out Annapolis with the skills of a landscape designer.

15. Reps, *Tidewater Towns*, p. 126.

16. In one example of Nicholson's pictorial use of the river in Annapolis, he had a section of land, extending from the harbor three hundred feet up to Statehouse Circle, set aside in 1696 "for planting or makeing a Garden[,] Vine[y]ard or Somerhouse or other use," and he conveyed the tract to himself, possibly with a view to establishing his own governor's residence there and commanding from it and its extensive garden setting a vista of the harbor (Reps, *Tidewater Towns*, pp. 132–33). This scheme anticipates the Palace Green vistas from the Governor's Palace in Williamsburg a few years later, except that the Palace Green leads nowhere, so to speak, whereas Nicholson's tract terminated beautifully at the river. The scheme proved abortive, but the diagonally lined Cornhill Street that subsequently bisected the tract and led straight to Statehouse Circle did establish a vista or pictorial link between the statehouse and harbor that would have pleased Nicholson. William Eddis, an Englishman who raved about "the new variegated beautiful prospects" at Yorktown and Williamsburg, saw the Governor's House in Annapolis in 1769 and left this revealing account of it: "The governor's house is most beautifully situated. . . . The garden is not extensive, but it is disposed to the utmost advantage; the center walk is

terminated with a small green mount, close to which the Severn approaches; this elevation commands an extensive view of the bay and adjacent country . . . and perhaps I may be justified in asserting that there are but few mansions in the most rich and cultivated parts of England which are adorned with such splendid and romantic scenery" (*Letters from America*, ed. Aubrey C. Land [Boston, 1969], pp. 11–13).

17. See Reps, *Tidewater Towns*, chap. 7, for a thorough account of how Nicholson went about laying out the town.

18. Sylvia Doughty Fries, in *The Urban Idea in Colonial America* (Philadelphia, 1977), chap. 4, suggests that the plan of the town, as carefully prescribed in the original legislative act calling for its establishment, was Nicholson's master plan for a new culture in the New World, recalling a Renaissance city in a so-called Wren-baroque style, where the arts and social graces could flourish and perpetuate civic pride.

19. *JHB*, 4:55.

20. *The History and Present State of Virginia*, p. 105.

21. This quarrel is described by Custis and Ludwell in papers among the Lee Family Papers, Section 46, 1/L51/f.64, Virginia Historical Society, Richmond; the relevant documents have been reprinted in *VMHB* 46 (1938): 244ff.

22. *The History and Present State of Virginia*, p. 105.

23. The "Act Directing the Building of the Capitoll in the City of Williamsburgh," passed by the Assembly with Governor Nicholson's approval on June 8, 1699, stipulated the sale of half-acre lots. See *JHB*, 3 (1695–1702):182–83, 196–99; and *LJC*, 1:276.

24. John Reps has conjectured that a garden plan included in both Evelyn's plan for London and his edition of de la Quintinie's *Compleat Gard'ner* may have inspired Nicholson's street and path treatment of the Capitol and Market Square areas (*Tidewater Towns*, pp. 169–79). The plan, less rare in the seventeenth century than Reps suggests, consisted of diagonal paths leading to the corners of a rectangular area. If Reps's conjecture is allowed, the formal treatment of the Capitol, together with such a garden plan as Evelyn's that may have inspired it, could have made gardens within the Capitol square all the more appropriate and interesting.

25. Jane Carson, ed., *We Were There: Descriptions of*

Williamsburg, 1699–1859 (Williamsburg, 1965), pp. 18, 19, 23, 24, 30.

26. "Act for keeping good Rules and Orders in the Porte of Annapolis," Archives of Maryland, 19: 498–504; cited in Reps, *Tidewater Towns*, p. 132.

27. A. J. Dézallier D'Argenville, *The Theory and Practice of Gardening*, trans. John James, 2d ed. (London, 1728), p. 95; cited in *Genius of the Place*, ed. Hunt and Willis, p. 130.

28. Tucker, "Letter," in Carson, ed., *We Were There*, p. 83.

29. Randolph was the son of Sir John (the colony's most distinguished lawyer in the early eighteenth century) and one of Williamsburg's most methodical and scientific gardeners; he wrote *A Treatise on Gardening* (ca. 1758–1764; first published in 1770).

30. See Custis to William Byrd II, August 12, 1724, Custis Letter Book, Library of Congress.

31. Lee Family Papers, Section 46, 1/L51/f. 64. I am assuming in this discussion that by the time Custis wrote his letter Spotswood had moved into the Palace. In a letter to Byrd on March 30, 1717, Custis denies being the governor's "court favourite" and affirms that he had "not bin with in the pallace doors nor exchanged one word with the governor this nine months" (*The Correspondence of the Three William Byrds of Westover, Virginia, 1684–1776*, 2 vols. [Charlottesville, 1977], 1:297). Even a year earlier, Ludwell had written to Sir William Blathwayt, complaining that although Spotswood was then living in "the best home that I have heard of in America" (that is, Palace) he was still cheating the king by being paid rent money for his private dwelling (Blathwayt Papers, Special Collections, CWFL). From this it would appear that Spotswood had moved into the Palace by March 1716.

32. On the question of land acquisitions for the Palace, see Patricia A. Gibbs, "Palace Lands" (March 1980), Research Report, Special Collections, CWFL.

33. For Finch's commission, see *EJC*, 4 (Oct. 25, 1721–Oct. 25, 1739):413.

34. Jefferson's drawing is in the Coolidge Collection, Massachusetts Historical Society, Boston, and has been published in Fiske Kimball, *Thomas Jefferson, Architect* (Boston, 1916).

35. This and other poems by Tucker are in the Tucker-Coleman Papers, Swem Library, College

of William and Mary, Box 62; for this poem, see Notebook 8, p. 14.

36. *The History of the College of William and Mary . . . 1693 to 1870* (Richmond, 1874), p. 21.

37. Most of the outhouses, including a smokehouse mentioned by Colonel Edward Hill in his description of the 1705 fire, were located on the west side. The Rochambeau and Desandrouins maps show clearly that this was the case; the buildings they depict to the east were connected with the Brafferton building and the President's House, neither of which existed before the 1720s. The maps also reveal just how large the western gardens were—the largest in town, apparently even larger than the Palace gardens.

38. The Robert Carter Diary, 1722–1727, is in the Alderman Library, University of Virginia, Charlottesville.

39. I am indebted to Lord Gooch of Benacre Hall, Suffolk, for permission to quote from the Gooch Papers.

40. William Dawson to the bishop of London, August 11, 1732, printed in *WMQ* 1st ser., 9 (1901): 220.

41. "The Journal of Ebenezer Hazard in Virginia, 1777," ed. Fred Shelley, *VMHB* 62 (1954): 405.

42. Later in the century the paling was supplemented by rows of trees. In the Frenchman's Map (figure 14) these trees are shown as a double row of dots; elsewhere on the map, such as around "Custis Square" and along both sides of the Palace Green, dotted lines clearly indicate the planting of trees.

43. Vegetables, too, would seem unlikely in that layout; yet when Josiah Quincy visited the town and college in 1773, both of which he thought were in rapid decline, he observed that "the college makes a very agreeable appearance, and the large garden before it, is of ornament and use" (cited in Carson, ed., *We Were There*, p. 27). Quincy's entire journal has been published as "A Journal, 1773," *Massachusetts Historical Society Proceedings* 49 (1915–1916): 424–81.

44. The Simcoe Map was found in England among the papers belonging to Lieutenant Colonel J. Graves Simcoe, commander of the Queen's Rangers in the Battle of Yorktown (Special Collections, CWFL).

45. *EJC*, 4:118. Crease may have started as college gardener in 1727; a special college statute that

year specified that "the Gardener" would be directed in his offices and salaries by the president and masters. The statute may also imply that a new stage of the gardens was then beginning (see *WMQ* 1st ser., 22 [1913–1914]: 292). Crease may have been residing in town as early as 1720, or earlier, though perhaps not as Spotswood's gardener; it depends on whether "Tom Cross," a valuable and competent gardener at Westover, was Byrd's garbled name for Crease. Three times in his "Secret Diary" for 1720 Byrd mentioned "Cross" as his "old" (that is, former) gardener from Williamsburg, who had been coming up to Westover on occasion to "lay out that part [of the garden] that was new" (*The Secret Diary of William Byrd of Westover 1709–12*, ed. Louis B. Wright and Marion Tinling [Richmond, 1941], pp. 378, 414, 491–92; hereafter cited as Byrd, *Secret Diary*).

46. York County Records, vol. 3 (Deeds, Bonds), p. 439.

47. *Virginia Gazette*, ed. William Parks, January 6–13, 1738.

48. *JHB*, 5:230. See also *JHB*, 5:277, 283.

49. *JHB*, 4:279–98 passim; 5:39.

50. "Correspondence of Alexander Spotswood," p. 229.

51. It is likely that the public was also paying for about six years' worth of gardening at his rented premises in town, where he lived before he could move into the Palace in 1716; this was paid out of a portion of the £150 rent stipend he received annually. See *EJC*, 3 (1705–1721):426, 432. See also Patricia Gibbs, "Palace Lands," p. 16n.38.

52. Spotswood's inclination to garden in a manner that Addison in *The Spectator* once mocked as Continental ostentatiousness is perhaps suggested by the one surviving volume of his library, bequeathed to the College of William and Mary upon his death. It is Piagnol de la Force's *Descriptions de Chateaux et Parcs de Versailles, de Trianon, et de Marly* (Amsterdam, 1715), from which he may have taken ideas for later garden designs at the Palace. And if he owned that volume on French royal parks, it is likely he also owned the book on French gardens translated in 1706 by the royal gardeners George London and Henry Wise, *The Retir'd Gardener*, as well as Evelyn's earlier translation of de la Quintinie's *The Compleat Gard'ner*, which Nicholson owned. See *The Offi-*

cial Letters of Alexander Spotswood, ed. R. A. Brock (Richmond, 1882), 1:xv–xvi; see also John M. Jennings, *The Library of the College of William and Mary, 1693–1793* (Charlottesville, 1968), p. 48.

53. "Memorandum," *WMQ* 2d ser., 10 (1930): 250.

54. W. W. Hening, *The Statutes at Large . . .* (Philadelphia, 1823), vol. 3 (1684–1710):482–84. Subsequent citations from the 1710 act are from this source.

55. *LJC*, 3 (1754–1774):1557. There is no record that this proposal was ever legislated. If its ideas were conceived by Spotswood himself, it is likely that they were executed.

56. A kitchen garden was also provided for in the "proposal." The 1710 act had ordered, not with any great originality, that it had to be in a "convenient" place, which meant near the house or the kitchen, but it is not possible to be any more precise about its location, since we do not know whether the kitchen was located in the west flanking building or (as it is now) in a dependency to the west above the south end of the canal. In any case, the kitchen garden was to be "enclosed with pailes," not with brick.

57. In 1713, before he began to fall out bitterly with Philip Ludwell, Spotswood tried to engineer an exchange of acreage with the planter whereby he would have given him forty acres of the governor's lands near Jamestown and Green Spring (with the required permission of the Board of Trade and Plantations) in exchange for forty acres of the woodland that Ludwell owned adjoining the Palace acreage. Cows and horses required sufficient grazing land, and Spotswood mentions using the land for convenient firewood; but beyond those needs, the exchange idea suggests his appetite for adjoining parkland, perhaps mostly for recreational uses.

58. See Isabel W. Chase, ed. *Horace Walpole: Gardenist* (Princeton, 1943), p. 25.

59. *The Theory and Practice of Gardening*, trans. John James (1712), p. 77. Grills of iron at ends of walks were common seventeenth-century European ornaments for extending the views of surrounding countryside.

60. The letter is dated September 18, 1727. Gooch's letter book, from which this citation is taken, is at Benacre Hall, Suffolk; I cite it with the permission of Sir Brian Gooch.

61. Cited in *The Genius of the Place*, ed. Hunt and Willis, p. 142.

62. See John Dixon Hunt, *Garden and Grove: The Italian Renaissance Garden in the English Imagination, 1600–1750* (Princeton and London, 1986), chap. 3, for a discussion of the *vigna* in the Italian and English gardens of the seventeenth and eighteenth centuries.

63. Nelson's letter is in the Nelson Letter Books, 1766–1775, p. 183, Virginia State Library, Richmond.

64. Botetourt's letter to the secretary of state is in PRO, CO 5, 1372, fols. 29–30. The more expressive letter to the unknown addressee is in the muniments room at Badminton House, Gloucestershire, and it is cited here with the permission of the duke of Beaufort. I am indebted to Graham Hood for drawing my attention to the latter citation.

Botetourt's inventory divided garden tools and implements into two classes: one set for the garden, the other for the park. See Graham Hood, ed., *Inventories of Four Eighteenth-Century Houses in the Historic Area of Williamsburg* (Williamsburg, 1974), pp. 5–19.

65. Feilde's letter of February 16, 1771, is at the Huntington Library, San Marino, Calif.

66. PRO, CO 5, 1353. After Thomas Jefferson became governor in 1779, there was authorization for "Hedging and Ditching" in the governor's "meadow" (Auditor's Account Books, 1779–1780, no. 3, p. 63, Virginia State Library).

67. See Byrd, *Secret Diary*, pp. 298–99, 481, 482.

68. Spotswood subsequently became Byrd's adversary politically; but by 1732, when Byrd visited the former governor at his estate in Germanna, on the upper reaches of the Rappahannock, they had been reconciled. Byrd later described Spotswood's gardens there, and his account is cited here as evidence of Spotswood's continuing enthusiasm for gardening in an increasingly natural style. Byrd was unimpressed by Spotswood's formal terraces and gardens close to the house, liking instead the more natural areas of the grounds. His short description in his essay "A Progress to the Mines" depicts a naturalized garden. He calls the house the "enchanted castle," speaks of deer around the house (recalling deer in Spotswood's park at the Palace), and mentions an avenue of cherry trees on the grounds. "The afternoon was devoted to the ladies," he commented, "who showed me one of their most beautiful walks. They conducted me through a shady lane to the

landing, and by the way made me drink some very fine water that issued from a marble fountain and ran incessantly. Just behind it was a covered bench." He later notes that he "took a turn on the terrace walk," though he judged that the grounds nearer the house contained "nothing beautiful but three terrace walks that fall in slopes one below another" (*William Byrd of Virginia: The London Diary [1717–1721] and Other Writings*, ed. Louis B. Wright and Marion Tinling [New York, 1958], p. 628; see also *The Prose Works of William Byrd of Westover: Narratives of a Colonial Virginian*, ed. Louis B. Wright [Cambridge, Mass., 1966], pp. 356ff.). Germanna must have had a very expressive, meditative character to induce Byrd to comment in this way about shady walks and a marble fountain.

69. Later in the century, at least after the Bodleian Plate was drawn (which does not show brick pillars in the brick walls), Governor Gooch, or someone during the building of the rear wing, enhanced the elegance and substantiality of these walls by increasing their height and adding regularly spaced oblique brick pillars, which were immediately or eventually topped with stone balls. Humphrey Harwood, the successful and ubiquitous Williamsburg builder, repaired these walls in 1788, seven years after the Palace had burned to the ground, by patching up the pillars and fashioning new balls and caps for them. See Harwood's Ledger, July 27, 1788, MS B25, Special Collections, CWFL.

70. Fragments of the Palace gate that were found by archaeologists revealed that it was similar to one dating from the eighteenth century that still exists at Westover: a triple-gate arrangement made in England.

71. See Mark R. Wenger's Colonial Williamsburg Foundation Architectural Report, "Reconstruction of the Governor's Palace in Williamsburg, Virginia" (1980), pp. 52ff., for a cogent account of Palace garden interpretation since the 1930s.

72. Access to that part of the garden was through the west gate on the main east-west axis path. Nothing is known of the gardens between the gate and the terraces as they were during Spotswood's time, although conceivably the kitchen garden was located there. Further north and within the north wall the ground sloped suddenly down into an area enclosed on three sides by the north wall, the wall separating the area from the North Gar-

den, and a wall or building alongside the uppermost terrace. What practical or ornamental use this enclosure was put to is unknown, but the protected character of the place and its proximity to what may have been a building—perhaps a greenhouse—apparently fixed to or part of the wall at the northwest corner would have made it an ideal area for a nursery garden. The Frenchman's Map shows what looks like a building at that corner, as does the Simcoe Map.

73. *JHB*, 5:277ff.

74. PRO, CO 5, 1318; reprinted in Mary R. Goodwin, "Governor's Palace" (May 1932), Research Report, Special Collections, CWFL, pp. 87–90.

75. *JHB*, 5:277.

76. *JHB*, 5:293. "Memorandum," *WMQ* 2d ser., 10 (1930): 250.

77. Beverley wrote in the revised edition of his *History* (London, 1722): "The third [public building] is a house for the Governor, not the largest, but by far the most beautiful of all the others. It was granted by the Assembly in Governor Nott's time, begun in President Jenning's time but received its beauty and conveniency from the many alterations and decorations, of the present Governor, Colonel Spotswood; who, to the lasting honor and happiness of the Country, arrived there, while this house was carrying up" (pp. 234–35). See also Jones, *Present State of Virginia*, p. 70.

78. Unequivocal recognition of Spotswood's gardening came during his lifetime, in 1738. Sir William Keith, governor of Pennsylvania from 1717 to 1726, praised him for the "laying out of Ground to the best advantage" at the governor's residence; and he went on to mention (but not, alas, describe) the "Improvements which he made to the Governor's House and Gardens." Sir William Keith, *History of the British Plantations in America* (1738), pt. 1, p. 172.

Chapter 3

1. Spotswood wrote to Bishop Compton on November 16, 1713: "These [seeds] are collected by a Gentleman now in this Country, a nephew of Mr. [Nicholas] Jekyll's of Castle Haningham [i.e. Hedingham] and one very curious in such things." Robert Alonzo Brock, ed. *The Official Letters of Governor Alexander Spotswood ... 1710–1722,*

Collections of the Virginia Historical Society, 2 vols. (Richmond, 1882–1885), 2:44–45.

2. This aspect of American gardening in the century has been well chronicled. See especially, U. P. Hedrick, *A History of Horticulture in America to 1860* (New York, 1950), pp. 85–90, 111–12.

3. Custis's letters to Collinson are in his Letter Book at the Library of Congress; a typescript by Maude Woodfin is on deposit at the Virginia Historical Society, Richmond. Most of the letters, or portions of letters, relating to gardening and plant exchanges have been published in *Brothers of the Spade: Correspondence of Peter Collinson, of London, and John Custis, of Williamsburg, Virginia, 1734–46*, ed. Earl G. Swem (Barre, Mass., 1957). Citations not included in that edition are taken from the typescript of the Letter Book. No adequate biography of Collinson is yet available. See, however, Ronald Webber, *The Early Horticulturists* (New York, 1968).

4. For a brief summary of Custis's life and career, see Jo Zuppan, "John Custis of Williamsburg, 1778–1749," *VMHB* 90 (1982): 177–97.

5. Custis Letter Book, typescript at Virginia Historical Society.

6. Letter to Perry, 1723, cited from Letter Book typescript. See also *Brothers of the Spade*, pp. 21–22, 23, 28, 45.

7. *Brothers of the Spade*, pp. 21, 23, 24.

8. Sir John Randolph and Isham Randolph, who had a residual interest in botany and gardening, apparently first put Custis and Collinson in touch with each other via a Virginia mountain cowslip also known as the Roanoke or Virginia bluebell, which grew in Custis's garden (*Brothers of the Spade*, p. 158n.57). For an account of Isham Randolph's botanical interests in the 1720s and 1730s, see Jonathan Daniels, *The Randolphs of Virginia, America's Foremost Family* (Garden City, N.Y., 1972), pp. 40, 50–52. See also *Brothers of the Spade*, pp. 23–25. For a brief description of Dungeness, Isham Randolph's plantation on the James River, and its garden, see Bartram to Collinson, December 1738, *WMQ* 2d ser., 4 (1926): 309; and Randolph to Bartram, p. 314.

9. By the end of his long life, Collinson had corresponded with all the leading botanists, professional and amateur, in America, including Custis, Byrd, John Bartram, John Clayton, John Mitchell, and Alexander Garden (of Charleston).

10. The only available printed source of the Collinson-Bartram letters is *Memorials of John Bartram and Humphry Marshall*, ed. William Darlington (New York and London, 1967); see pp. 89, 113. Later citations from Collinson's letters to Bartram are taken from this edition, as are all letters from Bartram.

11. *Brothers of the Spade*, p. 50.

12. Ibid., p. 64.

13. Unfortunately, Clayton, a close personal friend of Byrd II, Custis, and Mark Catesby, was not at home when Bartram paid a visit in 1738 to his plantation, Windsor, on the south side of the Piankatank River about forty miles north of Williamsburg. Clayton was one of the important contributors to the science of botany in colonial Virginia, corresponding not only with Collinson but also with Gronovius, Linnaeus, Bartram, Byrd, and many other botanists on both sides of the Atlantic. His Windsor plantation and his lucrative Gloucester County clerkship afforded him the leisure to travel widely in pursuit of Virginia plants and to grow them in his impressive botanical garden at Windsor, which he did for more than fifty years. When the Williamsburg physician John Galt visited Windsor in 1804, thirty years after Clayton's death, he was delighted to see a garden still flourishing with innumerable plants (Galt Papers, Special Collections, CWFL). For a biography of Clayton, see Edmund Berkeley and Dorothy Berkeley, *John Clayton, Pioneer of American Botany* (Chapel Hill, 1963). See also Richard Beale Davis, *Intellectual Life in the Colonial South 1585–1763*, 3 vols. (Knoxville, 1978), 2:852–55.

14. *Brothers of the Spade*, p. 27.

15. In his first known letter to Collinson, Custis mentions having received evergreens, for hedges and flower borders presumably, and reassures him that they "come safe to me and thrive very well; indeed, any tree may be transported if put in dirt and carefully minded." Collinson had already promised him horse chestnuts, "which tree I never saw," says Custis, "tho I was bred in England" (*Brothers of the Spade*, p. 24); cedars of Lebanon and Siberia; and some Italian evergreen oaks, which Collinson says, "Grow Tall and make a fine Hedge beare Cliping very Well" (January 25, 1737; ibid., p. 40). Collinson goes on to describe the chestnut's beautiful shape and blossoms, which "yeild a Delightfull prospect"; and

then he makes the interesting suggestion that "Rows of these Trees planted before your Houses next [to] the street att Williamsburg woud have a fine Effect" (ibid., p. 25).

16. *Brothers of the Spade*, p. 45.
17. Ibid., p. 65. In 1741 Custis announced that, thanks to the Persian lilac, his garden was "full of flowers this April of a very odoriferous smell and pretty small flowers" (ibid., p. 76).
18. *Brothers of the Spade*, p. 63.
19. Ibid., pp. 30, 34, 36–37.
20. Ibid., pp. 32–33, 36. Custis planted a good variety of trees sent to him by Collinson, including the cluster cherry, known as Cornish cherry, which produced "9 little trees" (ibid., p. 63) in the garden by 1739; cedar of Lebanon; larch trees; laburnum, which he said in 1736 were of "the quickest growth I ever saw" and had reached "4 or 5 feet high allready" (ibid., p. 33); Spanish Broom; "4 Buck thorn Berries Tree"; "4 small spruce Firr"; "4 silver Firrs"; pistaccio; almond; and horse chestnuts (ibid., p. 86). All these principally would have had a decorative function; shade doubtless was provided, for the most part, by native species.
21. *Brothers of the Spade*, pp. 33–34.
22. These included the sorrel, fringe, pearl, tulip poplar, red bud, chinquapin or chestnut, flowering dogwood (chiefly white), persimmon, honey or sweet locust, hickory, bayberry, wax myrtle, fragrant sumac, sassafras, black haw, cypress, umbrella (magnolia), toothache, ornamental sweet gum, cherry-laurel, and red and white mulberry.
23. *Brothers of the Spade*, p. 31. Catesby spent almost the entire second decade of the century in Williamsburg. Not much is known about him as a garden designer in England, but several passages, including the following from his preface to *Hortus Europae-Americanus* (1767), suggest his enthusiasm for the role of American plants in English gardens: "It will easily be imagined that . . . (the territory of the crown of Great Britain on the continent of America) must afford a plentifull variety of trees and shrubs, that may be usefully employed to inrich and adorn our [English] woods by their valuable timber and delightful shade; or to embellish and perfume our gardens with the elegance of their appearance and the fragrancy of their odours, in both which respects they greatly excel our home productions of the like kind" (p. i).

24. *Brothers of the Spade*, p. 69.
25. Ibid., pp. 29, 41, 51, 54, 29; *Natural History of Carolina, Florida, and the Bahama Islands*, vol. 1 (London, 1732), p. 27.
26. John Mitchell's garden in Urbanna, Middlesex County, must have been impressive. When he advertised it and his house for sale in 1745 (*Virginia Gazette*, November 21, 1745), he drew the reader's special attention to his plants: "a large garden containing many useful and curious plants and herbs." The most complete study of Mitchell is by Edmund Berkeley and Dorothy Berkeley, *Dr. John Mitchell, the Man who Made the Map of North America* (Chapel Hill, 1974).
27. *Brothers of the Spade*, p. 89.
28. Custis did not have much success with the moccasin flower, as he told Collinson: "I have sometimes by chance come across some and planted in my garden; but they never would continue above a year." *Brothers of the Spade*, p. 45.
29. *Brothers of the Spade*, p. 90.
30. Ibid., pp. 77, 31, 69.
31. Ibid., pp. 44, 46, 48–49. Custis's allusion to his Dutch box edging having been established for "many years" suggests that his gardens had contained well-established beds.
32. *Brothers of the Spade*, p. 55.
33. Ibid., pp. 61, 73, 74. His phileras were "quite destroyd," as were the yaupon and cassena trees, though his cedar, yew, and holly trees survived.
34. *Brothers of the Spade*, pp. 73, 75.
35. Letter dated January 15, 1724, Letter Book typescript, p. 50.
36. See *The Correspondence of the Three William Byrds of Westover, Virginia, 1684–1776*, 2 vols. (Charlottesville, 1977), 1:290, 341–42; hereafter cited as *Byrd Correspondence*.
37. The references to flower prints and flower pots are found in the Letter Book typescript, p. 177.
38. For an account of Bridges's career in Virginia, see Graham Hood, *Charles Bridges and William Dering: Two Virginia Painters* (Williamsburg, 1978).
39. *Brothers of the Spade*, pp. 27, 78.
40. Ibid., pp. 80, 53, 88.
41. Ibid., p. 58.
42. After George Washington acquired the property in 1759 through marriage to Daniel Parke Custis's widow, Martha, he rented it and then leased the house as a boardinghouse. In 1770 the grounds were praised in the *Virginia Gazette*

(Rind ed., October 4, 1770, p. 3) for their good pasturage rather than their ornamental pathways. Custis's grandson, John Parke Custis, wrote to Washington at Mount Vernon in 1778, imploring him to sell the Williamsburg land because Williamsburg "is declining fast, and the Houses on My Lots are in a wretched Situation; and are not fit to live in" (George Bolling Lee Papers, Virginia Historical Society, Richmond). When Washington put the land up for sale, he nevertheless asserted that it was located in "one of the most retired and agreeable situations in Williamsburg." Gardens were not mentioned, though several outbuildings were: a kitchen and well, large stable, and meathouse (smokehouse)—all on "four acres enclosed in one lot" (*Virginia Gazette*, November 27, 1778).

43. Since Byrd noted in his diary for July 20, 1720, that he had just walked with Custis in his garden, "into which he had put gravel," it is likely that gravel covered the garden paths. *William Byrd of Virginia: The London Diary (1717–1721) and Other Writings*, ed. Louis B. Wright and Marion Tinling (New York, 1958), p. 430.

44. Byrd kept notes on this trip, which he said were "like to swell into a volume" (*Byrd Correspondence*, 1:212). This journal has not been found, but Mark R. Wenger of Colonial Williamsburg discovered Perceval's journal from the same trip among the Egmont Papers in the British Library (Add. Mss. 47057 and 47058) and has edited them in *The English Travels of Sir John Perceval and William Byrd II: The Perceval Diary* (Columbia, Mo., 1989). Perceval's observations on gardens may be taken as clues to how Byrd himself probably responded to gardens of various styles as the two traveled north. He makes generous use of words like *prospect, variety, serpentine,* and *delightful* to describe landscape effects. He also records the prevailing European tastes for formality and symmetry in the gardens he saw.

45. For Byrd's letters to Southwell on this journey, see *Byrd Correspondence*, 1:209–15.

46. See William Brogden's two essays on Switzer: "Stephen Switzer, 'La Grand Manier,'" in *Furor Hortensis: Essays on the History of the English Landscape Garden in Memory of H. F. Clark*, ed. Peter Willis (Edinburgh, 1974), pp. 21–30; and "The Ferme Ornée and Changing Attitudes to Agricultural Improvement," in *British and American Gardens in the Eighteenth Century*, ed. Peter Martin and Robert P. Maccubbin (Williamsburg, 1984), pp. 39–43. See also Brogden's Ph.D. thesis, "Stephen Switzer and Garden Design in Britain in the Early Eighteenth Century" (Edinburgh University, 1973).

47. April 20, 1706; *Byrd Correspodence*, 1:259.

48. December 7, 1709; ibid., 1:273.

49. June 1710; ibid., 1:275.

50. Catesby arrived in Williamsburg on May 24, 1712, and stayed at the home of Dr. William Cocke, Virginia's secretary of state and a botanical enthusiast who had come to Williamsburg from England two years earlier. Within a few weeks of Catesby's arrival, Byrd invited him, his sister Elizabeth, and Dr. Cocke to Westover. Byrd and Catesby became friends immediately. "In the afternoon," Byrd noted in his diary, "Mr. Catesby, and I went into the swamp to see the nest of a humming bird and the Doctor followed along" (*The Secret Diary of William Byrd of Westover 1709–12*, ed. Louis B. Wright and Marion Tinling [Richmond, 1941], p. 534). Of particular interest to Catesby would have been the gardens. "Mr. Catesby and I walked in the garden," Byrd noted for May 26 (ibid., p. 535). Although a walk in his garden was a pastime that Byrd recorded in his diary frequently, the ones with Catesby during these weeks were not merely part of a domestic routine or pastime. By June 5, Catesby was making practical suggestions of design. Having walked with him "about the garden all the evening," Byrd stated that night: "Mr. Catesby directed how I should mend my garden and put it into a better fashion than it is at present" (ibid., p. 540). Catesby's visit occurred at a propitious time, just when Byrd was redesigning the gardens.

51. *William Byrd's Natural History of Virginia, or The Newly Discovered Eden*, ed. Richmond C. Beatty and William J. Mulloy (Richmond, 1940), p. 36. This work is not as useful to the garden historian as its title might suggest. Part of it is devoted to animals, and the sections on plants and trees lapse largely into tedious catalogues of species that may be found in the wild in Virginia.

52. See *William Byrd of Virginia: The London Diary (1717–1721) and Other Writings*, ed. Louis B. Wright and Marion Tinling (New York, 1958), pp. 128, 148, 150, 268; hereafter cited as Byrd, *London Diary*.

53. Ibid., pp. 267–68, 155, 175. John Macky, *A Journey Through England, In Familiar Letters from a Gentleman Here, to His Friend Abroad*, 4th ed. (London, 1722), 1:219.

54. *Another Secret Diary of William Byrd of Westover, 1738–41, With Letters and Literary Exercises 1696–1726*, ed. Maude H. Woodfin (Richmond, 1942), p. 337.

55. *Byrd Correspondence*, 1:327.

56. Byrd, *London Diary*, p. 378.

57. Ibid., pp. 385, 387, 389, 393.

58. Ibid., p. 507.

59. *Byrd Correspondence*, 2:752.

60. Ibid., 1:395. Byrd's descriptions of the wild scenery through which he traveled in 1728 on his expeditions to determine the boundary between Virginia and North Carolina are part of his journals, *The Secret History of the Dividing Line* (first published in *The Westover Manuscripts* [Petersburg, Va., 1841]) and the revised *History of the Dividing Line and Other Tracts from the Papers of William Byrd . . .*, ed. Thomas H. Wynne, Historical Documents from the Old Dominion, nos. 2 and 3 (Richmond, 1866). A modern edition has been published in *The Prose Works of William Byrd of Westover: Narratives of a Colonial Virginian*, ed. Louis B. Wright (Cambridge, Mass., 1966), pp. 41–336 (hereafter cited as Byrd, *Prose Works*). Citations from these journals are taken from this edition. Another edition is by W. K. Boyd, with a new introduction by Percy G. Adams, *The Histories of the Dividing Line Betwixt Virginia and North Carolina* (New York, 1967).

61. See Hunt, *Garden and Grove: The Italian Renaissance Garden in the English Imagination, 1600–1750* (Princeton and London, 1986), pp. 95–97. Hunt explains the classical Italian background of Shaftesbury's and Addison's thoughts about open landscape.

62. Byrd, *Prose Works*, p. 132.

63. Ibid., p. 265.

64. Ibid., p. 306. Byrd sits down by a clear stream on October 27 and responds to the murmur of the water as he might have next to a cascade in a garden, feeling the "composing" effect of the murmur upon his thoughts: "the murmur it made composed my senses into an agreeable tranquility" (p. 130)—precisely the associative effect that waterworks and grottoes were intended to have in the new English "classical" garden.

65. Byrd, *Prose Works*, pp. 116–17, 120–21.

66. For a seminal study of the artistic forces behind the emergence of landscape gardening, see Beverley Sprague Allen, *Tides in English Taste 1619–1800*, 2 vols. (Cambridge, Mass., 1937), 2: chaps. 17 and 18.

67. *Byrd Correspondence*, 1:355.

68. Ibid., 2:483.

69. Ibid., 1:408–9.

70. Ibid., 1:381.

71. Ibid., 2:486.

72. Bartram was not given to superlatives, so this is quite an endorsement. See Bartram Papers, Pennsylvania Historical Society, f. 21 (July 18, 1740). Bartram said nothing about a grotto or aquatic-like structure at Westover, although a letter by William Mayo in 1731 mentions that Mrs. Byrd desired shells, apparently for decorative purposes. A surveyor and friend of Byrd's who was assigned the fictional name Astrolabe in the *Secret History of the Dividing Line*, Mayo was writing to his new wife's brother about his orchards when he concluded with this request: "The last time I was at Colo. Byrds his Lady desired me to send to Barbados for some shells for her as Conk Shells Wilks & such Variety as may be got, let me beg the favour of you to get a small barrel full . . . & send them to Collo. William Byrd at Westover in James River" (*VMHB* 32 [1924], p. 56). At this time in Britain, shells were favorite ornaments for grottoes and rusticated garden buildings, which were often placed near water to create aquatic effects. With these shells, Mrs. Byrd may well have been planning to ornament some such garden feature.

73. *Memorials of John Bartram and Humphry Marshall*, pp. 113, 122. Byrd never mentions this greenhouse, but it must have been built after his return in 1726. During his period of intense plant collecting a greenhouse would have been essential. To these naturalists it appears to have been a major picturesque feature of the gardens.

74. He may not have been certain until 1720, when he speaks in his diary (July 4) of having "covered in" a building. This may have been his flanking brick kitchen, a building that, with his flanking library (built ca. 1709), determined the position of the main dwelling house in between (Byrd, *London Diary*, p. 425).

75. *Byrd Correspondence*, 1:400.

76. Shippen's is the most complete description of the gardens, especially with the plan he sketched; see *Westover Described in 1783* (Richmond, 1952). The original letter and sketch are in the Library of Congress.

77. For an original and detailed study of Westover House, see Mark R. Wenger, "Westover: William Byrd's Mansion Reconsidered" (M.A. thesis, University of Virginia, 1981).

78. Thomas Anburey, *Travels Through the Interior Parts of America* (New York, 1969; orig. pub. 2 vols., London, 1789; 2d ed., 1791), pp. 369–70.

79. François Jean de Chastellux, *Travels in North America, in the Years 1780, 1781, and 1782*, rev. and ed. Howard C. Rice, 2 vols. (Chapel Hill, 1963; orig. pub. London, 1787), 2:430–31.

80. Von Closen, *The Revolutionary Journal . . . 1780–83*, trans. and ed. Evelyn M. Acomb (Williamsburg, 1958), pp. 187–88 (February 26, 1782).

81. Shippen showed a portion of the perimeter of this garden with an uncertain wavy line, although its eastern brick wall is known to date from the eighteenth century.

82. Von Closen, *Revolutionary Journal*, p. 188.

83. Chastellux, *Travels in North America*, 2:430.

84. See Raymond P. Stearns, *Science in the British Colonies in America* (Urbana, Ill., 1970), pp. 280ff.; and Pierre Marambaud, *William Byrd of Westover, 1674–1744* (Charlottesville, 1971), pp. 80–83.

Chapter 4

1. John R. Stilgoe cites what he calls Nicholson's outdated seventeenth-century street plan for Williamsburg, with its attempt to stress form over use, as a reason for the town's failure to expand: "Annapolis and Williamsburg," he writes, "like most southern towns, never amounted to much, and it may well be that their curious street patterns prevented necessary expansion and the assembling of large lots. Even more than Charleston, they objectified out-of-date professional design." Stilgoe, *Common Landscape of America, 1580 to 1845* (New Haven and London, 1982), p. 93. As I argue in these pages, Nicholson's plan may not have encouraged physical growth, but it did create village-like neighborhoods or areas precisely where it was possible to acquire contiguous lots for gardens.

2. Jones, *The Present State of Virginia, From Whence Is Inferred a Short View of Maryland and North Carolina*, ed. Richard L. Morton (Chapel Hill, 1956), p. 71.

3. For Kimber's account of the town, see *WMQ* 1st ser., 15 (1907): 223.

4. Letter from Gooch, in Gooch Family Papers, Benacre Hall, Suffolk.

5. PRO, CO 5, 3/1740–44, p. 402. See also the Gooch Papers transcripts, vol. 3, p. 1015, Virginia Historical Society, Richmond. The Burgesses estimated that £1,300 was required to put the place right. This testimony differs, however, from that of Gooch's friend, Thomas Dawson, president of the college. In September 1750, Dawson wrote to the former governor, reporting that their friend Dr. George Gilmer, who "looks at your former House [the Palace]" frequently, feels "none can surely be equal to it." Dawson was a close friend of Gooch's, a fact that doubtless colored this message.

   As a footnote to the relationship between these two major figures in Virginia history, it is relevant to mention Thomas Wilson, an English friend of Gooch's and Dawson's. In the same letter in which he informed Dawson of Gooch's death on June 29, 1752, Wilson, on behalf of his wife, asked Dawson if he would procure and send from Virginia "a Variety of Shells, White Corral, Marine Plants & mosses & other beautiful Productions of Nature" for "a large Grotto that she is going to embellish wth. everything of the mineral fossil & [sperry?] kinds, & all Sorts of Shells from the different Quarters of the World" (June 30, 1752; Dawson Papers, Library of Congress; copy on microfilm, M-22-3, CWFL). The fad for grottoes in gardens had by this time reached its climax in England. This pursuit of minerals, as well as of plants, had been celebrated in 1732 in a poem by Dawson's brother, William, who had been president of the college before him: "Into The Mine descend / And view the kindred Ores their Masses blend? / Or else, in Search of Plants, excursive rove / Through the gay Mead and venerable Grove" (*Poems on Several Occasions*, ed. Ralph R. Rusk [New York, 1930], p. 27).

6. An instance of the House of Burgesses's earlier seriousness about maintaining the Palace gardens is its authorization in August 1726 that, owing to Drysdale's untimely death, his widow be approached about the purchase of "the remainder of the present Gardiner's [Thomas Crease] time, and that he

be employ'd in taking care of the said Gardens" in a supervisory capacity. See *EJC*, 4:114, 118, 134–35.

7. Burnaby, *Travels Through the Middle Settlements in North-America, in the Years 1759 and 1760*, 2d ed. (London, 1775), pp. 6–7.

8. Gordon, "Journal of an Officer in the West Indies Who Travelled over a Part of the West Indies, and of North America, in the Course of 1764 and 1765," in *Travels in the American Colonies*, ed. Newton D. Mereness (New York, 1916), p. 403.

9. "Journal of a French Traveller in the Colonies, 1765," *American Historical Review* 26 (1921): 71–76.

10. *The Journal of Claude Blanchard . . . 1780–83*, trans. William Duane, ed. Thomas Balch (Albany, N.Y., 1876), p. 141.

11. Eddis, *Letters from America . . . 1769–1777* (London, 1792), 1:4.

12. John Smyth, *A Tour in the United States of America* (London, 1784), 1:19.

13. Cited in Jane Carson, ed., *We Were There: Descriptions of Williamsburg, 1699–1859* (Williamsburg, 1965), p. 30.

14. Cresswell, *Journal . . . 1774–1777*, with a foreword by Samuel Thorneley (New York, 1924), pp. 206–8. In spite of Cresswell's praise of the "gentlemen's" gardens in Yorktown, I have been able to find little evidence of that taste.

15. Cited in Carson, ed., *We Were There*, p. 48.

16. *Tagebuch eines Bayreuther Soldaten . . . 1777 bis 1785* (Bayreuth, 1913); entries for the year 1781 have been reprinted in *WMQ* 2d ser., 22 (1942): 266–67.

17. Schoepf, *Travels in the Confederation . . .*, 2 vols., trans. and ed. A. J. Morrison (Philadelphia, 1911; orig. pub. Erlangen, 1788), 2:78–81.

18. *Virginia Gazette*, ed. Purdie and Dixon, 1766–1770.

19. These volumes included the Cambridge botanist Richard Bradley's *New Improvements of Planting and Gardening*, advertised for sale in 1771 and 1776 as a "general Treatise of Agriculture, displaying the Arts of Husbandry and Gardening" and known to have been part of Byrd II's library; Stephen Switzer's *Ichnographia Rustica*, which was in the libraries of Byrd, Jefferson, and John Mercer and was advertised for sale in 1751, 1764, and 1765 (Virginia Gazette Daybooks, 1750–1752, 1764–1766, Alderman Library, University

of Virginia); d'Argenville's *Theory and Practice of Gardening*, advertised in 1765, 1768, and 1770; William Chambers's *A Dissertation on Oriental Gardening* (1772); François Gentil's *The Retir'd Gardener* (edited by George London and Henry Wise, Queen Anne's royal gardeners, in 1706), which was owned almost certainly by Custis and George Washington; Batty Langley's influential *New Principles of Gardening* (1728); Thomas Whately's *Observations on Modern Gardening* (1770), owned by Jefferson and Mercer; and John Worlidge's *Systema Agricultura* (1669), owned by Byrd and advertised under the title *Dictionarum Rusticum* in 1770. For a survey of who owned what gardening books, see Helen Park, *A List of Architectural Books Available in America Before the Revolution* (Los Angeles, 1973).

20. *Virginia Gazette*, ed. Purdie and Dixon, November 6, 1766.

21. *Virginia Gazette*, ed. Purdie and Dixon, September 28, 1769; February 17, 1774, p. 3. The Rochambeau Map shows Hubard's garden to be larger even than the Palace garden, so it would seem he had good reason to advertise for gardening help. Indirect evidence suggests that this might have been a well-developed garden in town. Hubard acquired the land on Francis Street in the late 1760s, and in 1774 Nathaniel Burwell of Carter's Grove plantation sold Hubard one hundred cedar posts for his garden paling (Burwell Ledger, Special Collections, CWFL). Hubard's was one of several gardens along Francis Street from which one could command lengthy prospects southward toward fields and woods. Archaeological excavations on the site revealed that the house was correspondingly fine, "in the best style of the period." Archaeologists found there a colonial scythe blade, the most complete one that has been discovered in Williamsburg, and several bell glasses that were used to cover and protect plants. See Audrey Noel-Hume, *Archaeology and the Colonial Gardener*, Colonial Williamsburg Archaeological Series, 7 (Williamsburg, 1974), pp. 66–67, 81–82. Audrey Noel-Hume has noted that Hubard's book plate contains floral displays, which could have signified the importance of plants to him.

22. For some biographical information concerning Waller, see Littleton Waller Tazewell's "Sketch of His Own Family . . . 1823," ed. Lynda Rees Hea-

ton (M.A. thesis, College of William and Mary, Department of History, 1967). The history of the Waller family in Williamsburg is summarized by Andrew L. Riffe, "The Wallers of Endfield, King and William County, Va.," *VMHB* 59, no. 3 (July 1951): 337–52; 59, no. 4 (October 1951): 458–93. No personal evidence of Waller's interest in gardening exists; but in 1777 he paid Robert Carter for *Nature Displayed* (1739, 1759) by Noel Antoine Plucke—an influential English gardening manual in Virginia in the latter half of the century, the second volume of which was a rich fund of information on garden design, kitchen gardening, flowers, and trees, all well illustrated. Joseph Prentis of Williamsburg also owned this work; his copy of the second volume, which is owned by Colonial Williamsburg Foundation, is well worn with use. See Robert Carter's Account Book (1759–1775) in the Library of Congress.

23. The surviving copy is a tracing of Eliza's original drawing by her granddaughter Luty earlier this century. Until the early 1970s, the original was among the Blow Papers at Swem Library, College of William and Mary, but it is now lost. Mary Stephenson, who saw Luty Blow's copy at Tower Hill, was told by Luty Blow herself that she copied it from the original. See her note on the plan itself.

24. An attractive pavilion such as now stands in the Waller garden at this central point may well have been built in Williamsburg by Anthony Hay or by Benjamin Bucktrout. The latter advertised his ability in 1774 to build "all sorts of *Chinese* and *Gothick* PALING for gardens and summer houses" (*Virginia Gazette*, ed. Purdie and Dixon, September 1, 1774). The advertisement, although not related specifically to the Waller garden, indicates that a degree of sophistication had entered people's minds by that date as they set about enclosing and dividing their gardens.

25. This plan is among the Blow Family Papers, box 8, folder 6, Swem Library, College of William and Mary (hereafter cited as Blow Papers).

26. Blow Papers, box 33, folder 1.

27. Blow Papers, box 7, folder 1.

28. Blow Papers, box 24, folder 7.

29. These references are taken from the Jurgensen Collection and the Jeffcot Collection, Swem Library, College of William and Mary.

30. After Wythe moved to Richmond, the house

came into the hands of Col. Henry Skipwith, whose wife, Elizabeth, was William Byrd III's daughter and had grown up at Westover. Skipwith's brother owned Prestwould plantation in Mecklenburg County, Virginia, the garden of which was imaginatively designed and carefully planted by Lady Jean Skipwith (see chapter 5). Dr. Millington rented and then purchased the Wythe house from Col. Skipwith. Nothing is known of Millington as a gardener, or if even he was a gardener. According to a note scribbled at the bottom of the plan by "R.M.B." (a descendant of the family) in 1929, Millington's daughter, Kate Millington Blankenship, drew the plan while she and her family lived there. The extant plan is a copy; the original has been lost. Mrs. Martha Vandergrift, in her recollections, "Williamsburg in 1844," spoke of Dr. Millington's and his daughter's residence in the Wythe house. She also recollected that there still was a fine garden there then. Her reminiscences are in CWFL.

31. The house's history is summarized in "The George Wythe House," Research Report, Special Collections, CWFL.

32. *Thomas Jefferson's Garden Book, 1766–1824*, ed. Edwin Morris Betts (Philadelphia, 1944), p. 20. As indicative of Wythe's interest in practical gardening, Jefferson's letter to him of June 1790 may be quoted here. Jefferson appears to think that Wythe would be interested in hearing about the East Indian rice he has discovered in New York: "I enclose a few seeds of high-land rice which was gathered last autumn in the East Indies. if well attended to, it may not be too late to sow & mature it after you shal receive it. I have sowed a few seeds in earthen pots. it is a most precious thing if we can save it" (*Jefferson's Garden Book*, p. 151). On at least one occasion, Wythe ordered seeds from London; see Frances Norton Mason, ed., *John Norton and Sons: Merchants of London and Virginia* (Richmond, 1937), p. 53.

33. *Jefferson's Garden Book*, p. 533.

34. Ibid., p. 223.

35. The only obvious discrepancy is that the house in the plan is not wide enough; nor does it show the centrally placed structure at the bottom of the garden that appears in the Rochambeau Map, but this could have been torn down before the plan was sketched.

36. Excavations on the site revealed the remains of

three paths presumably in relation to which the garden either had to be designed or, at some point, was redesigned. One path was lined up centrally with the house and established the garden's chief east-west axis; it is the space in between the two garden areas in the Rochambeau Map and appears in the plan as a wide "gravel walk." The northern path was closer to the central one than was the southern one and made its way west in front of the outbuildings along the street. This path is not identified on the plan, but its position is apparent enough, as it is close to the north wall and is entered through a gate. The southern path proceeded west from a point southwest of the corner of the house, but its line was not as far south as the "dirt walk" or "garden path" shown in the plan as lined up with the dairy and extending along the church wall and the lilacs. The southern path, in fact, appears to be missing from the plan, unless Kate Millington Blankenship confused its position, which is not unlikely, since the relative distances she delineates between her paths match the excavated paths. See Ivor Noel-Hume, "George Wythe House, Archaeology Appendix to 1938 Report" (1958), CWFL.

37. Custis had Persian lilacs in his garden, "full of flowers"; the snowball or guelder-rose, with its snowball-like blossom, took its name from Philip Miller's *Gardener's Dictionary*.

38. Hoes and a glass bell jar were excavated in this area.

39. Little is known of Peyton Randolph's garden on the northeast corner of Nicholson and North England streets. Excavations on the site have revealed evidence of four early-eighteenth-century planting beds in which Peyton and his father, Sir John, appear to have experimented with asparagus from about the 1720s to the 1740s. These beds are the earliest for which any archaeological evidence in the Tidewater region exists. Laid out along the north-south and east-west axes, they appear to have been purely functional rather than symmetrical and ornamental. The deliberateness and care with which the gardeners provided drainage layers for these beds, instead of simply resorting to the more common raised planting bed used throughout the century, suggests an atypical experimental interest in growing vegetables that may have characterized Sir John and

Peyton Randolph and certainly did characterize another son, John, who kept a gardening diary (discussed in this chapter) that has survived. As Marley Brown III, Director of Archaeological Excavation for CWF, has put it: "The physical character of the planting beds found in the backyard of the Peyton Randolph house closely matches the description of asparagus beds contained in the advice of Judge Prentis and John Randolph, writing some sixty and eighty years later" ("Recent Evidence of Gardening in Eighteenth-Century Williamsburg," paper delivered at the Symposium on Landscape Archaeology, University of Virginia, September 27, 1987). For additional summaries and evaluations of the archaeological findings about the garden at the Peyton Randolph house, see the Colonial Williamsburg Foundation Archaeological Report by Marley R. Brown III, Andrew C. Edwards, and Linda K. Derry, "The Archaeology of the Peyton Randolph Houselot" (1986), chap. 5, pp. 54–60, and chap. 7, pp. 4–11, CWFL.

Peyton Randolph inherited the property in 1735 from his father, who supplied his English friends from time to time with American plants (see Richard Beale Davis, *Intellectual Life in the Colonial South 1585–1763*, 3 vols. [Knoxville, 1978], 2:849 and note 74; and Custis's undated letter from 1734 to Collinson, in *Brothers of the Spade: Correspondence of Peter Collinson, of London, and John Custis, of Williamsburg, Virginia, 1734–46*, ed. Earl G. Swem [Barre, Mass., 1957], pp. 23–24). It consisted of four contiguous lots between Nicholson and Scotland streets. When the house was advertised for sale in 1783, it was described as "pleasantly situated on the great square, with every necessary outhouse convenient for a large family, garden and yard well paled in . . . with several acres of pasture ground" (*Virginia Gazette, or, The American Advertiser* (James Hayes, Richmond), February 1, 1783, p. 3. On Peyton Randolph's death, an inventory of the property included an extensive list of gardening tools, including a wide assortment of hoes, six scythes with as many stones for sharpening them, "1 Garden Rake and Spade," and one wheelbarrow (see Graham Hood, ed., *Inventories of Four Eighteenth-Century Houses in the Historic Area of Williamsburg* [Williamsburg, 1974], pp. 24–26).

40. Hornsby's "Diary of Planting and Gardening,

1798–1803," is in the collections of the Missouri Historical Society, St. Louis.

41. The diary has been published in *WMQ* 1st ser., 7 (1899): 133–53. Blair makes a tantalizing allusion in the little "Diary" he kept in his 1751 almanac: "saw Amson's Gardens &c." (ibid., p. 137). The Desandrouins Map (figure 8) shows Dr. Amson's garden to be a very large one, due west of the Palace. Blair's allusion is intriguing simply because he felt that a sight of the doctor's garden was worth recording. There is some scattered evidence that doctors and apothecaries in Williamsburg, such as James Carter and Archibald Blair, took a professional interest in their gardens and plants as sources of medicinal remedies. Although they were not physicians, both Custis and Byrd maintained such an interest in plants. Amson seems even to have had a reputation as a horticulturist, for John Clayton mentioned him in a letter to John Bartram on September 1, 1760: "I have sent you, inclosed, some seed of a new plant, which I presume is a stranger in your northern [Philadelphia] parts of the world. Indeed, it grows here only in the southern parts of the colony. . . . I believe I told you that it was to be called *Amsonia*, after a doctor, here" (*WMQ* 2d ser., 6 [1926]: 319; reprinted from *Memorials of John Bartram and Humphry Marshall*, ed. William Darlington (New York and London, 1967), p. 408.

42. See Ayscough's advertisement for plants in *Virginia Gazette*, ed. Hunter, November 30, 1759.

43. For an informative account of the growth of commercial nurseries in the Chesapeake late in the eighteenth century, see Barbara Sarudy's detailed essay, "Nurserymen and Seed Dealers in the Eighteenth-Century Chesapeake," *Journal of Garden History* 9, nos. 3 and 4 (July–September 1989), especially her section on Peter Bellett, from which I learned much.

44. I am indebted to Barbara Sarudy's article, "Nurserymen and Seed Dealers," for bringing a few of these advertisements to my notice; see the appendix to her article.

45. See the Webb-Prentis Papers, Alderman Library, University of Virginia, box 2. Joseph Hornsby also ordered from Bellett. In his diary for March 1798, he notes he has sown "early Yorkshire Cabbage seed . . . from Bellett's. . . . 3 Rows Salmon Raddish seed from Bellett, next 3 Rows Turnip rooted Raddish seed from Bellett." On March 16 he noted: "Planted the South Asparagus Bed East side the main walk, with 4 Rows Roots at 1 foot distt. in the Row, the seed came from Mr. Bellett's, Williamsburg, which he calls the large Dutch Asparagus, the Plants were very fine" (Hornsby, "Diary"). Bellett apparently put his nursery up for sale in 1799 (but did not sell it); see his advertisement in the *Virginia Gazette & General Advertiser*, ed. Augustine Davis, November 12, 1799, p. 3. Bellett died in 1807.

46. Allusions to this little manuscript, which Randolph perhaps wrote merely for the use and benefit of his friends and acquaintances, suggest that it was published in the eighteenth century, possibly in 1793, but no such edition survives. As far as anyone knows, the volume was first published in 1816 as an appendix to John Gardiner and David Hepburn's *The American Gardener*. It was separately published in 1826 under the title *Randolph's Culinary Gardener*, with additions by "a native of Virginia" who mysteriously concealed his identity with the initial "M." Other editions, comments by Jefferson, and manuscript notes here and there identify the work as Randolph's. The diary has been published this century as *A Treatise on Gardening* (New York, 1924), hereafter cited as *Treatise on Gardening*. On Randolph's *Treatise*, see Sarah Stetson, "American Garden Books Transplanted and Native, before 1807," *WMQ* 3 (1946): 356–358.

47. *Treatise on Gardening*, pp. 21, 26, 50, 52.

48. Ibid., pp. 1, 3, 4, 9, 16.

49. For a discussion of the landscape gardening movement in England at this time, see Mavis Batey, "The High Phase of English Landscape Gardening," in *British and American Gardens in the Eighteenth Century*, ed. Peter Martin and Robert P. Maccubbin (Williamsburg, 1984), pp. 44–50; Christopher Thacker, *The History of Gardens* (Berkeley and Los Angeles, 1979), chaps. 13–14; Edward Malins, *English Landscaping and Literature, 1660–1840* (Oxford, 1966), chaps. 5–6. For a study of the development of landscape gardening over the whole of the eighteenth century, see David Jacques, *Georgian Gardens: The Reign of Nature* (London and Portland, Ore., 1984).

50. The house was removed from Williamsburg in the 1950s and sited on the James River in Newport News.

51. The ten acres of adjacent land were mentioned in W. W. Hening, ed., *The Statutes at Large of Virginia* (Richmond, 1820), 7:598–99.

52. In 1984 Colonial Williamsburg Foundation archaeologists excavated the southwest portion of the landscape, extending some 150 feet south of the house. The grading for a parking lot had long since destroyed much of the archaeological evidence of planting, however, and the existence of South England Street, modern buildings, and other parking lots made it impossible to embark on the scale of excavation that might have revealed eighteenth-century garden features. Archaeologists nevertheless found an eighteenth-century planting bed resembling the ones found behind (north of) the Peyton Randolph house and several agricultural trenches or planting strips. They also uncovered a semicircular arc of stake holes where the west wing of Randolph's house stood, which predated construction of the house in the late 1750s and point perhaps to John Randolph's early garden experimentation. Other garden features that were discovered, such as shrub holes and tree lines, were impossible to date owing to insufficient stratigraphic evidence. For a summary of the garden excavations done on the site, see Patricia Samford, Gregory J. Brown, and Ann Morgan Smart, "Archaeological Excavations on the Tazewell Hall Property" (Department of Archaeology, CWF, 1986), pp. 79–90.

53. *Virginia Gazette*, ed. Purdie, October 17, 1777.

54. *Norton and Sons*, pp. 249–50.

55. *Virginia Gazette*, ed. Purdie, August 21, 1778. One last point to make about Nicholas's garden is that his ward, Joseph Prentis, lived and studied law with Nicholas after his parents died in the 1760s. Himself one of Williamsburg's most sensitive and methodical gardeners in the last quarter of the century, Prentis probably learned from observing the gardening Nicholas did in the 1770s.

56. In 1770 Nicholas acquired from Governor Botetourt's estate a few gardening tools, most of which Botetourt had purchased from Governor Fauquier's estate in 1768, from bell jars to lawn rolling stones (see the Nicholas Account Books, Special Collections, CWFL). And in October 1773 Nicholas directed John Norton in London to send him "4 longest broad Grass Scythes with rings, handles and Iron wedges but no Sneeds nor cra-

dles" in addition to a number of whetstones for sharpening (*Norton and Sons*, p. 358).

57. *Norton and Sons*, pp. 184–85. That September letter included an order for the following, which may be taken as a representative list of the contents of a gentry kitchen garden, since several of these items required more careful cultivation than the average housewife was prepared to undertake: clover; early, middle, and late peas; Windsor and French beans; "orange" carrots; parsnips; early and hardy winter turnips; radishes; lettuces; spinach; celery; watercress; white mustard; cauliflower; sugar loaf; red, green, and yellow cabbages; red, purple, and white broccoli; prickly and green and white turkey cucumber; and melons and cantaloupes. His postscript reads: "If these Seeds are not quite fresh & good it will not be worth while to send them; many of those last sent faild to my great disappointment" (ibid.).

58. *Virginia Gazette*, ed. Hunter, April 4, 1755.

59. The legend is retold and the poem cited by Lyon G. Tyler, *Williamsburg the Old Colonial Capital* (Richmond, 1907), p. 254.

60. Richard Corbin, the owner of Bassett Hall by 1794, had a "Spring House" on the grounds. See Corbin Papers, Special Collections, CWFL, a document dated May 3, 1794.

Chapter 5

1. In her series of essays on Maryland colonial garden history, Barbara Sarudy provides an alternative view of Chesapeake (especially Maryland) gardens as having almost totally bypassed the influence of the English landscape garden, with its manifold variations. See especially "A Chesapeake Craftsman's Eighteenth-Century Gardens" and "A Late Eighteenth-Century Tour of Baltimore Gardens," both in *Journal of Garden History* 9, nos. 3 and 4 (July–September 1989). Her chief evidence is the fact that most gardens for which records exist contain areas near the main house that are geometrically laid out with straight paths. As I have already said, and again argue in this chapter, other factors, such as prospects, position, iconography, attitudes, and feelings, as well as practical considerations that had little to do with aesthetics or conscious choices to have a garden look this or that way, must also be taken into account. While the

straight lines of planting beds, walks, and so on were common to most gardens, it is misleading to speak broadly of formality versus informality. That Virginia plantation gardeners wished to retain their fenced-in and regularly shaped areas for reasons of convenience and economy is clear, but this does not mean they were unaware of English and continental landscape garden precedents; nor does it mean their designs remained unaffected by those practices. Geometrical shapes and straight lines were present even in the English landscape garden in the late-century high phase of the picturesque.

2. *Virginia Gazette*, ed. Purdie and Dixon, February 15, 1770; *Virginia Gazette*, ed. Purdie, October 17, 1777, p. 1.
3. McMahon, *The American Gardener's Calendar* (1806), p. 76.
4. *Tyler's Quarterly and Historical and Genealogical Magazine* 5 (July 1923): 8. Spooner's description first appeared as "A Topographical Description of the County of Prince George in Virginia, 1793," *Collections of the Massachusetts Historical Society* 3 (1794): 85–93.
5. Webb-Prentis Papers, Alderman Library, University of Virginia, Charlottesville.
6. Three categories of descriptions are used in this chapter. First, accounts were written for the most part by visitors to the colony. Residents were not, of course, insensitive to their own landscape; neither did they lack a sense of local attachment and place. It is simply a fact that people generally do not describe at length, for themselves or for others, where they live. They are not impelled, as travelers are, by sensations of discovery. For all his powers of natural description, for example, William Byrd II wrote little about the Westover gardens and nothing about the river that flowed next to them. He waited until he traveled to England or the North Carolina–Virginia border before he became descriptive. Diaries and journals of daily life in Virginia recorded private horticultural methods and data, but rarely the overall visual results of this work. More frequently, it is the traveler who can be relied upon to supply the views and prospects.

These travel commentators account for a second category of descriptions. A good number of them were Englishmen or Europeans whose descriptions presumably reflected European ideas about landscapes and gardens more carefully worked out than yet done in Virginia. Instead of distorting their descriptions, these ideas heightened their perceptions and enabled them to recognize lines of beauty and the inherent possibilities for landscape "improvement" in plantation gardens. Where a landscape garden had already been laid out, they can sometimes be counted on to understand what had been created and what could still be done.

A third category of descriptions, which is evident especially in Thomas Lee Shippen's romantic verbal pictures of Westover, includes those accounts written after the Revolution, when the landscape in the American mind took on a special beauty and meaning simply because it was American.

7. Burnaby, *Travels Through the Middle Settlements in North-America, in the Years 1759 and 1760*, 2d ed. (London, 1775), p. 13.
8. Ibid., pp. 32–33.
9. Schoepf, *Travels in the Confederation . . .*, 2 vols., trans. and ed. A. J. Morrison (Philadelphia, 1911; orig. pub. Erlangen, 1788), 1:93–96.
10. François Jean de Chastellux, *Travels in North America, in the Years 1780, 1781, and 1782*, rev. and ed. Howard C. Rice, 2 vols. (Chapel Hill, 1963; orig. pub. London, 1787), 2:380. Later, Chastellux added this note about Spring Garden: "The Author has since had an opportunity to see this garden, which answers the description given him of it, and is really most agreeable" (ibid., 569). Both Thomas Jones and his brother Walter were avid gardeners, and both cherished the memory of their famous uncle, Mark Catesby. In 1769, when Thomas was laying out the Spring Garden landscape, Walter (who was then in Edinburgh) could not resist a visit to his old relative's house in Suffolk. Earlier, while a student at William and Mary, Thomas had written enthusiastically to his brother at Spring Garden about a new edition of Miller's *Dictionary*: "If you have not supplied yourself with a Treatise upon gardening let me know if you want one and I can get one very well recommended by our gardener called Miller's Abridgement" (Jones Papers, Library of Congress). Walter eventually acquired his own house and garden at Hayfield, in Lancaster County. St. George Tucker alluded to it in one of his almanacs for 1792–1793, when he identified a peach stone that Jones had given him: "A red clingstone peach from Doctor Walter Jones's—a

very fine high flavoured fruit" (St. George Tucker Papers, Special Collections, Swem Library, College of William and Mary).

11. *Tyler's Quarterly and Historical Genealogical Magazine* 5 (July 1923), p. 8. Maycox and its gardens have completely disappeared.

12. Thomson, "Autumn," ll. 655–56, in *The Seasons*, ed. James Sambrook (Oxford, 1981), p. 170.

13. August 27, 1781; *The Journal of Lieut. William Feltman, of the First Pennsylvania Regiment, 1781–1782* (Philadelphia, 1853), p. 11.

14. A Yorkshire aristocrat, William Strickland, sixth baronet of Boynton, was also determined to see the principal seats of Virginia in the 1790s and included Maycox in an itinerary that encompassed Mount Vernon, Newcastle, Stratford Hall, Rosewell, Shirley, and Monticello. See his *Journal of a Tour in the United States of America 1794–95*, ed. the Reverend J. E. Strickland (New York, 1971), app. 1, pp. 225–27.

15. Von Closen, *The Revolutionary Journal . . . 1780–83*, trans. and ed. Evelyn M. Acomb (Williamsburg, 1958), p. 185.

16. Ibid., pp. 183, 187, 209, 212.

17. Shippen's letter to his father is in the Shippen Family Papers, Library of Congress; photostat in Special Collections, CWFL. That Stratford Hall's garden contained an orangery is a sign of its sophistication, although orangeries were not entirely uncommon in the colonial South. Westover, Mount Airy, and Eyre Hall in Virginia are known to have had them. Daniel Fisher, who lived in Williamsburg for a few years at mid-century, described an orangery in 1755 in the gardens of the Proprietor just outside Philadelphia. "What to me surpassed every thing of the kind I had seen in America," he wrote in his journal, "was a pretty bricked Green House, out of which was disposed very properly in the Pleasure Garden, a good many Orange, Lemon and Citrous Trees, in great profusion loaded with abundance of Fruit and some of each sort seemingly then ripe." Quoted in Louise Pecquet du Bellet, "The Fisher Story," in *Some Prominent Virginia Families* (Lynchburg, Va., 1907), 2:802. The entire journal is included in du Bellet's edition; for excerpts, see *WMQ* 1st ser, 27 (1908–1909): 100–139, 147–76.

18. *Virginia Gazette*, ed. Dixon and Nicholson, January 31, 1781.

19. Burwell III had inherited the estate, which amounted to nearly 5,000 acres, from his father in 1710, when he was still a minor. Therefore it must not have been until after 1721, when he came of age, that he seriously began to develop and ornament for himself an elegant residence. In 1736 an act passed in the House of Burgesses mentioned that Burwell "hath laid out great sums of money, in building a mansion-house, and other out-houses, and in making gardens, and other considerable improvements" (W. W. Hening, ed., *The Statutes at Large of Virginia* [Richmond, 1820], 4:534–37). Burwell IV inherited the estate when his father died in 1744, and it remained in the family until 1783, when his son sold it. In 1790 it was purchased by Henry Tazewell of Williamsburg, who had married Benjamin Waller's daughter. Tazewell's son, Littleton, who also owned Tazewell Hall in Williamsburg, wrote in his memoirs of how during a convalescence at Kingsmill he "commenced the life of a sportsman, spending all my time in the fields and woods" (Tazewell, "Sketch of His Own Family," ed. Lynda Rees Heaton [M.A. thesis, College of William and Mary, 1967]).

20. For a brief account of the archaeological excavations done at Kingsmill, see William M. Kelso, "Landscape Archaeology: A Key to Virginia's Cultivated Past," in *British and American Gardens in the Eighteenth Century*, ed. Peter Martin and Robert P. Maccubbin (Williamsburg, 1984), pp. 162–63; see also Camille Wells, "Kingsmill Plantation: A Cultural Analysis" (M.A. thesis, University of Virginia, 1976); and Mary R.M. Goodwin, "Kingsmill Plantation" (September 1958), Research Report, Special Collections, CWFL.

21. When the pillars were built is uncertain, but most likely they were part of the original scheme. The ubiquitous Humphrey Harwood charged Lewis Burwell V on August 22, 1778, for "takeing down Pillers" (Ledger B, Fol. 10, Special Collections, CWFL).

22. The Simcoe Map of the Kingsmill and Burwell's Ferry area shows at the far left a squarish garden enclosure, divided into four quadrants, which might well be this paled-in area (see figure 51).

23. Archaeologists are fairly confident about dating the steps to the period when the house was first constructed, before 1736, chiefly on the basis of the foundations.

24. On the general history of Carter's Grove, see Mary Stephenson, "Carter's Grove Plantation" (1964), Research Report, Special Collections, CWFL.

25. For evidence of the legal adjustments to Carter Burwell's inheritance of Carter's Grove and its implications about his intentions at the plantation, see Harold Gill, "Questions & Answers," *Colonial Williamsburg Foundation*, 4 (August 1983): 1–4.

26. As Lorena Walsh has put, "Nathaniel increasingly turned his home farm, like Green Spring, into a specialized unit geared to the comfortable living of its owner. By 1774 he had ceased to cultivate tobacco at Carter's Grove, and raised only enough corn for plantation use. Instead he grew more wheat and large quantities of oats to feed his horses, along with small patches of peas and barley. Quite possibly he had made improved meadows." Walsh, *The Study of Plantation Management* (forthcoming), chap. 5. Elsewhere she writes, "An organization change that most big planters did adopt was increasing specialization of home farm and adjacent quarter activities and workforces. . . . There, slave coopers, carpenters, shoemakers, smiths, gardeners, weavers, spinners, dairymaids, and domestics—along with occasional skilled indentured servants—worked under the close supervision of the planter, his wife, and the steward. . . . Cultivation of cash crops was often curtailed on the home farm; production of hay and oats for plantation horses, market gardening, milling, and livestock fattening were substituted" (chap. 6). See also her discussion of the nonagricultural emphasis at the home farm of Green Spring during the Ludwell family ownership in the eighteenth century.

27. It is no longer possible to enjoy from the house a view of the river as it meets the horizon because of woods and the U.S. Navy's mothballed fleet.

28. In 1775 the net agricultural profits at Carter's Grove were a mere £28, compared with £400 at Burwell's Fouaces Quarter near Williamsburg (Gill, "Questions & Answers," p. 3).

29. Very useful, since it is based on archaeological excavations, is Ivor Noel-Hume's *Digging for Carter's Grove*, Colonial Williamsburg Archaeological Series, 8 (Williamsburg, 1974). See also Kelso, "Landscape Archaeology," pp. 160–62.

30. On the basis of these discoveries, Colonial Williamsburg Foundation has restored the skeleton of the gardens.

31. One point of view about these steps is that their foundations may have disappeared over the years. The foundations of the terrace steps at Kingsmill were discovered to have been very shallow.

32. Richard Henry Lee's plantation, Chantilly, on the Potomac River appears to have had an enclosed garden rather like those of Kingsmill and Carter's Grove. It was laid out along a central or "Great Walk," with cross-paths dividing it into "squares." Judging by his "Memorandum Book" for 1776–1794, Lee planted mostly vegetables, herbs, and fruit in it. He kept a close watch on his produce and recorded in careful detail what he planted and where. On the other hand, the function of such notes as he kept is entirely practical and related to the domestic economy of the plantation. It is not likely that he would have recorded his ornamental planting in it. The "Memorandum Book" is at the Huntington Library, San Marino, California.

33. Beebe's manuscript journal, 1776–1801, in three volumes, is at the Pennsylvania Historical Society, Philadelphia. Volume 3, 1799–1801, contains the description of Pratt's garden.

34. No tree holes were found within the enclosed garden at Carter's Grove, but Burwell in any case would not have planted tall trees there to cast unwanted shade on plants and perhaps interrupt the prospect of the garden from the house. Ditches, probably planting ditches, were discovered along the inside of portions of the fencing, and these could have contained smaller trees or large bushes, as in Pratt's garden. Outside the paling, abbreviated archaeology proved inconclusive as to whether lines of fruit trees or even large orchards had been planted somewhere in the pastures. There was a ditch, again perhaps a planting ditch, outside the southernmost east-west fence, where trees may have served nicely to conceal the paling as seen from the river and to offer an element of naturalization. Perhaps this was where Burwell planted a few of the fifty poplar trees he purchased in 1750 for £100; the poplars aligned in front of the house today were not among these, for they were planted only about a century ago. In any case, Burwell would have undermined much of his gardening had he planted poplars there,

since they would have obscured the gardens and the prospects from the house. In 1781 Nathaniel Burwell planted three rows of trees somewhere outside the "garden" (Burwell Papers, microfilm, M96-1, Special Collections, CWFL).

35. *They Knew the Washingtons: Letters from a French Soldier with Lafayette and from His Family in Virginia*, trans. Princess Radziwell (New York, 1925), p. 164. Recent information has thrown some doubt on the veracity of these letters, the provenance of which remains unexplained.

36. The best source of information on Landon Carter's mind and achievements is Jack P. Greene's edition of *The Diary of Colonel Landon Carter of Sabine Hall, 1752–1778*, 2 vols. (Charlottesville, 1965); hereafter cited as *Landon Carter Diary*. See also William M.S. Rasmussen, "For Profit and Pleasure: The Art of Gardening in Colonial Virginia," *Arts in Virginia* 21 (Fall 1980): 18–27.

37. *Abraham Cowley: Essays and Plays*, ed. A. R. Waller (Cambridge, 1906), p. 411. Jack Greene discusses briefly Landon Carter's Horatian attitude in the *Landon Carter Diary*, 1:59–61.

38. *Landon Carter Diary*, 2:1123.

39. See Sarudy, "A Late Eighteenth-Century Tour of Baltimore Gardens."

40. Taken from Moncure D. Conway, *Barons of the Potomac and Rappahannock* (New York, 1892), pp. 138–41.

41. *Landon Carter Diary*, 2:1095.

42. Ibid., 1:254.

43. Ibid., p. 380.

44. Ibid., 2:673.

45. Ibid., 1:371.

46. Ibid., 2:1020.

47. Ibid., 1:526.

48. For a good account of this house and its owners, see Michael F. Trostel, *Mount Clare: Being an Account of the Seat built by Charles Carroll, Barrister, upon his Lands at Patapsco* (Baltimore, 1981).

49. "Diary of M. Ambler, 1770," *VMHB* 45 (1937): 166.

50. February 23, 1777, *The Works of John Adams*, ed. Charles F. Adams (Boston, 1851–1856), 2:435. It is interesting that Adams relished the element of surprise in the gardens as he descended from one terrace to another, which of course was characteristic of the new gardening in early-eighteenth-century England. In order to achieve this sur-

prise, the gardens had to be generously and skillfully planted. For a brief analysis of Mount Clare's gardens, see Sarudy, "A Late Eighteenth-Century Tour of Baltimore Gardens."

51. See *The Journal and Letters of Philip Vickers Fithian, 1773–1774*, ed. Hunter D. Farish (Williamsburg, 1957). This edition is hereafter cited as *Fithian Journal*.

52. *Fithian Journal*, pp. 32, 44, 63, 78.

53. Ibid., pp. 81, 30–31, 116; see also p. 123.

54. Ibid., p. 44.

55. Ibid., p. 81.

56. Ibid., pp. 81, 80.

57. Ibid., p. 61.

58. Ibid., pp. 94–95.

59. *Quebec to Carolina in 1785–86: Being the Travel Diary of Robert Hunter, Jr. a Young Merchant of London*, ed. Louis B. Wright and Marion Tinling (San Marino, Calif., 1943), p. 209. Blandfield, the home of the Beverley family, was built between 1760 and 1770. It is on the Rappahannock, close to Stratford Hall. For the gardens of Mount Airy to be compared to those at Blandfield is quite a compliment to the latter. The house stood in the center of a grand, complex, imaginative, and symmetrical landscape garden, only traces of which remain above ground today. A large semicircular lawn stretched out on the land side of the house, bisected by a ha-ha; the main drive approach to the house came up through the middle of the lawn to the front door. On the river side of the house, a large rectangular lawn, containing perhaps a bowling green, appears to have extended out from the house and down the sloping ground toward some terracing and the river. On either side of this lawn were two large gardens, enclosed perhaps by brick and divided into numerous planting beds. This rough outline of Blandfield's gardens is based partly on a small amount of archaeological excavation that has been carried out in them; there are plans for more extensive excavations, which will undoubtedly reveal the ornamental splendor of the landscape.

60. Hunter, *Quebec to Carolina*, pp. 214–15.

61. *Virginia Gazette*, ed. Rind, September 5, 1766, p. 3.

62. Arthur Shurcliff's measured drawing of Mount Airy in 1931 shows sketchy evidence of terracing, carved banks, the bowling green, and sunken gar-

dens. Shurcliff, "Southern Colonial Gardens," report on deposit in the Department of Architectural History, CWF. Archaeological excavations have not been carried out to substantiate the existence of these features and their dates.

63. The "Minute Book" is among the Tayloe Family Papers, MSSa/T 2118/a8, Virginia Historical Society, Richmond. I am grateful to Patricia Gibbs for bringing it to my attention.

64. A high level of gardening competence at Mount Airy is suggested by Robert Wormeley Carter's entry in his diary for July 17, 1780, where he notes that he had borrowed a gardener for some work at Sabine Hall: "Mt Airey Gardener came here & innoculated 4 peach trees & 1 mulberry; with Apricot & English Mulberries; gave him ten dollars" (Alderman Library, University of Virginia, Charlottesville).

65. Arthur Shurcliff measured the garden in 1928 and found clear evidence on the ground of a square garden. See his report, "Southern Colonial Gardens." The grounds have been restored with a square garden.

66. For a history of Marlborough plantation, see C. Malcolm Watkins, *The Cultural History of Marlborough, Virginia* (Washington, D.C., 1968).

67. On more than one occasion Mason supplied both George Washington and Thomas Jefferson with cuttings of fruit trees. To Washington, he sent New Town pippins, and he wrote to Jefferson as follows on October 6, 1780: "Almost all my Portugal peaches were stolen this year, before they were ripe; but I have saved the few stones I send you myself, & know they are the true sort. I have observed this kind of peach requires more care than most others, & if the trees are not tended, & the Ground cultivated, the fruit is apt to be coarse & harsh; with due culture the peaches are the finest I ever tasted. . . . The sooner the peach stones are planted the better" (*The Papers of Thomas Jefferson*, ed. Julian P. Boyd, vol. 4 [Princeton, 1951], p. 19).

68. The library also included gardening works by William Salmon, John Clayton, Philip Miller, Thomas Hale, Noel Antoine Plucke, Joseph Addison, and René Rapin. For information on Mercer's original library, I am indebted to Benny Brown, former Director of Research at Gunston Hall, who prepared a typescript inventory of it.

69. John Mason's description of the Gunston Hall gardens is among the John Mason Papers, MS Division, Library of Congress; Helen Miller cites it in her biography, *George Mason: Gentleman Revolutionary* (Chapel Hill, 1975), pp. 58–59.

70. *Journal of William Loughton Smith, 1790–1791*, ed. Albert Matthews (Cambridge, Mass., 1917), p. 64.

71. *The Diaries of George Washington*, ed. Donald Jackson and Dorothy Twohig (Charlottesville, 1976–1979), 1:327.

72. Miller, *George Mason*, p. 59.

73. Ibid.

74. For an account of the Skipwith family at Prestwould, see Susan McNeil Turner, "The Skipwiths of Prestwould Plantation," *Virginia Cavalcade* 10 (Summer 1960): 42–47. On the history of the house, see Sterling P. Anderson Jr., *Prestwould and Its Builders: Address Given at Prestwould, 28 September 1963* (Clarksville, Va., 1963), p. 2. For an impressionistic summary of Lady Jean's gardening activities, based on the manuscripts in the Special Collections of Swem Library, College of William and Mary, see Ann Leighton, *American Gardens in the Eighteenth Century: "For Use Or For Delight"* (Boston, 1976), pp. 271–91. Lady Jean's personal library is analyzed in fascinating detail for what it suggests about her inquiring intellect and diverse interests, gardening included, by Mildred K. Abraham, "The Library of Lady Jean Skipwith: A Book Collection from the Age of Jefferson," *Virginia Magazine* 91 (July 1983): 296–347.

75. Cited by Abraham, "The Library of Lady Jean Skipwith," p. 302.

76. Lady Skipwith's earliest mention of the island was in a 1792 list of "Cabbages sewn in this Island." All of the quotations from Lady Skipwith's gardening notes are from the Skipwith Papers, box 21, folder 10, Special Collections, Swem Library, College of William and Mary.

77. It is noteworthy, incidentally, that apart from Prince's Nursery in New York, Lady Skipwith's most prolific source of fruit specimens was St. George Tucker. For years he had specialized in fruit culture, first at Matoax plantation and then (beginning in 1789) in his Williamsburg garden with his new wife, Lelia. It is not unlikely that Tucker gave Lady Skipwith more advice on the subject than anyone else.

78. In addition to Miller's *Dictionary*, Lady Skipwith

owned *The Botanist's Calendar*, 2 vols. (London, 1797), and Benjamin Smith Barton's *Elements of Botany* (Philadelphia, 1803), but there is no mention of either in her notes. See Abraham, "The Library of Lady Jean Skipwith," pp. 327–28.

79. In observing that "American gardens may have retained their formality" because the untamed and wild landscape all around them had to be kept at bay rather than welcomed in, Barbara Sarudy cites the following description from the 1790s of the gardens at Belvedere, Governor John Eager Howard's home in Baltimore: "Situated upon the verge of the descent upon which Baltimore stands, its ground formed a beautiful slant toward the Chesapeake. From the taste with which they were laid out, it would seem that America is already possessed of a . . . Repton. The spot thus indebted to Nature and judiciously embellished was as enchanting within its own proper limits as in the fine view which extended far beyond them. The foreground possessed luxurious shrubberies and sloping lawns; the distance, the line of the Patapsco and the country bordering on the Chesapeake" (Thomas Twining, *Travels In America 100 Years Ago* [New York, 1894], p. 288). This description, however, is a tribute chiefly to the gardener, not the landscape. That is why Twining alludes to Humphry Repton, a popular professional English landscaper at the time. The spot or "situation" was obviously beautiful, and Twining loved it; but he was more interested in its being "judiciously embellished . . . within its own proper limits" with shrubberies and sloping lawns. See Sarudy, "A Late Eighteenth-Century Tour of Baltimore Gardens."

80. In 1732, for example, Yorktown reminded the Englishman Hugh Grove of the Thames beneath the Cliveden estate gardens. Yorktown stood elevated "like Black Heath or Richmond Hill and like that overlooks a fine river Broader than the Thames at those places and has likewise the prospect of a noble Bay. . . . I could compare Yorke to Cliveden overlooking the River" (manuscript journal, Alderman Library, University of Virginia, Charlottesville). One French traveler in 1765 summed up the character of Yorktown in this way: "This is a fine situation and a very pretty little town. . . . It is on an Elevated spot of ground by the side of the river to which it gives its name, on which it has a beautifull prospect" ("Journal of a French Traveller in the Colonies, 1765," *American Historical Review* 26 [1921]: 742). Lord Gordon also saw Yorktown that year and was taken with the town, which was "on the beautiful River of that name, which commands a full view of the River down towards the Bay of Chesapeake, and a pretty land view across to Glocester Town" (Gordon, "Journal of an Officer in the West Indies Who Travelled over a Part of the West Indies, and of North America, in the Course of 1764 and 1765," in *Travels in the American Colonies*, ed. Newton D. Mereness [New York, 1916], pp. 406–407).

Chapter 6

1. *The Writings of Thomas Jefferson*, ed. Andrew A. Lipscomb and Albert E. Bergh (Washington, D.C., 1903–1904), 11:283–84; hereafter cited as *Writings of Jefferson*.
2. Ibid., 13:78–79.
3. Julian Ursyn Niemcewicz, *Under Their Vine and Fig Tree: Travels through America in 1797–1799, 1805*, trans. and ed. Metchie J.E. Budka (Elizabeth, N.J., 1965), p. 98.
4. Washington may never have met John Custis, his wife's father-in-law by her first husband, Daniel Parke Custis; but he shared the collector's love of plants and, like Custis, obtained many of his plants through the post. Washington may well have seen Custis's famous Williamsburg garden before it began to deteriorate after Daniel Custis died.
5. The only good, detailed study of Mount Vernon's garden, especially its trees, is by Elizabeth Kellam de Forest, *The Gardens and Grounds at Mount Vernon: How George Washington Planned and Planted Them* (Mount Vernon, 1982). I am particularly indebted to de Forest for her account of Washington's planting.
6. Von Closen, *The Revolutionary Journal . . . 1780–83*, trans. and ed. Evelyn M. Acomb (Williamsburg, 1958), p. 212.
7. The numbers on this plan for the various features of the garden are used hereafter in the text.
8. November 12, 1787; *The Writings of George Washington*, ed. John C. Fitzpatrick (Washington, D.C., 1931–1940), 29:313; hereafter cited as *Writings of Washington*. In his diary for March 25, 1785, Washington wrote of planting some pine trees to help enclose the "Court yard": "Planted some of the

largest Pine trees on the Circular bank (the mound) which is intended to inclose the Court yard, Shrubberies, &ca. and Staked most of these wch. had been planted in the two Wildernesses" (*The Diaries of George Washington*, ed. Donald Jackson and Dorothy Twohig [Charlottesville, 1976–1979], 4:108).

9. From the beginning of his residence at Mount Vernon in the late 1750s, Washington conceived of the prospects from his hilltop as the centerpiece of future designs. He may even have translated them in his imagination to a classical landscape, a theme that his remodeling of the house in the Palladian style would have supported. On April 15, 1757, he sent an order to a distant relative in London for certain items related to his remodeling of the house; one of them was "A Neat Landscape after Claude Lorrain . . . £3.15.6" (Nina F. Little, *American Decorative Wall Painting, 1700–1850* [New York, 1952], p. 17).

10. As Washington told Vaughan in his letter of November 12, 1787, the willows flanking the gate at the western end of the bowling green were planted on artificial mounds (*Writings of Washington*, 29:313). These mounds not only encouraged the growth of the willows but also provided some attractive elevation at that end. In his diary Washington wrote that he created them in March 1786: "The ground being in order for it, I set the people to raising and forming the mounds of Earth by the gate in order to plant weeping willow thereon" (*Diaries of Washington*, 4:293).

11. *The Virginia Journals of Benjamin Henry Latrobe 1795–1798*, ed. Edward C. Carter II (New Haven and London, 1977), 1:165.

12. Ibid., p. 168.

13. Niemcewicz, *Under Their Vine and Fig Tree*, pp. 95, 96, 97–98. For the best study of Lorrain's influence, see Beverly Sprague Allen, *Tides in English Taste 1619–1800* (Cambridge, Mass., 1937), vol. 2.

14. *The Virginia Journals of Benjamin Henry Latrobe*, 1:165–66.

15. *Under Their Vine and Fig Tree*, p. 97.

16. *Journal of William Loughton Smith, 1790–1791*, ed. Albert Matthews (Cambridge, Mass., 1917), p. 63.

17. *Writings of Washington*, 32:182, 300. In the same October 1792 letter, he advises Whiting on where to plant some ivy: "The flowering ever-green Ivy, I want them to plant thick around the Ice house

upper side, not of the tallest kind, but of an even height. . . . The like at the No. East of the same lawn, by the other Wall [and if] the Path leading from the Bars to the Wild Cherry tree in the Hollow, was pretty thickly strewed with them (of the lower sort) and intermixed freely with the bush honey suckle of the Woods, it would, in my opinion, have a pleasing effect" (ibid., pp. 178–79).

18. *Diaries of Washington*, 4:75, 78.

19. *Writings of Washington*, 28:38.

20. *Diaries of Washington*, 4:104, 107, 163. In 1792 he laid out the gravel walks through the "wildernesses," instructing Whiting on October 14 to "gravel the Walks in the Pine labyrinths, on both sides of the Lawn West of the House" (*Writings of Washington*, 32:178). On Washington's trees, see de Forest, *Gardens and Grounds at Mount Vernon*, pp. 22–45.

21. For a good discussion of the Upper or North Garden, see de Forest, *Gardens and Grounds at Mount Vernon*, pp. 53–61.

22. The Lower Garden seems always to have been relegated to vegetables, fruit, and herbs and to have been used as a nursery for young or transplanted trees. It was planted in squares or rectangles and was partly terraced because of the sloping ground there. Niemcewicz mentions that this garden, which was "well cultivated and neatly kept" and tended by an English gardener, produced "all the vegetables for the kitchen, *Corrents, Rasberys, Strawberys, Gusberys*, quantities of peaches and cherries"; it also contained "lilies, roses, pinks, etc." (*Under Their Vine and Fig Tree*, p. 97). In back or south of it, on a gentle slope, Washington also had a vineyard, which doubled as a small orchard. That southern area, in other words, was essentially utilitarian. On January 13, 1786, Washington noted that he had "Laid out the ground behind the Stable, formerly a Vineyard, for a fruit Garden" (*Diaries of Washington*, 4:263). On October 14, 1792, he issued this directive to Anthony Whiting at Mount Vernon: "I would have what is called the Vineyard Inclosure cleansed of all the trash that is in it, and got in perfect order for fruit trees, Kitchen vegitables of various kinds, experimental grasses, and for other purposes" (*Writings of Washington*, 32:179).

23. "The Diary of the Reverend John E. Latta," July 3, 1799. The account of Mount Vernon by the Reverend Latta is taken from his unpublished jour-

nal, the location of which is unknown. A transcript of this paragraph is in the archives of Mount Vernon. On March 14, 1785, Washington recorded a few of his plantings in the Upper Garden, mentioning in the process some of its paths and features: "Planted the 9 young peach Trees which I brought from Mr. Cockburn's in the No. Garden—viz.—4 on the South border of the second walk (two on each side of the middle walk)—2 in the border of the Walk leading from the Espalier hedge towards the other cross walk and 3 under the South wall of the Garden; that is two on the right as we enter the gate & one on the left. The other Peachtree to answer it on that side & the two on the West Walk, parrallel to the Walnut trees were taken from the nursery in the Garden" (*Diaries of Washington*, 4:102).

24. See his letter to Tench Tilghman, August 11, 1784, *Writings of Washington*, 27:454–55. Washington engaged in some correspondence in 1789 with Mrs. Margaret Carroll of Mount Clare about the greenhouse and the nurture of rare and exotic plants (ibid., 30:404–05, 449, 461–62).

25. The Vaughan reference is cited from de Forest, *Gardens and Grounds at Mount Vernon*, p. 66.

26. *The Virginia Journals of Benjamin Henry Latrobe*, 1:165.

27. "The Diary of the Reverend John E. Latta," July 3, 1799. Closer to the house, in another enclosed but smaller area, Washington kept a botanical garden, where he could maintain close watch on the progress of some of his new acquisitions. "The intention of the little garden by the Salt House, &ca.," he wrote in a letter to Anthony Whiting in February 1793, "was to receive such things as required but a small space for their cultivation" (*Writings of Washington*, 32:328).

28. *Writings of Washington*, 29:205. Jefferson's landscaping has been the subject of a general and somewhat sketchy study by Ralph E. Griswold and Frederick D. Nichols, *Thomas Jefferson, Landscape Architect* (Charlottesville, 1978).

29. For an incisive discussion of the role of the American landscape in patriotic feelings during the Revolution, see Leo Marx, *The American Revolution and the American Landscape* (Washington, D.C., 1974).

30. *The Papers of Thomas Jefferson*, ed. Julian P. Boyd et al. (Princeton, 1950–), 13:269; hereafter cited as *Jefferson Papers*.

31. May 31, 1791, *Jefferson Papers*, 20:464.
32. Ibid., 9:445.
33. *Thomas Jefferson's Garden Book, 1766–1824*, ed. Edwin Morris Betts (Philadelphia, 1944), pp. 111–14; hereafter cited as *Garden Book*.
34. To William Hamilton, July 1806, *Garden Book*, p. 323. For a review of how French and English gardens influenced Jefferson, see *The Eye of Thomas Jefferson*, ed. William Howard Adams (Washington, D.C., 1976), pp. 319–36.
35. *Garden Book*, pp. 112–13.
36. Jefferson Papers, Library of Congress. For this reference I am indebted to William L. Beiswanger. See his elegant essay on Jefferson's garden architecture and design, "The Temple in the Garden: Thomas Jefferson's Vision of the Monticello Landscape," in *British and American Gardens in the Eighteenth Century*, ed. Peter Martin and Robert P. Maccubbin (Williamsburg, 1984), pp. 170–88; quotation at p. 182.
37. *Jefferson Papers*, 13:269.
38. *Garden Book*, p. 111.
39. *The Works of John Adams*, ed. Charles F. Adams (Boston, 1851–1856), 3:395, 402.
40. February 17, 1788, *Jefferson Papers*, 12:601; cited in *Garden Book*, p. xv.
41. From *Notes on the State of Virginia* (1787); cited in *Garden Book*, p. xv.
42. *Jefferson Papers*, 11:441. While residing in Paris in the 1780s, Jefferson drew a plan for a garden at the Hôtel de Langeac that exhibits the influence English gardens had had on him (see plate 1 in the American section of *British and American Gardens*, ed. Martin and Maccubbin).
43. For a clear review of a few of the literary and architectural sources of Jefferson's gardening temples and ideas, see Beiswanger, "The Temple in the Garden," and Beiswanger, "Thomas Jefferson's Designs for Garden Structures at Monticello" (M.A. thesis, University of Virginia, 1977).
44. Margaret Bayard Smith, *The First Forty Years of Washington Society*, ed. Gaillard Hunt (New York, 1906), pp. 73, 75.
45. Jefferson, Account Book, 1771, Coolidge Collection, Massachusetts Historical Society, Boston. Throughout, the descriptions from this manuscript are cited by Betts in the *Garden Book*, pp. 25–27.
46. When he revived the idea in 1809 and told Mrs. Smith about it, he spoke of including a monu-

ment to George Wythe, his professor at William
and Mary, on a mound "covered with a grove of
trees" (Smith, *First Forty Years*, p. 73). On Jefferson's reading behind this 1771 scheme, see Beiswanger, "The Temple in the Garden," pp. 170–
74.

47. Beiswanger's plan first appeared as plate 43 in
British and American Gardens. The numbers of the
features in the landscape that I have added to the
plan in figure 83 are cited in the text that follows.

48. For an account of this tradition, see G. R. Hib-
bard, "The Country House Poem of the Seventeenth Century," *Journal of the Warburg and Courtauld Institutes* 19 (1956): 159–74.

49. On this temple, see Beiswanger, "The Temple in
the Garden," p. 172.

50. On nymphaeums in the Renaissance villa, see
David R. Coffin, *The Villa in the Life of Renaissance
Rome* (Princeton, 1979); and Otto Kurz, "Huius
nympha Loci: A Pseudo-classical Inscription and
a Drawing by Dürer," *Journal of the Warburg and
Courtauld Institutes* 16 (1953): 171–77.

51. Beiswanger provides a translation of the inscription in "The Temple in the Garden," p. 174.

52. A correct version of Pope's poem may be found in
*The Twickenham Edition of the Poems of Alexander
Pope*, vol. 6, ed. Norman Ault (London and New
Haven, 1964), p. 248. Beiswanger plausibly sur-
mises that Jefferson got the idea for his grotto and
nymph from Pope's description of them in his letter to Edward Blount, June 2, 1725 (*Correspondence of Alexander Pope*, ed. George Sherburn
[Oxford, 1956], 2:296–97); Jefferson owned a
copy of Warburton's edition of Pope's *Works* that
contained the letter. See Beiswanger, "The Temple in the Garden," p. 172.

53. Dr. Syntax was the eccentric hero of William
Combe's parody of English picturesque im-
provers like William Gilpin. Combe supplied the
verses to accompany Thomas Rowland's colored plates and drawings of Dr. Syntax's travels
throughout Britain in search of the picturesque.
The highly successful work was entitled *The Tour
of Dr Syntax in search of the Picturesque* (1809).

54. See plate X in the *Garden Book*. It was probably
early in the first stage of landscaping that Jefferson laid out the semicircle of trees and shrubs
facing the house.

55. See Beiswanger, "The Temple in the Garden," pp.
174–76.

56. The arrangement was recorded on October 15 in
Jefferson's 1771 Memorandum Book.

57. Beiswanger, "The Temple in the Garden," pp.
174–76.

58. On March 31, 1774, Jefferson specified the dimensions and shape of this garden platform or
terrace: "laid off ground to be levelled for a future
garden. the upper side is 44.f. below the upper
edge of the Round-about and parallel thereto. it is
668. feet long, 80 f. wide, and at each end forms
a triangle, rectangular & isosceles, of which the
legs are 80.f. & the hypothenuse 113. feet" (*Garden Book*, p. 50). Jefferson's first mention of building a garden wall at Monticello, on April 11,
probably referred to the stone wall below this
new garden terrace.

59. William M. Kelso, the resident archaeologist at
Monticello, directed the excavations. He has ana-
lyzed his findings in "Landscape Archaeology: A
Key to Virginia's Cultivated Past," in *British and
American Gardens in the Eighteenth Century*, pp.
163–68.

60. See Beiswanger's discussion of this pavilion and
the temples that Jefferson planned for the vegetable garden but did not build, "The Temple in the
Garden," pp. 183–84.

61. For an account of the archaeology on the site of
the garden pavilion and the uncovering of what
may have been the ha-ha ditch, see Kelso, "Landscape Archaeology," pp. 166–67.

62. See Kelso, "Landscape Archaeology," p. 166. The
orchard has been replanted using the same holes
that Jefferson specified.

63. His complete description appears in François de
la Rochefoucauld-Liancourt, *Travels Through the
United States of America* (London, 1799), 2:69–
72.

64. The plan is in the Jefferson Papers, Massachusetts
Historical Society.

65. *Garden Book*, pp. 359–60.

66. As William Beiswanger has pointed out ("The
Temple in the Garden," p. 180), Jefferson was
also fascinated by the European gardens he saw
in the 1780s, especially by examples of the
"fantastic" and "sentimental"—this in spite of
Whately's censure of such artificial and theatrical
tricks in *Observations*, p. 120. It is surprising, for
example, that in the hermitage at Wilhelmsbad,
in Hanau, Germany, Jefferson thought that a sen-
try box covered with bark to look like the trunk

of an old tree was a "good idea" and "may be of much avail in a garden." He could read about such fantasies in a few late-eighteenth-century pattern books he owned. For Jefferson's responses to these fantastical operations of the garden art, see his "Memorandums on a tour from Paris to Amsterdam, Strasburg, and back to Paris 1788. March. 3," *Jefferson Papers*, 13:8–36; the account of Wilhelmsbad is on p. 17.

67. July 10, 1805, Jefferson Papers, Massachusetts Historical Society; cited in *Garden Book*, pp. 303–304. Henry Home, Lord Kames, was the author of *Elements of Criticism* (1762), a book that Jefferson owned.

68. On Woodlands, see James D. Kornwolf, "The Picturesque in the American Garden and Landscape before 1800," and especially Elizabeth McLean, "Town and Country Gardens in Eighteenth-Century Philadelphia," both in *British and American Gardens in the Eighteenth Century*.

69. Jefferson Papers, Library of Congress; cited in *Garden Book*, p. 323.

70. In 1793 Parkyns published *Six Designs for Improving and Embellishing Grounds*, which may have influenced Jefferson. Parkyns was back in Scotland by 1804, so apparently Jefferson just missed him. There is no evidence that Parkyns did any work for Jefferson at Monticello. For an account of Parkyns's life and career as a landscape gardener, see A. A. Tait, *The Landscape Garden in Scotland 1735–1835* (Edinburgh, 1980), pp. 200–202.

71. Jefferson Papers, Library of Congress; cited in *Garden Book*, p. 323.

72. Jefferson Papers, Massachusetts Historical Society; cited in *Garden Book*, p. 349. To Anne Cary Randolph on February 16, 1808, he wrote: "the first time I come home I will lay out the projected flower borders around the level so that they shall be ready for the next fall" (Jefferson Papers, Massachusetts Historical Society; cited in *Garden Book*, p. 364).

73. This plan also shows the broom wilderness or labyrinth in a pinwheel design (no. 13 on figure 82). Jefferson had mentioned this before, but it is unknown if it was laid out. In an 1808 memorandum, Jefferson made some notes for altering it (*Garden Book*, p. 384).

74. *Garden Book*, p. 360.

75. Smith, *First Forty Years*, p. 68.

76. Jefferson Papers, Library of Congress; cited in *Garden Book*, p. 416.

77. Jefferson Papers, Library of Congress; cited in *Garden Book*, p. 427.

78. *Writings of Jefferson*, 12:369–70.

79. Sarah Nicholas Randolph, *The Domestic Life of Thomas Jefferson* (Charlottesville, 1947), p. 349.

80. Jefferson Papers, Library of Congress; cited in *Garden Book*, p. 455.

81. James A. Bear Jr., ed., *Jefferson at Monticello* (Charlottesville, 1967), p. 46.

82. *Horace Walpole: Gardenist*, ed. Isabel Chase (Princeton, 1943).

83. Letter to John Page, cited in *Garden Book*, p. 3.

Chapter 7

1. The complete title of this treatise was *Observations on the Formation and Management of Useful and Ornamental Plantations; on the Theory and Practice of Landscape Gardening; and on Gaining and Embanking Land from Rivers or the Sea.*

2. This essay was published in *The Literary Journal* 2, no. 12 (December 31, 1803); for a modern reprinting of the essay, see Laurence Fricker, "John Claudius Loudon: The Plane Truth?" in *Furor Hortensis: Essays on the History of the English Landscape Garden in Memory of H. F. Clark*, ed. Peter Willis (Edinburgh, 1974), pp. 76–88. On Loudon, see also David Jacques, *Georgian Gardens: The Reign of Nature* (London and Portland, Ore., 1984), pp. 164–83, 189–96; and Rudi J. Favretti and Joy Putnam Favretti, *Landscapes and Gardens for Historic Buildings* (Nashville, Tenn., 1978), pp. 34–37.

3. McMahon is discussed by John W. Harshberger, *The Botanists of Philadelphia and Their Work* (Philadelphia, 1899), pp. 117–19; and Favretti and Favretti, *Landscapes and Gardens for Historic Buildings*, pp. 37–41. The latter includes a particularly useful summary of McMahon's adaptation of Repton and other eighteenth-century landscapers.

4. In her article on William Faris's Annapolis garden diary, dating from 1792–1804, Barbara Sarudy generalizes that designs "for most Chesapeake gardens appeared to strive for uniformity in every part" ("A Chesapeake Craftsman's Eighteenth-Century Gardens," *Journal of Garden History* 9,

nos. 3 and 4 [July–September 1988])—a point of view I have addressed elsewhere in this book. Yet she has gleaned from Faris's diary several garden features that we know existed in Virginia gardens throughout the century and that may still have been prevalent at the turn of the century and could well have characterized both Prentis's and Tucker's gardens: geometric garden beds containing both vegetables and flowers, garden paths lined with boxwood, front gardens dominated by flowers, separate utility and ornamental gardens, herbs included in the same beds with vegetables, nursery beds at the very rear for tulips and boxwood cuttings, the occasional arbor with seat, beehives, statues, fruit trees, and flower pots. Also on Annapolis gardens, see Barbara Paca-Steele (with assistance from St. Clair Wright), "The Mathematics of an Eighteenth-Century Wilderness Garden," *Journal of Garden History* 6, no. 4 (1986): 299–320; and Mark P. Leone, "Power Gardens of Annapolis," *Archaeology* 42 (March–April 1989): 34–41.

5. Colonial Williamsburg Foundation owns most of the Prentis library; other extant volumes are at the Alderman Library, University of Virginia, and in the possession of Dr. and Mrs. Joseph P. Webb and their family. In some cases the volumes bear the bookplate of John, Joseph's brother. What is known of the books in this library indicates both literary and gardening interests. The library includes Pope's *Works*, the *Spectator*, Dr. Johnson's *Dictionary*, Lord Orrery's edition of Swift, *Paradise Lost*, Prior's *Poems on Several Occasions*, Pope's 1725 edition of Shakespeare (with Governor Dunmore's bookplate), Swift's *Miscellanies*, Sterne's *Tristram Shandy*, Mandeville's *Fable of the Bees*, and a number of works on religion, travel, and geography. His gardening books included Noel Antoine Plucke, *Spectacle de la nature: Or, Nature Display'd* (7th ed., 1750, "Translated from the Original French, By Mr. Humphreys"); Philip Miller's *Gardener's Kalendar* (9th ed., 1751) and *Gardener's Dictionary*; Arthur Young's, *Rural Oeconomy* (2d ed., 1773), which is inscribed, "J Prentis Wmsburg 17th May 1776"; *Meditations and Contemplations* by James Hervey (17th ed., 1764), which included a lengthy discourse, "Reflections on a Flower Garden"—a volume which Prentis gave his daughter Eliza; Bernard McMahon's *The American Gardener's Calendar, adapted to the climate and seasons of the United States* (Philadelphia, 1806); and John Gardiner and David Hepburn's, *The American Gardener, Containing . . . Copious Instructions for the Cultivation of Flower Gardens, Vineyards, Nurseries, Hop-Yards, Green Houses, and Hot Houses* (Washington, D.C., 1804), which is inscribed, "Mrs. Basset to Jos Prentis 1809." The inventory of Prentis's books was performed in 1810 and is among the Prentis Papers, Small Collections, Swem Library, College of William and Mary, Williamsburg.

6. Prentis grew up in the family house (now called the William Prentis house) on Duke of Gloucester Street, attended the College of William and Mary, and, after his parents died in the 1760s, lived with Robert Carter Nicholas as his ward on South England Street. See "Green Hill," Research Report, Special Collections, CWFL.

7. Prentis's correspondence is in the Webb-Prentis Papers, Manuscripts Department, accession no. 4136, Alderman Library, University of Virginia, Charlottesville. Since the collection is being reorganized, it is not always possible to cite box numbers; cited hereafter as Webb-Prentis.

8. Webb-Prentis, accession no. 4136. The letters between Joseph Sr. and Joseph Jr. from 1796 to 1809 may be found in box 8.

9. Webb-Prentis, accession no. 4136: Robert to Joseph Prentis, December 2, 1800; Meade to Prentis, August 1796 and June 13, 1797.

10. This poem was written inside a letter from Thomas Nicolson to St. George Tucker, July 30, 1795, and is endorsed in Tucker's hand, "Letter to Barraud, Aug. 4, 1795" (Tucker-Coleman Papers, box 19, folder July 1795, Special Collections, Swem Library, College of William and Mary, Williamsburg).

11. Prentis's "Monthly Kalendar" (in his "Account Book and Garden Book, 1774–1788," Webb-Prentis, accession no. 4136-b) is a narrative of detailed gardening instructions for every month of the year, in the style of a gardening manual. Vegetables and herbs, both common and rare, commanded most of his attention, and he includes advice on methods of pruning and how to preserve produce over the winter. In addition to the ordinary vegetables and herbs, he was especially interested in asparagus, as he was later at Green Hill. He also grew the less common eggplant, artichokes, salsify, feverfew or featherfew used medicinally, rue (known as the herb of grace), tansy,

and okra. In the ornamental vein, he also mentions nasturtiums and "Slips of box."

12. The "Directions about Gardeng" that were included in the "Garden Book" for 1774–1788 focused almost exclusively on vegetables and fruit. A noteworthy exception is his direction for "Dressing Borders," where he wrote that in February one should thoroughly clean "Beds and Borders" and that this "gives a liveliness to the Surface, is pleasing to the Eye, and well worth the Labour." The manuscript is in the Webb-Prentis Papers, accession no. 4136-b.

13. When Prentis moved to Green Hill in 1778, the original six lots attached to the house had become eight, occupying four acres or most of the block bordered by Henry, Prince George, Nassau, and Scotland streets. These four acres, which, according to an 1810 deed of sale, consisted of "the Gardens both on the east and west side of the yard," must not be confused with the ten or more acres that Prentis managed to acquire by 1790 and on a few of which he farmed—"convenient for pasturage," as he noted in the 1790 advertisement (see "Green Hill," Research Report, Special Collections, CWFL). The Williamsburg College Map of 1791 (in CWFL) shows that some of this land was located to the north and west of his block, so that in effect he was flanked by his own lands. The lots to the west were attached to a dwelling house and had belonged to Frances Hubard, wife of James, whose other Williamsburg property has already been mentioned.

14. *Virginia Independent Chronicle and General Advertiser*, June 30, 1790.

15. Tucker to Fulwar Skipwith, [no month] 10, 1809, Tucker-Coleman Papers.

16. *The Phoenix Plough-Boy*, ed. Bruff and Repiton, November 5, 1828; repeated in the November 12 issue.

17. See John Charles, "Recollections," typescript in CWFL, pp. 9–10. With allowance for the subjective and tentative nature of this kind of historical evidence, historians have found that Charles's memory was surprisingly sound and accurate.

18. Webb-Prentis, box 8.

19. Ibid.

20. Tasks the judge wanted his son to tell Ellick to perform in September 1803 included the laying of new gravel on the walks and perhaps in the yard and the harvesting of wood for the winter: "Gravel to be got in a large Quantity Pompey to cut wood for winter, Ellick and Charles to keep the Gardens clean. . . . When the turnips are well in Leaf, tell Ellick to weed them about 8 inches a part in the Row, and to weed the ground very clean between them." For more sowing, he adds, there were turnip seeds "in the press in Study" (Webb-Prentis, box 8).

21. November 17, 1808, Webb-Prentis, six letters from Wickham, 1807–1822 (the letters after 1809 are to Joseph Jr.).

22. September 23, 1808, Webb-Prentis.

23. *Thomas Jefferson's Garden Book, 1766–1824*, ed. Edwin Morris Betts (Philadelphia, 1944), p. 89. According to the 1809 inventory of Prentis's estate, Ellick and his fellow gardeners had plenty of tools with which to work, including: "four old spades, 2 old shovels, garden reel, 7 old hoes, 2 scrapers, pair [of] steps, one cutting spade, 2 dung forks, 2 grubbing hoes, 3 rakes, 2 pitch forks, 2 wooden rakes with iron teeth, 2 water pots, 2 wheel barrows, one pair shears, one grind stone" (Prentis Papers, Special Collections, Swem Library, College of William and Mary, Williamsburg).

24. March 11, 1809, Webb-Prentis.

25. March 7, 1807, Webb-Prentis.

26. Joseph Sr. to Joseph Jr., January 20, 1806, Webb-Prentis. It is not clear what plant from his garden Prentis had in mind when he instructed his son to forward several "Bushes" across the river; "ten or a dozen bushes [are to be] taken up, and they ought to be separated so as to have one root in a place." There was no danger of denuding the garden, since "they will furnish the whole Town if they are wanted. . . . a few of the seed is also sent."

27. This is a manuscript volume, "Account book and garden book of Joseph Prentis," accession no. 4136-b, 1775–1779, 1784–1788, Webb-Prentis. The plants Prentis wrote about are the following: artichokes, Jerusalem artichokes, beans, Margaran beans, broccoli, cauliflower, currants, celery, "Chamomile Flowers," gooseberries, onions, parsley, strawberries, raspberries, spinach, parsnips, salsify, peas, lettuce. Among the directions for specific jobs, he singled out "Dressing Borders," "Dung your Grounds," and "Gathering Seeds."

28. October 1802, Webb-Prentis.

29. In September 1803, when the paling around the gardens was in an advanced state of decay, Prentis makes a similar distinction about the "small Garden": "The pales and Planks to the little garden was in a ruinous state, and cannot be worth repairing except with old timber. It is probable they can put them up so as to last a short time— the little Garden wants new ti[m]ber in every part" (Webb-Prentis).

30. Recent archaeological excavations have discovered the precise location of this graveyard; see Marley Brown, Amy Bennett, and Thomas Higgins, "Archaeological Examination of the Davis Lot, Prentis Corner, and Contested Property" (1985), Department of Archaeological Research, CWF.

31. August 26, 1805, Webb-Prentis.

32. Prentis Papers.

33. Ibid.

34. This poem, "The Bermudian," has been printed in Mary H. Coleman, *St. George Tucker, Citizen of No Mean City* (Richmond, 1938), p. 2; it was first published in Hull, England, in 1808.

35. Henry Tucker and Anne Tucker to St. George Tucker, Tucker-Coleman, box 4, folders August 1772 and May 1772.

36. Tucker-Coleman, box 4, folders July 1768, January 1772, August 1772, and August 1775.

37. August 11, 1773, Tucker-Coleman, box 5, folder August 6–16, 1773; "Almanack," 1774, Tucker-Coleman, box 61.

38. Transcripts, TR/27/.1, pp. 2–3, 12 (Journal to Charleston—1777), Special Collections, CWFL; Journal to Charleston (1777), Tucker-Coleman, box 6, folder March 1777.

39. James Madison wrote to him from Loch Lomond in Scotland in September 1775: "If you can conceive a Prospect of Vales, Lakes, Woods, cloud-capt Mountains, Rocks and Seas, at once bursting forth upon the sight to be delightful, it was here we enjoyed it" (Tucker-Coleman, box 5, folder September 1775). See also Martha Bland to Frances Bland Randolph, May 12, 1777, Tucker-Coleman, box 6, folder April–May 1777.

Tucker was apparently struck by a passage of landscape description that he wrote in his 1793 "Almanack," next to which he drew a line to draw attention to it: "How sweet is the landscape before us!—the distant mountains mingle with the azure, and all between is the finest penciling of na-

ture. The verdant lawn, the tufted grove, the dusky tower, the hanging wood, the winding stream and tumbling water fall, compose the lovely picture before you" (Tucker-Coleman, box 61). In 1774, on a trip alone to some unspecified destination in the north, he recorded this impression of a landscape scene: "Beautiful Country. Number of Farms, Orchards, & Meadows with Haycocks" (Tucker-Coleman, box 61).

40. Tucker-Coleman, box 5, folder 107.

41. July 12, 1786, TR/27/.1, Special Collections, CWFL; Tucker-Coleman, box 13, folder July 1786. All subsequent quotations describing the 1786 tour are from this manuscript.

42. Tucker-Coleman, box 13, folder July 1786.

43. They went out of their way to visit William Prince's already famous "Nursery Garden," where they were introduced to choice fruit specimens, several of which they ordered for the Matoax gardens and the gardens of Fanny's brother, Theodorick Bland. These included "six New Town Pippins, six Newark Pippins, six Green Gage Plumbs, six Carnation Cherries, six May Duke Cherries, six Apricots of the best kind, six Bergamot Pears, six two pound Winter Pears . . . half a bushel of Clover seed (Red) and half a bushel of Orchard Grass" ("Almanack," 1786, Tucker-Coleman, Box 61). William Prince operated one of the most successful nurseries in America at the end of the eighteenth century. So great was the demand for his plants from all over the nation that he published a catalogue in 1827 of the "American Trees, Shrubs, Plants, and Seeds, Cultivated and for sale at the Linnaean Botanic Garden and Nurseries, near New York."

44. TR/27/.1, Special Collections, CWFL; Tucker-Coleman, box 8, folder September 1780.

45. St. George to Frances Tucker, July 11, 1781, Tucker-Coleman, box 9; TR/27/.1, Special Collections, CWFL.

46. A few of Fanny's letters to Tucker in Williamsburg in 1787, the year before she died, indicate that he had planted a number of trees at Matoax over the preceding years. "Your peaches, plumbs, and apricots," she wrote, "look indifferently, [but] the cherries, apples, and pears well." A few days later she added, "your trees look charmingly" (Tucker-Coleman, box 14, folder April 17–30, 1787). Matoax had a sad end. The Randolphs sold it about 1794, and then it burned in

the early nineteenth century. When John Randolph, Fanny's son, returned to the ruins in 1816, he was overcome with nostalgia and grieved over what had befallen his boyhood home. He recorded his feelings in a letter in 1820; although he did not finish his description, it is poignant: "I went to Matoax for the last time four years ago. I cannot repeat the trial. If they had left the trees, the noble trees, and beautiful shrubs, I could have borne the destruction of the houses and gardens and orchard. These could have been replaced, but now . . . " A few years later he looked back again: "From my earliest childhood I have delighted in the groves and solitudes of poor old Matoax. I now recall several of my favorite seats where I used to ruminate, 'chewing the cud of sweet and bitter fancies,' all bitter now" (cited in William Cabell Bruce, *John Randolph of Roanoke 1733–1833* [New York and London, 1922], 1:40).

47. Tucker-Coleman.

48. *Virginia Gazette and Weekly Advertiser*, ed. Nicholson and Prentis, September 14, 1782.

49. This summary of Tucker's house renovations and the information that follows about the house are taken from "St. George Tucker House," Research Report, Special Collections, CWFL. One of the lots, the northernmost one on the Green, had been the site of the Williamsburg theater, but by the 1760s it had disappeared.

50. Tucker wrote this autobiographical sketch for Richard Rush, Comptroller of the Treasury in Washington; it has been printed in *VMHB* 43 (1934): 219.

51. 1790 "Almanack," Tucker-Coleman, box 61.

52. According to the "Memo" ("Virginia Almanack," 1792, Tucker-Coleman, box 61), Tucker particularly liked peaches, stones of which he obtained from plantations such as Sabine Hall, Corotoman, and Hayfield. His cousin Donald Campbell sought his advice on fruit on November 9, 1794: "I inclose you Mr. Prince's list of Trees and woud thank you to point out to me the best kinds of Cherries Peaches Plumbs Apricots Nectarines Pears and early apples" (Tucker-Coleman, box 18, folder November–December 1794).

53. Philip Barraud to St. George Tucker, October 14, 1791, TR/041/.1, p. 1, Special Collections, CWFL; and Barraud to Tucker, August 24, 1796, Tucker-Coleman, box 19, folder 1796.

54. Tucker to Cary, October 8, 1795, TR/27/.1, p. 4, Special Collections, CWFL.

55. Nothing at all is known of Dr. Greenway's studies.

56. *The American Museum* was published for a time, carrying pieces both scientific and literary.

57. October 13, 1796, Tucker-Coleman, box 21, folder 1796; July 11, 1800, box 22, folder July 1800; August 4, 1798, TR/04/.1, Special Collections, CWFL; May 20, 1814, Tucker-Coleman, box 33, folder May–June 1814.

58. Fanny Coalter to John Coalter, April 11, 1810, TR/04/.2/FB(T), Special Collections, CWFL.

59. The Palace Green always represented for Tucker a social as well as a visual focus in the town, which is one reason he liked the position of his house and garden. In a poem entitled "Lines, supposed to have been found upon the Palace-green at Williamsburg, on May-day, 1816" (Tucker-Coleman, box 62, notebook 8, p. 14), he evokes a feeling for the society of the Palace Green, and Palace and college gardens, that he enjoyed during these years:

> O! the sweet, bewitching Scene,
> Palace-grounds, or College-green,
> When the Beaus, and Belles, assembling;
> Beaus, their secret thoughts confiding;
> Belles, their smiles, and Blushes hiding,
> Frowns, and careless looks, dissembling.

Dr. Barraud once called the Palace Green "Tucker Green."

60. An 1815 inventory of the Tucker household lists eighteen cows, not just two, so there had to be pasturage for them somewhere in or near the town. Perhaps two cows were kept in one corner of their Nicholson Street property. When Tucker first suggested the idea of a house in Williamsburg to his first wife, he also mentioned buying a little farm close to the town.

61. TR/27/.2, p. 42, Special Collections, CWFL; Lelia Tucker to Frances Bland (Tucker) Coalter, May 30, 1809, TR/27/.2; Lelia Skipwith Carter Tucker to Frances Bland (Tucker) Coalter, October 10, 1809, TR/27/.2; Lelia Skipwith Carter Tucker to Frances Bland (Tucker) Coalter, March 17, 1808, TR/27/.2.

62. See "Almanack," 1793, for August 25; an entry for March 1793 in "Almanack," 1792; and a March entry in the "Almanack," 1804 (Tucker-Coleman, box 61).

63. Tucker-Coleman, box 61.

64. John Coalter to St. George Tucker, January 21, 1813, Tucker-Coleman, box 32, folder January 19–31, 1813.

65. Tucker-Coleman, Box 80, folder 4 (1800–1809).

66. Washington Irving, "The Author's Account of Himself," *The Sketch Book of Geoffrey Crayon, Gent.* (New York, 1890), p. 10.

67. "Lines Composed a Few Miles Above Tintern Abbey," lines 95–99, *The Complete Poetical Works of Wordsworth*, ed. Andrew J. George, Riverside Edition (Cambridge, 1932), p. 92

68. "I Wandered Lonely as a Cloud," lines 21–22, ibid., p. 311.

69. *Poems of Freneau*, ed. Harry Hayden Clark (New York, 1929), pp. 268–69 (ll. 45–48, 53–56).

Conclusion

1. "The Gift Outright," in *The Poetry of Robert Frost*, ed. Edward Connery Lathem (New York, 1966).

2. Meade's letter to Prentis is in the Webb-Prentis Papers, Manuscripts Department, accession no. 4136, Alderman Library, University of Virginia, Charlottesville; a transcript is in TR/30/.1, pp. 40–47, Special Collections, CWFL.

3. Letter to William Mason, November 27, 1775, *The Correspondence of Horace Walpole*, ed. W. S. Lewis (New Haven, 1955), 28:234.

4. Preface to *The American Gardener's Calendar* (1806), p. iii.

5. Loudon, *Encyclopedia of Gardening*, p. 401.

Bibliographical Essay

While the notes to the individual chapters in this book include all the historical texts and the scholarship that lie behind my account of Virginia garden history from Jamestown to Jefferson, this essay provides a more selective, introductory bibliographical guide to the subject. In addition to listing the relevant works, I have tried to suggest briefly the value and particular contribution that many of them have made, directly or indirectly, to this relatively new field of art, cultural, and social history.

The sketch is divided into five parts: the first reviews general garden histories; the second, British garden history from the seventeenth to the early nineteenth centuries; the third, American garden history of the same period; the fourth, garden history of Virginia and the Chesapeake region, including primary sources not specifically relating to garden history but illustrating how people thought of the landscape; and the fifth, studies in fields other than garden history that have a bearing on my subject. Unless especially relevant, I have not included the seventeenth- and eighteenth-century primary sources on gardening that appear in the notes. Manuscript sources are specified in the notes and summarized in the Preface. Unless otherwise indicated, the place of publication is London.

General Garden Histories

The best standard general history of world gardens is Christopher Thacker's *The History of Gardens* (Berke-ley and Los Angeles, 1979). Derek P. Clifford's *A History of Garden Design* (1966; 2d ed. 1973), though older, is still sharp and useful. A broad sweep of the subject was also provided by Marie-Luise Gothein, *A History of Garden Art* (1928). See also Edward Hyams, *A History of Gardens and Gardening* (New York, 1971), and Rosemary Verey, *Classic Garden Design* (New York, 1984). On the subject of exchangeability or mutual influence of urban and country gardens, see Nicholas Purcell, "Town in Country and Country in Town," in *Ancient Roman Villa Gardens*, ed. Elisabeth B. MacDougall, Dumbarton Oaks Colloquium on the History of Landscape Architecture, 10 (Washington, D.C., 1987), pp. 187-203; and Judith A. Kinnard, "The Villa Gamberaia in Settignano: The Street in the Garden," *Journal of Garden History* 6, no. 1 (1986): 1–18.

British Garden History Literature

In the last fifteen years there has been an explosion of writing on garden history, especially in and about Britain. Morris Brownell has assessed this essentially scholarly phenomenon in " 'Bursting Prospect': British Garden History Now," in *British and American Gardens in the Eighteenth Century: Eighteen Illustrated Essays on Garden History*, ed. Peter Martin and Robert P. Maccubbin (Williamsburg, 1984). That volume contains nine additional essays on British garden history, although its principal value lies perhaps in the eight essays on American garden history (more on these below). John Dixon Hunt and Peter Willis's *The Genius of the Place: The English Landscape Garden, 1620–1820* (1975), an anthology and commentary on the English landscape garden, made readily available for the first time many texts central to the development of this art form. More recently, in *Garden and Grove: The Italian Renaissance Garden in the English Imagination, 1600–1750* (Princeton and London, 1986), Hunt has somewhat revised existing assumptions about English garden history by documenting the largely classical and Italian Renaissance inspiration for English gardens in the seventeenth and eighteenth centuries. He has also edited a special issue of the *Journal of Garden History* on Anglo-Dutch gardens (vol. 8, nos. 2 and 3 [1988]), which includes his own essay on the Dutch influence in England, "Reckoning with Dutch Gardens" (pp. 41–60). See also Tom Turner's history, *English Garden Design: History and Styles since 1650* (Woodbridge, Suffolk, 1986).

Other definitive studies of the English garden that bear on the present study are: Beverly Sprague Allen's old solid standby, *Tides in English Taste 1619–1800*, 2 vols. (Cambridge, Mass., 1937), the first volume of which contains a chapter on "The Revolution in Garden Design"; Nikolaus Pevsner, ed., *The Picturesque Garden and Its Influence Outside the British Isles*, Dumbarton Oaks Colloquium on the History of Landscape Architecture, 2 (Washington, D.C., 1974); Roy Strong, *The Renaissance Garden in England* (1979); David Jacques, *Georgian Gardens: The Reign of Nature* (London and Portland, Ore., 1984); Edward Malins, *English Landscaping and Literature, 1660–1840* (Oxford, 1966); Christopher Hussey, *English Gardens and Landscapes 1700–1750* (1967); Morris Brownell, *Alexander Pope and the Arts of Georgian England* (Oxford, 1978); Peter Martin, *"Pursuing Innocent Pleasures": The Gardening World of Alexander Pope* (Hamden, Conn., 1984); Peter Willis, *Charles Bridgeman and the English Landscape Garden* (1977); John Dixon Hunt, *The Figure in the Landscape: Poetry, Painting, and Gardening during the Eighteenth Century* (Baltimore, 1976) and *William Kent: Landscape Garden Designer* (1987); and Dorothy Stroud's two books, *Capability Brown*, 2d ed. (1975) and *Humphry Repton* (1962). On John Loudon, see Laurence Fricker, "John Claudius Loudon: The Plane Truth?" in *Furor Hortensis: Essays on the History of the English Landscape Garden in Memory of H. F. Clark*, ed. Peter Willis (Edinburgh, 1974), pp. 76–88. For an encyclopedic survey of British botanical litera-

ture to the end of the eighteenth century, the reader could not do better than refer to Blanche Henrey's *British Botanical and Horticultural Literature Before 1800* (1975). A good recent study of Philip Miller is Hazel Le Rougetel, *The Chelsea Gardener: Phillip Miller, 1691–1771* (Portland, Ore., 1990).

General American Garden History to 1826

The first historical effort at an assessment of American gardens was the Englishman William Cobbett's *The American Gardener*, published in London in 1821. There are no comprehensive modern studies that are appropriate to mention here.

British and American Gardens in the Eighteenth Century contains eight essays on American garden history that present new perspectives on colonial gardening and suggest it was an active art form in the cultural life of the period. All or parts of five of them are on colonies other than Virginia: James D. Kornwolf, "The Picturesque in the American Garden and Landscape before 1800"; John Flowers, "People and Plants: North Carolina's Garden History Revisited"; Abbott Lowell Cummings, "Eighteenth-Century New England Garden Design: The Pictorial Evidence"; Elizabeth McLean, "Town and Country Gardens in Eighteenth-Century Philadelphia"; and George C. Rogers Jr., "Gardens and Landscapes in Eighteenth-Century South Carolina."

Mount Clare's gardens, in Maryland, which I describe for comparative purposes in chapter 5, have received valuable attention by Michael F. Trostel in *Mount Clare: Being an Account of the Seat built by Charles Carroll, Barrister, upon his Lands at Patapsco* (Baltimore, 1981). On Maryland gardens specifically, *The Journal of Garden History* published a double issue, "Eighteenth-Century Gardens of the Chesapeake" (vol. 9, nos. 3 and 4 [July–September 1989]) containing five very fine essays by Barbara Wells Sarudy, in which (among other theses) she contends that the increasingly naturalized style of the English landscape garden had little effect on the essentially geometric or "formal" shapes of most American colonial pleasure gardens. The titles of her essays are: "Gardening Books in Eighteenth-Century Maryland" (pp. 106–10), "Nurserymen and Seed Dealers in the Eighteenth-Century Chesapeake" (pp. 111–17), "Genteel and Necessary Amusements: Public Pleasure Gardens in Eighteenth-Century Maryland" (pp. 118–24), "A Late

Eighteenth-Century Tour of Baltimore Gardens" (pp. 125–40), and "A Chesapeake Craftsman's Eighteenth-Century Gardens" 141–52). See also Mark P. Leone's essays, "Power Gardens of Annapolis," *Archaeology* 42 (March–April 1989): 34–41, and "Interpreting Ideology in Historical Anthropology: Using Rules of Perspective in the William Paca Garden in Annapolis, Maryland," in *Ideology, Power, and Prehistory*, ed. Daniel Miller and Christopher Tilley (New York, 1984), pp. 25–35.

Less scholarly in character than all the above, but readable and interesting, is Ann Leighton's *American Gardens in the Eighteenth Century: "For Use Or For Delight"* (Boston, 1976); there is much good information in this book, though the author maddeningly neglected to cite many of her sources. A book that is less historical but more practical from the point of view of American garden preservation and restoration is *Landscapes and Gardens for Historic Buildings* (Nashville, Tenn., 1978), by Rudi J. Favretti and Joy Putnam Favretti.

Chesapeake and Virginia Garden History and Landscape

A number of late-sixteenth- and seventeenth-century accounts and promotional tracts about Virginia and the New World include early responses to its landscape as a type of "garden of the world." A few of these are: Thomas Hariot, *A brief and true report . . .* (1588), ed. R. G. Adams (Ann Arbor, 1931); George Percy, *Observations Gathered Out of 'A Discourse of the Plantation of the Southerne Colonie in Virginia by the English'* (1606), ed. David B. Quinn (Charlottesville, 1967); *Newes from Virginia: The Lost Flocke Triumphant* (1610), ed. W. F. Craven (New York, 1937); Ralph Hamor, *A True Discourse of the Present Estate of Virginia* (1615), ed. A. L. Rowse (Richmond, 1957); *A Perfect Description of Virginia* (1649); William Bullock, *Virginia Impartially Examined . . .* (1649); and Thomas Glover, *Account of Virginia* (published in the *Philosophical Transactions* of the Royal Society on June 20, 1676; rpt. Oxford, 1904). See also the evocative descriptions of Bermuda, well known to Shakespeare before he wrote *The Tempest*, that were brought back to England in 1610 by the survivors of a Virginia-bound expedition, led by Thomas Gates and Sir George Somers, that was shipwrecked on the island: an "unauthorized" pamphlet by Silvester Jourdan, a member of

the crew, *A Discovery of the Bermudas, Otherwise Called the Isle of Devils* (1610); the Virginia Company's "official" account, *A briefe declaration of the present state of things in Virginia* (1616); and William Strachey's report, *The True Repertory of the Wrack and Redemption of Sir Thomas Gates*, dated July 15, 1610, and eventually published in *Purchas His Pilgrims* (1625).

These and other accounts, or portions thereof, have been published in *Tracts and Other Papers, Relating Principally to the Origins, Settlement, and Progress of the Colonies in North America . . . to the Year 1776*, ed. Peter Force, 4 vols. (1836–1846; rpt. Gloucester, Mass., 1963). A few were assessed in the eighteenth century by William Stith, Virginia historian and professor at the College of William and Mary, in his *History of the First Discovery and Settlement of Virginia* (Williamsburg, 1747; available in modern editions by Morgan P. Robinson [1965] and Darrett B. Rutman [1969]).

An earlier history of Virginia, more promotional in character than Stith's, that contains long descriptions of the fauna and flora of the colony is Robert Beverley's *History and Present State of Virginia* (first published in 1705 and then revised and extended in 1722), ed. Louis B. Wright (Chapel Hill, 1947). Leo Marx, in *The Machine in the Garden* (Oxford and New York, 1964), calls Beverley's book the first full treatment of the New World pastoral ideal by a native American. See also the later history by Hugh Jones, *The Present State of Virginia, From Whence Is Inferred a Short View of Maryland and North Carolina*, ed. Richard L. Morton (Chapel Hill, 1956). For a good and convenient analysis of promotional literature generally in the colonial period, see Richard Beale Davis, *Intellectual Life in the Colonial South, 1585–1763* (Knoxville, 1978), vol. 1, chap. 1.

There have been several good modern studies of the Edenic and other metaphors contained in responses to the Virginia landscape, among them: Peter A. Fritzell, "The Wilderness and the Garden: Metaphors of the American Landscape," *Forest History* 12 (1968): 16–22; Roderick Nash, *Wilderness and the American Mind* (New Haven, 1967); Lewis Simpson, *The Dispossessed Garden* (Athens, Ga., 1975); and Bernard W. Sheehan, *Savagism and Civility* (Cambridge, 1980). On the patriotic feelings engendered by the American landscape during the American Revolution, see Leo Marx, *The American Revolution and the American Landscape* (Washington, D.C., 1974).

During the eighteenth century almost nothing was

published on or specifically for colonial gardening; the little there was consisted of horticultural manuals, practical guides mainly to kitchen gardening. Even in this vein, however, most eighteenth-century gardeners in North America depended, with some adaptation for soil and climate, on what amounted to their horticultural bibles: the Englishman Philip Miller's *Gardener's Dictionary* (1724, etc.) and *Kalendar* (1732, etc.). Miller occasionally alluded to southern colonial botanical gardeners and the plants they discovered in the region. The most famous general practical guide to gardening in America at the beginning of the nineteenth century was by Jefferson's friend, Bernard McMahon, *The American Gardener's Calendar* (Philadelphia, 1806), adapted to the climate and seasons of the United States. It went through several editions in the century. The only native Virginian work to appear in print was John Randolph Jr.'s less ambitious *A Treatise on Gardening By a Citizen of Virginia* (written ca. 1758–1764; published in 1816, 1826, and 1924), chiefly a manual of practical gardening tasks and advice but also containing a few tips on ornamental gardening. Marjorie Fleming Warner considered the importance of Randolph's *Treatise* in "The Earliest American Book on Kitchen Gardening," American Historical Association, *Annual Report* (Washington D.C., 1923). Joseph Prentis's detailed gardening "Monthly Kalendar," which records his plantings in Williamsburg in 1775 and 1784–1788, unhappily remains unpublished; the manuscript is in the Alderman Library, University of Virginia. For an informative account of early gardening books in America, see Sarah Stetson, "American Garden Books Transplanted and Native, before 1807," *William and Mary Quarterly* 3 (1946): 343–369.

The early history of botany and horticulture in the colonial South has been well told. After his sojourn in Virginia from 1712 to 1719 and in other southern colonies from 1722 to 1726, Mark Catesby settled down again in England and eventually wrote extensively of North American natural history in his two books, *The Natural History of Carolina, Florida, and the Bahama Islands*, 2 vols. (1731–1743) and *Hortus Europae-Americanus* (1767). The former was the first truly scientific, extended account of southern colonial natural history. A complete biography of Catesby is available in George F. Frick and Raymond P. Stearns's *Mark Catesby: The Colonial Audubon* (Urbana, Ill., 1961). Good general analyses of botanical study in this period are U. P. Hedrick, *A History of Horticulture in*

America to 1860 (New York, 1950); Raymond P. Stearns, *Science in the British Colonies of America* (Urbana, Ill., 1970), which focuses particularly on the southern colonies; and Alice M. Coats, *The Plant Explorers* (New York, 1969). For a study not limited to the colonial period, see Joseph Ewan, *A Short History of Botany in the United States* (New York, 1969). See also Richard Beale Davis' endlessly useful *Intellectual Life in the Colonial South*, vol. 2, pp. 811–65, 954–61. Other good accounts of early botany are Ronald Webber's *The Early Horticulturists* (New York, 1968); Jonathan Daniels's *The Randolphs of Virginia, "America's Foremost Family"* (Garden City, N.Y., 1972), which considers Isham Randolph's botanical interests in the 1720s and 1730s; and John Prest's more recent *The Garden of Eden: The Botanic Garden and the Re-Creation of Paradise* (New Haven and London, 1981). Also relevant is John W. Harshberger's *The Botanists of Philadelphia and Their Work* (Philadelphia, 1899).

There is a biography of the Bartrams by Ernest Earnest, *John and William Bartram: Botanists and Explorers 1699–1777, 1739–1823* (Philadelphia, 1940). John Bartram's letters (especially to Peter Collinson) have been edited by William Darlington, *Memorials of John Bartram and Humphry Marshall* (New York and London, 1967). Edmund Berkeley and Dorothy Berkeley have published the definitive study of the Reverend John Clayton, the so-called first Clayton, *The Reverend John Clayton, A Parson with a Scientific Mind* (Charlottesville, 1965); the older biography by Walter T. Layton, *The Discoverer of Gas Lighting, Notes on the Life and Work of the Reverend John Clayton, D.D., 1657–1725* (1926), is still very useful. Joseph Ewan and Nesta Ewan have done the same for Banister, *John Banister and His Natural History of Virginia, 1678–1692* (Urbana, Ill., 1970). Banister's important "Catalogue" (1686) of Virginia plants was published by John Ray as an addendum to his *Historia Plantarum* (3 vols., 1686–1704). The second John Clayton, the clerk who was also a brilliant naturalist and the author of *Flora Virginica* (1739–1743, 1762), is also the subject of a biography by Edmund Berkeley and Dorothy Berkeley, *John Clayton, Pioneer of American Botany* (Chapel Hill, 1963). Clayton's university-trained botanical friend, Dr. John Mitchell, who exerted a great influence on American botany and European perceptions of it, is the subject of yet another specialized study by Edmund Berkeley and Dorothy Berkeley, *Dr. John Mitchell, the Man Who Made the Map of North America* (Chapel Hill, 1974). John Lawson's seminal survey of the natural history of North Carolina, *A Description of North-Carolina* (1718), has been edited by H. T. Lefler in *A New Voyage to Carolina* (Chapel Hill, 1967); see also Frances Latham Harriss, ed., *Lawson's History of North Carolina*, 2d ed. (Richmond, 1952).

William Byrd II's Anglo-Virginian botanical activities are described by Pierre Marambaud in *William Byrd of Westover, 1674–1744* (Charlottesville, 1971). His published correspondence contains many letters to and from British naturalists like Sir Hans Sloane and James Petiver about Virginia flora and fauna: see *The Correspondence of the Three William Byrds of Westover, Virginia 1684–1776*, 2 vols. (Charlottesville, 1977). Byrd's interest in the subject is also amply evident in a modern edition, *William Byrd's Natural History of Virginia, or The Newly Discovered Eden*, ed. Richmond C. Beatty and William J. Mulloy (Richmond, 1940; orig. pub. in German in Bern, 1737), and in his *Secret History of the Dividing Line* (1st ed. by William K. Boyd; New York, 1927) and the revised *History of the Dividing Line* (1st ed. by Edmund Ruffin; Boston, 1841), published in *The Prose Works of William Byrd of Westover: Narratives of a Colonial Virginian*, ed. Louis B. Wright (Cambridge, Mass., 1966) (another edition of the two histories is by W. K. Boyd, with a new introduction by Percy G. Adams [New York, 1967]). There is no biography or study of John Custis, but his plant exchanges with his English correspondent, Peter Collinson, are scrupulously documented in their letters, edited by Earl G. Swem in *Brothers of the Spade: Correspondence of Peter Collinson, of London, and John Custis, of Williamsburg, Virginia, 1734–46* (rpt. Barre, Mass., 1957; orig. pub. in American Antiquarian Society, *Proceedings* 58, pt. 1 [Worcesester, Mass., 1949]). See also Mary Frances Goodwin, "Three Eighteenth-Century Gardens: Bartram, Collinson, and Custis," *Virginia Quarterly Review* 10 (1934): 218–33.

There are three essays on Virginia gardens in *British and American Gardens in the Eighteenth Century*: Peter Martin, " 'Long and Assiduous Endeavours': Gardening in Early Eighteenth-Century Virginia"; William K. Kelso, "Landscape Archaeology: A Key to Virginia's Cultivated Past"; and William L. Beiswanger, "The Temple in the Garden: Thomas Jefferson's Vision of the Monticello Landscape." The essays by Kelso and Beiswanger are on Monticello. See also my essays on Williamsburg: " 'Promised Fruites of Well Ordered Towns'—Gardens in Early 18th Century Williamsburg," *Journal of Garden History* 2, no. 4 (1982): 309–

24; and "The Role of the Garden in the 'Making of a Town': Williamsburg, Virginia," *Studies in Eighteenth-Century Culture*, 12 (Madison, Wis., 1983), pp. 187–204. A fine modern study that links archaeology to garden history and focuses mostly on Williamsburg is Audrey Noel-Hume's *Archaeology and the Colonial Gardener*, Colonial Williamsburg Archaeological Series, 7 (Williamsburg, 1974).

As is the case with other aspects of colonial American garden history, the critical and scholarly literature on eighteenth-century Virginia plantation gardens is quite limited. Apart from unpublished research and archaeological reports and master's theses, few studies are available; the reader should consult the notes to chapters 4 and 6 for references to them. For a survey of "historic" Virginia gardens that is now more than half a century old and made no pretensions to scholarship, the reader can refer to *Historic Gardens of Virginia*, ed. Edith Tunis Sale, rev. ed. (Richmond, 1930). One unique and unpublished piece of work must be mentioned: Arthur Shurcliff's "Southern Colonial Gardens," on deposit in the Department of Architectural History, Colonial Williamsburg Foundation. Shurcliff, the landscape architect who laid out the earliest of the gardens in the Colonial Williamsburg Historic Area, methodically visited many of Virginia's plantation gardens, or what was left of them, measured them, and compiled this volume from his drawings. There is almost no archaeological evidence, and even less research, behind Shurcliff's drawings and conjectures, but at least he recorded what there was to see on the ground in the late 1920s and 1930s.

In addition to William Kelso's article on archaeology mentioned above, one of the very few published studies based on archaeological work at a plantation is Ivor Noel-Hume's *Digging for Carter's Grove*, Colonial Williamsburg Archaeological Series, 8 (Williamsburg, 1974). Two reports on Bacon's Castle and Green Spring, both unpublished but worth mentioning here because of the gardens' early dates, are Nicholas Luccketti, "Archaeological Excavations at Bacon's Castle Garden, Surry County, Virginia," James River Institute for Archaeology, Inc. (June 1987), and Louis R. Caywood, "Excavations at Green Spring Plantation" (Yorktown, 1955). See also Caywood's article, "Green Spring Plantation," *VMHB* 65 (1957): pp. 67–83.

Landon Carter's gardens at Sabine Hall have been fortunate to be the subject of an informative and well-written article by William M.S. Rasmussen, "For Profit and Pleasure: The Art of Gardening in Colonial Virginia," *Arts in Virginia* 21 (Fall 1980): 18–27. Those gardens are, in addition, documented better than most by virtue of Carter's diary, which was edited by Jack P. Greene, *The Diary of Colonel Landon Carter of Sabine Hall, 1752–1778* (Charlottesville, 1965). Another (more narrative) diary that sheds considerable light on Robert Carter's gardens at Nomini Hall over the space of a year was edited by Hunter D. Farish, *The Journal and Letters of Philip Vickers Fithian, 1773–1774* (Williamsburg, 1957). For an impressionistic account of Lady Jean Skipwith's gardens at Prestwould, see Ann Leighton, *American Gardens in the Eighteenth Century.*

Not surprisingly, Thomas Jefferson's landscaping is far better documented and more completely analyzed than anyone else's in the colonial period and for half a century after. The best general study of Jefferson as architect is still Fiske Kimball's *Thomas Jefferson, Architect* (Boston, 1916). Two books have since appeared on his landscaping specifically. Edwin Morris Bett's edition of *Thomas Jefferson's Garden Book, 1766–1824* (Philadelphia, 1944) is a mine of information on Jefferson's planting at Shadwell and Monticello, and Betts added extracts from Jefferson's letters and other writings to fill in the biographical context; he also included extensive notes and commentary. Neither must one overlook William Howard Adams's *The Eye of Thomas Jefferson* (Washington, D.C., 1976), which contains an incisive and revealing section on gardening and landscape, "The Pleasures of Nature" (pp. 314–51). A less satisfactory study is Ralph E. Griswold and Frederick D. Nichols's *Thomas Jefferson, Landscape Architect* (Charlottesville, 1978). See also William Beiswanger's more recent essay, listed above, on Jefferson's designs for garden buildings at Monticello. On Jefferson's dealings and friendship with Bernard McMahon, the Philadelphia naturalist, see Joseph Ewan, "Bernard M'Mahon, Pioneer Philadelphia Nurseryman, and His American Gardener's Calendar," *Journal of the Society for the Bibliography of Natural History* 3, pt. 7 (October 1960): 363–80.

Amid a stream of essays about Mount Vernon over the years, two reliable and careful studies are especially notable: Robert B. Fisher, *The Mount Vernon Gardens: A Brief Description of Their Origin and Restoration, Complete Plant Lists, Plans, and Other Illustrations* (Mount Vernon, 1960), and Elizabeth Kellam de Forest, *The Gardens and Grounds at Mount Vernon: How George Washington Planned and Planted Them* (Mount Vernon, 1982). An early glimpse of the gar-

den restoration at Mount Vernon comes from M. F. Anderson, "Mount Vernon's Restoration," *American Landscape Architect* 6 (March 1932): 8–11. In his journals, Benjamin Latrobe left some descriptions of the gardens (*The Virginia Journals of Benjamin Henry Latrobe 1795–1798,* ed. Edward C. Carter II [New Haven and London, 1977]), as did Julian Ursyn Niemcewicz (*Under Their Vine and Fig Tree: Travels through America in 1797–1799, 1805,* trans. and ed. Metchie J.E. Budka [Elizabeth, N.J., 1965]).

Contemporary descriptions of other plantations are scarce, but there are some good ones late in the century. The most detailed is Thomas Lee Shippen's of Westover, which has been published as *Westover Described in 1783* (Richmond, 1952). Others that contain garden descriptions of varying length and detail, especially of plantations along the James River, are: Thomas Anburey, *Travels Through the Interior Parts of America* (New York, 1969; orig. pub. 2 vols., London, 1789; 2d ed., 1791); the Reverend Andrew Burnaby, *Travels Through the Middle Settlements in North-America, in the Years 1759 and 1760,* 2d ed. (1775); Johann David Schoepf, *Travels in the Confederation 1783–1784,* 2 vols., trans. and ed. A. J. Morrison (Philadelphia, 1911); Baron Ludwig Von Closen, *The Revolutionary Journal . . . 1780–83,* trans. and ed. Evelyn M. Acomb (Williamsburg, 1958); and François Jean de Chastellux, *Travels in North America, in the Years 1780, 1781, and 1782,* rev. and ed. Howard C. Rice, 2 vols. (Chapel Hill, 1963; orig. pub. London, 1787). In addition, numerous other descriptions of plantations (and of Williamsburg) may be gleaned from Jane Carson's two very handy editions: *Travelers in Tidewater Virginia, 1700–1800: A Bibliography* (Williamsburg, 1965) and *We Were There: Descriptions of Williamsburg, 1699–1859* (Williamsburg, 1965).

As I have suggested, writing on colonial southern gardening was highly romantic and impressionistic until the 1980s; little use was made of documentary sources, and there was not much in the way of archaeological excavation to assist writers. Three examples are Alice B. Lockwood's *Gardens of Colony and State: Gardens and Gardeners of the American Colonies and of the Republic Before 1840,* 2 vols. (New York, 1934) and Henry C. Forman's two books, *Jamestown and St. Mary's: Buried Cities of Romance* (Baltimore, 1938) and *Tidewater Maryland Architecture and Gardens* (New York, 1956). Dorothy Hunt Williams, *Historic Virginia Gardens: Preservations by the Garden Club of Virginia* (Charlottesville, 1975 ed.), has long been used for its traditional survey of some major Virginia gardens restored by the Garden Club of Virginia, and it still provides a valuable overview of these important landscapes; but because few of the restorations it records (and their plans) are based on extensive research or archaeological excavations, it must be consulted cautiously.

Related Studies in Fields Other than Garden History

In *Common Landscape of America, 1580 to 1845* (New Haven and London, 1982), John Stilgoe analyzes in a broad and inclusive manner the arrangement and uses of landscape "belonging to the people"; his attention to Americans' attitudes to various forms of landscape raises a number of interesting ideas relevant to gardening. Equally stimulating is Rhys Isaac's pioneering work, *The Transformation of Virginia, 1740–1790* (Chapel Hill, 1982), which chronicles how Virginians thought about and used their land throughout the colonial period. Although neither of these books is about gardening, both ought to be required background reading for anyone trying to assess the developing nature and function of gardens in the colonial mind.

Seventeenth- and early-eighteenth-century efforts at pleasure gardening had to cope with considerable natural, economic, and social obstacles. A number of studies deal with the latter, of which the following are especially illuminating. For a detailed and statistically fascinating account of the physical hardships endured by seventeenth-century Virginia settlers, see Edmund S. Morgan, *American Slavery, American Freedom: The Ordeal of Colonial Virginia* (New York, 1975). On the lot of women, see Julia C. Spruill's *Women's Life and Work in the Southern Colonies* (New York, 1972). The prominent and perplexing role of climate in determining how successfully people farmed and gardened has been considered by Karen Ordahl Kupperman, "The Puzzle of the American Climate in the Early Colonial Period," *American Historical Review* 87 (December 1982): 1262–89. On the history of climate, see also a special issue of the *Journal of Interdisciplinary History* (Spring 1980).

On the character of immigrant elitism in late-seventeenth-century Virginia, see Carole Shammas's fresh view of the subject, "English-Born and Creole Elites in Turn-of-the-Century Virginia," in *The Chesapeake in the Seventeenth Century: Essays on Anglo-American Society*, ed. Thad W. Tate and David L. Ammerman (Chapel Hill, 1979). Richard Bushman has also suggested new relationships in "American High-Style and Vernacular Cultures," in *Colonial British America: Essays in the New History of the Early Modern Era*, ed. Jack P. Greene and J. R. Pole (Baltimore, 1984).

More traditional descriptions of the social classes and their ways of life are Louis B. Wright, *First Gentlemen of Virginia* (San Marino, Calif., 1940); Thomas J. Wertenbaker, *The Planters of Colonial Virginia* (Princeton, 1922); Richard Beale Davis, *William Fitzhugh and His Chesapeake World, 1676–1701: The Fitzhugh Letters and Other Documents* (Chapel Hill, 1963); and (for a later period) Carl and Jessica Bridenbaugh's *Rebels and Gentlemen: Philadelphia in the Age of Franklin* (1942).

Using findings from archaeological excavations, Fraser D. Neiman, in *The 'Manner House' Before Stratford* (Stratford, Va., 1980), explains that the layout of late-seventeenth-century plantation grounds was generally practical and little disposed to the ornamental. In *Tidewater Towns: City Planning in Colonial Virginia and Maryland* (Charlottesville, 1972), John Reps considers the several historical and cultural sources and factors that determined the layouts of Williamsburg, Annapolis, and other colonial capitals. Sylvia Doughty Fries, in *The Urban Idea in Colonial America* (Philadelphia, 1977), analyzes how colonial town planning reflected ideals of a new culture in the New World.

Index

A

Adams, John, 117, 145, 164, 213n.50; on American land-scaping, 147, 148
Addison, Joseph, xxiii, 47, 70, 197n.52
Allen, Major Arthur, *see* Bacon's Castle
Ambler, Mary, 117
American Museum, The, 178
Amson, Dr., 208n.41
Anburey, Thomas, 75
Andros, Governor Edmund, 20, 193n.75
Annapolis, Md., 30, 35, 36, 165, 195nn.14 and 16. *See also* Nicholson, Governor Francis
Apthorpe, Mr., 176
Argenville, A. J. Dézallier d', *Theory and Practice of Garden-ing*, 37, 45, 205n.19
Ashe, Thomas, 5
Ashley River, S.C., 112
Athawes, Samuel, 47
Audley End (Essex), 66
Ayscough, Christopher (gardener), 92

B

Bacon, Edmund, describes Monticello, 163
Bacon's Castle, 7, 10–13, 11 (fig. 5), 12 (fig. 6), 131, 190n.30
Badminton House (Gloucestershire), xx, 19
Baltimore, 92, 117
Banister, John (English botanist), 15, 16, 17, 193nn.62 and 70; contribution to the Westover gardens, 19
Barraud, Dr. Philip, 177, 180; letters to St. George Tucker, 178, 179

Bartram, John, 16, 55, 56, 57, 72, 87, 192n.52, 208n.41; describes Westover, 203n.72
Bartram, William, 171
Bassett, Burwell, 96
Bassett Hall (Williamsburg), 46, 80, 94, 96, 209n.60; gardens of, 166; landscape of, 96–98; plan of grounds, 96 (fig. 48), 97 (fig. 49)
Bathurst, Allen, first earl of, 37
Beebe, Lewis, describes Maryland garden, 113
Beiswanger, William L., 217n.36
Bell Champ (England), 144
Bellett, Peter, 166, 208n.46
Bellett's nursery (Williamsburg), 92 93, 95, 98
Belvedere (Baltimore), 215n.79
Belvidere plantation (Richmond), 102 (fig. 50), 131
Benjamin Waller House (Williamsburg), 84–87; gardens of, 86, 91, 98; plan of the gardens, 84, 85 (fig. 43), 206n.23
Berkeley, Lady, 8
Berkeley, Norbone, Lord Botetourt (governor of Virginia), 47, 83, 198n.64
Berkeley, Sir William, xviii, 7, 8, 10, 11, 190n.26; *A Perfect Description of Virginia*, 5. *See also* Green Spring plantation
Beverley, Robert, xviii, xiv, 5, 26, 64; attitude toward Nicholson's design of Williamsburg, 34; describes the College of William and Mary gardens, 21; describes Westover, 23, 26; enthusiasm for plants and river set-tings, 15; *History and Present State of Virginia*, xxiii, 4, 15, 16, 17, 26, 71, 191n.45, 192nn.55 and 62, 193n.73, 199n.77; praises Spotswood's gardens, 53
Beverley Park (Virginia), xviii, 15
Blackstone's island, 104
Blair, James, 8, 19, 20 (fig. 7), 40, 43

Blair, John, 92, 208n.41

Blakiston, Nathaniel (governor of Maryland), 8

Blanchard, Claude, 81

Bland, Martha Dangerfield, 175

Bland, Richard, 115

Blandfield plantation (Virignia), 121, 131, 213n.59

Blankenship, Kate Millington, 87, 206n.30. *See also* George Wythe House

Blathwayt, Sir William, 10, 19, 196n.31

Blenheim Palace (Oxfordshire), 68, 146

Blow, George, 84, 86, 87

Blow, Richard, xix, 87, 175; plan of his Norfolk house, 84, 85, 86 (fig. 44)

Bobart, Jacob (English botanist), 18

Bodleian Plate, 8, 23, 25 (fig. 10), 36, 41, 49, 169; detail of Governor's Palace gardens, 43, 44 (fig. 21), 194n.88

Bore, Chevalier de, 36, 82

Borghese, Villa (Rome), 30

Boston, 29, 87, 102

botanical gardens, 192n.52

Bowdoin, Peter, 93, 171

bowling greens, 100, 131; Blandfield, 213n.59; Green Spring, 7; Mount Airy, 123, 213n.62; Mount Clare, 117; Mount Vernon, 140, 142, 216n.10; Nomini Hall, 119; Sabine Hall, 116, 117

Boyle, Charles, fourth earl of Orrery, 68, 69, 71

Boyle, Richard, third earl of Burlington, 145, 51

Boyle, Robert, 17

Brackly Lodge (England), 66

Bradley, Richard, 114, 125, 205n.19

brick garden walls: Governor's Palace, 50; Kingsmill, 105; Mount Vernon, 137, 143; Pleasant Hill, 101; Westover, 69, 74, 77

Bridgeman, Charles, 45, 66, 145

Bridges, Charles, 63

Brompton Park nurseries (England), 65

Brown, Lancelot ("Capability"), 68, 164, 167, 184

Bruton Parish Church (Williamsburg), 39, 91

Bucktrout, Benjamin, 206n.24

Bullock, William, 18

Burnaby, Reverend Andrew, 81, 101, 102, 131

Burnet, Thomas, *Sacred Theory of the Earth*, 191n.45

Burr, Aaron, 128

Burwell, Carter, 107–9, 112, 114. *See also* Carter's Grove plantation

Burwell, Lewis, 104, 105, 107

Burwell, Lewis III, 104, 211n.19

Burwell, Nathaniel, 108, 113. *See also* Carter's Grove plantation

Byrd, Mrs. Maria Taylor, 69

Byrd, William I, xviii, 4, 14, 17, 18–19, 25, 26, 64; sends botanical notes to Sloane, 192n.45, 193n.67

Byrd, William II, xviii, xix, xxi, 4, 7, 8, 15, 16, 18, 19, 26, 43, 45, 48, 49, 54, 55, 56, 57, 59, 62, 64–77, 65 (fig. 33), 79, 82, 83, 87, 102, 104, 114, 127, 141, 174, 183, 197n.45, 198n.68, 202n.50; description of landscape, 69–71; *Journey to the Land of Eden*, 69; *Natural History of Virginia*, 67, 78, 202n.51; *Secret Diary*, 10; *Secret History of the Dividing Line*, 69, 70, 71. *See also* Westover plantation

Byrd, William III, 69, 74, 75, 77, 102

C

Cadignan, Chevalier Dupleix de, 82

Calvert, Charles, Lord Baltimore, 68

Campbell, Archibald, third duke of Argyll, 67, 72, 174

Campbell, Donald, 174

canal, Governor's Palace gardens, 50, 51 (fig. 25)

Capitol building (Williamsburg), 23, 35, 36, 44, 196n.24

Carter, Edward, 151

Carter, Frances Anne Tasker, xix, 117, 118, 130

Carter, Landon, 4, 100, 114 (fig. 62), 115. *See also* Sabine Hall plantation

Carter, Mrs. Charles, painting of, 119 (fig. 64)

Carter, "Councilor" Robert, xix, 4, 80, 117, 119, 120. *See also* Nomini Hall plantation

Carter, Robert "King," 40, 64, 108, 114

Carter, Robert Wormeley, 214n.64

Carter's Grove plantation (Virginia), 92, 101, 104, 107–14, 123, 131, 212n.26; archaeology at, 212n.34; gardens of, 107, 112, 113; grounds of, 109; painting of, 113 (fig. 61); reconstructed garden plan, 110 (fig. 59); restored gardens, 109 (fig. 58); view from gardens, 108 (fig. 57)

Cary, Henry, 53

Cary, Mathew, 177, 178

Castle Howard (Yorkshire), 18

Catalogus Plantarum, 58 (figs. 27a–b)

Catesby, Mark, xvii, 54, 56, 66, 178, 195n.8, 201n.23, 202n.50, 210n.10; *Natural History of Carolina, Florida, and the Bahama Islands*, 59, 60 (fig. 28)

Caversham House (Berkshire), 145

Chambers, William, *Dissertation on Oriental Gardening*, 205n.19

Chantilly plantation (Virginia), 104, 131, 212n.32

Charles, John, reminiscences about Williamsburg, 170

Charles County (Md.), courthouse landscape plan (1697), 6, 7 (fig. 2)

Charleston, S.C., 4, 5, 29, 87, 102; described by St. George Tucker, 175

Chastellux, François Jean de, 77, 102, 103, 210n.10; describes Westover, 75

Chaumiere (Kentucky), 184

Chelsea Hospital, London, 23, 25

Chiswick House (Middlesex), 51, 145

Church, Angelica, 148

Cirencester Park (Gloucestershire), 37

Claremont (Surrey), 112, 145, 146; garden plan of, 146 (fig. 80)

Clayton, Reverend John, 15, 16, 17, 18
Clayton, John (so-called second), 57, 59, 79, 87, 178, 200n.13, 208n.41; *Flora Virginica*, 192n.53
Cleve plantation (Virginia), 119
Clifts plantation (Virginia), 188n.9
climate, effects on Virginia gardening, xx–xxi, 187n.4, 188nn.4 and 7
Cliveden (Buckinghamshire), 34, 67 (fig. 34)
Coalter, John, 180
Cocke, Dr. William, 202n.50
Cocke, Elizabeth, 59
College Creek, 104
College of William and Mary, xviii, 8, 18, 28, 79, 89, 92, 165, 166, 173, 194n.79; Dutch influence on, 21, 23; gardens of, xvii, 19–25, 28, 29, 40, 41, 42, 197nn.37 and 43; student describes hopes for new capital, 29
Collinson, Peter, xx, xxi, 55, 56, 57, 58, 59, 60, 61, 63, 64, 71, 72, 200n.15
Compton, Henry, bishop of London, 8, 16, 19, 20; gardens at Fulham Palace, London, 5, 17
Cook, Moses, 31
Corotoman plantation (Virginia), 131, 177, 223n.52
Courthouse (Williamsburg), 82
Cowley, Abraham, 114, 115
Crease, Thomas (gardener), 41, 42, 92, 197n.45
Cresswell, Nicholas, 82
Crossy Hall (Lincolnshire), 51, 52 (fig. 26)
Custis, John, xvii, xix, xx, xxi, xxiii, 7, 8, 16, 19, 37, 38, 43, 54, 55, 56–64, 77, 78, 79, 80, 83, 84, 87, 91, 98, 101, 166, 182, 183, 196n.31, 200n.15, 201n.20; quarrel with Governor Spotswood, 38
Custis Square (Williamsburg), 36, 37, 38, 56, 64, 201n.42. *See also* Custis, John

D

Dan River, 126, 128
Dawson, Thomas, 204n.5
Dawson, Reverend William, 40, 41
Day, Jonathan, 63
Dedmans, Samuel, 130
Desandrouins (French colonel), map of Green Spring plantation, 8
Desandrouins Map of Williamsburg, 21, 22 (fig. 8), 36, 50, 64, 89, 95, 96, 172, 197n.37, 208n.41
Digges, Edward, 4, 8
Dismal Swamp, 174; described by St. George Tucker, 175
Dr. Syntax, 150, 218n.53
Doehla, Johann, 82
Dorchester, N.C., 175
Downing, Andrew Jackson, 164, 185
Drysdale, Governor Hugh, 80
Duke, Colonel Henry, 48
Dungeness plantation (Virginia), 200n.8

Durazzo, Count, 148
Durdans (Surrey), 68
Dutch gardens, xviii, xxii, 21–22, 63, 65, 187n.1, 194n.83
Dyrham Park (Gloucestershire), 10, 19. *See also* Blathwayt, Sir William

E

Eagle's Nest plantation (Virginia), *see* Fitzhugh, William
Eddis, William, 36, 81
Elm Hill plantation (Virginia), 127, 129
English gardens, 3
Eppes, Francis, 163
Esher Place (Surrey), 146 (fig. 81), 147
Euston Hall (Suffolk), 66
Evelyn, John, 19, 20, 21, 23, 30, 31, 66, 125, 196n.24

F

Farquharson, John (gardener), 92
Felix Hall (England), 65
Feltman, William, 103
ferme ornée, xxiii, 141, 146, 148, 151; as realized at Bassett Hall, 96; as realized at Monticello, 161
Fielding, Lady Dudley, 68
Finch, Philip, 39, 40
Fithian, Philip, 120; describes Mount Airy, 121; describes Nomini Hall, 117, 118, 119
Fitzhugh, William, xviii, 4, 14, 64, 191nn.36 and 41, 192n.45
flower gardens, 113, 128, 130, 131; Governor's Palace, 49; Monticello, 159, 160, 162; Mount Airy, 123; Mount Vernon, 143; Prestwould, 129
Force, Piagnol de la, 197n.52
Fort Washington, N.Y., described by St. George Tucker, 176
French gardens, xii, xiii, 63, 65, 73, 103, 197n.52
Frenchman's Map of Williamsburg, 33 (fig. 14), 50, 64, 81, 197n.42
Freneau, Philip, 181
Frost, Robert, 183
Fulham (Middlesex), 67
Fuller, Thomas, xix
Furber, Robert, *The Flower Garden Displayed*, 62 (fig. 29), 63

G

gardenesque, 167, 171
garden fences, ornamental, 87
garden tools, 209n.56, 221n.23
Gardiner, John, and David Hepburn, *The American Gardener*, 208n.46

Gates, Sir Thomas, 5

Gentil, François, *The Retir'd Gardener*, 205n.19

George Wythe House (Williamsburg), 80, 166, 206n.30; archaeological excavations in garden, 89; contemporary plan of gardens, 84, 87, 88 (fig. 45), 89, 90, 91, 99; fruit of, 89, 91; gardens of, 87–91, 98, 207n.36; plan of restored gardens, 90 (fig. 46)

Gerard, John, *Herball*, 125

Germanna estate (Virginia), 43, 53, 198–99n.68

Glover, Thomas, *Account of Virginia*, 18

Gooch, Governor William, 39, 40, 79, 80, 199n.69; describes Governor's Palace gardens, 47

Gordon, Lord Adam, 36, 81

Governor's "Park" (Williamsburg), 39 (fig. 19), 45, 46, 47, 48 (fig. 23)

Governor's Palace (Williamsburg), xvii, xviii, xix, 8, 79, 80, 92, 105, 166, 194n.1; gardens of, xviii, xxiii, 30, 38, 39 (fig. 19), 40, 42–53, 74, 199n.72; garden walls, 199n.69; kitchen garden, 198n.56; lands of, 45, 46 (fig. 22)

Grayson, Colonel William, 143

Green Hill (Williamsburg), 84, 166, 168, 178, 221n.13, 222n.30; gardens of, 29, 168–72, 221n.20, 222n.29

Green Spring plantation (Virginia), 7–10, 9 (fig. 3), 11, 13, 28, 69, 92, 189n.21, 190n.26; sports and pastimes at, 10; painting by Latrobe, 10 (fig. 4). *See also* Berkeley, Sir William

Gresham College, London, 8

grottoes, 203n.72, 204n.5; at Monticello, 150

Gunston Hall (Virginia), 123, 143, 164; gardens of, 123–26; library of, 214n.68; modern plan of the gardens, 123, 124 (fig. 68)

H

Hagley Park (Worcestershire), 147

ha-ha: Blandfield, 213n.59; Governor's Palace, 45; Monticello, 153, 154; Mount Vernon, 140; Westover, 76

Hamilton, William, 147, 158

Hamor, Ralph, 5

Hampton, Wade, describes Prestwould, 128

Harvey, Captain John, 5

Harwood, Humphrey, 199n.69

Hayfield plantation (Virginia), 223n.52

Hayward, Nicholas, 191n.36

Hazard, Ebenezer, describes College of William and Mary gardens, 41

Hill, Colonel Edward, 197n.37

Hill, John, his plan of Prestwould, 127, 128

Home, Henry, Lord Kames, 158

Homer, 47

Horace, 47, 55, 114, 115

Hornquarter plantation (Virginia), 103

Hornsby, Joseph, 166; his gardening diary, 91, 92

Hôtel de Langeac, Jefferson's plan of gardens, 217n.42

House of Burgesses, 33, 80, 115

Howard, Charles, 18

Howard, Governor John Eager, 215n.79

Hubard, James, 84, 205n.21

Hungars plantation (Virginia), 93, 171

Hunt, John Dixon, 21, 23, 70

Hyde, Henry, earl of Clarendon, 7

I

icehouse: Mount Vernon, 216n.17; Bassett Hall, 96, 98

Irving, Washington, on American landscape, 181

Isaac, Rhys, 26

Italian Renaissance gardens, xviii, xxii, 30, 47, 101, 112, 115, 129, 187n.1, 194n.80; influence of, 21, 33

J

Jamaica, N.Y., described by St. George Tucker, 175, 176

James, John, 45

James River, 18, 101, 102, 103, 104, 107

Jamestown, 3, 4, 5, 7, 189nn.13, 16, and 18; Ambler House, 6; surviving terraced garden wall foundations, 5, 6 (fig. 1)

Jefferson, Thomas, xix, xxiii, xxiv, 44, 65, 87, 89, 91, 93, 101, 103, 129, 134, 135, 136, 144–63, 165, 166, 167, 168, 171, 173, 180, 181, 182, 183, 217n.42, 218nn.58 and 66, 219n.72; on advantages of American landscape, 144, 147; his Garden Book, 151; his gardening ideas, 148–50; influence on American landscaping, 164; sketches of and for Monticello grounds and gardens, 151 (fig. 83), 152 (fig. 84), 154 (fig. 86), 156 (fig. 89), 157 (fig. 90), 159 (fig. 91), 160 (fig. 92), 161 (fig. 93), 162 (fig. 94); sketch of Governor's Palace, 40, 50, 81; visits English gardens, 145–47. *See also* Monticello

Jennings, Colonel Edmund, 21

Johnson, Colonel Philip, 96

Jones, Hugh, *Present State of Virginia*: describes the College of William, 21, 23; describes Williamsburg, 29, 79

Jones, Thomas, 102, 210n.10

Jones, Walter, 210n.10

Jukes, Francis, painting of Mount Vernon, 137, 138 (fig. 76)

K

Kames, Lord, *see* Home, Henry

Kearney, Major James, drawing of the "Virginia Peninsula," 34 (fig. 15)

Keats, John, 181

Keith, Governor William, praises Governor's Palace gardens, 199n.78

Kelso, William, 218n.59

Kent, William, 145, 164

Kentucky, 101

Kimber, Edward, 79

Kingsmill plantation (Virginia), 73, 101, 104–107, 109, 112, 113, 211n.19; archaeological excavations of, 105 (fig. 52); excavated garden features of, 107 (figs. 54–56); gardens of, 105; modern plan of the gardens, 106 (fig. 53); shown on Simcoe Map, 105 (fig. 51)

King's Weston (Gloucestershire), 19

Kinnard, Judith, 30

Kip, John, *Britannia illustrata*, 125

kitchen gardens, Governor's Palace, 45, 209n.57

Knight, Henry Payne, 167

Knyff, Leonard, *Britannia illustrata*, 125

Kornwolf, James, 4

L

Langley, Batty, *New Principles of Gardening*, 205n.19

Latrobe, Benjamin, 8, 147, 162, 189n.21; describes Mount Vernon, 137, 140–43; painting of Green Spring, 10 (fig. 4); paintings of Mount Vernon, 137 (fig. 74), 138 (fig. 75)

Latta, Reverend John E., describes Mount Vernon, 143, 217nn.23 and 27

Lawson, John, xxiii, 4, 16, 17, 71, 192n.55

Leasowes (Shropshire), 141, 146, 147

Lee, Richard Henry, 212n.32

Lee, Thomas, 104

Lee, William, 7

Lightfoot, Philip, 37

Lister, Dr. Martin (English botanist), 18

Locke, John, 20, 38, 195n.8

London, George (royal gardener to Queen Anne), 19, 65, 197n.52

Lorrain, Claude, 140

Loudon, John Claudius, 167; *Encyclopedia of Gardening*, 185

Ludwell, Philip I, 8, 19, 190n.26

Ludwell, Philip II, xix, 8, 10, 38, 43, 64, 196n.31, 198n.57

M

Macky, John, *Journey Through England*, 68

McMahon, Bernard, 162–63, 167, 184; *American Gardener's Calendar*, 101, 168

Madison, James, 175, 222n.39

Magazine (Williamsburg), 37 (fig. 17)

Market Square (Williamsburg), 36, 81, 82, 177

Marlborough plantation (Virginia), 125, 131

Marvell, Andrew, 29

Mason, George, 123, 125, 214n.67. *See also* Gunston Hall

Mason, John, describes Gunston Hall, 125–26

Matoax plantation, 131, 168, 175, 176, 177, 220n.46

Mattaponi River, 101, 103

Maussion, Helene-Louise de Chastenay, 113, 114

Maycox plantation (Virginia), 75, 101, 103, 131, 183

Meade, David, 75, 101, 103, 166, 169, 180, 183, 184, 185. *See also* Maycox plantation

Mease, James, 89

Mercer, John, 83, 125

Michel, Francis Louis: describes College of William and Mary, 23, 194n.86; sketch of Wren Building, College of William and Mary, 23 (fig. 9)

Middle Plantation, Va., 7, 20, 28

Middleton Place (Charleston), 112; modern plan of the gardens, 111 (fig. 60)

Miller, Philip, *Gardener's Dictionary*, xxi, 83, 93, 114, 130, 210n.10

Mill Hill, Collinson's garden at, 55

Millington, Dr. John, 87

Missen, Maximilian, 31

Mitchell, Dr. John (botanist), 16, 59, 201n.26

Monticello (Virginia), xxiii, 44, 55, 74, 103, 131, 134, 144–63, 165, 166, 184; aerial view, 156 (fig. 88); drawing of Garden Pavilion, 155 (fig. 87); first stage of gardens, 151–53; gardens of, 144, 148, 218n.58, 219n.73; modern plan of the grounds, 149 (fig. 82); painting of, 163 (fig. 95); second stage of gardens, 154–61; view of Montalto, 154 (fig. 85). *See also* Jefferson, Thomas

Moore, Thomas (poet), 96

Morgan, Edmund, 4

Morristown, N.J., 175

Mount Airy plantation (Virginia), 70, 80, 120, 121 (fig. 66), 131, 164, 213n.62, 214n.64; gardens of, 121, 123; modern plan of the gardens, 122 (fig. 67). *See also* Tayloe, John I

Mount Clare plantation (Maryland), 10, 117

Mount Vernon (Virginia), 55, 104, 123, 125, 131, 134, 135–44, 161, 166, 184; aerial view, 135 (fig. 72); aquatint by George Parkyns, 140 (fig. 79); gardens of, 136, 140–44, 216nn.9, 10, 17, 10, and 22; paintings of, 138 (figs. 75 and 76), 140 (fig. 78); plan of the restored gardens, 139 (fig. 77); Vaughan's plan of the gardens, 136 (fig. 73). *See also* Washington, George

Murray, John, Lord Dunmore (Governor of Virginia), 47, 48

N

Nelson, Thomas, 103

Nelson, William, 47, 108

Nervi, Italy, 148

Newenham, Sir Edmund, 144

New Hall (England), 65

New York City, 29, 87; described by St. George Tucker, 176

Nicholas, Robert Carter, 36, 37, 80, 95, 96. *See also* Robert Carter Nicholas House

Nicholson, Governor Francis, xvii, xix, xxiii, 21, 29, 30-31, 34, 36, 38, 39, 40, 79, 81, 82, 93, 193n.71, 195n.8, 196nn.18 and 24; design of Annapolis, 195n.16; design of new capital of Williamsburg, 30, 204n.1; his library, 30, 195n.7. *See also* Williamsburg

Nicholson, James (gardener), 92

Niemcewicz, Julian, describes Mount Vernon, 135, 140, 141

Nomini Hall plantation, xix, 70, 80, 101, 114, 117, 120, 123, 130; gardens of, 118–19; painting of, 120 (fig. 65)

Norfolk, Va., xiii, 174

North Carolina, 26

Norton, John, 95, 96

Nott, Governor Edward, 42

O

Olmsted, Frederick Law, 185

orangeries, 211n.17

orchards: classical precedent, 47; Bassett Hall, 96, 97; George Wythe House, 91; Governor's Palace, 45, 47, 48, 49; Green Spring, 8; Monticello, 89, 153, 156 (fig. 89); Mount Airy, 123; Nomini Hall, 119; Prestwould, 129; Sabine Hall, 115; St. George Tucker House, 177, 180; Tower Hill, 84; Westover, 67, 72

Otway, Anne Taylor, 71

Ovid, 47

P

Page, John, 34, 145, 177

Painshill Park (Surrey), 147

Palace Green (Williamsburg), 36, 38 (fig. 18), 39, 40, 87, 89, 165, 166, 173, 177, 179, 223n.59

Pamunkey River, 102

Parke, Daniel II, 19, 20

Parke, Dunbar, 61

Parke, Frances, 56

Parkyns, George Isham, 158, 219n.70

Patapsco River, 117

Peale, Charles Wilson, 134; his painting of Mount Clare, 117

Perceval, Sir John, 65; his *English Travels*, 202n.44

Percy, George, 3, 26

Perry, Micajah, 56

Petersburg Intelligencer, 93

Peticolas, Jane Bradick, painting of Monticello, 163 (fig. 95)

Petiver, James (English botanist), 5, 78, 192n.55

Peyton Randolph House (Williamsburg), 37, 91, 98, 207n.39. *See also* Hornsby, Joseph

Philadelphia, 29, 87

picturesque, 4

Pierce, William, 5

plantation gardens: descriptions of, 101–104; general patterns, 100–101, 131–33, 183–85; seventeenth-century expression of social aspirations, 13–14

plant exchanges, xx. *See also* Byrd, William I; Byrd, William II; Collinson, Peter; Custis, John

Pleasant Hill plantation (Virginia), 101, 131

Pliny the Younger, 17, 192n.60

Plucke, Noel Antoine, *Nature Displayed*, 206n.22, 214n.68, 220n.5

Plunkenett, Leonard (English botanist), 18, 19, 55, 78

Pope, Alexander, xxiii, 31, 47, 145, 150, 164

Popple, William, 195n.8

Port Royal, Bermuda, 173

Portsmouth, Va., xiii, 175

Port Tobago plantation (Virginia), *see* Wormeley, Ralph II

Potomac River, 104, 117, 118, 119, 123, 125, 137, 141

Povey, Thomas, 8

Powhatan plantation (Virginia), 87

Pratt, Henry Routh, 113

Prentis, Joseph, xix, xxiv, 36, 80, 91, 93, 101, 165, 167, 168–72, 181, 182, 183, 184, 209n.55, 220n.6, 221nn.26 and 27; Monthly Kalendar and Garden Book, 170; 220n.11, 221n.12; library of, 220n.5; local attachment to Williamsburg, 166. *See also* Green Hill

Prentis, Joseph Jr., 169, 172

Prentis, Margaret, 169

Prentis, Robert, 169

Prestwould plantation (Virginia), 126, 127, 177; contemporary plan of the grounds, 127 (fig. 69); gardens of, 127–30. *See also* Skipwith, Lady Jean

Price, Uvedale, 167

Prince, William, nursery (New York), 222n.43, 223n.52

promotional literature, 4

Purcell, Nicholas, 30

Q

Quincy, Josiah, 197n.43

Quintinie, Jean de la, *The Compleat Gard'ner*, 30, 125, 197n.52

R

Randolph, Anne, 159

Randolph, Ellen, 158

Randolph, Frances Bland, 175

Randolph, Sir John, 200n.8

Randolph, John, 37, 166; gardens of, 94–95; *Randolph's Culinary Gardener*, 93–94, 98, 196n.29, 207n.39, 208n.46

Randolph, Isham, 200n.8

Randolph, Martha Jefferson, 144